Thinking Through Your Writing Process

Thinking Through Your Writing Process

Judith Barker-Sandbrook

McGraw-Hill Ryerson Limited

Toronto Montreal New York Auckland Bogotá Caracas Hamburg
Lisbon London Madrid Mexico Milan New Delhi Paris San Juan
São Paulo Singapore Sydney Tokyo

"Erosion" by E.J. Pratt, reprinted by permission of University of Toronto Press,
© new edition, 1989. Copyright 1931 E.J. Pratt

Excerpt from "Nationalism and the Pacific Scandal," by A.A. Den Otter, Canadian
Historical Review (LXIX, 3, 1988), University of Toronto Press.
© University of Toronto Press. Reprinted and amended by permission of
University of Toronto Press and the author.

"The Writer" from *The Mind-Reader*, copyright © 1971 by Richard Wilbur,
reprinted by permission of Harcourt, Brace Jovanovich, Inc.

ISBN 0-07-549644-5

3 4 5 6 7 8 9 10 D 8 7 6 5 4 3 2 1

Printed and bound in Canada

Cover and text design by Kirk Stephens

Canadian Cataloguing in Publication Data

Barker-Sandbrook, Judith.
Thinking through your writing process

ISBN 0-07-549644-5

1. English language—Rhetoric.   I. Title.

PE1408.B37 1989   808'.042   C89-095208-6

Every reasonable effort has been made to find copyright holders of quotations.
The publishers would be pleased to have any errors or omissions
brought to their attention.

Wonder is not precisely knowing
And not precisely knowing not . . .

—Emily Dickinson
"Wonder Is Not Precisely Knowing"

To the memory of Margaret Laurence,
with wonder and appreciation.

Judith Barker-Sandbrook, M.A., B.Ed., is an Ontario Academic Courses teacher of English. She has been an instructor of writing workshops for the Scarborough Board of Education and piloted the Ontario Ministry of Education's Contact North teleworkshop writing program. She was awarded the Distinguished Achievement Award for Excellence in Educational Journalism (Special Publication) by the Educational Press Association of America for "Launching Independent Learning" (*Forum*, March/April 1988). She co-authored *Thinking Through the Essay* (McGraw-Hill Ryerson, 1986), *101 Independent Study Projects for the OACs in English* (OSSTF Resource Book, 1986) and *The Politics of Africa's Economic Stagnation* (Cambridge University Press, 1985). She has also published a teacher's resource manual on independent learning with the Scarborough Board of Education.

CONTENTS

Readings

CHAPTER *Two*
Writing with Style 65

Readings

CHAPTER *Three*
Writing in Contemporary Styles 109

Readings

PART *B*
Branching Out

CHAPTER *Four*
Writing the Elements of Narrative—and More 157

Readings

CHAPTER *Five*
Writing Non-Fiction Prose 201

Readings

CHAPTER *Six*
Writing Short Stories, Drama, and Poetry 261

Readings

PART C
Writers' Resources

CHAPTER *Seven*
Writers Writing 329

CHAPTER *Eight*
Workshop Supplement 371

ACKNOWLEDGEMENTS

Thanks to my family—Richard and Samantha—and all the other special people who assisted with the manuscript at various points in its preparation and review, especially:

Debra Wells, Erika Krolman, Janice Matthews, and Edith Carlson, McGraw-Hill Ryerson Ltd.;

Blair Martin and Craig Stewart, student reviewers;

Dr. John Lundy, Head of English, Sudbury Board of Education;

Bill Murtha, Head of English, Northumberland & Newcastle Board of Education;

Neil Graham, Co-ordinator of English, Scarborough Board of Education;

Peter Fergus, Co-ordinator of English, Ottawa-Carleton Board of Education;

Pat Currier, Assistant Head of English, Victoria County Board of Education.

A special thanks to the student writers whose work is included in this book and the companion guide, A HARMONY OF MANY VOICES.

Alison Calder	Tanya Kanigan
Greg Hollyer	Sarah Lee
John Hunter	Richard Lees
Blair Martin	Melanie Misanchuk
Anne Malcolm	Bridget Newson
Ghislaine McDayter	Joanna Norland
Ali Norman	Rita Schepok
Pat O'Keefe	Beth Singleton
Zenovia Sadoway	Cameron Stewart

Chad Vankoughnett
Courtney Walker
Debra Wood

A portion of the proceeds from *Thinking Through Your Writing Process* is donated to the Canadian Writers' Foundation, a federally incorporated benevolent fund which has assisted needy Canadian writers since 1931.

PROLOGUE

To the Teacher
Intended Audience and Organization of Book

Thinking Through Your Writing Process is intended for *senior students of writing*; it fosters communication and thinking skills through the writing program at the heart of every English classroom.

Parts A and C build general language proficiency for students of core English, studies in literature, and the writer's craft. Part B applies learning about style to writing in many genres and modes with an emphasis on contemporary non-fiction.

Chapters One through Six guide students through the learning/teaching cycle:

- **Fore-words** organizes and motivates.
- **Foundations**, a practice section; builds core skills, attitudes and knowledge through reading, writing, listening, speaking, observing, performing, viewing, and thinking critically and creatively.
- **After-words**, a summative section; draws together central learning and delves deeper into topics of special interest. Questions and exercises are organized into four categories:
  - *Reading and Responding*   Longer passages and questions encourage careful reading and creative thinking about writing.
  - *The Writing Folder*   Suggestions invite students to apply "Foundations" learning. They may revise and polish works-in-progress or begin fresh pieces for summative evaluation. Topics suggest points of departure for individual adaptation.
  - *Independent Learning*   Sample projects can be easily adapted to meet specific curriculum requirements and individual interests.
  - *The Writer's Notebook*   Spontaneous writing encourages students to: review learning, reformulate and extend experience, assess personal growth, plan remediation, and build bridges to new learning.
- About **Word Processing**   Activities are easily adapted to individual circumstances. Teachers may wish to consult their school's computer experts. See also the instructor's guide, *A Harmony of Many Voices*.

An Invitation to Students of Writing

"Are you writing a story, Mum? Am I in it? Don't tell about . . ." The study door flies open and in dashes my daughter.

The answer is both yes and no. You'll find elements of story—setting and plot of sorts, and plenty of characters, dialogue, and dramatic tension. The characters are students of writing much like you; with them, you'll explore the challenge of this program—to enhance your verbal confidence and creativity. Instructional materials open up the world of writing for senior students who write with reasonable proficiency but want to refine communication and thinking skills.

There is no magic formula to meet this challenge, but three steps will point you in the right direciton. First, think of yourself as a person who writes—an individual with a story to tell. Next, set personal goals. Whether you wish to build a strong foundation for post-secondary education or compose the perfect advertisement or sports column, you can make a unique contribution to the class. Finally, adopt a risk-taking attitude; a willingness to experiment and objectively assess results will carry you a long way toward your goals.

To begin in your program, reflect on the widsom of the Chinese proverb below and consider its possible significance for your growth.

Give me a fish, and I will eat today.
Teach me to fish, and I will eat for a lifetime.

PART
A

Building the Centre

C H A P T E R
One

The Writers' Workshop

A. FORE-WORDS

Warm up for activities in this chapter with discussion and writing. The quotations and questions below may help you begin.

T.S. Eliot   "It's much better to stop [after three hours of composing] and think about something else quite different."

Chinese Proverb   "I hear and I forget/I see and I remember/I do and I understand."

Alan Ziegler   "A workshop is for puttering around in. . . ."

1.   Imagine yourself preparing for an activity at which you excel—a sport or a craft, perhaps. Describe how you feel. Recall the preparation and practice phases in which you acquired the tools to excel at this activity.

2.   List the skills, attitudes, and knowledge you'd need to pass along to a friend who wishes to excel at this activity.

3.   What must the friend contribute to the learning process? *How* would you teach these skills, attitudes, and dimensions of knowledge?

B. FOUNDATIONS

When it comes to words,
it's a matter of who's to be
Master, that's all.

—Humpty Dumpty

As a senior student, you're ready to assume responsibility for your progress as a writer. You're ready to build a strong foundation to meet a variety of language-related challenges. You're ready to become a self-confident writer with a repertoire of critical and creative strategies at your disposal.

Let's set out to master the writer's tools of the trade. It's the first day of school. Take a quick look into a writer's workshop where you'll become a frequent visitor.

Scene: An instructor and a class of senior students are sitting in a circle.

Instructor: Okay, who's next? Something about yourself as a writer—your interests or goals.
Tarvo: Well, you know me from last year . . . I want to write a play this year, something incredible.
Kirsten: I hope we'll spend time on writing science reports. I'm not big on drama.
Sasha: I like informal pieces—nothing heavy.
Craig: Maybe we'll be able to publish a student newspaper? Journalism's my main interest.
Kirsten: What do we need for next class? Someone from last semester's group mentioned a Writer's Notebook. What's that? Last year we had writing folders, but . . .

Kirsten is on the right track. She is one of the students who will share experiences in a writing program similar to yours. Like the others, she is a composite character who reflects reality but is not real. Although these students' program may differ somewhat from yours, you'll benefit from the example of their collaborative problem-solving.

The Writer's Notebook Kirsten mentioned, which may take many forms, is one piece of equipment you'll need. It is a *discovery book*—a place for spontaneous exploration and experimentation. You'll also require a writing folder—perhaps a file or separate section in your notes—for works-in-progress. Computer facilities are a bonus, but not a prerequisite.

Now, let's begin crafting your writing tools. Activity One focuses on two fundamental communication skills: listening and speaking. Good writers are active listeners. They sharpen their senses by attending to a message's form and content, and they acknowledge receiving information. Remember your annoyance the last time someone's gaze wandered as you talked?

Appropriate responses include verbal signals, facial expressions, eye contact, and body language—cues that the message has registered. Recall strategies include visual and sound associations. At the same time, effective speakers encourage their audience by careful attention to the message's content and form, including clear enunciation and controlled pitch and pace.

Activity One   Learning to Listen and Share
Purpose

- to build listening, speaking, and interaction skills
- to break the ice

1.   Get acquainted—or learn something new about classmates. Break into two circles. One person speaks directly to the individual on the left. In turn, share your name and a writing preference (perhaps something you'd enjoy composing, such as a short story, or what you like to wear or eat when you write). Add something else characteristically *you*—a favourite colour, word, nickname, sport, or musical group. As you listen, link each name, face, and detail.

2.   The person spoken to repeats the speaker's words: "Your name is . . . You like . . ." Continue until everyone has spoken.

3.   Repeat the process, but this time:
a.   speak to the person on the other side
b.   add another of your writing preferences.

4.   One circle re-forms inside the other. A volunteer in the outer circle introduces the person on each side to the inner circle and shares preferred techniques of active listening. Observe the same rules of response. Continue until everyone has spoken.

5a.   Discuss the experience, including patterns in the type of information shared; recall techniques employed and your comfort level during this activity.
b.   Reflect on your learning in written form.

Another tool writers require is keen observation skills. The nineteenth-century French novelist Flaubert reportedly spent long days on his balcony noting changes in light through coloured glass. American author Henry James said that a writer is someone on whom "nothing is lost"; those observations then flower into vivid perceptions. And British poet William Blake assured his comrades, "You can see what I [see], *if you choose.*"

Activity Two introduces you to observing like a writer by switching on your mental movie camera.

Activity Two   Observing with Your Camera Eye
Purpose
- to hone observational skills
- to practise visualization, using "talk aloud" and camera-eye recorder techniques

1.   Work with a partner or small group. Imagine yourself at home in a specific room, looking through the lens of a movie camera. Focus on details that create atmosphere, such as colours, shapes, textures, odours, and even tastes. Talk aloud about the landscape you visualize, using non-evaluative phrases, for example, "the window is grimy in the bottom right-hand corner," rather than "I see on my window a disgusting blob." In other words, record without value-laden comments.

a.   Visualize yourself with your camera standing in the doorway: Are you facing north, south, east, or west? What is directly in front of you, and to the right and left, under your feet, above your head? Be precise: a camera sees all.

b.   Next, visualize yourself moving to the centre of the room and turning forty-five degrees to your right: How has the perspective changed? Continue until everyone has taken a turn.

2.   At home, reflect on the accuracy with which you were able to recall the room. In your Writer's Notebook, enter a comment about your observations.

3.   Rediscover with fresh eyes familiar objects, clothing, structures, food, and people. Imagine what might strike you on first sight. For a week, record detailed observations in your Writer's Notebook about colours, shapes, lines, textures, sensations, odours, sounds, actions, reactions, idiosyncrasies, and so on.

Your Writer's Notebook plays an important role in crafting your powers of objective observation. It may be a writer's most valued possession. Sometimes called a journal or diary, it's a place to reflect, pose questions, evaluate progress, and think through issues. You'll also engage in *freewriting*—a technique of creative thinking in which you keep your pen moving across the page for a set time without pausing to reflect on grammar or expression.

Practise this process in Activity Three as you reflect on writing experiences and explore how others have used their notebooks.

Activity Three   Exploring the Writer's Notebook
Purpose

- to discover creative uses for the Writer's Notebook
- to experiment with freewriting
- to reinforce camera-eye observational skills

1.   Experiment with freewriting for approximately ten minutes. Switch off the nagging voice of doom that says, "I don't know what to write," or "This isn't a proper sentence, you dummy." (*Tip:* If you can't turn it off, incorporate its whispers into the flow and stroke them out later. Or try Henriette Klauser's "invisible ink" technique. Placing carbon paper between two pages, write on the top page with a empty ball-point pen. Being unable to reread as you write may help keep your "critic in line."* If you're composing at a computer, turn off the screen.) Attempt to *see* as an outside observer, rather than emphasizing personal opinions. This first entry might reflect on your reactions to the group work and sharing you've done in this class.

2a.   As you read the following passages from published writers' notebooks and interviews, note the variety of motivations and uses for such record-keeping. If you've written a notebook or journal in the past, you may wish to reflect on similarities and differences.

Emily Carr   "I used to write diaries . . . but I was in terror that someone would read [them] and ridicule me . . . I wonder why we are always ashamed of our best parts . . ."

Joan Didion   "The point of my keeping a notebook has never been, nor is it now, to have an accurate factual record of what I have been doing or thinking . . . instead I tell what some would call lies. . . . How it felt to me; that is getting closer to the truth about a notebook. Remember what it was to be me; that is always the point."

Anne Frank   "I want to write, but more than that, I want to bring out all kinds of things that lie buried in my heart."

Penn Kemp   "[In my journal] I'm usually trying to figure something out. It's an analytical journal. It's a puzzle—I'm looking at a dream image or something that has bothered or elated me. . . . In order to write, in order to live, we must

---

*   This phrase is used by Henriette Klauser.

become conscious of what we are doing and use it, manipulate it creatively. You have this two track system; you're the creative source pouring through and at the same time you're aware of how to shape it. The left brain provides a funnel or a form through which the source can pour."

Anaïs Nin   "I had to find one place of truth, one dialogue without falsity. This is the role of the diary."

b.   Brainstorm many ways to experiment in your Writer's Notebook. Do not censor ideas. Begin each statement with a different trigger verb. The following examples may promote ideas:

The Writer's Notebook provides a chance to

- practise . . . dramatic language
- collect . . . anecdotes
- evaluate . . . progress
- imagine how to . . .

- interview . . . yourself
- debate . . . ethics
- hypothesize . . .
- innovate . . .

Compare your work with that of your classmates. You may wish to post a master list on a bulletin board for future reference and revision.

3.   Working with a partner or small group, compose a brief first draft which reflects your learning about the Writer's Notebook. You may wish to use one of these suggestions:

- a humorous announcement about the publication of a notorious writer's or politician's journals
- a found poem (see Glossary, page 406)
- a satirical set of rules for keeping a Writer's Notebook
- an excerpt from a talk-show interview with a living writer or celebrity whose journals have recently been published.

You've probably observed that writers such as Didion and Carr explore their "writing selves" in their notebooks. In "Setting Goals," we'll examine how establishing individual and group goals may enhance personal growth.

Setting Goals

Awareness of your personal learning goals is another powerful writer's tool. A goal is a target or ideal to work toward. A short-term goal might be to complete an assignment by tomorrow, whereas a long-range goal may have a series of steps. A realistic goal is based on *fact*—that is, you have good reason to believe it is achievable within a measurable period of time. Goals are tentative statements, not to be regarded as carved in stone. Frequent reflection on goals, individually and with others, is part of the dynamic process of learning and living.

Prize-winning Canadian cartoonist Lynn Johnston notes that setting goals and disciplining yourself to meet them are crucial for successful living. First, define what you wish to accomplish. Then collaborate with peers and the instructor to meet individual and common goals and/or restate and refine goals in light of on-going experience. Before moving on to Activity Four, you may wish to discuss these issues as a class or freewrite about them in your Writer's Notebook. Completing the statements and answering the questions below may focus your thoughts.

- In this workshop my main goal is to . . .
- I believe this goal is achievable because . . .
- Reaching this goal is important to me because . . .
- Challenges I must meet include . . .
- Plans to meet this goal include . . .
- I will measure my success by . . .
- What are our group aims for this writing program?
- How can we work together to achieve these goals within the confines of circumstances and the course of study?
- Are our individual goals conducive to our group goals?
- How can we help each other meet individual and group goals?

You may wish to post a copy of group goals on your bulletin board for future reference and revision. Or compare your goals with those composed by Tarvo's class, which are listed below. The list answers "What may a successful student achieve from this writing program?"

Goals for the Writing Program

- explore language potential and creativity
- build confidence in communication skills
- share writing and ideas with others
- develop patience and tact
- refine independent and collaborative skills
- master composing at a word processor
- assess with objectivity writing by self and others

This portrait and your group goals form an appropriate centre for an important classroom tool—the bulletin board. A showcase to mount works-in-progress, reminders, and memorabilia, the bulletin board is a visual symbol of shared purpose.

Help your teacher to build an aesthetically pleasing atmosphere in which to collaborate. For example, an appealing room may exhibit cartoons and line drawings—created by students or clipped from publications—depicting humorous situations about writing. The cartoon below is one example. Or post photographs of classmates engaged in thinking-through-writing situations. (*Tip*: Focus on faces. Your school's yearbook editor may be interested in obtaining copies for publication.)

FEIFFER®

Feiffer © 1987 Jules Feiffer. Reprinted with permission of Universal Press Syndicate. All rights reserved.

Posters of authors, media personalities, and other artists or creative people in any field add stimulating colours, lines, and shapes. Keep in mind, however, that bright colours and shapes distract some people. Visual noise fatigues, just as background music stimulates creativity in some and disorients others. You might compromise by confining displays to a back wall.

Learning Strategies

Preferences for visual and auditory stimulation are just two ways learners differ. An understanding of how learning styles affect the writing process may also help you get the most out of your program. The term "learning style" refers to ways individuals perceive and process information. Research into brain function is still in its infancy. Learning experts disagree on many points. However, the following skit may help you gain a general sense of your learning preferences and those of your peers.

Scene: Senior students compare notes while waiting for class to begin. The schedule calls for language instruction.

Craig: I wish people wouldn't lecture us about how to fix sentences. I like to do things myself . . . learning means *discovering* things, exploring *"what if"* on my own. Then I might like to coach my kid brother—or you.
Kirsten: No way. I want the teacher to give me *information,* to help me look into ideas. I often ask, *"What* do I need to know?" I want to be shown how to use semicolons. Otherwise, I feel uncomfortable . . . as if something's missing, you know?
Sasha: Yeah, sometimes that's okay—sometimes. But I want to know *how* . . . . How does the semicolon work? I want to see and touch things I learn about—hands-on practice and less talk.
Tarvo: Well, I want to know *why* things happen and why I need to know them. Tell me what difference knowing why you use the semicolon will make to my writing, and I might want to study it.

Chances are you, too, have a preferred way to learn. Do you recognize yourself in one or more of the comments? There is no one right way to learn. However, most successful students are flexible. An effective writing program takes account of individual needs by offering diverse activities, as well as by challenging participants to stretch their repertoire. Another look at the students' dialogue above links learning styles to specific classroom situations.

As Tarvo is a sociable "people person," who prefers to discuss ideas with classmates and values emotions highly, brainstorming and role-playing help him meld learning with personal experience. He hopes to work with children's theatre. When his imagination is stimulated, he is especially innovative and empathetic. Tarvo may need encouragement in personalizing abstract ideas.

Kirsten is a logical learner who likes to analyze concepts and link ideas. She benefits from lectures and teacher-led discussion, and values the opinions of experts. An observer, Kirsten draws back from the occasionally hectic workshop to watch and reflect. As hers is a no-nonsense approach, Kirsten prefers writing reports, reviews, and other forms of non-fiction. She may need encouragement to experiment with new approaches and ideas.

Sasha is a practical learner who absorbs new information by tinkering and practising. In earlier grades she excelled at worksheets and hands-on activities which challenged her common-sense strengths. In the workshop, she prefers practising and personalizing new concepts. Practical field research, including work-study activities, is welcome. Sasha prefers the instructor to act as her coach and facilitator.

The workshop's freedom is ideal for Craig's active and individualistic learning style. Because of his penchant for self-motivated discovery, Craig enjoys independent study and class presentations. Inventive and curious, he often plays with concepts. Craig excels at writing experimental poetry and fiction, but also enjoys the adventure of investigative journalism.

Of the four students, Craig is most likely to try something new. Before moving on to Activity Four, read the personal essay by Penney Kome, "There's a First Time for Every Day" (page 54) and speculate on how Kome's approach to life could help you develop your writing skills.

In Activity Four, apply the information about learning style preferences and risk-taking to yourself and your peers; it may assist planning to meet varied learning needs, but should not be used to pigeonhole individuals.

Activity Four Examining Learning Strategies

Purpose

- to apply concepts about learning strategies to yourself

- to consider ways to use this information

- to reflect on personal implications for writing performance

1. Complete this exercise in small groups. Then discuss highlights of your discussion with another group.
a. Which learning style of the four described on pages 12 and 13, or composite of two of them, most closely resembles your learning preferences? Which is most unlike you? Justify.
b. How might this introduction to learning styles enhance your ability to

- select an appropriate independent learning project

- meet the needs of your writing partner

- choose a peer editor or work group?

2. Co-write with your group a humorous skit reflecting a real or imaginary situation in which different learning styles have created difficulties. Share your work with another group.

3. In your Writer's Notebook reflect on
a. your reactions to the concept of learning styles
b. the role you played in the co-writing process and how this may be a reflection of your learning style.

4. In your writing folder, compose the first draft of a memo to yourself, your writing group, or your instructor about a "first" you could experiment with in writing, or a fresh approach to try soon. Keep in mind these criteria for effective memos:

- Employ straightforward language—that is, rely on active verbs and lean sentences and avoid "window dressing" in the form of unnecessary adjectives and adverbs or big words.

- Attempt to sound appropriately formal and business-like, but not pompous.

- Keep it brief and to the point; if you state your thesis (the main argument) in the first paragraph, you'll help yourself and your reader stay interested and on track.

- Be specific by referring to concrete examples—people, places, situations, events.

5.   In your Writer's Notebook, summarize your planning and drafting process for the memo; store this information for later use. Keep in mind these criteria for effective summaries:

- Use active verbs, strong nouns, and few adjectives and adverbs.

- Compose brief sentences, stating the main idea at or near the beginning of each.

- Stick to a strict recounting of "the facts"; do not editorialize by including personal comments.

Your Learning Preferences and Your Writing Process

Learning preferences, along with the temperament, attitudes, and feelings you bring to the task of writing, influence your success almost as much as your current skill level. In a successful workshop participants endeavour to accommodate individual differences. One way of achieving this is by balancing time for personal reflection with opportunities for exchanging ideas.

If, like Sasha, you want quick results, developing patience to hone your writing skills will be a personal challenge. Or perhaps like Craig you enjoy experimenting and speculating, in which case you may have difficulty bringing your work to closure. On the other hand, you may need to be alone, as Dr. Anthony Storr points out in his thoughtful analysis of the creative process, *Solitude: A Return to Self* (Collier Macmillan). Activity Five encourages you to explore possible relationships between learning preferences and writing performance.

Activity Five   Reflecting on Attitudes About Writing
Purpose

- to continue investigation of your learning and writing preferences

- to practise self-assessment

- to focus on attitudes, values, and habits which may affect writing performance

1.   In your Writer's Notebook, assign each item a number rating which best describes your current position.

1 = does not describe me   5 = describes me well

a.   I enjoy working in a congenial atmosphere in which students and the instructor support each writer's needs.
b.   I like to experiment with creative thinking strategies, employing techniques to open up the world of writing through inventing, imagining, innovating, and discovering.
c.   I am looking forward to reading a range of work by professional and student writers.
d.   I am eager to read advice from professional writers.
e.   I like to work in both open-ended and structured peer-group situations.
f.   I enjoy shared decision-making.
g.   I enjoy participating in oral activities to stimulate writing, e.g., storytelling and dramatic arts exercises such as role playing.
h.   I feel generally positive about developing objective self- and peer-assessment skills for writing.
i.   I enjoy enhancing my ability to write for various purposes and in a variety of situations.

2.   Your teacher may ask you to discuss your responses as a class or to share your reactions in small groups. Each statement refers to a learning/teaching strategy frequently employed in collaborative writing programs.

3.   In your Writer's Notebook, freewrite about the implications of your answers for your writing progress. Do your answers to the quiz and the subsequent discussion of responses help you predict with which students you would work best in a writing group?

4.   In your writing folder, compose the first draft of a letter in which you attempt to persuade a classmate that you would be well-matched writing partners. Keep in mind that your task is to mount a logical argument, based on your knowledge of learning styles and attitudes to composing.

Up to this point we've explored preferred learning styles and the attitudes you bring to writing. Now let's focus on our core concern—the act of writing and how it is accomplished. We'll begin by eavesdropping on Tarvo as he gazes into his locker:

> Whatever happened to plain old writing? Somebody decided it's a process. Kirsten says she looked up "process" in *Webster's*. It says: "a natural phenomenon marked by gradual changes that lead toward a particular result." What's natural for me isn't the same as for Sasha. And what are these "gradual changes"? A guy can't win. You think you've got it licked in

grade 9—you put on your Walkman and whip off a not-half-bad 20-Minute Essay Special. Then somebody says you need three copies with a lot of stuff crossed out on the first two. A guy just can't win.

You may share Tarvo's frustration; how best to teach writing is an old and thorny issue. Perhaps you've tried different approaches and are still puzzled about what works best for you.

What does research tell us about how to write well? Professor Donald Murray sums up the lesson when he says that there is no one right way to write—no lock-step, magic formula, "just alternatives.... All writing is experimental." Indeed, the discovery process bears a striking resemblance to the best scientific methodology. As David Suzuki points out in his auto-biography, *Metamorphosis: Stages in a Life*, scientific experimentation is not a linear process proceeding neatly from one objective to another. Rather, like most problem-solving, it requires following "your curiosity . . . into blind alleys and down side streets, often landing you far away from where you intended."

Nonetheless, successful writers share core strategies they've adapted to their needs. You'll examine these strategies and consider how to make them your own. But first, a little background about brain function and the thinking-writing process is in order.

When people talk about the process of writing, they are referring to a zig-zag process through which we form thoughts. Our best writing grows from an interplay of what are popularly known as the left and right brain lobes. In most right-handed people, the left lobe contributes diction and structure to writing. The right lobe brings colour, verve, and rhythm. The opposite is true of most left-handed people. Each site enhances the other; your best writing is a joint product of the analytical and creative.

However, most people have a dominant "side" of the brain which is most easily stimulated; the result may be "unbalanced" writing. Kirsten's work is strongly analytical, but tends toward the unimaginative. On the other hand, Tarvo may get carried away with colourful writing which lacks focus and structure. In the following paragraphs, we'll examine strategies to foster "whole brain" writing for all types of learners. *The process is generic; that is, it provides a valuable approach for any type of writing.*

As senior students, you're probably familiar with this breakdown of the process of writing:

- prewriting—exploring and planning

- writing and revising—drafting, rethinking, redrafting, editing, polishing, proof-reading

- postwriting—publishing and assessing.

HERMAN®

1/21

©1988 Universal Press Syndicate

**''I can't remember: Are accountants
'left brain' or 'right brain'?''**

These phases are presented sequentially for instructional purposes. In fact, they *intersect* just like a seed which simultaneously sprouts vertical and horizontal roots. And you won't necessarily nurture each piece of writing through all the phases; you may decide to bail out after a first draft. You might distinguish steps by visualizing yourself playing different roles—donning a new cap for each.

First, you're the **explorer**, the creative thinker. Your ideas brew just under the conscious surface. Students like Tarvo and Craig often find this phase easiest. To encourage the creative flow, try one of these activities they enjoy or consult Writer's Resource Three (page 385):

> snapping fingers, swimming lengths, jogging at a steady pace, daydreaming, listening to music, brainstorming, doodling, drawing or painting, talking "around the edges" of your topic, researching data, freewriting, word association, and metaphorical or divergent thinking techniques.

You'll note these activities involve repetitive motions which allow the analytical mind to switch off. Indeed, Albert Einstein had to take great care when shaving. The stroking blade stimulated sudden recognition of a solution he was not consciously pondering, sometimes causing him to cut himself.

Next, you'll need to play the role of writer as **planner**, the architect who juggles and sifts ideas. Writers like Kirsten often excel at this phase. As you jot down preliminary ideas, your analytical and creative faculties organize and search for connections, patterns, and relationships until you identify a working blueprint. For students like Craig, a word processor enhances this brainstorming-organizing-reorganizing process because it facilitates experimentation. And for Sasha, the hands-on practice builds the confidence to take risks. For information on specific planning techniques such as mapping, see the Workshop Supplement (page 387).

When you feel ready, jump into the role of writer as **builder** of scaffolding. Some people feel they're diving into a cold bath. However, Nobel Prize-winning novelist William Faulkner offered sage advice: "Get it down. . . . Take chances. It may be bad, but it is the only way you can do anything really good." Capture the main ideas and connections without heed to the niceties of phrasing or syntax. Tarvo finds he's most comfortable when he writes as if he's talking directly to his audience. Indeed, this tactic helps any writer keep the style appropriate for the audience and occasion.

At this point the writer's critic is at its most strident. But if you can silence rushing anxieties, you'll "hear" the right lobe's contribution. Visualization may help: picture yourself gleefully ignoring your critic. Assert yourself and send it packing.

Whether you're writing a scholarly essay or a one-act play, you may elect to compose chunks out of sequence. You do not have to follow the dictum: "begin at the beginning and go until the end." Keep the momentum up as long as you're comfortable. For a lengthy piece, experts suggest breaking in mid-thought or paragraph. Then pick up where you left off. If work is progressing poorly, you might consider the advice of H.G. Wells: "If you are in difficulties with [writing], try the element of surprise: attack it at an hour when it isn't expecting it."

When the first draft is finished, put the writing aside—preferably overnight. Store it in your writing folder. If you're using a word processor, you'll want to print this first version.

A cautionary note: If you're a writer who revises-in-process, arrows, circles, and lines to indicate new trains of thought are useful. On a word processor, you might mark places for later changes with symbols (asterisks or question marks). Experts advise caution with the revise-in-process strategy; the internal critic's whispers, "change that word" or "that's dumb—fix it now," may cause premature shut-down and writer's block. It may also slow progress. Dorothy Parker, an American writer of short stories, who spent six months composing just one, said: "I think it out sentence by sentence—no first draft. I can't write five words but that I change seven."

Next, don your **reviewer** cap to re-see, re-hear, reshape—in short, to revise. Your goal is to wrest order from chaos: to shape and pare and sculpt. Reading the piece aloud exposes false notes and redundancies. Step outside yourself; see and hear the words as others might experience them. Focus on overall content, organization, and style. Leave fine points of word choice and spelling for the editing phase.

You may complete a self-revising step before engaging in a peer conference. For a sample self-conference form, see the Workshop Supplement (page 379). Or you may move directly to a peer conference. In either case, key tools are your eyes and ears, your intuition, and an open mind. Gordon Lish, former editor of *Esquire* magazine, urges his students to "stay open for business"; this is difficult for writers who become prematurely committed to their words. Poet Penn Kemp notes that revision may, indeed, be an ongoing process of re-hearing and rewriting previously published work:

> When I'm performing [my poetry] or playing with it in public . . . I always find something new so the piece keeps happening. I've been working with one piece for about fifteen years; it's my favourite piece, and I just keep finding more patterns.

As you read to your partner, listen with fresh ears. Professor Lucy Calkins, who has worked with students from kindergarten through university, describes the conference as a process of learning to interact with your own writing. Although experienced writers often function as their own audience at this stage, they too may benefit from comments. For sample peer-conference scenarios and forms and organizers to focus your discussion, see the Workshop Supplement.

The conference is an interactive process of negotiating meaning, but control should always stay with the writer. Note suggestions for later reflection and/or complete relevant forms and checklists. If you're working at the screen, enter comments before they're forgotten, or experiment with revisions with your partner by your side.

Fifth, you're the writer as **reconstructor**, tapping your critical faculties to reshape, delete, and refine. Craig excels at resequencing paragraphs, but Kirsten is strongest at eliminating whole sections to clarify and refine form and content. Flaubert rewrote one paragraph at a time—sometimes a dozen times— casting out the trite, the redundant, and the dull. In a week, he composed two polished pages; the other dozen he discarded. Chekhov, a master of the modern psychological short story, struck out the beginning and end of many pieces.

The prolific modern novelist Joyce Carol Oates is an avid rewriter. In an interview with Michael Schumacher, she said:

I revise endlessly, tirelessly—chapters, scenes, paragraphs. . . . I don't like to push forward with a story or novel unless it seems to me that the prose is strong enough to be permanent, even though once the work is finished I will want to rewrite it. The pleasure *is* the rewriting: the first sentence can't be written until the final sentence is written. This is a koan-like statement, and I don't mean to sound needlessly obscure or mysterious, but it's simply true. The completion of any work automatically necessitates its revising. . . . Since we are all quite different, I can't presume to say [there is one right way to sharpen revision skills]. Reading, with an objective eye, is a necessity—trying to *see* one's work as if it were the work of another, setting aside involvements of the ego. . . . Revision is in itself a kind of artwork, a process of discipline and refinement that has to be experienced . . .

Store the revised draft(s) in your writing folder. They mirror a valuable inner journey and facilitate assessment of progress.

Now it's time to play the **editor**; you'll edit, polish, and proof-read in this fine-tuning phase. Focus on those all-important small touches that give your work flair and naturalness. As Pulitzer Prize-winning journalist William Zinsser notes, you owe readers clarity. Arrange words for maximum impact on your audience. The French poet Baudelaire reportedly kept a printer waiting several months as he repolished a few lines. Have you been as diverting or entertaining as possible? A wry comment or paradoxical turn of phrase may entice the audience to read further. These small details are part of your style—those outlandish touches that are uniquely yours.

You may wish to complete a self-editing phase before collaborating with an editing partner. Listen in while Sasha scrutinizes her work:

Okay, what did Kirsten point out last time? No sense making the same mistakes. I repeated "she said . . . he said" again. Where's that thesaurus she gave me?

Take pride in polishing the details of your craft. Make the first impression a favourable and lasting one. Focus on conciseness, word choice, and effective use of rhetorical devices.

When acting as someone's editor, wield a light, almost invisible, hand. Using checklists and organizers, such as the Workshop Supplement samples, prune, tidy, shape, spot digressions, and check transitions. But leave the style intact; it's the writer's personality expressed on paper. Poet and dramatist T.S. Eliot lauded his editor, Ezra Pound: ". . . he didn't try to turn you into an imitation of himself"; rather, Pound looked for "what you were . . . doing."

Few of us are our own best proof-readers. That's one reason newspapers employ professionals. Exchange work with other students or read your work aloud to a writing partner who may have a second copy.

At last, it's time for the writer as **publisher** to enjoy the pleasures of having others hear or read your work. You've put forth a lot of effort and will probably want to show off the results beyond your peer-writing group. Practising writers in all fields usually welcome the opportunity to read from their work at public gatherings and seminars. One mark of a professional is an eagerness to learn from other practitioners. You may, in fact, have an opportunity to create a class publication as suggested in Chapters Five and Six.

Your class might stage a Writers-in-Residence Day, in which student-authors volunteer to read their work. Or if you've written children's stories, you could read them to elementary classes. Yearbook editors are always looking for good material. These experiences build confidence and reinforce the reality of an audience. You might collaborate with your teacher to develop ideas for sharing. Activity Six on page 22 will get you started.

Benefit from the technology in your school. Desk-top publishing and computer networks open up options for sharing many types of writing with a wide audience without the formality of a commercial publisher. George Bernard Shaw, for one, would have welcomed a technology to bypass this "intermediate parasite." At the University of Toronto, engineers and computer scientists engage in daily exchanges of articles and messages with colleagues around the world who've joined their computer network. Exchanging ideas and problems facilitates professional growth.

Finally, think of yourself as the **evaluator**, locating strengths and weaknesses and developing plans to remedy problems the next time you revise—or begin a fresh assignment. You've been assessing and reflecting on your writing throughout the composing process. However, your teacher may ask for formal summative self- and peer-evaluation. The forms on page 382 may help focus your thoughts.

The assessment process develops objectivity about your own writing and that of others. Eric Fromm, a respected psychologist and philosopher, offers an enlightening perspective on this concept: "Objectivity does not mean de-tachment, it means respect, that is, the ability not to distort and to falsify things, persons, and oneself." You'll find practice helps you pull together your feelings about a piece of your work. Reflecting on learning in your Writer's Notebook is often a most valuable step in the self-evaluation process.

Before assessing your classmates' work, you'll want to practise balancing tact with candour. Activity Six provides one such opportunity. But first, pause to give yourself a pat on the back. If you've taken Zinsser's advice, you will have "believed in yourself, taken risks, dared to be different, pushed yourself to excel." Chances are you're on the road to writing well. And if you're feeling dissatisfied with your current piece, think of the next one. After all, Hemingway's philosophy was, "I have tried simply to write the best I can; sometimes I have good luck and write better than I am."

Activity Six Practising Conference, Revision, and Editing Skills

Purpose

- to sharpen conference, revision, and editing skills

- to raise awareness of conference etiquette

- to practise distinguishing among revision, editing, and polishing phases

1.   Work as a class. If word processing facilities are available, you might display a passage on a large monitor or crystal panel on an overhead projector. Otherwise, print the piece on an overhead transparency or blackboard. Read the passage which appears on page 404 of the Workshop Supplement, or work with one provided by your instructor. Offer the kinds of constructive comments you would like to receive. Don't nit-pick. The following generic conference questions drafted by senior students focus on clarity of thought and purpose, logical development of ideas, and overall impact. Use them to focus your conference.

- Does the opening represent the real beginning?

- Is the topic clear from the outset?

- Do transitional devices help the reader follow the flow?

- Is material presented in the most effective order?

- Do any thoughts need clarification?

- Is language tailored to purpose, tone, and audience?

- What sounds and images work well or fail?

- Is content clear, apt, substantial?

2.   Work with a partner. One person assumes the role of writer and the other is a conference partner. Role play a conference about another piece of writing from this book. You may wish to tape the interaction and compare notes with another group. These suggestions may help you begin:

> This part confuses me. Is something missing? What can you fill in to help me follow your train of thought? I'm not sure what the most important idea in this passage is. How can you give it more emphasis? This middle section seems redundant—what's the key point?

Or reverse roles. The "writer" asks questions such as:

> What do you hear me saying? Describe my voice as you hear it. What are the characteristic traits of my voice? What do you visualize and hear when you read my work?

3.   Reflect in your Writer's Notebook about the role play, noting what you have learned about conference etiquette. Then consider how the wisdom of the following proverbs might enhance future interaction:

- Actions speak louder than words.
- Fools rush in where angels fear to tread.
- The sun loses nothing by shining into a puddle.
- Never tell tales out of school.
- Today you; tomorrow me.
- A trouble shared is a trouble halved.
- We must learn to walk before we can run.

4.   With a partner, read Writer's Resource Two: Tips for Successful Conferences. Using its suggestions, your own experience, and the proverbs listed above, compose your own conference tips.

5.   In your writing folder, co-write a skit modelling an editing conference between two students; show clearly the types of concerns belonging to this phase of the writing process. Consult the "Editing Checklist" form (page 384).

6.   Pick a short piece of writing in your folder—a draft essay, letter, memo, skit, announcement, or interview from previous activities—which you wish to revise. Hold a peer conference about the selection. Obtain written comments.

7.   The following list summarizes typical student concerns about writing activities discussed above. You may wish to work in pairs—one person assuming the role of the instructor—to answer these questions.

> **Kirsten:**   Must I use peer editors? Why can't I always write in one form/genre?
> **Tarvo:**   Why can't I plan my revisions mentally and make just one copy? How can I give helpful advice when some of my skills are weak?
> **Craig:**   How do I know when to quit?
> **Sasha:**   How can I write when I'm not feeling inspired?

Under what conditions do you produce your best writing? Do you need the pressure of a deadline or plenty of "worry time"? Famous writers have their preferences, too. For example, Schiller, a German poet, stored rotting apples under his desk lid; the odour stimulated his composition. Flaubert worried himself into knots in his dimly lit study late at night. Hemingway composed standing up with his elbows resting on the top of a highboy.

There's no one right way to go about writing. But strong writers develop the ability to write in a variety of circumstances for different purposes and audiences, as you'll explore in Activity Seven.

Activity Seven   Identifying Your Personal Composing Process

Purpose

- to explore personal composing processes and their implications for writing performance

- to share composing processes in order to enhance co-operation

1.   In your Writer's Notebook, predict how you might react in the following situation: You decide to enter a writing contest. Within three days, you are to complete the first draft of a novel. The prize is $5000 and a contract for publication. Consider mental and physical preparations. Would you type, write by hand, or use a word processor?

2.   Read "The Three-Day Novel Writing Contest" by Judy Keeler (on page 52). Then complete these questions in groups.
a.   What attitudes and resources does the writer bring to the event? How may these factors influence performance?
b.   If you were to make a filmstrip of Keeler's composing process, what would each frame portray?
c.   Review the Writer's Notebook entry about your composing process (Activity Four, question 5). Does this reflection shed light on the contents of your personal filmstrip?

3.   In your writing folder, draft a personal essay about your attitude to new experiences. Analyzing Kome's essay (on page 54) with a partner may help you decide where to position your thesis, and the types of evidence, transitions, and structural development you'll employ. For additional review, see the Workshop Supplement, Writer's Resource Five. Or consult a reference such as A. Dawe's *Copyright Canada* (Macmillan, 1979) or Stewart, Kowler, and Bullock's *Essay Writing for Canadian Students* (Prentice-Hall, 1985).

4.   In your Writer's Notebook, draft your Writer's Profile. Reflecting on how you completed question 3 or the memo in Activity Four and using the items listed below may help you begin:

- where you like to write

- getting ready to write

- strengths and areas you'd like to improve

- emotions as you tackle a new assignment

- attitudes about the likelihood of improvement

- the importance of verbal skills in your future.

5.   Share your profile with your writing group. What are the implications of these findings for working together?

6.   You may have read about the popular notion of personality types. The so-called Type A individual is a hard-driving, goal-oriented perfectionist who is uncomfortable when not in control. The Type B person appears relaxed, adapts well to life's vicissitudes, and enjoys the daily process of living.
a.   Which personality type do you most closely resemble?
b.   What are the likely benefits and disadvantages of each character type from the point of view of writing?

7.   In your Writer's Notebook, speculate on how the wisdom of the following proverbs may refine your composing process:

- A bad workman blames his tools.

- Experience is the best teacher.

- Genius is an infinite capacity for taking pains.

- Nothing is certain but the unforseen.

- Nothing ventured, nothing gained.

- Old habits die hard.

- Self-praise is no recommendation.

The Writer and the Word Processor

Is there a "type" of writer who particularly enjoys composing on a word processor? Preliminary research attests to varied responses, but advocates and detractors speak with equal vigour. In Activity Eight, you'll explore your feelings about composing on a word processor and then consider the reactions of two professional writers.

Activity Eight   Exploring the Word Processor
Purpose

- to explore feelings about and gain experience in composing on a word processor

- to reflect on the writer's interaction with the word processor

- to examine the word processor's effects on creativity

Note: Students without word processing facilities or experience should skip questions 2, 4c., 5, 7.

1.   Discuss these issues in small groups:

- your previous experience and comfort level with word processing and how it has affected your writing

- if you're new to the word processor, predict how you might react to an opportunity to build word processing skills and give reasons.

2.   Working alone or with a partner at the keyboard, compose a skit, story, nonsense verse, or ballad. Use at least seven of these words: toenail, top hat, ship, rabbit, puppet, map, panel, pen, computer. Then reflect on these questions in your Writer's Notebook:

> How did you begin? Where did you look as you composed? How did the plot or story-line develop? How did you feel during this experience? What sense of ownership do you feel for the story? How did your composing process differ from working with a pen?

3.   After reading "In the Mode: Personal Computers and Creativity" (page 60) and "The Joy of *Writing*" (page 56), comment on the following in your Writer's Notebook (or computer file):
a.   Which article "sounds" more like your current position?
b.   Select one comment that interests you and react to it.

4.   Complete these exercises with a partner:
a.   Explain the computer metaphors Wilson discusses. Give other examples currently in use.
b.   Compare Lancashire's and Frye's reactions to word processing (page 62) with Norland's frustrations with her typewriter (page 404).
c.   The sense of disembodiment Wilson reports has also been cited by the American writer Kurt Vonnegut, Jr., who claims to feel distanced from the words on the screen even though he has been closely involved in their selection. Speculate on how this reaction could have a positive effect on revision.

5.   According to Professor Robert Logan, the word processor may harness personal creative forces. Left-brain composing processes are modified or complemented by the spatial right-brain function. The visual interaction with the screen stimulates writers' creative processes. The screen becomes a canvas on which quick brush strokes encourage the process of making meaning or discoveries. Have you experienced similar reactions?

6.   The process of writing can be compared with the growth of a seed; after a period of inactivity, it germinates or sprouts in all directions. Although such proliferation may be facilitated by a word processor, it also occurs with traditional writing methods. Compose a Writer's Notebook entry at the keyboard in which you comment on this idea in light of a personal example. Is the process happening as you work?

7.   Researchers say writers "talk" to the computer screen.

a.   Have you experienced this or a similar phenomenon?

b.   In your writing folder, draft a dialogue between yourself and the word processor about your composing process. Role playing this situation with your writing partner or speculating on how one of these proverbs relates to your writing process may help you begin:

- After dinner rest awhile, after supper walk a mile.

- Practice makes perfect.

- There's a remedy for everything except death.

- Procrastination is the thief of time.

- Make haste slowly.

- Old habits die hard.

In Chapter Two, we'll take a second look at the development of your word processing skills. Meanwhile, whether you compose at a word processor or with a pencil and paper, you'll craft a strong foundation of skills which enhance writing confidence and creativity.

The Artisan at Work

Practitioners of writing—journalists, poets, advertising copywriters, and song-writers—generally offer three pieces of advice to aspiring writers. You'll notice that we've discussed aspects of items one and two in previous sections of this chapter.

- Become a practised observer of yourself.

- Become a keen, objective observer of life.

- Learn what you can from whomever you can.

Activities Nine and Ten focus on item three—what we can learn from professionals about their art and craft, and how to unleash creative potential.

The comments in Activity Nine were written by prominent Canadian authors specially for the readers of this book. Together, they represent a wealth of experience in a variety of fields.

Activity Nine   Learning from Practitioners of Writing
Purpose

- to explore comments from practitioners of writing about their composing processes

- to explore links between critical and creative thinking
- to focus on language

1a.   Read the following comments; record appealing phrases, clever language usage, and spontaneous responses—fleeting thoughts or associations—in your Writer's Notebook.
b.   Note comments that "say" something with which you identify.
c.   Be prepared to deliver an in-role dramatic reading of one passage to your class or writing group.

Pierre Berton

Read! Read! Read!
Write! Write! Write!
Rewrite! Rewrite! Rewrite!

June Callwood

The act of writing is a part of the act of living. The quality of a writer's interior life and the richness of the experience which informs the writing are both gained by thoughtful investment in reading, reflection and activities. Writers are like spiders, who spin their webs out of their own essence. No one can write interestingly with only a little insight. Writers-to-be need to work on grammar, sentence structure and vocabulary, but most of [all] they need to work on their own personal growth.

Robert Fulford

You do not have to begin at the beginning. You can begin at the end or in the middle or anywhere else. It took me 13 years to learn this. If there is one part of your writing project of which you feel totally in command (there usually is), then write that first: a scene, a piece of description, some analysis. It will give you confidence to go on with the rest. You can of course alter it later to fit in with the whole work.

No one can come into your room and rip words out of your typewriter or word processor without your consent. Therefore, do not be ashamed of writing something silly, thoughtless, or juvenile. At the end of three or four hours at the typewriter it is better to have written something bad than nothing at all—bad writing can be revised, white paper can't be helped at all.

Write something every day.

Read, every day, something you know to be good, even a few thousand words, just to remind yourself what it's all about.

Always have at least two writing projects in the works. When the one you're working on becomes so hopeless you can't bear to look at it, shift to the other one—which now appears wonderfully attractive. Go back to the first one later.

Remember, in the darkest moments of despair, that there has never been a writer, however talented, who didn't to some extent share the feelings of inadequacy you are having now.

Phyllis Gotlieb

My most intense pleasure in writing comes when I am working at a novel, plodding along in my agonizing manner, wondering if what I am doing will interest anybody—and suddenly I get what can only be called a vision: a screaming computer, a crimson telepathetic leopard, a gilled woman swimming under water in a big fishbowl. I know I must get this vision into the work, because it brings it to life, but—it will change the course of the story and shapes of the characters, and how will it fit in? Then I realize, sometimes, that this new idea answers the questions and solves the problems that have been slowing me down, and I can move forward with new energy. At other times I look back and find that I have been subtly and unconsciously preparing for this lightning flash through the whole course of the novel: in either case when the vision meets the work it is as if an electric current were being joined to illuminate a city.

Lynn Johnston

Some days you're "on." Some days you reach a vacuum—the thing is to have faith that the "on" day will return and to use the "empty" time to go over old material and read through others' work who stimulate and encourage. I'll read Bombeck, if I'm really low on batteries.

Have a routine, set goals for yourself, and reach those goals. Many *talk* about doing something and never do it—why? Because they're poor disciplinarians. A writer has to be his own worst slavedriver, and once the project's done, he has to be his own worst critic.

Joy Kogawa

I spent years in the disciplined pursuit of the technique of writing, seeking the right words and so on, but a turning point came when my pen's struggle was enlisted in my heart's greater need for a sense of rightness in my life and in my understanding of the world. I became less interested in getting the precise words and more interested in having my life more precisely "in tune" and writing became a tool to that end. It seems to me now that the years of discipline in technique were a preparation for the time when the skills would be needed, and I've learned to trust a process that seems to be at work whether I understand it or not as I go along. What matters most to me in writing is a rigorous discipline of trust.

Anne Marriott

The experience which most significantly influenced me as a young writer was hearing Ira Dilworth, a former high-school principal . . . and a CBC director read T.S. Eliot's *The Wasteland* at a house gathering of poets and would-be's. I had grown up with Keats and Shelley and loved them, but suddenly I heard this incredible, amazing new kind of poetry, doing all sorts of fantastic things that I hadn't realized were possible. A whole new world broke suddenly open in front of me, and nothing in writing or reading was ever the same.

Farley Mowat

What makes a writer? In a nutshell: *writing* makes a writer. That is the first and most important dictum. There are few others.

Peter C. Newman

It [writing] is the toughest and yet most satisfying career there is. The perfect word, phrase, sentence, paragraph—that's what you live for and die for—and yet only you can define its perfection! I recommend writing to no one as a way of life, because failure will leave you feeling defeated and worthless; success will consume you.

Jean Sonmor

The most surprising thing I've learned about writing is that words drown each other out. Pack a sentence with $50 words and watch the spontaneity and color drain out. What's left is a cumbersome mess with no deftness and little style.

2.   In groups:

a.   Summarize the main idea of each passage in one grammatical sentence.

b.   Rank quotations in descending order according to their perceived value for students of writing. Justify. Compare your rankings with another group's, accounting for differences. Draft a compromise ranking.

3.   Role play responses to the questions which follow. One person plays the author and another the interviewer:

- Phyllis Gotlieb is asked: "In what way does the visual image you speak of 'solve' problems that have slowed you down?"

- Joy Kogawa is questioned by a high school student: "Suppose that writing in a way that brings your life more nearly 'in tune' doesn't sell.

Would you continue in this mode or consciously return to your earlier, 'disciplined' approach?"

- Peter Newman is interviewed by a local celebrity: "How do you prevent success from 'consuming' your talent?"

- June Callwood is asked by a Student Services counsellor: "How can a person 'work on growth' "?

6.   In your Writer's Notebook, reflect on the role play. You might ponder a surprising comment, striking phrase, or technique.

7.   In the time allotted by your instructor, write the first draft of a persuasive essay in response to one of the following:
a.   Whose work would you be most interested in reading after thinking about these comments?
b.   Each person's composing process is unique.

You may wish to revise this timed writing for inclusion in your writing folder.

In their comments, the quoted Canadian writers emphasize creative or undefined sources of power. This idea is not new. Carl Jung, the renowned Swiss psychoanalyst, recommends play as the ideal medium for fostering personal creative powers: "Without . . . playing with fancy no creative work has ever come to birth." Thus, creative play becomes a valuable tool for the student writer. If you're a learner like Kirsten, you may need to practise feeling comfortable with these exercises. Activity Ten uses holistic strategies to unlock your creativity.

Activity Ten   Experiencing Left Lobe and Right Lobe
Purpose

- to experience your right and left modes of being

- to experience a differentiation between left and right lobes

- to warm up for writing through visualization

1.   Your teacher or a student familiar with visualization techniques will talk you through these exercises by Canadian poet Penn Kemp. Begin by closing your eyes and relaxing. You may wish to play background relaxation music to facilitate the process.

Exercise One   Clasp your hands together. Which thumb rests on top? Try the other thumb in that position. Is it comfortable?

Imagine you have a series of building blocks in front of you and are about to build your dream home. Using your right hand only, construct that home in the air in front of you, paying careful attention to the way you work. Do you visualize the home in detail or as a whole? Are you constructing it step by step? Are you working from a plan or a blueprint? Are you thinking along vertical or horizontal lines? Is your attitude conceptual or practical?

Now reverse hands. Construct your home with your left hand, using the same building blocks. Note the differences in the ways the two hands move the building blocks.

Exercise Two   Place your attention completely in your right side. Inhabit it fully. Feel your right toes, your right foot, leg, hip, side. Stretch your right side; wriggle the fingers of your right hand. Circle your right shoulder. Feel the right side of your neck, of the head, your right ear, your right cheek, your right eye. Get a feeling of what it is like to be completely right-sided. Breathe in and out of your right nostril, covering your left with your left hand. You're in new territory; explore it. Scribble, doodle, or draw with your right hand. Note if it feels loose or tight, how it holds the pen.

If you were a colour, what colour would you be? Draw the geometric shape that represents your right side. What texture are you? What weight? What season is it? What mood? Of the four elements, which are you? Which direction? What country does your right side come from? What is its environment? Its time period? Its gender? If your right side were an animal, what would it be? Listen for its sound. What emotion does it convey? Let the sound become comprehensible, a word, a phrase, or sentence that you can get on paper. What are the qualities of your right side—its personality? Let your right side present to you a symbol of itself. See that symbol in its setting. Sharpen your focus so it is as clear and distinct as possible. Your right side has something to tell you it has been meaning to say for years. Let the words well up of their own accord, without any direction or interference from you. Now let that message take the form of a story or poem. Keeping your left eye covered, write down what it has to say.

Repeat with the left side before beginning question 2.

2.   Complete one or more of the following activities in your Writer's Notebook.
a.   Freewrite about a word, image, or association that comes to mind following the visualization experience.
b.   Reflect on the visualization experience in your Writer's Notebook.
c.   Compose a found poem or a haiku using words and phrases from the advice of the Canadian writers (on pages 28 to 30) or other sources.
Did the visualization exercise facilitate this writing assignment?

3.   Draft a work for your writing folder. You might prepare a
a.   visualization exercise for your writing group

b.   research essay, report, or debate about the value of visualization for senior students of writing

c.   formal letter to a school board official, arguing for or against visualization as a thinking-through-writing stimulus. (Refer to classmates' reactions as well as your own.)

What does the concept of creativity entail? How can we measure it? Are the mental processes that stimulate invention in the sciences and the arts similar? Is as much creativity required to write an outstanding scholarly essay as is that needed for a brilliant piece of poetry? Although there are no pat answers, let's continue to examine the concept of creativity in Activity Eleven.

Activity Eleven   Exploring the Concept of Creativity
Purpose

- to explore a concept through varied creative and critical thinking strategies

- to recognize clichés and stereotypes

- to distinguish between fact and fiction or myth

1a.   In a small group, brainstorm your associations with the concept of creativity. For example, consider colours, sounds, people, events, and places. (If word processing facilities are available, you might begin a database about creativity.)

b.   Complete this sentence: A creative person is someone who . . .

2.   Compose three generalizations you believe to be true about creativity. Compare lists. Identify stereotypes or other patterns which suggest clichéd thinking.

3.   Reflect on occasions when you felt creative. Are there common elements? What feelings accompany these occasions? Compare responses.

4a.   In the library, locate sayings or quotations about creativity. What commonly held assumptions are, in fact, myths?

OR

b.   Assess the validity of each of the following statements. Justify your responses with evidence. (Record *how* you went about obtaining and validating evidence.)

- The only real writing is poetry, drama, and prose fiction.

- A real writer waits for inspiration to "hit" before writing.

- A real writer writes one effortless draft.

- You're born with creativity, or you're just out of luck.
- You have to know exactly what to say before you can begin.
- Flawless grammar and spelling guarantee effective writing.
- Nothing important about writing skills can be taught.
- You must write a certain number of drafts to get an A.
- You can't help anybody write until your mastery is flawless.
- Analyzing admirable samples of the writer's craft is either harmful to your unique writer's voice or may stifle your creativity.

5.   Read these quotations which reflect the views of individuals from diverse backgrounds. Apply your learning to composing and debating resolutions about creativity.

Jerome Bruner   "... if ever there was a silent process it is the creative one.... [The essence of a creative act is] one which produces effective surprise."

Charlotte Brontë   "... the writer who possesses the creative gift owns something of which he is not always the master—something that ... strangely wills and works for itself."

Gerhard Gollwitzer   "Talent is a slippery concept."

Morton Hunt   "The unconscious, though one cannot force it, will not produce new ideas unless it has been painstakingly stuffed full of facts, impressions, concepts ... "

Aldous Huxley   says we must "be shaken out of the ruts of ordinary perception."

George Kneller   "Creativity ... [means looking] afresh at what we normally take for granted."

Arthur Koestler   writes: "Every creative act involves ... a new innocence of perception liberated from the cataract of accepted belief."

Edward Lindaman   Discovery is made from the "mundane and trivial," illuminated by a "readiness to put the pieces together in an entirely new way and see ... patterns where only shadows [had] appeared."

Abraham Maslow   "A musician must make music, an artist must paint, a poet must write ... to be ... at peace."

David Suzuki   "... *satori* means the unfolding of a new world [through intuition] hitherto unperceived [through logic]."

C. AFTER-WORDS

Reading and Responding

1.   Study the cartoon by Jules Feiffer (page 11).

a.   Cite evidence from this chapter and personal experience(s) suggesting others share the character's anxiety.

b.   Account for the perceived distinction between the skills required for creative writing and those required for a profession such as accounting. Is the perception justified?

2.   Read Davies's "We Must Sing with the Voices God Gave Us" (page 45). Of the Canadian writers presented in this chapter, whose composing process is most similar to that of Davies?

3.   Compare your writing "eccentricities" to those McLeod discusses in "Create Eccentrically" (page 55). What are the implications of these habits for your present and future success?

4.   Read "Creative Writing Co-op" (page 57) and the following excerpt from "Chorus of Many Voices" by Beverly Daurio.

> A workshop is always a chorus of many voices, critical, praising, encouraging, refining. You may leave a workshop, but the voices remain with you, helping through the long hours of revision.

a.   Predict whether you would enjoy the University of Victoria's creative writing program. Give reasons.

b.   How might Daurio's experience help you make the most of your writing program?

5.   Read the following quotation from Alison Griffiths, who writes on business in collaboration with her husband, David Cruise:

> It started as editing each other's stuff, and sort of expanded. . . . It was very efficient. We work very closely together. David does about 75 pecent of the first draft, then we send it back and forth for a while, and I do the second draft. . . . As the outline becomes more complete, it is necessary to do more and more research. . . .

a.   Compare their composing process with those discussed by Sweet and Blythe in "Collaborwriting" on page 92.

b.   On the basis of your experience to date with co-authorship, predict the role you might play in such a partnership.

6.   Refresh your knowledge of essay form, by comparing several samples from this chapter; the essays by Davies, Pearson, Kome, and Hathaway work well. Consider such features as:

a. clarity and placement of thesis
b. structure and organization
c. techniques of unity, coherence, and emphasis
d. types and quality of evidence.

The Writing Folder

1. The famous historian Edward Gibbon wrote, "Conversation enriches the understanding, but solitude is the school of genius; and the uniformity of work denotes the hand of a single artist."

Use this quotation as a starting point for a reflective personal essay or a piece of formal argumentation about the importance of balancing togetherness and solitude in a successful writer's workshop. (To review essay form, see question 6 above and Writer's Resource Five—Writing Essays on page 402).

2. Revise and polish a draft from your folder.

3a. In a letter convince a friend about the merits of peer conferencing. The letter should reflect your learning to date. If you belong to a computer network, you could send the letter to a student in a similar writing program.

OR

b. In a formal essay, persuade the head of your school's history department that in-class peer conferencing could improve the quality of written assignments.

4. Compose "Ten Commandments for Writers" or "Ten Commandments for Workshop Members." Use material from the comments by writers in this chapter, as well as your own experience. Elaborate on each dictum.

5. Prepare your own cartoon strip or collaborate with a friend to depict experiences in your writing program. Display the work on the bulletin board or cover of your writing folder. You may wish to revise the captions or create new strips reflecting your group's progress.

6. In a personal essay, vignette, or skit:
a. parody the idea of the creative "vision"

OR

b. explain what you've learned about your creative potential.

7. Compose a dial-a-lecture for a younger student troubled by writer's block. The advice should reflect learning from this chapter.

8. Write both sides of a debate based on a comment or concept from this chapter. Review quotations, comments, or readings for ideas. Check your resolution with your instructor at the planning stage.

9.   Assume the role of a radio interviewer. Compose the questions and answers of an interview with a Canadian writer whom you admire. The figure might be a sports or music columnist, a children's writer, or perhaps a cartoonist such as Lynn Johnston. Your work should reflect your learning about the writing process.

10.   Write a role play which models *one* of:
a.   a conference between two workshop members (revision or editing/polishing stage)
b.   a conference between a student and teacher (revision or editing/polishing stage)
c.   a peer coaching session in which a computer wiz demonstrates how to use the word processor.

11.   In a descriptive essay, show your mastery of the fine art of observing like a writer. Vividly recreate the details of a room or person without relying heavily on adjectives and adverbs.

12.   React to one of this chapter's opening quotations (page 4). You might write an expository essay or a skit exploring the statement.

Independent Study

For general tips on the **process** and **product** of **independent study**, see Writer's Resource Four (page 394).

1.   Investigate the writing processes of a Canadian whose work you admire. Consider a writer who publishes in a local newspaper or community magazine. Use print resources including primary works by the writer; non-print sources might include documentary films, and radio or personal interviews. Define a specific topic with your teacher. An in-class visit by the writer could form part of the oral component and/or play segments of an interview tape.

2.   Locate a work/study placement in a local publishing house or newspaper. Exploring options at small community newspapers and magazines may prove fruitful. Develop a specific project around your experience in consultation with your teacher and work-placement supervisor.

3.   Work with a local elementary teacher on a specific aspect of the class writing program. Define a topic for your written and oral report with the co-operation of both teachers. (*Note:* An excellent source of ideas for developing children's imagination is Richard de Mille, *Put Your Mother on the Ceiling: Children's Imagination Games.* Donald H. Graves's *Writing: Teachers and Children at Work* provides equally helpful tips about working with elementary school children's writing.)

4.   Survey students about the effects of word processing on their writing processes. Design the project and questionnaire in consultation with your teacher. Your written project might include a short story, dramatization, or journal entries reflecting learning.

5.   Research a concept or issue dealt within this chapter and write a formal essay or report that reflects your learning. Or review one or more books about the concept. You might take a close look at the literature on one of:

- creativity   · imagination
- writer's block   · collaborative writing
- writers' notebooks

The Writer's Notebook

1.   To assess your understanding of concepts about writing as a process, you may wish to compose a Quick Quiz or use the one printed below.

Informal Quick Quiz

In your *notebook*, mark each item T (True) or F (False).
a.   To write authentically you must always select your own topic.
b.   Professional writers promote one "best way" of writing.
c.   There are patterns in advice from professional writers from which others may benefit.
d.   Because of different learning style preferences, some students may adapt more comfortably to peer conferences than others.
e.   According to current research, the left and right brain hemispheres have totally different functions.
f.   Research has clearly established that reading and analyzing the work of professional writers and peers is harmful to the growth of your personal writing style.
g.   To revise means to look for spelling and grammar errors.
h.   The primary function of a writing partner is to find mistakes before the teacher does.
i.   The instructor is responsible for producing strong writers.
j.   Writing is an art and a craft; although some have more talent than others, most people improve through rehearsing the process.
k.   Most published authors find writing easy.

2.   Freewrite in response to one of these statements:

Graham Greene   "Writing is a form of therapy. . . ."

Alexander Pope   "A little learning is a dangerous thing. . . ."

Ben Jonson   "Learn to be wise and practise how to thrive."

3.   Revise your Writer's Portrait (from Activity Seven, question 4) characterizing your strengths and problem areas. You'll rework this draft as your course progresses.

READINGS 1

Training Your Muse: Seven Steps to Harnessing Your Creativity

Marshall Cook

. . . If only you could control [the] lightning strikes [of creativity]. If only your muse, that mischievous stranger who seems to take such delight in catching you off guard, could be taught to perform its magic at your bidding.

It can.

You can create a literary lightning rod to draw inspiration to you when you need it. You can teach your muse to work in harmony with its more orderly mental partner, the editor and critic, the bookkeeper and the schedule-maker that gets you through your day-to-day tasks in competent if unspectacular style.

You can bring order out of your creative chaos with a seven-step process for creating "inspired" moments. I've used the process successfully for years, and I've seen my students create more and better work with it than they ever thought possible.

Step 1: Feed the Muse

Your body must have good food to thrive. Your intellect needs the stimulation of new ideas. And your muse craves experiences, both first- and second-hand, to create with.

Your own experiences are your first and best source of creative inspiration. If an experience has meaning for you, it will probably have meaning for others, too. . . .

Your subconscious mind stores all experiences and sense impressions, shapes them, creates them anew. You use this storehouse of pictures, smells and feelings whenever you dream or remember. Memory isn't a computer-like retrieval of static bits of information, but rather an active reshaping of those bits. Dreaming also involves a creative chewing on experience that defies and transcends the logic of the conscious mind.

The trick is to harness that creative energy and use those stored experiences in your writing.

Begin by keeping a journal. Give your writing muscles a vigorous daily workout. You'll also be compiling a priceless source of ideas for later on. Record your experiences and impressions, describe the people you meet, capture bits of dialogue heard in passing, write yourself notes on your greatest work-in-progress, your life.

If possible, write your journal entries first thing in the morning, even if it means setting the alarm for half an hour earlier. On first waking up, you're still in touch with your muse, which has been happily creating dream movies for you all night. You'll establish and reinforce the connection between your sub-conscious inspiration and your conscious writing. . . .

Play "what if?" with your experiences, past and present. "What if" this happened instead of that? "What if" I had said that instead of this? ("What if" is a lot like "If only I'd . . ." except that here the only axe you have to grind is the sharp edge of your creativity.) . . .

Experiences don't have to be unusual in order to feed the muse. Everyday life can convert into the richly detailed vision so important for successful fiction and nonfiction.

Try to see familiar sights as a traveler from another country—or another planet—might see them. Vary your routine. Habit is necessary for survival, but too much habit is harmful to your creative health. Get up at 4 a.m. and visit that 24-hour coffee shop you've previously frequented only for lunch. Take your dirty clothes to the coin-operated laundry, even though you have a perfectly good washer and drier in the basement. Arrive early for the movie and listen to the people sitting around you.

Second-hand experience, though not as vivid as your own, can be an even broader source of inspiration and is just as real to your muse. . . .

Read widely. If you read 20 of the same type of book, you may be reading the same book 20 times in terms of what it can teach you as a writer. Branch out. Let one subject suggest another, one writer recommend a friend. When I discovered that Ken Kesey's favorite writer was Larry McMurtry, I sought out McMurtry's novels for myself and have enjoyed—and learned from—everything he has published.

Read as a writer. Analyze how the writers you admire achieve their effects. Consciously study their technique. Rather than spoiling your enjoyment of their work, you will certainly enhance it while learning more about your craft.

Make idea-gathering a regular part of your routine—and your non-routine—day. You'll soon find yourself with more ideas than you'll ever be able to write about. . . .

Step 2: Nurture the Idea

The idea may come as gradually as a sunrise. It may flash across the sky like a shooting star. But come it will, because you've given your muse plenty of experience to feed on and create with.

Be ready for that inspiration. Respect it and the process you went through to create it. But don't be too quick to draft a query letter or novel outline based on it. Make the idea prove its worth. Creative people must entertain lots of silly ideas in order to receive the occasional strokes of genius.

Beyond a short entry in your journal, don't even write the idea down yet. With specific form and shape on paper come limits. When you write the idea down, you squeeze the mighty stream of its possibilities down to a trickle. Of the hundreds of ways you might develop the notion, you've limited it to only one.

It's too early for that. Carry the idea around in your mind. Nurture it with your attention. Every time it enters your consciousness, examine it from every angle. Let your muse play with it while your conscious mind sleeps or goes about other tasks.

What if you forget it? Fine. If the idea wasn't strong enough to keep your muse engaged, it wasn't worth writing about anyway. If it's worth keeping, it will take on a life of its own, putting on flesh, gaining strength and clarity, becoming as independent as an adolescent. Soon you won't be able to forget it if you try.

Then you know you have a winner.

Step 3: Ignore the Idea

After several days or even weeks of pampering your idea with your attention, consciously banish it from your mind. Set a date and time to begin writing in a few days—literally make an appointment with yourself—and then gently but firmly send the idea packing every time it comes tugging at your sleeve.

This will give your muse time to play with the idea uninterrupted by your more-inhibited conscious mind. And it will also frustrate your muse. Why would you want to do that? Because the more frustrated the muse becomes, the more creative it gets, almost like an ignored child trying to gain attention with wild stunts. That's why so many of your best ideas come in response to seemingly unsolvable problems.

While you're letting the idea incubate, engage in wordless recreations. Knit, jog, listen to classical music, paint the living room ceiling (this is recreation?). The pressure to shape ideas into words on paper will build in you even as your muse works ever harder on your behalf to develop an idea worth paying attention to.

Exercise is especially beneficial at these times. Aside from the obvious physical benefits of movement to offset hours of sitting, exercise will refresh mind and spirit, leaving you better prepared to wrestle words onto paper. And exercise will help you keep in touch with your creativity. Just as marathoners report breaking through to an uplifting, almost primitive second wind, so writers receive inspiration while running, swimming, bicycling or hang-gliding. While no marathoner, I run almost every day. If I'm letting an idea simmer (which is almost always), I invariably come back from a run full of solutions to problems, even though I haven't consciously thought about them.

If you read during this waiting period, stay away from anything too closely related to the kind of writing you plan to do. Otherwise you may find your style becoming contaminated by the writer you're enjoying. If you're getting ready to write fiction, catch up on some research or a good how-to book. If yours is a nonfiction project, enjoy your favorite mystery writer.

At this stage, don't tell anybody about the idea. You'll spread precious words on air instead of paper. Your muse will delight in sharing the idea. It doesn't care what form the storytelling takes. The joy, after all, is in the telling. But when you later ask it to guide you in putting the story on paper, it's likely to respond, "What for? We already told that one."

"Yes. But this time somebody might *pay* us to tell it," you reply.

"Ho-hum," the surly muse counters.

You can train your muse to work with you, but you can't bribe it with promises of fame and fortune. It's incorruptible. It creates strictly for fun.

Step 4: Welcome the Idea Back

So many of my students at writing conferences and workshops tell me they'd write more if they "only had the time." I tell them to file that excuse right next to "Why bother? Editors won't buy a story by a _____ from _____ anyway" (fill in your own favorite deficiencies, real or imagined). If you really want to write, you'll make the time for it.

That appointment you made with yourself at the beginning of Step 3 should be the most important date you keep all week. Your writing deserves more than leftover scraps of time. It should have prime time, when you're fresh and alert. After all, writing contributes to your personal growth and may even contribute to others' as well. Does that sound too lofty? Where would you be without your books, newspapers and magazines? This is important business you're about, this sharing of your vision on paper.

As the appointed time draws near, quiet your mind. Empty it of all distractions and concentrate totally on your story or article or poem or novel. If this sounds a lot like meditation, so be it. Whatever you call it, it's an important step in attracting the lightning of inspiration. Think about what you will say, not how you will say it. Visualize. Give tangible shape and form to every abstract idea.

There's nothing more real for you in all the world at this moment than the idea you want to write about.

Ideally, you'll do this mental preparation in a special "writing place." It needn't be fancy. Mine is a second-hand desk stuck in the corner of the basement behind the furnace. It's a long way from the book-lined, sky-lighted loft of my fantasies, but it's all mine, and it's for writing only. When I go to my writing place, my muse knows it's time to create.

If it makes you feel better to have a talisman along, go with the feeling. I'm not sure I could write without my "Lake Wobegon Whippets" baseball cap, but I'm not about to find out.

As a part-time writer with a fulltime job, a wife and child, and a jogging habit, I find that I must carve these writing sessions out of early mornings, late nights and rainy Saturdays. If I can't be in my writing place when I have time to write, I make wherever I am a writing place. I write in doctors' offices, airport terminals and faculty lounges. I love my typewriter, but a lunch bag and a pencil will do just fine. Wherever I am, the writing gets done.

Step 5: Create!

As you concentrate on your idea, you should at some point become overwhelmed by the impulse to write. If you find yourself becoming overwhelmed instead by the impulse to sleep or play Monopoly, go back to Step 1 and start over with a more compelling idea. If your idea can't keep you interested, you certainly can't expect it to entertain a reader.

If you've followed Steps 1 through 4, you should be so ready to write that you can't not write. Rush to your table, seize your quill pen (or whatever) and begin. You've trained your muse to work on schedule. You've captured that summer lightning.

If you find yourself staring into space for ten minutes at a stretch, go back to Step 4 and visualize until you're truly ready to write. Dreaming time is for dreaming. Writing time is for writing. You might need to start another project or revise a rough draft. Don't worry. Writer's block is no enemy. It's often a message from your muse telling you an idea isn't quite ready yet.

I've had articles and stories flow smoothly on the first try. But others have required false starts and temporary abandonment. Several years ago, I set out to write a story based on the painful experience of spending a day hunting for my runaway son. Each time I began, I ran into a wall. I could phrase the problem in terms of some technical matter: Where to begin? Which point of view to adopt? How much to tinker with the actual experience? But the real problem was that I was still too close emotionally to the experience to write about it for publication. My muse was warning me not to proceed with the project. I made a journal entry and went on to other ideas.

The story has a double happy ending. My wife and I found our son and had the kind of cleansing talk that parents of teenagers would recognize. And I was finally able to go back to my journal entry and create from it a story that sold on first try to *Working Mother*, my first sale to a "slick" magazine.

If the idea is ready, write steadily and rapidly, with intensity and joy. Capture the flow, the vitality, the excitement. Don't be afraid to enjoy the process. Remember, your muse is in it for the pure joy of it, and if writing isn't at least a little bit of fun, you should probably do something else, something easier, like becoming a human cannonball.

Give no thought to writing style. Style is a by-product of who you are. If you write honestly, you'll sound like yourself, which is exactly who you should sound like. The world doesn't need another Andy Rooney or Erma Bombeck. The world needs you, with your unique vision, insight and energy.

Take chances. This is no time for timidity. You can revise for clarity and coherence later, but you can't breathe life into a stillborn manuscript. Believe in your vision.

Lock out the older sister who never thought you'd amount to anything, the uncle who considers writing a waste of time, the English teacher who wrote "awkward" in the margins of your compositions. This is no time for editors, critics or other harpies. "Do not disturb. Muse at work."

How long should you work? How many breaks should you take? It depends on your rhythms and your stamina. Some of us are sprinters, some middle-distance runners, some marathoners. If you feel like taking a break, you should probably take one. When the pain begins to exceed the joy, it's probably time to quit. If things are going well, you may lose all track of time and not feel the need for any breaks at all. You'll have locked out the timekeeper along with the editor.

I recently put this process to a rather

extreme test by entering the Eighth Annual Three-Day Novel Writing Contest, sponsored by Pulp Press of Vancouver. The rules were simple: Begin writing on or after midnight, Friday, Aug. 30, and finish on or before midnight, Monday, Sept. 2. In between, create a novel of between three and 713 pages (some sense of humor, those folks at Pulp Press).

I carried characters and plot possibilities around for weeks ahead of time, exploring every "what if?" my muse conjured for me. A week before the contest, I banished it all from my mind. By Friday afternoon, I was raring to write. Filled with anticipation (72 hours to write!) and anxiety (a novel in three days?), I lay down at 11:30 p.m., closed my eyes, cleared my mind of all save my novel, and let the story come flooding back in.

At exactly midnight I fed my typewriter a sheet of paper and typed my name and address and the title of what I hoped would turn into a novel.

Seventy-one hours and 40 minutes later (I finished with a whole 20 minutes to spare) and with time off for eating, sleeping and jogging, I had a 30,000-word novel called *The Boy Who Saw the Numbers*. My muse, tethered to a truly absurd schedule, amazed, delighted, and surprised me throughout. In the midst of a three-day frenzy, I learned not to hurry. I relearned that a writer must at times be willing to sacrifice for the writing and never the other way around. And I relearned the oldest and best lesson of all, that a writer must write honestly and simply.

Step 6: Sustain the Flow

If you don't have the luxury of 72 uninterrupted hours for writing and can't finish your project in one sitting, don't wait until you stumble to a stop, unable to think of what comes next. Stop in mid-thought, even in mid-sentence. Know exactly what will come next. Make another appointment with yourself to continue your work, and, again, let nothing short of fire or flood deter you from

keeping that appointment. When you return to your work and finish that interrupted thought or sentence, the words will begin to flow almost as if you never stopped.

Step 7: Revise

Perhaps you were hoping for a writing process that would somehow give you permission to skip this step. Me, too—but I haven't found one yet. Revision is an essential step in the struggle Hemingway defined as "trying to get the words right." You've created something vibrant and alive. But it might also be incoherent to everyone except its creator.

Set your masterpiece aside for a cooling-off period—the longer the better. James Michener is reported to store his manuscripts for a full year, while he goes off to research the next mega-novel. For us mere mortals, something well short of a year will have to do, but make sure it's at least overnight.

You must approach your work objectively. That's why the cooling-off period is essential. If you revise immediately after creation, you'll view your work as new parents view their baby. Who would revise a newborn? This is no time for doting. It's time to welcome the editor back into the workplace for a rigorous session of critical evaluation and revision. Now the editor is your friend. It's that editor, after all, who keeps you from making a fool of yourself in public and who enables you to communicate your brilliant ideas to others. You didn't want your editor to interfere with your muse, because creating the rough draft isn't an editor's job. But now you need that editor's help. And you'll find that your editor has been thinking about your project and has plenty of opinions and plans for improvement to offer.

In your newly-created work, you'll discover both less and more than you expected. The work may be quite rough. Grammatical howlers may abound. But your editor knows how to smooth out the jagged prose. You may have omitted things you were certain you were going to include. But your editor may now realize that the piece is better off without them.

And in their place will be ideas you didn't know you had, images and associations that crackle with originality and vitality. These are the gifts of the subconscious. You and your muse will have created a work of authentic vision, unique in all the world.

And you will have learned how to harness that most exciting and powerful of natural phenomena, the lightning of creative inspiration.

We Must Sing with the Voices God Gave Us

Robertson Davies

I suppose there must be as many ways of writing novels as there are authors, and, in our time, when literacy is supposed to be in danger, there are hundreds of thousands of authors. Industry, though praiseworthy, will not produce a good book. . . . If you really mean to write a book you will find your own way of doing it.

Nevertheless countless people, many of whom wish to become authors, want to know how an author works. The *Star* has asked me to tell you how I work. I wish the answer were more interesting.

Very briefly, what I do is this: I yield to a theme, I ponder over it, I make a mass of notes, then I begin writing and write every morning from 9:30 until 12:30, Sunday included, until the book is done; I have it professionally typed, I revise the text rigorously, then I have it retyped and send it to my agent, who sends it to the publishers and takes care of all the business arrangements. All told it takes about three years.

Sounds simple and clear, doesn't it? But let us look a little more closely.

I said I "yielded" to a theme. Like all writers, I get great numbers of letters and many of them are from students who ask, bluntly, "where do you get your ideas from?" The answer, which they are reluctant to believe, is that I do not "get" ideas; ideas get me. I do not invent plots; they arise in my mind, beginning usually with some mental picture that will not go away. It demands to be examined and thought about. And as I think about it something like a plot emerges. It is not always a plot that I particularly like, but it likes me and won't go away.

That is why I have written to countless aspiring writers that if they do not have any ideas that demand to be written about, perhaps they should consider seriously whether writing is the life for them. In the words of my old friend, Nicholas Goldschmidt, "In the world of art, if you haven't got it, you've had it."

Did I say I "pondered?" Yes, I did, and I know it sounds pretentious, as if "think about" would not be grand enough for what I do. But "pondered" is the right word, because I do not think coherently about my theme. I let it present itself in a variety of shapes, and offer me characters and situations I know I cannot use. Then, as the pondering becomes more and more insistent, I begin to make notes, and that is often the longest part of the work of writing a novel. I try to be tidy about the notes, numbering and indexing them in a special book, and sometimes the notes fill 150 to 200 closely written pages. As the notes swell in number I read them over, and wonder what I can make of them. Because somehow or other, a way must be found of telling the story.

This presents real difficulties and sometimes several methods will have to be explored before the right one declares itself. Shall it be first person narration, and if so shall there be more than one narrator? If this method is chosen, how do I deal with the problem that there are things in the story that no single person can know? Sometimes, as in

What's Bred In The Bone, there are things no human being can know, but which the reader must be told, and then I have to call on spirits who have special knowledge. I have been sharply criticized for this, but if the critics can do it any other way, they are at liberty to try.

The method of narration is profoundly characteristic of the author, and no two authors have precisely the same character. Henry James is leisurely and profuse; Graham Greene is so compact as sometimes to be telegraphic. Who would wish either man to be other than what he is? Dickens whoops and guffaws and weeps in print; Thackeray is coolly ironic, and both are right. Tolstoy seems not to know when to shut up; Stendhal measures out his narrative like an apothecary. Flaubert agonizes over every word and Trollope writes his daily stint without, apparently, crossing out a line. Both have their immense virtues. Balzac intrudes his personality on every page, and E.M. Forster hides himself behind a veil, but a single, unattributed paragraph would enable us to identify either man. Only critics, those great and good men, would wish any author to write in a way other than his own. As the Welsh proverb has it, "we must sing with the voices God gave us."

My own way of writing has been called, in a very complimentary phrase, magic realism— a mingling of realism based on close observation with elements which most people find quite out of this world, though not out of the world as it appears to me. I write of life as I perceive it to be, and luckily for me quite a large number of readers, in several languages, want to hear about it.

Then comes the actual writing. If I have suggested above that I am a pattern of industry, I only wish it were so. I try to write every day, but now and then I am tired, or written out, or even ill. I have never written a book in my life without having to pause for some wretched illness to take its course. This happens, I think, to everybody. Even Bernard Shaw, who presented himself to the world as a man without weaknesses and a monster of assiduity, reveals in his diaries (which we now have) that often he sat idle at his desk, utterly used up, eating boiled sweets, for which he had a childlike passion.

Then of course there is the Black Dog, the horrible, depleting depression to which Byron gave that name; when the Black Dog is on me, I look upon myself and curse my fate, and trouble deaf heaven with my bootless cries. I have never known or heard of an author who was a stranger to the Black Dog.

Somehow, however, the book gets itself written, and now and then the passages written when the Black Dog was at his most malignant may be the best.

The book, once written, must cool off. That is while my secretary is at work. It takes quite a while for a typescript of 500 or 600 pages to be transcribed in that neat, elegant, enviable professional form, in which every flaw is pitilessly revealed.

This is where the real fun begins. Revision! Cutting off some of the fat, but not all. Tightening and tidying. Making sure that the heroine does not have red hair on page 100 and raven locks on page 300. Catching shameful, pretentious mistakes, misquotations, and follies so stupid that the author blushes at them. Above all, shining up the vocabulary.

This does not mean substituting fancy words for common ones. More often it means substituting plain but strong words for flabby ones. It means giving every line of dialogue, so far as possible, the right flavour for whoever is speaking, and making the words spoken give the clue to how they are spoken, so that it is not necessary to fall back on nonsense like, " 'Do you love me?' she wailed, clenching her hands till the nails drew blood from the flesh."

I try to write, so far as I can, dialogue in Standard English. Slang may be outdated by the time the book is in print, and attempting to write dialogue that suggests the speech of an uneducated person very quickly becomes patronizing. A word or two should be sufficient to show the level of literacy to which a character belongs. If the reader is attentive, a too-elegant expression, or a snatch of professional jargon, tells all that need be told.

Revision could go on indefinitely, and the author must know when to call a halt. Too much revision can ruin a book, just as too much kneading may spoil a loaf of bread.

What might keep it alive? Not being a best seller, certainly. Try reading a few best sellers of days gone by and see for yourself. Read *The Rosary* by Florence Barclay or *If Winter Comes* by A.S.M. Hutchison; best sellers once, but who reads them now? What keeps a book alive is what Nabokov calls "the more or less irrational '*shamanstvo*' of a book;" the Russian word means enchanter-quality. It is not essential in a best seller, which is a commercial product, but a book must possess it if it is to live.

After that, the fate of the book rests with its readers, and the author reflects that, if he is lucky, some of those readers have not yet been born.

Writers, unless they have very bad habits, tend to live long lives, and go on writing so long as they can drag themselves to the—oh yes, the typewriter. I write on a machine, a simple affair; I don't want a word processor. I process my own words. Helpful people assure me that a word processor would save me a great deal of time. But I don't want to save time. I want to write the best book I can, and I have whatever time it takes to make that attempt.

I am old-fashioned enough to think that a book is a work of art. That is to say, the unique result of a unique temperament. Many are not, but that is what a real writer wishes to produce.

Art, as somebody—I think it was a Roman—has said, is long.

15 Great Creative-Block Busters

Nancy Hathaway

When I moved into my first apartment, I was thrilled to be living alone because it meant I wouldn't have to hide my writing from the prying eyes of roommates. Virginia Woolf wrote of the need for a room of one's own. At long last, I had one. I set up my portable typewriter, hitherto used only for term papers, and prepared to write.

Because I had a regular daytime job, my plan was to write in the evening. But night after night, I found ways to avoid even looking at the typewriter. Whenever possible, I went out. The rest of the time—which was most of the time—I allowed fatigue and phone calls to interfere, along with plenty of other distractions ranging from the need to cook something complicated to the need to read a novel. And if I actually *did* sit at that rickety linoleum-top table and roll a sheet of white bond paper into the typewriter, nothing came. My mind went blank, and I ended up writing letters. After six months, I had not finished a single story. I figured I would never be a writer.

My experience is far from unusual. Creative block can happen to anyone in any field. Scientists, educators, business people, and bureaucrats are as susceptible as artists, though artists are especially familiar with its patterns of paralysis. Artist Eugenia Butler describes a bout with block this way: "I was slowing things down, putting glue into the works, and I couldn't stop it. The work wasn't coming, the shows weren't coming, and I couldn't work. I didn't *want* to work. It *hurt* to work. Yet work was the most important thing in the world to me."

Writer's block has garnered the most press, and, indeed, it is probably the best-known of all forms of creative block. Short-story writer

Katherine Mansfield (1888-1923) described it in her journal: "Wasting time. The old cry—the first and last cry—why do ye tarry? Ah, why indeed? My deepest desire is to be a writer, to have 'a body of work' done. And there the work is, there the stories wait for me, *grow tired*, wilt, fade, because I will not come. And I hear and *acknowledge* them, and still I go on sitting at the window, playing with the ball of wool. . . ."

According to Los Angeles psychiatrist and media consultant Carole Lieberman, M.D., 75 percent of professional writers experience writer's block at least once in their careers. During that time, most manage to eke out a few words, but 18 percent of them cannot write at all. What do they do instead? Simple. They procrastinate—like mad. They get sick. They panic. They overeat. They feel confused, afraid, angry, and guilty. And all the time, at the back of their minds, they hear this awful chorus that says *you're not doing your work.*

Some creative people never feel this way. They seem to be tuned into an endless, unblocked stream of ideas. What's their secret? Possibly, they have a greater tolerance for the process of creativity, which involves a natural ebb and flow of productivity. "I don't think that writer's block exists, really," says prolific author Joyce Carol Oates. "I think that when you're trying to do something prematurely, it just won't come." So perhaps the trick is to not panic when you've reached the point where your ideas need incubation time. This notion of allowing for a natural gap in your productivity is supported by Virginia Valian, Ph.D., visiting professor of linguistics and psychology at the University of Rochester: "In each piece of work there comes a point where . . . you've got to take it one step further, and you don't know what that one step is. That's when people are the most nervous and anxious and upset."

This is when a cacophony of fears sings in your mind. These include the fears of: taking a risk, making a change, being too old, looking foolish, the unknown, what we might find if we really look, not being able to produce (regardless of track record), and, last but not least, criticism and failure.

The fear of criticism and failure looms especially large when you're trying something new. After all, new ideas can be bad ideas. Yes, you and your work *will* be judged. "But your fantasies of how others will react come from your own self-doubts," explains Dr. Lieberman. "For example, if you are unsure of your own intellect, you may imagine that others will find you stupid."

No wonder creative blocks arise. They conveniently obliterate the problem of dealing with reactions to your work. No work, no criticism; no criticism, no pain. Instead, there will be the sorrow (not to mention the dwindling income) that comes from closing off parts of yourself.

Getting Unblocked

So, how do you cope with this mental paralysis? One thing is certain: if you're blocked, whatever you're doing now isn't working. Doing it harder or doing it more often won't help, though it's tempting to think otherwise. You have to change your approach. Some of the following suggestions require a shift in attitude; they are mind games you can play to psych yourself into a creative mood. Other suggestions involve simple exercises to get going again and physical changes in your method of working.

Expect the Unexpected.   "One of the things that happens when you're feeling blocked is that you're not going with the ideas that are coming up," says Butler, who has had major successes and major blocks. Often, the ideas you get aren't the ideas you *hoped* to have, so you reject them and let your true creativity slip between your fingers. "I had been a very intellectual, art-about-art kind of artist, so at first when my gut instinct wanted me to make art furniture, I ignored it," Butler says. Fortunately, she finally gave in to the urge. Her recent projects include 20 pieces of furniture she made for the film *Ruthless People*.

A breakthrough is always unexpected and seldom easy. "It is not a mere expansion of awareness; it is rather a kind of battle," writes Rollo May, Ph.D., in *The Courage to Create*. "A dynamic struggle goes on within a person, between what he or she consciously thinks on the one hand, and, on the other, some insight, some perspective that is struggling to be born."

To give birth to a new idea, first be receptive to it. This may mean abandoning other ideas of which we've grown fond. Picasso said, "Every act of creation is first of all an act of destruction." So, mixed in with the pleasure—indeed, the joy—of breakthrough, there may be some anxiety or guilt.

Drop Your Guard. Get in touch with *all* your feelings and memories, no matter how painful they may be. When you put up a shield to protect yourself from unwanted emotions, you also cut yourself off from a rich creative source. One of the ways to ferret out your feelings is to start each creative session with what Dr. Lieberman calls personal inventory. Ask yourself, "How do I feel?" and answer the question in as many ways as you can. Consider how you feel physically and emotionally. "You're most creative when you're most in touch with these feelings," Dr. Lieberman says. "It doesn't matter whether you're hungry and jittery or tired and lonely and your feet hurt. The point is to identify what you're feeling. Unguardedness produces the best work," adds Dr. Lieberman.

Think of Yourself as Creative. "For a long time, I was too scared to be an artist," says Anna Homler, a successful performance artist who has done shows on both coasts. "I was intimidated by the image of the artist. I thought I wasn't thin or tortured enough." Getting past such internal stereotypes is a major step, for the importance of self-image cannot be overestimated. Roger Von Oech,

Ph.D., author of *A Whack on the Side of the Head* and a consultant in creative thinking to many corporations, reports that when psychologists studied a group of people who worked for a major oil company, they discovered that a single trait distinguished the creative people there: "The creative people *thought* they were creative, and the less creative people didn't think they were."

Change Your Environment. If you're indoors, move outdoors. Try working at the public library. Go to a different place, even if that means sitting in a coffee shop for an hour or moving your chair to the other side of the desk. But be careful: getting hung up on creating the perfect office or the ideal studio can be a trap.

If you usually listen to music when you work, try silence. Consider changing the hours you work: get up earlier to work first thing in the morning—or work in the evening and go to bed an hour later.

Change Your Tools. "Frequently, people think that barriers to creativity are some invisible, vague, mysterious goo," says Richard Byrne, Ph.D., former dean of the Annenberg School of Communications at the University of Southern California and one of the country's foremost advisers on technology and the management of change. "Sometimes it's a lot simpler than that. It could be that you need a quieter typewriter."

Other suggested changes: use crayons instead of paints, a fountain pen instead of a computer, index cards instead of legal pads, a tape recorder instead of a notebook.

Change Your Project. For example, write a play instead of a speech or a list instead of a report. Keep in mind that you can return to your original project later. During my creative-block period, I wanted to write fiction. But it meant so much to me that I froze up. When I started working on nonfiction (which involved a major shift in the way I viewed myself), I felt less threatened and was soon able to write fiction as well.

Change Your Goals. "Break the task into the smallest possible parts," recommends Valian. The more intimidating the overall task, the more important this is. The smaller the goal, the less threatening. The boost you get from *reaching* small goals—whether jotting down an idea on an index card or making one small pencil sketch in a pocket-size notebook—can spur you on to increased activity.

Or change the way you measure your output. If you set quantity goals for yourself ("I'll get up when I've written three pages"), change them to time goals ("I'll work for two hours") to increase your sense of accomplishment.

Play. Take a break. Give your unconscious mind an opportunity to come up with solutions. Especially fruitful moments are the transitional ones between work and play, between waking and sleeping. If your creative work is detailed and intellectual, do something physical. If you're wrestling with an abstraction, turn to something concrete such as a jigsaw puzzle. Fool around with clay or play the harmonica. You don't have to spend all day at it: 15 minutes can be enough. Taking time out to meditate may also help. Or indulge in a pleasant daydream—imagine yourself in the sunlit meadow or tropical paradise of your choice. It doesn't really matter what you do, as long as you enjoy it.

Sleep on It. "In the shadowy period before dozing off, you might drop your question, your problem, or your dilemma into your mind like a letter into a mailbox," writes Philip Goldberg in *The Intuitive Edge: Understanding Intuition & Applying It in Everyday Life.* "A hazy thought, the merest idea, will be better than a precise verbal statement. Drop it in, and let it go." Have a notebook near your bed, and in the morning, grab it before you do anything and scribble madly. You'll be surprised at what appears.

"Freewrite." Even if you're not a professional writer, you may find the following exercise helpful. "Force yourself to write, without stopping, for ten minutes," says Peter Elbow in *Writing with Power.* "Sometimes you will produce good writing. . . . Sometimes you will produce garbage. . . . You may stay on one topic, you may flip repeatedly from one to another; it doesn't matter. . . . The only point is to keep writing." If you can't think of anything to say, write about that—keep the pencil moving. Elbow adds, "If you're a blocked writer, 'free-writing' will help you overcome resistance and move you gradually in the direction of more fluency and control."

Brainstorm. Sit down with a pad of paper or a cassette, flash the problem you are facing in your mind, and then record every single idea—every word, thought, phrase, image, sound, and feeling—you can think of, no matter how silly, impossible, embarrassing, or off the point it may seem. Write as much as you can as fast as you can. Don't stop to assess the ideas. The best way to get an idea, to paraphrase two-time Nobel laureate Linus Pauling, is to get *a lot* of ideas. Your only goal should be quantity.

The rewards of brainstorming come from being uninhibited, but that takes practice. "After some practice, your mind will come up with an inexhaustible fount of ideas," says Byrne. You can judge them later. Perhaps only one or two will be possibilities, but at least the creative juices will be flowing.

Think Like a Child. Ask "How come?" "What if?" "Why not?" You may find yourself stretching your imagination wide enough to come up with the answers. Don't worry if you can't use them; at least you're breaking through your paralysis.

Be Contrary. Reverse things. Don't take it from the top. Start at the end or in the middle. Put the first part last. Shuffle things around. Do the opposite of whatever you usually do, and revel in your spirit of rebellion.

Do the same thing with analogies. Compare your subject to the most outlandish thing you can think of: dinosaurs, a teapot, the solar system, a pencil, the ocean, the Wars of the Roses. "Simply take an object, a concept, or an event and look for qualities, functions, or processes to associate with the problem under consideration," writes Goldberg.

Seek Out Solitude.   Many people are afraid of solitude. But most of the time, being alone is a prerequisite for creative insight. "If we are to experience insights from our unconscious, we need to be able to give ourselves solitude," writes May.

Mozart wrote of this process: "When I am, as it were, completely myself, entirely alone, and of good cheer—say, traveling in a carriage, or walking after a good meal, or during the night when I cannot sleep; it is on such occasions that ideas flow best and most abundantly. *Whence* and *how* they come, I know not; nor can I force them."

Visualize.   Finally, visualize yourself completing the project in as much detail as you can. "If you can imagine doing it, you are likely to do it," says Valian. "And if you can't imagine doing it, you will not do it no matter how wonderful it sounds."

The creative urge is a strong one, and it is not one to be ignored. If you feel blocked, try *anything* to actualize your dream. Why? Choreographer Martha Graham explained it best to colleague Agnes de Mille: "There is a vitality, a life-force, an energy, a quickening, that is translated through you into action. And because there is only one of you in all of time, this expression is unique. And if you block it, it will never exist through any other medium and [it will] be lost. The world will not have it. It is not your business to determine how good it is nor how valuable nor how it compares with other expressions. It is your business to keep it yours clearly and directly, to keep the channel open. You do not even have to believe in yourself or your work. You have to keep open and aware directly to the urges that motivate you. Keep the channel open."

"I Wish I Could Do Something Creative"*

Many people feel a strong desire to "do something creative," but they have no special talents (or so they think) and can find no outlet for that desire. This yearning usually doesn't go away; if left untended, it can cause depression. The reason is simple: having no creative outlet can feel like living in a windowless room. Regardless of how we express it, creativity is a basic need. "As children, we discover something new every day, but as adults, most people lose that combination of curiosity and playfulness," observes Carole Lieberman, M.D., a Los Angeles psychiatrist. "Being creative means discovering something new."

It also means not having to adapt to the wishes of anyone, whether that person is an employer, a parent, or a picky partner. Being creative means being willing to lose control, to fool around, to experiment, and to accept the possibility that the project you're involved in—whether it's building a miniature village in your basement or inventing a salad—may turn out to be a real mess. That kind of creative expression provides what is often available nowhere else: total freedom for your imagination. Finding a creative outlet, Dr. Lieberman says, "offers an area of life where you don't have to be in control, where you can leave things to your imagination and not worry about the finished product. It's not that you don't care. You care—but it's the *trip* that's important."

Fortunately, there are alternatives to a bad case of frustrated creativity. "The main thing is to be willing to take lots of risks," stresses Dr. Lieberman. "Go through the catalog of a community center or an extension university and pick whatever course strikes your fancy.

. . . .

* This section of Hathaway's article is separate from what precedes it; in the original publication of "15 Creative-Block Busters," it appeared at the end of the article and was boxed.

Don't allow your internal critic to limit what you should or shouldn't choose as a creative activity."

One woman who had been a social worker for many years did just that. She had no idea how to find an outlet for her creativity; in fact, she wasn't even sure she was "creative." Eventually, though, she was desperate enough to find out. She signed up for a half dozen workshops—in weaving, landscape architecture, t'ai chi ch'uan, dance, acting, and stained glass. She knew she couldn't be good at, or even enjoy, all those activities, but that knowledge took the pressure off her experimentation. She didn't *have* to come up with a winner.

As it turned out, she did respond to one of these classes. She apprenticed herself at a stained-glass workshop and later opened a small studio in her house. She was commissioned to design a couple of windows, exhibited several pieces in a group show, and eventually found herself working, creatively and contentedly, as a professional stained-glass maker. In about a year and a half, she changed her life completely.

The Three-Day Novel Writing Contest

Judy Keeler

The Three-Day Novel Writing Contest received a lot of attention the year I entered it, in 1982. Writers made a big to-do renting hotel rooms and locking themselves into windowless warehouses. One not only acquired the latest VDT, but also had gourmet treats and champagne delivered to keep his creative juices from going hungry.

But the stories of how books get written in 72 hours is often at least as interesting as the works themselves. It is no small task to turn out a page of prose in an hour or less, nor to write for 72 hours without much, if any, sleep.

It was certainly three days that I'll never forget.

When I entered the contest, all I knew was that I wanted to write a story about Jamaica. And I had serious doubts about whether I could do it. I used my last $50 to buy food . . . saving enough cash to take the bus home from North Bay in case I couldn't get a ride. On Labor Day weekend, when everyone else was playing tennis, walking dogs, [and] closing up cottages . . . I was packing paper, typewriter ribbons, candles and socks to head north to a cabin in the bush that belonged to a friend. And it *was* the bush.

Luckily, I found some people who were driving to North Bay who let me ride with them, even though they were already overcrowded and the trunk of the car sloped to the ground. It was 10 at night before we arrived. No driveway, no lights greeted us. My companions tried to talk me out of this craziness. But even lured by the comforts and company of friends, I knew that if I didn't get settled and started, I never would. The contest began in two hours.

Helped through the swamp that led to the door, with my cooler, typewriter, and assorted luggage, I opened the cabin door to find old horse harnesses, tires and dead mice. The little house was a shambles. Repressing my first urge to spend the next 12 hours cleaning, I put a sheet across the doorway from the kitchen to the living room and decided to live in the kitchen.

The kitchen, with the voice of a creek outside the window, a big old red stove, country tables and a couple of chairs, was by far the best of the disaster areas. There was no phone, no electricity and no running water. Two kerosene lamps were my light, and water was brought in with buckets. There was an outhouse.

In a way, it was ironic. The wooden cabin and the high rolling hills behind looked like the setting in Jamaica where my story was about to take place. As I began at midnight, the first thing I did was thumbtack a series of snapshots I had taken in Jamaica to the boards of the kitchen wall—and set up my typewriter. Reggae tapes provided the other source of inspiration as I began writing.

The moment I sat down, I was stricken with fear. What if I could not finish, what if I could find no plot, what if there were bears when I went out in the middle of the night alone? Chasing away these nightmares, I took out legal-sized paper and began to write, and write, and write. The story poured out. . . . I promised myself not to go for walks in the country, and not to discuss my work with a friend who was to drop by once a day to see that I was all right. Going to Jamaica in my imagination, playing with images at my fingertips, I could have been anywhere. People I knew in a remote village called Windsor Forest became the basis for characters I put into the book.

The title was born from reality, too. One morning at breakfast near Negril, I was writing in a journal. On the front of the book I wrote, "JAH TRAVELS" (Jah is Jamaican patois for God). A teenage boy approached me and, standing over my shoulder, said, "Ah . . . Jah travels wi' de lady." Two years later, Jah Travels became the title.

By the time I reached page 50 it was Saturday night, and I had the feeling of being halfway through. I knew the secret of getting to the end was pacing and the endurance to keep awake. But at this point my work was handwritten, and no one, but no one, would be able to read that set of hieroglyphics. To the typewriter. From then on, all but the most difficult of passages went straight onto the page, with little correction or proofreading. A writer's horror.

I typed all night beneath the moon, beside the creek that spoke to me in far-away patois. The little fireflies I saw outside dancing in the grass were jumbies, Jamaican spirits ready to pinch, surprise or frighten. Even two kerosene lamps and a dozen candles placed in empty bottles around the room did not shed enough light. I was certain my book and the cabin would go up in flames. Eyes blurred, back tired, I could barely read the page. The sentences didn't make sense. I prayed for clarity.

My furious pounding at 3 a.m. disturbed no one. There was nothing but a sliver of moon and countless stars. By this time I was so tired that I decided I must cat-nap; I could stay awake no more. But being tired didn't matter. All that mattered was the next sentence.

The candles were ashes when I reached the final stretch Sunday morning. When I felt famished, there were camembert, smoked oysters, fruit and cheese to munch on, not to mention lots of Jamaican Blue Mountain coffee. I was up against time and fatigue, and taking breaks only encouraged me to quit. But by 2 in the afternoon I was on the last lap, and I knew I had earned a walk. So I set out to the fields, but I soon felt cabin and typewriter calling me back.

When my friend came at 4:30 to chop wood and see if I needed anything, he invited me to join his family for a dinner break. Anticipating the poor lighting situation, he somehow knew I would not want to stay at the cabin. A nearby friend of his offered me a place to finish my book undisturbed. Not only was this place an idyllic log cabin, right on a lake, it turned out I knew the owner. Throwing a few logs on the fire to break the chill, I . . . sat underneath a real lamp to pound out the last pages of Jah Travels.

When I finished, of course, I couldn't sleep. So we sang and played guitar until dawn, when the post office opened and I could put the book in the mail. I still couldn't sleep for another 16 hours, at which point I collapsed in a hammock and had a dream: I was standing on a rock on an island in Muskoka, where I spent many childhood summers. This magical island called Monte Cristo, had a rock facing the wild westerly wind, and a bent pine that I felt was a holy, spiritual place. It was always on this rock that I stood when my friend's parents were busy closing up the cottage and the kids were getting in the last swims, and I made promises to myself.

One of them was that one day I would write a book.

There's a First Time for Every Day

Penney Kome

On my way to an Olympic hockey game, I overheard a woman complaining how much she hates to get lost. I had to laugh to myself. Getting lost can be the very essence of adventure, as any seasoned traveller knows. I've been getting lost, and found again, for 10 years now. It comes with exploring new territory. In the long run, the result is progress.

You see, for 10 years I've made a point of doing something for the first time every day. Feeling myself getting stuck in a rut, I consciously decided to risk something new every day.

Newness is a risk, you know. Psychologists say that most people avoid change because it unsettles them. That's why so many people, when they travel, insist on having their regular food. A huge bowl of cornflakes proudly displayed in the breakfast buffet at a Stockholm hotel attests to how loath people are to forgo the familiar.

Oddly enough, I found that my philosophy of "firsts" actually diminished my risks. As is the case with many people, I'm reluctant to try to do new things unless I know I can do them well, for fear of looking foolish. When my goal is simply to collect a "first," however, then the focus shifts to my own personal best.

For instance, I was reluctant to try roller skating when it was a fad, from fear of falling and looking silly in front of more experienced skaters. With my new philosophy, I tried skating, and I did in fact fall, but it didn't matter. I'd done what I set out to do. In a writer's life of delayed gratification, I'd achieved a small goal for the day.

I soon figured out that I could tackle big goals by breaking them down into little daily "firsts." The first year of living this way was heady stuff. I got my first driver's licence, first car, first project grant, first cross-Canada trip, first contact lenses, and first apartment alone.

I began to worry about running out of "firsts", which led me to clarify what I meant by that term. Actually, I decided, anything goes: visiting a new place, reading a new author, meeting a new person, trying a new recipe—these are just a few of the possibilities. Buying something new will do, but only in a pinch.

There's no need for heroics, just a change in routine. I fondly remember the first time I downed tools in the middle of the day and went to a movie; or the first time I realized that, Mother's injunctions notwithstanding, I really didn't have to eat everything on my plate.

A friend said that my philosophy reminds her of a man she knows. After several harrowing years in combat during the Second World War, during which he saw the deaths of literally hundreds of men under his command, he emerged with the resolution to "have a little fun every day." Rather than being embittered, he decided that fun is as important as anything else you can accomplish in life.

Firsts are not always fun, however. My first experience with public speaking was utterly nerveracking. Like many others, I became a writer because, for me, writing was easier than talking.

It was an ordeal to stand in front of an audience—especially when, as it turned out, I was saying something unpopular—that left me both exhausted and exhilarated. Not only had I achieved my first for the day, I'd overcome a lifelong fear. But I did it for the "first."

When offered an opportunity for a "first," of course, I have to weigh the potential benefits against potential losses. Sometimes I use Gloria Steinem's guideline: "What's the worst that could happen? Will I die?" With public speaking, at least, the answer is no. Other times, it's not that simple. . . .

It goes without saying that some questions are too important to be decided on the basis of "firsts." You wouldn't accept the first proposal of marriage, say, simply because it was a first. . . .

My tenth year of "firsts" has been as exciting as the beginning year. The list includes: first marriage, first step-child, first baby, first house purchase, first time living in the West, first major award, and first European speaking engagement. The risks have gotten bigger since I started living this way, and so have the rewards.

As I watched the Winter Olympics on television, it occurred to me that many of the competitors were teenagers. For most of them, this was their first Olympics. My heart was in my throat watching the risks that some of them took. Whether or not they won medals, whether they got lost in the airports and on the streets of Calgary, I'm sure that all of them would say that their lives are richer for their "first."

Create Eccentrically

Carol McLeod

A novelist explained, at a writers' workshop held recently in New Brunswick, how detailed lists help her create saleable fiction. "I draw up lists of everything—places, physical characteristics, speech patterns—you name it. I even draw maps of the towns and houses my characters live in. It really helps me visualize the story."

One particularly smug man in the audience eyed her skeptically, "Don't you think it's all just a bit eccentric?"

"Perhaps," she shrugged. "My only regret though is that it's not an eccentricity I can claim as my own—I've copied it from Sinclair Lewis."

Establishing work habits that provide motivation is one of the keys to successful writing. Creativity cannot be bound by convention. Some of the world's greatest writers have had quirks that would make the smug man at the New Brunswick workshop cringe in horror.

Foremost on the list is Samuel Johnson, who developed an entire repertoire of peculiar mannerisms. To steady his resolve and focus his imagination, Johnson would immerse himself in complicated mathematical calculations. Whenever he felt the need to break up his feelings into more manageable units, he would reach out and touch the posts he passed as he walked the streets of London. Indoors, he would pace the floor as if he were measuring it, then test it for firmness and finally trace geometric patterns with his heels and toes.

Less compulsive was Jane Austen, who had an obsessive secrecy about her writing. With no room of her own in which to work (a situation Virginia Woolf would later use as a theme), Austen used to sit at a small mahogany desk in the family dining room writing on small scraps of paper that she could slip into a drawer if someone came in unexpectedly.

Honoré de Balzac had an entirely different quirk. Getting up at midnight, the author of *La Comédie Humaine* would don a monastic white robe, then write until daylight. He spent the rest of the day correcting proofs and conducting his business affairs. After supper he would fall into bed, only to begin again at midnight. To fortify himself in his grueling pace, he drank cup after cup of black coffee—an estimated 50,000 cups during his creative period alone.

For Charles Dickens inspiration came not from a cup but rather from a mirror. A gifted actor, Dickens would often rush from his desk to a nearby mirror where he would gesticulate and make violent facial contortions before returning to his desk to write down the scene he had just acted out.

Slightly more sedate was Hans Christian Andersen, who relaxed by creating elaborate and sophisticated paper cuttings. More than interconnected dolls, Andersen's cuttings included everything from sprites and swans to horrible demons and naked witches.

Friedrich Nietzsche, the great philosopher-writer, liked to work amid the doves in Venice's Piazza San Marco. When failing eyesight finally drove him indoors, Nietzsche shut himself up in an airless attic and refused to work unless his desk was strewn with rotten apples.

Of less peculiar makeup were L.M. Montgomery and John Galsworthy, whose eccentricities may seem more familiar to many writers. While Montgomery could only work when closeted alone in absolute silence, Galsworthy could write anywhere—even on a train speeding through the English countryside.

Considerably more self-centred was Somerset Maugham who, in the latter stages of his career, depended upon ego massage to foster his creativity. Working in his study before a wall of expensively bound books, Maugham insisted that a collected set of his own novels be placed directly at eye level.

For Hugh Garner, an extremely sensible man and winner of the 1963 Governor General's Award for Fiction, selling his novels to the general public was just as important as selling them to editors. Whenever he found his books out of stock in major stores, he would descend upon his publishers demanding to know what was wrong with their distribution system.

Other writers have had their own eccentricities—more or less bizarre. But one thing remains clear: no quirk, no matter how outrageous, should be rooted out if it helps get the story written. If it works for *you*, forget the smug individual who might appear at your next workshop and carry on.

The Joy of *Writing*

Alan Pearson

In this age of increasingly sophisticated writing tools, I have recently spent several years wanting a fountain pen, not a ballpoint, a *fountain* pen. And, being a professional writer I thought I deserved the best. Unfortunately, because writing—to use Dylan Thomas's phrase—pays a mouse's ransom in remuneration, the matter had to be given careful thought. I took a year to justify the purchase.

Now I'm the proud owner of a top-of-the-line Shaeffer; it's golden, has fine ridges along the length of its barrel and gleams in sumptuous splendour in the desk light as I work on the virgin sheet!

The colour is pretty, but it's also symbolic: it continuously says, *gold* is what its efforts will yield. Ian Fleming, after the success of his first book, *Casino Royale*, had a golden typewriter made for him as a spur to commercial effort.

I had wanted to go back to the fountain pen because it had come to my attention that most of the writers I admire are or were handwriters: Gore Vidal, Laurie Lee, de Beauvoir, Capote, and almost all the poets. And it wasn't just a literary thing: Jack (*The Eagle Has Landed*) Higgins, Eric Ambler, and Helen MacInnes among many other "pop" writers write books the hard way. There have to be some compelling reasons.

By the process of writing by hand I discovered them for myself. The first thing to be noticed is that you work in *silence*; this appeals to me, not only because it's conducive to orderly thought, but because I don't have to put cotton wool in my ears as I do when I type.

Then there is that ease of making changes; no more thought-disruptive twisting of the typewriter roller backward and forward. Word changes and the addition of new clauses are carried out with the stroke of a pen.

And then there is the esthetic pleasure as you note the lush flow of Royal Blue ink flowing from the gleaming nib.

Finally, there is a lot to be said for being able to write easily in bed, on a bus, in a chair or on a beach if the mood takes you. By contrast, the intransigent typewriter demands you sit upright, separated from the page where the creation takes place. Also, you have to *rivet* the delicate thoughts noisily to the paper. Surely this is all wrong; thoughts *flow*, they don't come out like a rain of tin tacks on the skin of a drum.

Many typewriter addicts believe the machine will make more work possible, but this is not so. Consider the paucity of output of most of today's novelists compared to that of their Victorian counterparts. I am a touch typist, and I've found my output is the same no matter what compositional method I use. The explanation is that a writer's output is determined by the rate at which he or she can generate ideas and put them into good sentences.

But what about word-processors? someone will ask. As far as I'm concerned, they are another example of technology in search of an application—useless for the real writer. They are essentially a business tool. Proponents of this intrusive hardware say, "But you can add paragraphs and sentences so easily."

My answer to that is that I get paragraphs in the right place most of the time from the start. But, in any event, adding or subtracting them is easy. To subtract one you cross it out; to add one you write it on the left-hand side of the exercise book you write in, with an arrow to indicate where it should go. For that you need a $5000 word processor?

Edmund Wilson once said that English prose began to decline at about the time the typewriter was invented. I'm inclined to agree.

It is true the designers of these alluring pieces of high tech hardware are dedicated and expensively educated specialists, but what I should like to know is this: will they *ever* be able to design anything that can compete in simplicity and usefulness with my super fountain pen?

Creative Writing Co-op

Lori Thicke

A one-of-a-kind programme at the University of Victoria in British Columbia is turning out trained and experienced Creative Writing graduates ready to be assistant editors, publicity persons, copy editors, proofreaders, typesetters, newspaper reporters and radio broadcasters. What is the programme that delivers so much? It's the Creative Writing Co-op and it blends the aesthetic with the academic and transforms both into on-the-job experience.

"Co-operative education isn't a new concept," says Robert Allington, the Creative Writing Co-op coordinator, "but traditionally it has involved science-oriented studies like physics and biology." Co-op programmes in the humanities are rare, and the Creative Writing Co-op at the University of Victoria is the first in Canada to offer students work terms to complement the creative and literary bent of their studies.

The idea of dove-tailing university and relevant paid work experience comes to this country via Dr. Howard Petch, the University of Victoria president who initiated co-operative education when he was the president of southern Ontario's Waterloo University. But that was only the first step. The former chairman of the Creative Writing Department, Dr. Dave Godfrey, "went out knocking on doors to get the Co-op started," according to Allington. "He had to convince the skeptics of co-op education at the university whose orientation really has been in the sciences."

Godfrey is now teaching publishing procedures, one of the core classes of the co-op programme. "Everybody said it wouldn't work," he recalls. "After a while I started thinking it wouldn't work myself. I've never had so many sleepless nights." However, the Creative Writing Department now has one of the most successful co-op programmes in the university by virtue of the number of students matched to employers each year and the fact that all the graduates from the programme are now employed in their field.

As publisher and editor of the *Agassiz Advance* in B.C., Allington himself was a co-op employer before he came to the university. "They sold me on the programme. They convinced me cooperative education had benefits for both the student and the employer. I got involved because I believed in it."

How does the Co-op work? "Students still complete the regular requirements for a BA or a BFA degree," explains Allington. "Students are offered workshops in fiction, poetry and drama, and such courses as publishing procedures, graphic arts, journalism, and photo journalism. At the completion of their second year, they are eligible for their first four-month work term. The employers receive résumés, interview the applicants, and make their decision. By the time the student graduates, she or he will have held four temporary positions."

Although the positions *are* temporary, students are treated like any other employee, with the concomitant responsibilities. And while many co-op positions are partially funded by the federal government—a boon to employers—the student receives a regular working wage. The only difference is that at the end of the work term, the student goes back to school.

The types of jobs filled are as varied as the students themselves. Ken Faris, now finishing his final work term at Agriculture Canada, spent last summer working with Crabtree Publishing in Toronto. "As part of my work for Crabtree, I spent two weeks in the Arctic

taking pictures for an educational book I was putting together on the Inuit for grades five, six, and seven."

With the Co-op, Faris has been across Canada and as far afield as India; he has worked as a reporter and photographer on weekly and bi-weekly newspapers in the interior of BC and in 1984 he arranged a placement for himself in Hyderabad, India, as an editorial assistant for an international agricultural research institute funded by the United Nations.

Most co-op positions are in B.C., however, with a sprinkling available in several other provinces, particularly Alberta and Ontario. "This past summer, students could apply to be an editorial assistant for a small publishing house on the West Coast, a publisher's assistant in a larger establishment in Toronto, a typesetter for a Vancouver printing firm, an information services officer for a large oil company in northern Alberta, a reporter in the Yukon, and assistant editor for a children's publisher in Hamilton, or a radio broadcaster on Vancouver Island," says Allington.

Past positions held by students include some unusual jobs: one student was a ghost writer, several others have been involved in computer software documentation, and a co-op student originally hired as a radio broadcaster ended up hosting a feature television programme.

Co-op students possess a variety of talents, and eligibility requirements for the programme are stiff. Says Allington, "Only a small percentage of applying students are actually accepted. Only the best students are chosen."

Those who have been accepted into the programme are, naturally, enthusiastic. "After working at four different jobs I have several alternatives for when I graduate. Two of my four employers have offered me work when I complete my degree," says Faris.

Allington is equally positive about the benefits for students. "By the time they graduate, they will have at least sixteen months on-the-job experience in writing-related fields. No matter how students decide to earn their living with their pens, whether they want to write the Great Canadian Novel, or edit the manuscripts of others, or make a contribution in other ways, that experience will benefit them."

However tantalizing the benefits, co-op students find themselves having to make sacrifices. Many students have had to postpone romantic involvement because joining the co-op means they are on the go every four months. Married students are often reluctant to enter the programme, not wanting to leave their spouses behind as they move to a new job location.

For Jane Hamilton, who recently completed an extended work term with Crabtree Publishing, where she was in charge of all the artwork, the greatest frustration was "getting ready to move and not knowing where I was going." It's not uncommon for placements to be finalized only weeks before the student is expected to move to the new location. Students must, usually within a few days, go to a town or city they don't know, find a place to live, and start a new job. Says Hamilton, "It's like Outward Bound: they throw you in the jungle and you either sink or swim or get eaten by the monkeys." But, she adds, "The job made up for the hassles. I learned things I wouldn't have learned otherwise and got a lot of great experience." The co-op programme, she says, "gives you the opportunity to find out what you can do."

The benefits of co-op do not accrue just to the students. As Allington says, "From my own experience and the experience of other employers I've talked to, it's often difficult to find somebody—particularly in small business, and most publishers fall into that category—who is qualified and wants to move where you are. With the co-op, the employer gets an enthusiastic worker, somebody who's already made a commitment to writing or writing-related fields as a career path—who really wants to learn, who digs and hustles."

Jean Paton, director of operations for Simon and Pierre Publishing in Toronto, which has recently become a co-op employer, agrees. "The energy and enthusiasm a student brings is valuable to a company like ours."

Ellen Godfrey, president of Press Porcepic in Victoria and a long-standing co-op employer, believes that it is necessary for literary publishers to have "the combination of someone who knows something about publishing and who has a literary sensibility. It's very important to have someone with a liberal arts education in my firm. (Someone) widely read and well educated." In addition to this, she values the "practical experience" of co-op students. "In a small company everybody needs expertise in all areas. (They) should be able to understand the process from beginning to end." Godfrey says that hiring co-op students "who already have the basis upon which the knowledge they need can be added," saves her time. "I have recommended it to friends across Canada."

Although Bobby Kalman, publisher and editor-in-chief of Crabtree Publishing, initially felt she was "taking a chance" in hiring not one but two co-op employees, she says she found the students "well trained and very professional. (They) really know what they want to do and realize how valuable the experience is. They appreciate the opportunity and are not just looking at it as a job. I wouldn't hesitate to hire someone from the co-op even on a full-time basis because the experience they get working for publishers makes them realistic—they know what publishing is really about."

Ellen Godfrey believes the Creative Writing Co-op is the way for all education to go. "It clarifies what you intend to do with your degree. Co-op is the beginning of where people keep moving between work and education for the rest of their lives."

In the Mode: Personal Computers and Creativity

Paul Wilson

Last August I bought a word processor, which was in fact a microcomputer outfitted with a special set of programs that allowed me to use it as a souped-up typewriter. It was not cheap: most good word processing systems cost several times more than a good electric typewriter, but in my line of work—translating and writing—there were strong practical considerations in favour of getting one. I was just putting the final polish on my translation of a 900-page novel that had gone through a total of four retypings, two of which I did myself. The combined expense of that work—most of it mindless drudgery—could have paid for a machine that could eliminate that kind of repetition forever. So despite some misgivings, I took the plunge.

Once I'd bought the thing, I realized that I had also purchased entry into the mysterious world of computer technology. Everyone knows this world exists, just as everyone knows it is making big changes, analogous to those brought about by the internal combustion engine and the telephone. But most of the technology is invisible and hard to understand without some practical, "hands on" experience of it.

My first big discovery was that I had completely misunderstood the term "computer literacy." I had thought it was something you could achieve by reading books, and so I read a lot about computers before finally buying one. But now I realized that almost nothing of this had really sunk in, and it was only after some time with the machine that I gradually began to grasp, or at least was better able to conceptualize, what was going on.

Part of it was becoming familiar with the strange terminology. Expressions like "booting up," "saving to disc," "scrolling," "swapping," and "buffer" slowly began to make sense. Far from getting in the way of understanding, as they had seemed to do when I first read the manuals, they were, I now realized, vivid metaphors that help one to visualize invisible operations. I was especially intrigued by the notion of "scrolling" the text through the monitor or "window." It was like a direct link back to a pre-book culture, and it made me feel a strong, if somewhat improbable, sense of continuity with the scribes of ancient Alexandria.

A lot of computer jargon has come into our everyday speech, and this is a sure sign of its vigour, its usefulness, and its appeal to people's ears. Two of the most familiar expressions are "hard" and "soft," and in a way they point straight to the heart of the new technology. Computers are essentially a "soft" or malleable technology. They can be made to receive, store, manipulate, organize (the French word for computer is "ordinateur"), and transfer information, but the machine itself is inert, dumb, and useless until it is configured to operate in a certain way by the appropriate "software" and given specific instructions by the user. The only limits to its potential are in the "hardware"—that is, in the design and capacity of the chips, the other electronic parts, and the peripheral devices that constitute the physical apparatus—and in the imagination and intelligence of those who design and use the software.

This is where the analogy with a typewriter breaks down. Suppose a writer buys a computer to write a book. Very quickly, he will discover that in addition to making the everyday chores of writing and revising much easier, the computer can also be used to connect him, via the telephone, to what are called data bases, essentially electronic libraries where he can search for the information be needs. When he finds it, he can then "download" the data into his computer and transfer it to his own data base, which he stores on floppy discs. Moreover, he can "log on" to a network of other computer users, find those who share his professional and personal interests, and use the computer to trade information, compare notes, and exchange letters. Finally, when the book is finished, he can send the "manuscript" electronically to a publisher. And all this has been accomplished with the help of billions of tiny, angelic bits of electricity dancing endlessly variable quadrilles on the head of a microchip. It is the variability of that dance that is the key.

Of course, even if you only use the microcomputer to write with, it is still a very useful tool. And that was my second discovery: although personal computers may have a power that is awesome to contemplate (according to *Scientific American,* if the aircraft industry had evolved as spectacularly as computers have over the past 25 years, a Boeing 767 today would cost $500 and could fly around the world in 20 minutes on five gallons of fuel), and they may be surrounded by an aura of mystic potential for transforming the world, but basically they're just a tool.

As the strengths and limitations of this tool became clearer to me, I began to see that for all the extravagant claims being made, the computer had not really supplanted the "older" technology at all. My typewriter was still indispensable for addressing envelopes, filling out forms, and writing short letters, and pen and paper were still as useful as ever for taking notes and editing. Looking up words in the dictionary was often faster, and always more interesting, than "accessing" the computer's spelling program, as useful as that may be. And you can't read a floppy disc on the subway, at least not yet. So in fact, we are living in a continuity of technologies that stretch from the space age all the way back to neolithic times, if not beyond. To put it another way, John Henry may have died trying to beat the steam drill, but his nine-pound hammer is still on sale at the corner hardware store. In that sense, at least, I have stopped thinking of the computer as a threat.

The third thing owning a computer made me realize was how much of what the average layperson sees and reads about computers is hype, or at least hyperbole. Like so many important inventions, the computer is still very much a technology in search of new applications, and this is especially true of personal computers, which in the past three years have become a multi-billion dollar growth industry. This marketplace is teeming with contenders, from corporate colossi like IBM—which has only recently entered the personal computer sweepstakes—to tiny, hole-in-the-wall operations manufacturing what are sometimes called clones, computers cobbled together from spare parts to run on software meant for the established makes. In addition, there is a thriving cottage industry producing hundreds of thousands of programs and hardware "enhancements" to expand the capacity of existing computers. Each day, as computers become more powerful and versatile, and as the radius of the market extends beyond buffs, fanatics, and serious, informed users, the claims become more extravagant and less precise. In this situation the buyer, more than ever before, had best beware. . . .

How are writers themselves taking to the new technology? Over the past five months I've conducted a random and very unscientific survey. Among those who actually work with a word processor, statements like "I'd never go back" or "I don't know how I ever managed without it" are common. Writers who work to deadlines in particular find them indispensable. Many praise what they call the "pliability" of the text—meaning that you can play with it on the screen and get it right before committing it to paper; others say that the very ease of the physical act of writing seems to free the imagination.

Speculations on whether the computer actually helps people to write better vary widely, largely because the creative process itself is a far greater mystery than any technology. But there is one thing on which just about everyone agrees: the machine really comes into its own during the rewriting process. Writers like bp Nichol, who may go through many different drafts of a poem or script, find that it sharpens the editing process. "Hand-edited text makes it difficult sometimes to see through the layers of your intention," Nichol says. "A word processor is the perfect tool for working through that to a point of clarity."

In this connection Ian Lancashire, a professor of English at the University of Toronto and author of *Computer Applications in Literary Studies*, raises an interesting point. "Writing on a computer," he says, "takes the process of writing—which on paper is like a monologue—and turns it into a dialogue." Studies made in the U.S. have shown that students who use word processors tend to have a dialogue with themselves as they write, although they are not always aware of it. "With a word processor, it is much easier to shift your perspective to that of the reader. You view the work as a fluid landscape rather than as something fixed and immutable." Lancashire also believes, on the basis of practical experience in the classroom, that the computer has a great potential for teaching technical people and civil servants how to write clearly.

Enthusiasm for word processing among writers and scholars is far from unanimous. When I heard a rumour that Northrop Frye was writing the next volume of *The Great Code* on a word processor, I wrote to ask him what his feelings were. "I'm afraid I'm still a Luddite in regard to computers," he replied. "I start all my writing in longhand, eventually graduate to the typewriter, and after a series of revisions on typed copies I get what I am after. What bothers me about composing on the typewriter, and would continue to bother me on a word processor, is seeing what I have written facing me. I write so slowly that early drafts look like a kind of accusation."

Frye's response echoes the feeling of many established humanities scholars and writers who feel that their own writing and research-

ing patterns are too set to change, and there is probably no real reason why they should, particularly since writing habits are so strongly individual. But the new technology has raised a host of other concerns as well, especially among those who are sometimes called "heavy users." The problems are well known: many secretaries who have to spend long hours each day in front of a video display terminal complain of back and eye strain, migraine headaches, menstrual cramps, spontaneous abortion, and a curious form of distress described as "a sense of disembodiment" or "loss of body perception." The usual explanation is that it has something to do with the electromagnetic radiation emitted by the screen. Frank Zingrone, a founding member of the degree program in communications at York University, and communications consultant Eric McLuhan feel they have found a physiological explanation having to do with the different functions of the right and left sides of the brain.

Zingrone told me that when the eye is presented with a pictorial image it tends to range widely and wildly over it, looking for detail that interests it. When presented with print, however, it fixates, and jerks forward as it reads. Once a reader loses interest in the material, the eye tends to resume the wandering that is its natural state. Each of these eye activities is related to one hemisphere of the brain—the wandering mode to the right, the fixed, linear mode to the left. Zingrone and McLuhan speculate that if you spend long hours a day at a terminal doing boring work, the two modes are in constant conflict, thus causing stress, which in turn leads to other, more familiar symptoms. If few writers complain of the ill effects of using computers, Zingrone suggests this is because they are interested in what they are writing on the screen, thus minimizing the stress.

Like every new technology, computers are provoking a lot of questions. Is this the dawn of a new age of information, or are we simply in for an era of unprecedented information pollution that threatens to smother our culture in banality and may even endanger individual freedom as we know it? The stage for great changes has already been set, and a wide array of computing power once reserved only for large institutions now is available to individuals and groups, both through the marketplace and through a growing variety of public institutions and networks. Those who feel that computers are a threat to culture or human freedom would have a stronger case if the technology were being deliberately held back for exclusive use by governments and police forces, as it is in the Soviet bloc, for example. In this context, the growing interest of small business and members of the cultural community—writers, journalists, academics—in computer technology is a hopeful sign, provided, of course, that its great potential is used for more than just self-aggrandizement.

At the moment, the present trends to exploit the technology culturally in this country seem entirely natural in the Canadian context. Enterprises like Swift Current, Stan Bevington's on-line printing and publishing operation, and Dave Godfrey's championship of large, easily accessible computer networks all reflect a view of the Canadian tradition in which railway lines, national broadcasting systems, and complex communication between artists and their audience are felt to be essential to the country's problematic integrity. Of course such problems are never solved by technology alone. The important thing, as always, will be what gets communicated. And that, as always, depends on minds of flesh and blood.

CHAPTER
Two

Writing with Style

A. FORE-WORDS

Warm up for activities in this chapter by discussion and writing. These quotations and questions may help you begin.

William Styron   "Good style is the product of long, hard practise and writing."

Robert Cormier   ". . . choose [your] words . . . with the reader in mind."

Anton Chekhov   "The art of writing is the art of abbreviation."

1.   Brainstorm your associations with "style" and define it.

2.   Are there objective criteria to judge "good style" for clothes, music, film, and writing? Justify.

3.   Why is communicating with style important for your present and future success?

B. FOUNDATIONS

Style matters. But the pursuit of style is delicate and elusive, and requires a lifetime commitment to language proficiency, reading, and personal growth. In this chapter, you'll work toward one aspect of that goal: the development of a clear, concise writing style to express your writer's *voice*. We'll focus on three concerns raised by our students of writing.

Tarvo: *Why* does style matter?
Kirsten: *What* is good style? There seem to be so many.
Sasha: *How* do I acquire good style? Is there a secret formula?

Craig's concern, "*What if* we need more than one basic style for post-secondary success?" is the focus of Chapter Three.

Let's get our bearings with a quick look at what John Dryden said about writing with style in "The Art of Poetry":

> Observe the language well in all you write,
> And swerve not from it in your loftiest flight.
> The smoothest verse and exactest sense
> Displease us, if ill English give offence:
> A barbarous phrase no reader can approve;
> Nor bombast, noise, or affectation love.
> In short, without pure language, what you write
> Can never yield us profit or delight. Take time for
> thinking; never work in haste;
> And value not yourself for writing fast.
> A rapid poem with such a fury writ,
> Shows want of judgment, not abounding wit.
> More pleased we are to see a river lead,
> His gentle streams along a flowery mead,
> Than from high banks to hear loud torrents roar,
> With foamy waters on a muddy shore.
> Gently make haste, of labour not afraid:
> A hundred times consider what you've said:
> Polish, repolish, every colour lay,
> And sometimes add, but oftener take away.
> 'Tis not enough when swarming faults are writ,
> That here and there are scatter'd sparks of wit;
> For each object must fix'd in due place,
> And differing parts have corresponding grace:
> Till, by a curious art disposed, we find
> One perfect whole, of all the pieces join'd.

Dryden's subject is the writing of poetry, but his comments apply to all forms of discourse. Before reading on, discuss writing tips contained in the poem. Is the advice given in this eighteenth-century composition still timely? Cull a preliminary list of style tips for your Writer's Notebook.

Before delving into the complexities of "good style," let's consider Tarvo's query. Why does communicating with style matter? You're probably not planning to be Shakespeare, after all.

The Pleasurable and Practical "*Why*" of Style

Learning to communicate with style enhances the quality of your life. Perhaps because we take words so much for granted our awareness of style is dulled. Listen to toddlers playing with words; observe their delight. Listen to children chanting skipping songs in the schoolyard; observe their pleasure in the rhythm of language. In Activity One, we'll take time to listen to words that sound good.

Activity One   Listening to Words That Sound Good
Purpose

- to enjoy a variety of sound patterns
- to begin a collection of words that sound good
- to review connotation and denotation

1.   Get into a listening frame of mind. A volunteer student or the teacher begins by reading this passage in a steady voice.

> Imagine you're in a quiet country lane meandering downhill toward a rushing brook. On either side of the brook, heavy willow boughs trail in the water. You hear the chirps of birds over the rushing water. Can you see them? What colour are they? . . . You stop, remove your sneakers, dangle your toes in the dark wetness. What do you hear? How does the water feel on your skin? What odours fill the air?

When you're ready, move on to the next question.

2.   Volunteers read to the class or groups. Listen and enjoy.

- Tarvo and Sasha enjoy the rhythm of "Gus: The Theatre Cat" by T.S. Eliot:

> Gus is the Cat at the Theatre Door.
> His name, as I ought to have told you before,
> Is really Asparagus. That's such a fuss
> To pronounce, that we usually call him just Gus.
> His coat's very shabby, he's thin as a rake,
> And he suffers from palsy that makes his paw shake.
> He was, in his youth, quite the smartest of Cats—

But no longer a terror to mice and to rats.
For he isn't the Cat that he was in his prime;
Though his name was quite famous, he says, in its time.
And whenever he joins his friends at their club
(Which takes place at the back of the neighbouring pub)
He loves to regale them, if someone else pays,
With anecdotes drawn from his palmiest days.
For he once was a Star of the highest degree—
He has acted with Irving, he's acted with Tree.
And he likes to relate his success on the Halls,
Where the Gallery once gave him seven cat-calls.
But his grandest creation, as he loves to tell,
Was Firefrorefiddle, the Fiend of the Fell.

'I have played', so he says, 'every possible part,
And I used to know seventy speeches by heart.
I'd extemporize back-chat, I knew how to gag,
And I knew how to let the cat out of the bag.
I knew how to act with my back and my tail;
With an hour of rehearsal, I never could fail.
I'd a voice that would soften the hardest of hearts,
Whether I took the lead, or in character parts.
I have sat by the bedside of poor Little Nell;
When the Curfew was rung, then I swung on the bell.
In the Pantomime season I never fell flat
And I once understudied Dick Whittington's Cat.
But my grandest creation, as history will tell,
Was Firefrorefiddle, The Fiend of the Fell.'

Then, if someone will give him a toothful of gin,
He will tell how he once played a part in *East Lynne*.
At a Shakespeare performance he once walked on pat,
When some actor suggested the need for a cat.
He once played a Tiger—could do it again—
Which an Indian Colonel pursued down a drain.
And he thinks that he still can, much better than most,
Produce blood-curdling noises to bring on the Ghost.
And he once crossed the stage on a telegraph wire,
To rescue a child when a house was on fire.
And he says: 'Now, these kittens, they do not get trained
As we did in the days when Victoria reigned.
They never get drilled in a regular troupe,
And they think they are smart, just to jump through a hoop.'
And he'll say, as he scratches himself with his claws,
'Well, the Theatre's certainly not what it was.
These modern productions are all very well,

But there's nothing to equal, from what I hear tell,
    That moment of mystery
    When I made history
    As Firefrorefiddle, the Fiend of the Fell.'

• Kirsten is struck by the vivid images of this passage from Kate Chopin's novel, *The Awakening*:

The walk to the beach was no inconsiderable one, consisting as it did of a long, sandy path, upon which a sporadic and tangled growth that bordered on either side made frequent and unexpected inroads. There were acres of yellow camomile, reaching out on either hand. Further away still, vegetable gardens abounded, with frequent small plantations of orange or lemon trees intervening. The dark green clusters glistened from afar in the sun.

• Craig is intrigued by the experimental sound patterns in bill bissett's "iul tell yu a storee she sd":

                    i beleev
            yuv livd manee lives
                n ths is th culminaysyun
        if you can let go uv dredging for downrs n
            advocate sharing n leisure recreaysyunal
                time in th post compewtr age thr can
        b at last freedom if yu promote n realize
                equalitee in access to evreething n
            kindness loving help n if yu let go uv
        yr grudges guilt envees feers see yr own
            possibul happeeness yu can entr th
    streem pass thr th island uv
    swallows it is all within seeing
        heering trace touch taste th softlee
    ink spilling silkee ways uv th stars wher
        ther ar othr lives waiting for yu whn
    th time is aftr yet anothr long sojurn
            yu accept th strength n entr th
        pleides yuv alredee livd on venus
    th erth will b alrite livd on venus
    th erth will b alrite th almost
        liquid lite uv dawn embracing th
    wild flowrs it is a changing
            place

2a.   In your Writer's Notebook, speedwrite about your favourite passage from question 1. Focus on words' sounds, shapes, and textures.

b.   Draft a paragraph for your writing folder, responding to one of these quotations. (You may wish to illustrate your paragraph with references to the passages by Dryden, bissett, Eliot, Chopin and/or your favourite stylist.)

Michele Landsberg   ". . . words are more powerful than anything armies can blast each other with."

William Golding   "I have a life-long love of rhythm, sound, and particular rhyme."

Sheila Watson   Words are "charged with all sorts of possibilities which may explode at any minute."

3.   Start a collection of words that sound good in one section of your Writer's Notebook. Beside each word, record associations—colours, textures, sounds, shapes—whatever comes to mind.

4a.   Review the distinctions between connotative and denotative language in the Glossary (page 406). Which of the words in your "Words that sound good" list have strong connotations?
b.   Read "Self" by Peggy Rosenthal (page 104). With a partner, discuss what the passage adds to your understanding of connotation and denotation.

5a.   Question family members about your early use of language; perhaps they recall your first words, play noises, or phrases you enjoyed in stories and songs. Do these words or sounds shed light on present preferences or associations?
b.   If your family speaks more than one language, ask your parents or older siblings if you mixed phrases or sounds.
c.   Consider the implications of your answers to a. and b. for your present and post-secondary writing success.

Regardless of your post-secondary plans, the ability to communicate with style enhances your options and likelihood of success. Salespeople, nurses, graphic artists, and corporate managers all need a strong command of oral and written language. In Activity Two, explore the importance of language in the workplace with your present and future needs in mind.

Activity Two   Communicating with Style in the Workplace

Purpose

- to explore the practical value of effective oral and written communication

- to distinguish between connotative and denotative language and examine the impact of each on audience reaction

- to practise active listening, summarizing, and paraphrasing

1.   List incidents illustrating the value of clear communication outside of school. You might reflect on your part-time job or situations your parents have mentioned.

2.   In pairs, read "Communicating with Style in the Workplace":

> *Greg Hollyer and Heather Forsythe have worked in a variety of jobs related to business and industry. They are graduates of Queen's University's engineering program. Forsythe also completed a Master of Business Administration degree. In this interview, she shares her on-the-job experience and the insights that helped her meet language-related challenges.*

GH: . . . let's get down to a specific example illustrating the importance of strong communication on the job.

HF: Last summer, I worked on a consulting project. A key part was oral presentations to clients. The boss stressed a strong verbal style to communicate energy and humour. Communication style—words, voice, and body language—keeps the audience tuned in.

GH: In business and industry, working with others in groups or teams is a common strategy. How does this relate to the need for strong communication?

HF: Well, in business school we did a lot of group activities to prepare for teamwork—particularly collaboratively written final reports and oral presentations. Working together can lead to conflict; a lot of the conflict comes from poor listening.

GH: How do you resolve team conflicts?

HF: The only way to get passed differences is to really hear what each of you is saying. One course concentrated on active listening—paraphrasing each other's words and repeating them aloud until you're sure you understand each other.

GH: How does this relate to individual communication strengths?

HF: Everybody on the team needs effective style. A friend told me about a collaborative writing experience that shows why. Her partner had trouble with awkward sentences and linking ideas. He was functionally literate, but his writing style was unpolished. She had to spend more than her share of time shining up his sections of their report. In the workplace you're under pressure to produce high-quality written work in co-operation with others. Over time, a weak writer becomes a burden and may be resented. . . . Probably the single most important thing you'll do out of high school is interact and communicate with other people. . . . In business, communicating with style is more important than any kind of number-crunching or analysis.

3.   In your Writer's Notebook:

a.   Write a letter to Forsythe or Hollyer posing questions or reacting to an intriguing statement.

b.   Reflect on the importance of Forsythe's arguments for your post-secondary plans.

4.   In a small group, practise your collaborative skills. But before you begin, (re)read Writer's Resource Two, Strategies for Successful Peer Conferences (pages 374–385), and consider how this material may enhance your co-writing skills.

a.   Draft a monologue reflecting your thoughts as you practise speaking skills on tape.

b.   Or compose a dialogue between co-workers struggling to write a collaborative report.

Exchange assignments with another group and obtain both oral and written peer comments on your work.

5.   Working with a partner:

a.   Audiotape a précis of the Forsythe-Hollyer interview. (To review précis techniques, see page 390).

b.   Listen to another team's work, noting differences in interpretation, emphasis, or ideas. Then paraphrase the précis aloud to them.

Now that we've considered Tarvo's query about *why* style matters, it's time to focus on Kirsten's and Sasha's concerns: *what* good style is and *how* it may be acquired. As you work through Activities Two to Eight, compose a master list of five key style ingredients.

Five Key Ingredients of Strong Style

Let's go back to John Dryden. Suppose he were to visit your classroom today. You invite him to join an oral reading of the following prose passages written over the last two hundred years. In its time, each has been judged "good writing"—appropriate for publication by respected presses. As you listen to a volunteer read, ponder the styles you prefer and their suitability for your present writing needs. What would Dryden's reaction likely be?

Bruno Bettelheim

"Children's playings are not sports and should be deemed their most serious actions," Montaigne wrote. If we wish to understand our child, we need to understand his play. Freud regarded play as the means by which the child accomplishes his first great cultural and psychological achievements; through the play he expresses himself. This is true even for an infant whose play consists of nothing more than smiling at his mother, as she smiles at him. Freud also noted how much and how well children express their thoughts and feelings through play. These are sometimes feelings that the child himself would remain ignorant of, or overwhelmed by, if he did not deal with them by acting them out in play fantasy.

Joseph Conrad

He was an inch, perhaps two, under six feet, powerfully built, and he advanced straight at you with a slight stoop of the shoulders, head forward, and a fixed from-under stare which made you think of a charging bull. His voice was deep, loud, and his manner displayed a kind of dogged self-assertion which had nothing aggressive in it. It seemed a necessity, and it was directed apparently as much at himself as at anybody else. He was spotlessly neat, apparelled in immaculate white from shoes to hat, and in the various Eastern ports where he got his living as ship-chandler's water-clerk he was very popular.

Charles Dickens

It was the best of times, it was the worst of times, it was the age of wisdom, it was the age of foolishness, it was the epoch of belief, it was the epoch of incredulity, it was the season of Light, it was the season of darkness, it was the spring of hope, it was the winter of despair, we had everything before us, we had nothing before us, we were all going direct to Heaven, we were all going direct the other way—in short, the period was so far like the present period, that some of its noisiest authorities insisted on its being received, for good or for evil, in the superlative degree of comparison only.

Lynne Hancock

She was only two months but she looked like an old woman. Her thin body was frail and heavily lined, her tiny face incredibly wrinkled. She lay on a hot-water bottle in a room heated to a stifling 80°F in honour of her tropical origins. A miniscule huddle of long spindly limbs wrapped tightly around her nakedness, a thumb held constantly in her mouth. Shiny, black blobs of eyes stared up from a frightened little face. She was an ugly, black, scrawny, bug-eyed spider. I could scarcely conceal my disgust.

Dylan Thomas

I remember the smell of the sea and the seaweed, wet flesh, wet hair, wet bathing-dresses, the warm smell as of a rabbity field after rain, the smell of pop and splashed sunshadows and toffee, the stable-and-straw smell of hot, tossed, tumbled, dug and trodden sand, the will-and-gaslamp smell of Saturday night, though the sun shone strong, from the bellying beer-tents, the smell of the vinegar on shelled cockles, winkle-smell, shrimp-smell, the dripping-oily back-street water-smell of chips in newspapers, the smell of ships from the sundazed docks around the corner of the sandhills, the smell of the known and paddled-in sea moving, full of the drowned and herrings, out and away and beyond and further still towards the antipodes that hung their koala-bears and Maoris, kangaroos and boomerangs, upside down over the backs of the stars.

Do these passages stand up to Dryden's criteria for good writing? Measure each according to the points on your list.

Next, check to see if your list mentions authentic, distinctive language. Reread two passages. What makes each "sound different"? Each has a flavour and texture of its own. This quality is called *voice*—the medium through which the writer conveys character and commitment to the audience. Voice contributes an almost indefinable quality that makes each person's style as unique as a thumb print. And it's the first and most fundamental ingredient of "good style"—**Ingredient One: Good style expresses the author's voice.**

In Activity Three, identify characteristics of voice through active listening and collaborative writing. If your writer's voice is weak, don't be discouraged. It will blossom with time, patience, and experimentation.

Activity Three   Listening for Voice
Purpose

- to practise identifying elements of voice

- to listen for characteristics of your writer's voice

- to collaborate with others

1.   Take turns reading "You Will *Not* Become a Writer When You Grow Up" (page 94), and "Collaborwriting" (page 92).
a.   Next, tape and listen closely to a reading of one paragraph from each. Briefly describe how each style differs. Compare notes with others.
b.   What do you think you know about each writer, judging from his or her writer's voice? Justify.
c.   Complete the same exercise using passages by Bettelheim, Dickens, and so on.

2.   Do this exercise anonymously—type if possible, perhaps at the word processor.
1.   Freewrite for fifteen minutes in response to one of these quotations.

Norman Mailer   "Style is character."

William Zinsser   "When we say we like a writer's style, what we really mean is we like his personality as he expresses it on paper."

b.   Your instructor or a student will collect and randomly redistribute papers to your writing group. Can you identify the writer? How? Exchange papers and repeat the experiment. (*Note:* This exercise works best when you've been together in writing groups for a few weeks. You may wish to repeat it several times during the course.)

3.   Discuss characteristics of your partner's voice revealed in writing. Listen for patterns in phrasing and syntax, rhythm, and use of slang. What other clues can you add to this list?

4.   In your Writer's Notebook, reflect on your partner's comments about your style. What pleases or surprises you?

5.   Working with a partner, compose a new version of the same topic you selected in question 2. Compare voice(s) in the jointly written passage with your individual work. Is one writer's voice dominant? Was this reflected in *how* you collaborated? If you worked on a word processor, who typed? Discuss experiences with other partners.

6.   In your writing folder, draft an essay which explains or argues a point about the writer's voice. You might select one of these topics:
a.   your understanding of the concept
b.   an analysis of voice in two passages above
c.   characteristics of your writer's voice.

A second key ingredient of good style is mentioned by both John Dryden and contemporary American writer Kurt Vonnegut, Jr.—**Ingredient Two: Good style is clear and concise.**

Read Vonnegut's "How to Write with Style" (page 106). Then apply his rules in Activity Four.

Activity Four   Writing with Style
Purpose

• to rank a variety of writing styles according to criteria

• to determine personal preferences

• to compose in a clear, concise style

1.   Vonnegut doesn't offer technical advice. Freewrite about how this approach may reflect his views on writing.

2.   Compare Dryden's and Vonnegut's ideas. Do they convey essentially the same message?

3.   As you read aloud the following passages, ponder your stylistic preferences. Which writer might you enjoy conversing with? Why? (*Note:* Authors' names have been removed to encourage reactions to *writing,* not

reputation. The source, era of publication, and intended reader/audience provide context.)

a.   From a speech delivered in the 1950s:

It is a privilege to help man endure by lifting up his heart, by reminding him of the courage and honor and hope and pride and compassion and pity and sacrifice which have been the glory of his past.

b.   From a letter to the editor in the *Toronto Star* on August 24, 1987:

. . . . Obviously you fail to see the inherent contradiction in your position. You cannot individualize learning and standardize evaluation. Such pedagogical schizophrenia undermines the learning process. For example, children who are learning at their own speed require individualized ongoing evaluation that emphasizes and measures individual achievement; children who are faced with standardized evaluation, which defines and measures arbitrary achievement levels by grade or by age, must attempt to learn at an arbitrarily imposed speed which may or may not be appropriate for them as individuals.

c.   From contemporary prose fiction:

In the late summer of that year we lived in a house in a village that looked across the river and the plain to the mountains. In the bed of the river there were pebbles and boulders, dry and white in the sun, and the water was clear and swiftly moving and blue in the channels.

d.   From contemporary prose fiction:

I prod . . . [the June bugs] with a fingernail. They're not alive. Death hasn't tarnished them, however. Their backs are green and luminous, with a sharp metallic line down the center, and their bellies shimmer with sheer copper.

e.   From contemporary prose fiction:

There was a boy who lived on the seashore. There he played and grew and wondered. . . . With his flute he shaped the sand and the water, twisting them into shapes of his mind. The shells that were washed lonely and tired on the beach, he moulded with his hands, changing them from flat, ugly shards to burning sunrises of his life.

f.   From contemporary prose fiction:

Wooed and wed. Wife. A knife of a word that for all its final bite did not end the wooing. To my wonderment.

g.   From nineteenth-century prose fiction:

The studio was filled with the rich odour of roses, and when the light summer wind stirred amidst the trees of the garden, there came through the open door the heavy scent of lilac, of the delicate perfume of the pink-flowering thorn.

4.   In your group, rank the passages from 1 (lowest) through 7 (highest) according to the criteria of clarity and conciseness, and the author's expression of distinctive voice.

5a.   Write sentences imitating the style of one writer you admire. Try for similarities in

*   types of diction (e.g., balance of connotative and denotative words)

*   sentence construction (e.g., characteristic placement of phrases, subject, and verbs)

*   variety of sentence structure

*   rhetorical devices/figures of speech

*   overall flavour and texture of the style.

b.   In your Writer's Notebook, reflect on whether this experience of imitation may hinder or help the growth of personal style.

6.   In your writing folder, draft a descriptive or argumentative paragraph in a clear, concise style. Experiment with something which is new for you—perhaps unusual word placement or a stylistic technique you admired in one of the above passages. Record and listen to an audiotape of this writing. What characteristics of voice do you hear? Get a second opinion.

The third ingredient of good style is implicit in both Dryden's and Vonnegut's advice—**Ingredient Three: Good style shows rather than tells.**

Although *forms* of showing vary, the basic principle is a constant in written and oral communication. The more you *show* your audience as opposed to direct telling, the more successful is your communication.

Dialogue is one popular "showing" device. Read this passage from the novel *Marya: A Life* by Joyce Carol Oates.

"A going-away party? For you?" Wilma said.
"For Clarence Michalak and me, not just *me*." Marya said, slightly embarrassed. "He's going into the army."
"It's the night before you leave??"
"Well—I can have everything packed and ready. I won't really be taking much," Marya said.

In under fifty words, Oates vividly imprints a scene on our minds. We are more likely to remember that Marya and her aunt have grown apart, that they feel uncomfortable in each other's company, than if Oates had simply recounted these details.

You've already encountered other popular techniques of showing in non-fiction. Review articles by Gibson (page 94) and Blythe and Sweet (page 92).

Look for examples of how they *show*, instead of telling, through their use of

> contrast, comparison, action and reaction, direct speech or quotation, sound or sight imagery (especially appeals to the senses), factual detail or example, and conflict.

Then move on to Activity Five to reinforce your knowledge of "show, don't tell."

Activity Five   Recognizing and Applying Techniques of Showing

Purpose

- to enjoy oral language individually and with others
- to identify and employ "showing" techniques
- to practise working under time constraints

1.   In groups, volunteers read aloud brief samples of memorable writing. You might select a children's classic, such as *Dr. Seuss* or *Alligator Pie* (by Dennis Lee). As you listen, imagine a pleasant, secure place—perhaps somewhere you enjoyed as a child. Conjure up pictures, colours, shapes, sounds, and associations.

a.   After each reading, reflect in your Writer's Notebook about memorable words and phrases. What proportion of these words have positive connotations? Provide examples.

b.   If you wish, share your responses with one or more peers. Are there similar patterns in the responses?

2.   Read this excerpt from William Zinsser's *On Writing Well*.

> . . . Besides wanting to write as well as possible, I wanted to write as entertainingly as possible. When I tell aspiring writers they should think of themselves as part entertainer, they don't like to hear it—the word smacks of carnivals and jugglers and clowns. But to succeed you must make your piece jump out of a newspaper or magazine by being more diverting than anyone else's piece. You must find some way to elevate your act of writing into an entertainment. Usually this means giving the reader an *enjoyable surprise*. Any number of methods will do the job: *humour, anecdote, paradox, an unexpected quotation, a powerful fact, an outlandish detail, a circuitous approach, an elegant arrangement of words*. These seeming amusements, in fact, become your "style." When we say we like a writer's style, what we really mean is that we like his personality as he expressed it on paper. Given a choice between two traveling companions—and a writer is someone who asks us to travel with him—we choose the one who makes an effort to brighten the trip.

After (re)reading passages by Chopin (page 70), Conrad (page 74), and one other author, make a list of examples illustrating how each writer "brightened the trip" through "showing."

3a.   Examine an unpolished passage from your Writer's Notebook or writing folder. Label specific ways you've "entertained" or "brightened the trip." Does your work reflect the advice of John Metcalf in "Soaping a Meditative Foot?"

- "Take pride in the placing of words."

- "Know the weight, colour, and texture of *things*."

Make point-form notes about possible revisions to incorporate more "showing."

b.   Assess the effectiveness with which the authors of two or more passages from pages 73 to 75 employed techniques of showing.

4a.   In a small group, brainstorm techniques of showing that are most suitable for formal expository and argumentative essays. (*Tip*: Scrutinize sample essays for ideas.)

b.   Co-write a short essay in which you apply your learning.

c.   Hold a peer conference about the draft with another group.

5.   In your writing folder, draft two short pieces of writing for different audiences—for example, a formal argumentative essay for your instructor and a pep talk persuading a young sibling to give up a bad habit. Which techniques of showing are most appropriate for each? Justify.

A fourth element of good style is appropriate language. Vonnegut refers to "keeping it simple." Dryden speaks of "pure" language. Both pieces of advice add up to—**Ingredient Four: Good style uses appropriate language.**

The issue of appropriate language is a complex one. Language advances our goals if we dress it carefully for specific occasions. As senior students, you're familiar with the perils of wearing jeans and a T-shirt to a formal job interview, or using slang or offensive language in a conversation with your principal. Similarly, wise writers tailor language to purpose, audience, and content. Activity Six reviews how to do this.

Activity Six   Tailoring Language to Meet Your Needs
Purpose

- to recognize that different purposes, audiences, and content require varying levels of language

- to understand how altering the level and type of language creates varied tones and moods

- to apply this information to your writing

1.   With your writing group, review the concepts of purpose, audience, tone, mood, and level and type of language by perusing "Matching Writing Variables," printed at the end of this activity. Clarify problems with your instructor before moving on to question 2.

2a.   (Re)read articles by Gibson (page 94), Kome (page 54), and the Royal Bank Letter (page 249). State the apparent purpose and audience of each.
b.   Find specific examples that illustrate how language in each piece is tailored to different audiences, purposes, and content.

3.   With a partner:
a.   Assess the suitability of language in several of the pieces on page 77 to their audiences. Justify.

OR

b.   Hold a peer conference about the suitability of language in your work from Activity Five, question 5.

4.   If you have not done so already, write a clear statement of audience and purpose on each draft in your writing folder. Then in your Writer's Notebook:
a.   Reflect on apt use of language in one draft from your writing folder. Note possible revisions. Or perform this exercise with a partner's work.
b.   Write several guidelines to improve this aspect of your work. Guidelines might sound like this: "To make my language less stilted, I'll imagine I'm talking to . . ." or "Watch out for. . . ."

5.   In your writing folder, complete one of these assignments:
a.   Compose a formal essay which evaluates the validity of this statement: "In writing, purpose is first; then, decide how to achieve it." Be sure to explain how other variables are interconnected with purpose. Draw your proof from the works listed in question 2.

OR

b.   Draft a short essay for two audiences—one for a formal occasion, the other informal. Annotate your drafts, indicating examples of word choice altered for audience.

Matching Writing Variables

These five steps will help you work through your options with any type of writing. Note that each decision builds upon the one(s) that precedes it and should be viewed as part of a whole package.

1. Purpose

WHY am I writing this piece?

To . . .

amuse	illuminate	ponder
argue	inform	record
educate	inspire	reflect
empathize	interpret	report
encourage	persuade	
entertain	please the senses	

2. Audience

FOR WHOM am I writing this piece?

For . . .

- preschoolers   • young adults   • adults

Note: Research your audience by examining sample books and/or back issues of relevant magazines and newspapers. Note format, types of content, style, vocabulary, use of illustrations, and so on.

3. Tone

What ATTITUDE will I adopt toward my subject?

The tone will be . . .

- humorous   • sombre

- playful   • impersonal

Note: In oral expression, the speaker reveals tone through diction *and* vocal inflections, pacing and body language. In written communication, tone must be revealed through diction and stylistic features strong enough for readers to "hear." The writer may *assume* a tone toward a topic to achieve a desired effect; this may be called adopting a *persona* or mask.

4. Mood

What is the EMOTIONAL ATMOSPHERE to which my audience will respond?

Types of mood:

- just about any human emotion

- may be close to or opposite to the tone

Mood, the complement of tone, is created by the writer's attitude. It is the audience's emotional response to the writer's tone. The interrelationships look something like this:

writer + attitude → tone of PASSAGE → mood → audience response

Note: Mood (reader response) may vary.

5. Level of Language

How FORMAL should my language be, given previous choices?

Formal Standard English is commonly used in high school and university essays; business, legal, and professional documents, reports; high quality newspaper reports and editorials.

Characteristics

- idiomatic
- impersonal
- authoritative
- unadorned (focus on denotative diction)

Avoid

- use of first person ("I," "my")
- directly addressing the audience ("you")
- contractions
- colloquialisms, slang

Informal Standard English is commonly used in the everyday speech of educated people; memos and letters to friends; fiction, drama, poetry, contemporary journalism (columns, interviews, feature articles), and advertising.

Characteristics

- idiomatic
- invitational
- personal (uses "I," "you," and so on)
- adorned (may use blend of connotative and denotative diction, figures of speech to enhance audience response)
- distinctive writer's voice shines through

Avoid:

- stuffy phrasing or jargon and dense paragraphs
- devices which distance the audience

Non-Standard English is commonly used in passages of dialogue, dialect in personal essays, fiction, drama, poetry, and New Journalism to create a specific effect.

Characteristics:

- does not follow standard rules of usage and/or grammar but resembles informal English in other ways

- rich depiction of reality may be created through slang

Note: Each of these levels of language is appropriate in specific circumstances. One rule of thumb: tailor language to suit both purpose and audience; if in doubt, check with your instructor.

Another aspect of appropriate language concerns sensitivity to its power. As an evolving force, which reflects society's altered values, appropriate language changes. For example, consider this statement: "The artist wants his audience to enjoy his work." What assumption does this statement make? Why may it offend? If you want language to work *for* you, consider rephrasing in a non-sexist way. One of these strategies may work: rewrite the statement in the plural; recast to eliminate pronouns; or use "you" as this book does. Activity Seven explores this aspect of language in more depth.

Activity Seven   Recognizing and Avoiding Sexist Language

Purpose

- to appreciate the dynamic quality of language

- to recognize that sexist language may offend your audience

- to practise rephrasing sexist language

1.   Working alone, brainstorm words and phrases you associate with the notion of "sexist language." List them in your Writer's Notebook. Discuss these associations with a partner.

2a.   After reading the excerpt from *The Handbook of Non-Sexist Writing* (page 102), discuss the authors' thesis and the evidence employed. What biases, if any, do the authors betray through their choice of language and proof?
b.   With a partner, scrutinize samples of your writing folder work for sexist language. What changes might be in order?

3.   Co-write or role play one of these situations:
a.   an interview of the authors on a television talk show
b.   a parody of a politician or sportscaster trying to avoid sexist words.

4.   Investigate policy about sexist language which may affect your functioning in school and the workplace.
a.   Locate your school board's policy.
b.   Explore rules about the writing of textbooks used in schools.
c.   How may government and business policies on sexist language affect your performance in the workplace? Invite a guidance counsellor to discuss language in the workplace.

5.   Discuss sexist language with a foreign-language teacher. How does English compare in this regard with French, German, or Italian, for example?

6.   In your Writer's Notebook:
a.   record words which are difficult to use neutrally (e.g., sportsmanship, craftsmanship) and think of possible alternatives.
b.   freewrite about your reactions to this subject.

7a.   Formulate and debate resolutions about the use of sexist language in your writing program. As you prepare your work, reflect on the most persuasive types of evidence.
b.   In your writing folder, draft an argumentative essay based on a debate topic.

Next, let's examine that quality of language most enjoyable for the reader—**Ingredient Five: Good style uses lively language.**

Activity Eight instructs on a variety of language-related problems that may detract from writing with style. Since needs and interests are unique, focus on writing techniques of benefit to you. The suggestions are *starting points* for further exploration. Remember that these concerns are best attended to at the editing stage of writing.

Activity Eight   Techniques of Lively Writing
Purpose

- to review language problems which detract from writing

- to practise objective self- and peer assessment

- to identify and plan for personal language needs

In pairs, work through the following exercises. You may wish to divide the review into several sittings. Each response invites you to scrutinize your writing and plan revisions.

1.   "My editing partners claim my language needs more 'punch.' What does punch mean, and how do I get it?" A "punchy" piece of writing almost jumps off the page to engage the reader. Here are several suggestions:

a. *Use vivid verbs and forceful nouns, not a clutter of modifiers.* A vivid verb is dynamic. It conveys a precise impression. For example, "The boy *walked* home at a *snail's pace*" is less effective than "The boy *straggled* home." Why?
Verbs of being often offend with their listlessness; overuse of "seem," "look," "appear," "be," and "become" weaken the force of your presentation. For example, "It looks as if I can come to the party" is less effective than "I expect to attend the party." Why?
Compose your own example, showing a weak and improved version. Examine several paragraphs of your writing. Note examples of listless verbs.
A strong noun conveys a precise image. For example, "The tiny little man walked to his broken-down house" is less effective than "The dwarf trundled to his hovel."
Compose your own example of a weak and improved version. Examine your work, noting flabby nouns.

b.   Heed George Orwell's advice: *"Never use a big one when a small one will do."* William Hazlitt concurs: "I hate anything that occupies more space than it's worth. . . . I hate to see a parcel of big words without anything in them."
Compose your own weak and improved examples. Examine several paragraphs of your writing or that of your partner. Note sentences to rework.

c.   *Use the active voice whenever possible.* For example, "It has been found that water flows faster downstream" is less effective than "Water flows faster downstream." Justify.
Compose one example of ineffective use of the passive voice; then write an improved version. Examine several paragraphs of your work; rework passive verbs.

d.   *Use words accurately.* These commonly confused and abused words are from Sasha's "words to watch" page in her Writer's Notebook:

affect/effect	allude/refer	allusion/illusion
already/all ready	alright/all right	alternate/alternative
all together and altogether	among/between	amount/number
ante/anti	bi/semi	can/may
continual/continuous	different from/different than	disinterested/uninterested
economic/economical	eminent/imminent	farther/further
fewer/less	imply/infer	

Quiz your partner about these distinctions. Survey samples of your writing; note phrasing to correct.

e.   *Vary the word order and length of your sentences to highlight ideas and break up auditory monotony.* For example, "She never dropped anything when the phone rang" is less arresting than Salinger's "She was a girl who for a ringing phone dropped exactly nothing."

Which word order is most effective? Why?

A good writer never loses sight of personal goals.

(subject + verb + direct object)

Always keep personal goals in sight when writing.

(understood subject + verb + object)

Personal goals should always be kept in sight by a good writer.

(object + verb in passive voice + subject)

Edwin Peterson, a retired professor from the University of Pennsylvania, suggests the "pencil rule." Lie an ordinary sharpened pencil with the tip pointing to the right. Now, model your sentence after the pencil; put the most important idea where the tip points, the second most important idea at the beginning where the eraser rests, and the "connectors" in between. Consider, for example, the different effect or emphasis created by each of the following:

She was, after all, a lady. (pencil sentence)
A lady she was, after all.
And after all, she was a lady.

f.   *Generally, short sentences are more effective.* Their dynamic tension propels the reader forward. To avoid boring the ear, however, vary sentence length.

Read an excerpt from your work to a partner; listen for appealing rhythm or music. Which sentences almost hum? Which plod and splutter? Consider revisions.

2.   "What is meant by 'clichéd diction' or a 'trite expression'? I'm told my writing lacks freshness."

Certain commonly employed phrases bore or even irritate the reader. It's a case of familiarity breeding contempt. Clichés erect walls between your voice and audience. You want to sound like yourself, not hundreds of others.

Consider whether the following statements entice you to sit up and take notice:

Her eyes were as blue as the sky.
Jane was as beautiful as a princess.
Dave had his heart set on playing lead guitar.

Examine your writing for a passage which "rings true." Ask your partner for an opinion.

3. "What is a 'corruption of language' "?

a. *Certain "illogical" words are now in common use.* For example, "ize" at the end of a word means "to make like." What is the logic of such words as "hospitalize" and "computerize"?

b. *You'll find nouns incorrectly used as verbs.* For example, conference, a noun, is used as a verb—to conference and conferencing. As we noted with sexist language, usage alters. Until new usages are legitimized in dictionaries, avoid them. See also Safire's "Bizbuzz" (page 250) and French's "Yuppies . . ." (page 93). Examine your writing for language corruptions.

In your Writer's Notebook freewrite about what this activity has highlighted concerning your language needs. Discuss this assessment with the teacher. Plan a program of remediation, or work with a peer coach. Every few weeks, assess your progress and consult your instructor about revised goals.

C. AFTER-WORDS

Reading and Responding

1.   Bob Blackburn, a commentator on language uses and abuses, contended in his column "English, Our English" that "English usage is changing for the worse" in newspapers, radio, and television.

a.   Does your experience bear out this opinion? Justify with specific examples.

b.   Would Eugene Forsey, writer of the following letter to the editor, likely agree with Blackburn?

> In your editorial "Service Non Compris" (April 6), you say that when the postal clerk in Moncton, N.B. kept asking a French-speaking customer all his questions in English, "At length, a francophone clerk noticed what was happening and interceded."
>
> My dictionary says that "intercede" means "plead (*with* person *for* another)".
>
> Didn't you mean "intervened?"

c.   Propose specific solutions to mitigate this trend.

2.   After reading the selections by Anderson (page 91), Lessing (page 96), and French (page 93), analyze their stylistic elements. Present your findings in chart form and use as your headings the five ingredients of good style listed in this chapter.

3.   Suppose you are to write an essay, for examination purposes, analyzing the style of a sight passage.

a.   State a hypothetical purpose, audience, tone, mood, and level of language.

b.   Do passages written by one or more of Dickens, French, and Swift and Miller exemplify suitable style and level of language for this purpose? Justify.

4.   Read short stories or essays by a stylist you admire. As you read, respond in your Writer's Notebook. Include words that "sound good" and make comments which demonstrate your understanding of good style. You might begin with Doris Lessing's "Through the Tunnel" (page 96). Other excellent prose stylists include Margaret Atwood, Margaret Laurence, Farley Mowat, Alice Munro, Bertrand Russell, and E.B. White.

The Writing Folder

1.   Revise and polish one or more of your drafts from the activities in this chapter.

2.   Write a humorous or reflective essay, or a skit set in the future. Your audience could be your school's yearbook readers and the subject our changing language. To get started, reflect on words, usages, or punctuation conventions that may be defunct when your children are senior students. (Be sure you've read French's "Yuppies . . ." on page 93 before you begin.)

3.   Compose a spoof on authors tormenting themselves over style. For ideas see comments by or about authors such as Flaubert (page 23), Peter Newman (page 30), Farley Mowatt (page 265), or Bartlett's *Familiar Quotations*.

4.   Use appropriate techniques of "showing" to persuade two audiences about the merits of slang in certain situations. You might begin with Carl Sandburg's statement: "Slang is a language that rolls up its sleeves, spits on its hands, and goes to work."

5.   Assess the merits of two pieces of writing published for different purposes and audiences on the same topic. Use criteria you have learned about the webbed interrelationship of purpose and audience and other writers' choices to guide your assessment.

6.   Experiment in an essay with a technique of showing which is new to you. Then comment on how you approached the assignment and felt about the process of risk-taking.

Independent Study

1.   Heed Samuel Butler's advice: "Do not hunt for subjects, let them find you." Peruse your Writer's Notebook entries and writing folder for ideas on which to base a project.

2.   Flaubert reportedly sat all night cupping his head in his hands trying to "squeeze" out the right word from his "unfortunate brain." Research other writers' views of the "agonies of style." Apply your knowledge in an imaginative way. For example, create a one-act play about a writer searching for an authentic voice, or compose a report or a mock symposium of writers on writing. Interesting research sources include:

- Geoff Hancock, *Canadian Writers at Work* (Toronto: Oxford University Press, 1987)

- Bruce Meyer and Brian O'Riordan, *In Their Words* (Toronto: Anansi, 1984)

- V.S. Naipaul, *Finding the Centre* (Markham: Penguin, 1985)

3.   Research one aspect of our changing language. You might investigate: how words change; acceptance of new words into dictionaries; or comparative changes in English and Romance languages. Negotiate a written format such as a short story accompanied by a brief research paper.

4.   Investigate dialects of Canadian English using print and interviews with one or more new Canadians—perhaps students at your school. Reflect your learning in an imaginative form appropriate to the focus of your course. (*Note:* If you decide upon a short story or a piece of New Journalism with dialect, use it sparingly. See also Chapters Five and Six.)

5.   Working with an elementary teacher, create original crossword puzzles or other language games to enhance children's vocabulary. Plan a report with the instructor.

6.   Investigate literacies required in the post-secondary field you plan to enter. You might interview older students or people practising in the field, as well as job placement counsellors. Include written sources. Define a specific focus with your instructor. The written product might be a play or research paper.

The Writer's Notebook

1.   Compose a quick quiz about the key concepts in this chapter; exchange it with a friend. Or reflect on your growth as a stylist, focusing on strategies you have used or will use to enhance your language.

2a.   Freewrite about the growth of your writing process; identify prewriting and revising strategies that work for you.
b.   Are you taking full advantage of word processing facilities?

3.   Review your Writer's Profile and revise it in light of recent growth.

READINGS 2

Whatever Happened to Plain English?

Doris Anderson

Much as we would all like to be fluent in at least one other language, I find it more and more difficult to cope with plain English—because English isn't plain anymore. As with so many other things in our complex world, English tends to be used in such a specialized and peculiar way by each particular group or profession, that sometimes we seem to be in danger of becoming a modern-day Tower of Babel.

For example, why can't we talk about "poor people" anymore? We know we have them by the millions. We call them "underprivileged" or "culturally deprived." In the days when I was poor, I would have been insulted to be called "culturally deprived." I was poor. No money.

And why can't we come flat out and say people are trying to get ahead instead of saying they have "upward mobility"? And when conditions are getting worse, what's the matter with stating this fact instead of saying they are "escalating downward"?

Why is it we never have discussions anymore? Why do we always have "seminars"? And why can't we just do things instead of "effect" them? When people don't want to do something, why can't they say "no" instead of "opting out"? And when someone doesn't like a situation, does it help to say he's "alienated"?

. . . .

From *Chatelaine*, June 1967. © Maclean Hunter, 1967.

And while we're on the subject of people—what happened to them? When did they become "human resources" or "human factors"?

On the other hand, it's easy to understand why we talk of the "credibility gap" instead of "how much will the public swallow". But instead of saying "at this point in time" wouldn't it be easier just to say "now"? And if something doesn't come off, isn't it simpler just to call it a flop instead of an "abortive attempt"?

In speaking of children the verbiage is even thicker. We never say a child is bad or naughty. He is "aggressive" or "displaying his aggressions." He is never spanked or punished. He is "adjusted" (like a little machine). If he's behaving, he's never called a good child (heavens, no!). He's "well adjusted." When he is learning something, he is being "oriented." And when he can't learn something, he has a "learning disability." He doesn't even sit in a schoolroom anymore. He's in a "learning laboratory." When he goes to look something up, he goes, not to an old-fashioned library, but to a "resource centre."

It's true and trite to say every limp and worn cliché in our language laundry bag such as "bright as a new penny," "clean as the driven snow" was once a new verbal invention. But even the most clever language creations, in our age of rapid communication, become rapidly crushed and soiled.

And I don't mind that. What I do mind is the gimmickry that we load on the way we talk and write. Our infatuation with jargon builds no bridge of better understanding between people. It builds little walled-in societies where you need a special language key to participate. And that isn't what language is for, is it?

Collaborwriting

Hal Blythe
Charlie Sweet

The authors are professors of English at Eastern Kentucky University. Their work includes short stories, articles, and scripts for both educational and commercial television. Each weekday—forty-eight weeks a year—Blythe and Sweet meet for two hours between classes at a fast-food restaurant. In this excerpt, they explain their process of collaborwriting.

. . . For almost ten years we have collaborated on over 250 published works, and all of them are products of a single methodology on whose cornerstone is inscribed WRITING DEMANDS DISCIPLINE. . . . Each writing session is structured. While we absorb the first jolt of caffeine, we talk over anything interesting we've run across in the media or personal experience. "Where do you guys get all your ideas?" we're always being asked at writers' conferences. Essentially we're both sponges absorbing information, events, and personalities around us. It's in this initial and informal brainstorming conversation that we hear ourselves and each other talking. Somehow this process gives us a focus on ideas that might otherwise escape our attention; thus this interchange becomes a primary advantage of team-writing. Then, too, we subscribe to what we call the three-burner theory. Besides the primary piece we're bringing to a boil on any given day, we like to have a second starting to bubble, and a third we've just put on the stove. Usually we jot down what we discuss and try to rough out vaguely what we might do with it. One day we might come up with a query letter for *Writer's Digest* while another time we might mention a key idea to help bring a bubbling plot to a boil.

Stage two is the read-through of what we wrote the previous session. Hal's reading the material aloud helps us correct any problems in form and content. Misspellings, overused sentence patterns, unnatural-sounding dialogue—all are exorcised at this point in our daily ritual. Further, this reading shifts us into the flow of the piece. It is here that we leave the booth. . . .

Stage three is the actual writing. Charlie plays scribe because Hal writes as though he has a medical degree. Here as in everything else the collaboration is total. Our idols Manny Lee and Fred Dannay (Ellery Queen) divided up the chores so that one wrote the plot outline, the other filled in the story, and on Fridays they met to revise. *We, on the other hand, write every word facing each other across the paper-filled formica.*

During this stage we usually work from a rudimentary outline constructed in an earlier session. It's a free exchange of ideas. Hal might, say "What if . . . ?" and Charlie will pick up the cue and supply some details. If we reach the point in the wood at which the roads diverge and Hal wants to travel one way while Charlie the other, we talk out the situation until we both take the same path. The more we write together, the less we encounter divergences and the more we seem to be able to finish each other's sentences. We usually work out scenes by dramatizing the parts. A scene really comes alive when Hal, playing Mike Shayne, interrogates Charlie the Gat. Once, in fact, we got so wrapped up in the role-playing that an . . . employee who overheard but didn't know us, asked almost hopefully, "Are you guys . . . detectives?" Three cheers for credibility! We try to end each writing session at an exciting juncture, making the starting point of the next day's writing easier.

Stage four is the only time we work alone. Every night Hal does any necessary research for the next day and handles our correspondence. Meanwhile, Charlie plays with our newest investment, transferring the day's material onto a floppy disk and running off a copy for the next day's proofreading. Changing over to a [word processor] has improved both the quality and the quantity of our writing. We're more open to revision since the magic of word processing makes the chore easier than in the old days, when even a minor change meant a totally retyped manuscript. Our word count—and yes, we do consider that part of the discipline—has more than doubled. When Charlie types, he also provides an extra reading.

The next day we repeat the cycle. When the project is ready to be taken off the burner and presented for consumption, we do a final read-through, checking for any errors in logic and mechanics. The finished product, [by] then, usually has been through at least five readings in part or in whole.

... Maybe our collaborating isn't so much two heads, but, as psychological studies are showing, an instance of being able to integrate Charlie's right brain with Hal's left brain. We're not saying we're a pair of half-wits, but that we have complementary personalities. ...

Yuppies, Baby-Boomers Find Their Way into New Roget's

William French

Peter Mark Roget, eminent nineteenth-century British physician and scientist, could scarcely have imagined the consequences of his interest in words. When he first published his thesaurus in 1852, all he intended was to provide his contemporaries with a handy guide to clear thinking and writing. But he unwittingly founded an industry and a family fortune, as well as bestowing immortality on his surname. Roget and Thesaurus are now as inseparable as Gilbert and Sullivan, or Campeau and takeover.

Thirty million copies later, the newest edition of the unique reference work, edited by Betty Kirkpatrick, has just been published in Canada. ... It replaces the edition pub-

lished six years ago, and contains 11,000 new entries—dramatic evidence of the ability of the language to adjust to rapid social change. The new entries provide an impressive guide to the preoccupations of the eighties.

Among the words and phrases listed for the first time or with new meaning are acid rain, aerobics, AIDS, arbitrage, baby-boomer, baglady, cellular radio, cursor, designer drug, glitterati, lean cuisine, necklace (as in South Africa), nuclear winter, rubber bullet, SDI, video disk and yuppie. A latter-day Rip Van Winkle awakening from even a 20-year sleep would find most of those words incomprehensible.

Some of them are meaningless even to those of us who are reasonably awake. This may be due to cultural differences between North America and Britain, where the thesaurus is compiled. And since Roget's is not a conventional dictionary but closer to a dictionary of synonyms, the meaning of such words usually must be deduced. A good example is "manky": the index refers us to unclean, where we find under the subhead insalubrious: "foul, offensive, nasty, grotty, manky, yukky; abominable, disgusting, repulsive." Clear enough?

John Crosbie will have a marvelous time using the new Roget's to prepare more speeches on free trade. He can attack opponents as "Scribaceous sieverts and jarming oncogenes." I don't know what it means, but it certainly has a more authoritative ring than his libelling of fakirs and philosophers and encyclopedia salesmen.

One reason why this edition of the thesaurus is so comprehensive is that the operation is now computerized. Language specialists search journals, magazines, newspapers and other sources to find new words and phrases. Their discoveries are fed into the database and cross-referenced with much greater ease and accuracy.

Dr. Roget probably wouldn't have been surprised by the concept of the computer, even 150 years ago. He had an inquiring mind and a thorough grasp of scientific prinicples. Early in the nineteenth century, for example, he presented a paper on the effects of seeing a moving object through slats. He had observed that when he watched the wheel of a passing carriage through the venetian blinds in his basement, an image of the wheel was retained on the eye's retina for a fraction of a second after the wheel disappeared from view. His discovery was pursued by other scientists, notably Faraday, and eventually led to the invention of motion pictures.

Dr. Roget, whose family background was French Huguenot, created the thesaurus almost as a postscript to an eventful career. He had already retired when he decided to classify and organize the English language, not alphabetically but according to subject. Early in his career as a lecturer and writer he began to keep a notebook of related words and phrases, on which he drew to help give variety to his speeches and articles. It took him four years to organize and expand his notes, but the result was published by Longmans in 1852, when he was 71. The full title was Thesaurus Of English Words And Phrases Classified And Arranged So As To Facilitate The Expression Of Ideas And Assist In Literary Composition. Many a gormless speech-writer has had occasion to bless him since.

The public was enthusiastic from the start, and by the time Roget died at 90 he had produced several revised and expanded editions. The project remained in the family when Roget's son John, a lawyer, took over and produced several new editions until he died in 1908. Then *his* son, Samuel, an electrical engineer, stepped in to oversee what had become a valuable property. Soon after, fortune smiled again; the boom in crossword puzzles created a huge new market for Roget's, and between 1911 and 1929 there was at least one new edition every year. Samuel Roget sold the family rights to Longmans in

1952, and when he died the following year, the Roget connection ended. Longmans is still the originating publisher; it's almost as good as having a monopoly on the Bible.

"Goodbye! farewell! adieu! au revoir! auf Wiedersehen! arrivederci! adios! be seeing you! see you later! cheerio! ciao! bye-bye! ta-ta! so long! pleasant journey! have a good trip! bon voyage! God be with you!"

You Will *Not* Become a Writer When You Grow Up

Sally Gibson

"Mummy, I want to be a writer."
"What did you say?"
"I want to be a writer."
"Don't you ever, *ever* say that again."
"But, Mummy, I only. . . ."
"No, I mean it. If you ever say that again, I'll march you straight upstairs to bed. No dinner. And no story."

I haven't quite sunk this low, yet. But I've come close, very close. In the face of all my parental exhortation, at least one of my daughters persists in the perverse notion that she should become a writer when she grows up. What rot!

Where did we go wrong? Maybe it was the bouncing rhymes and bedtime stories. Maybe we should have shoved books like *Montessori Dress for Success*, or *Recess Risk Takers* or *The One Minute Speller* or *Power Napping* under the Christmas tree instead of *Corduroy* or *Pippi Longstocking* or *Anne of Green Gables*. And the Greek myths—the Greek myths were a definite mistake, except perhaps for Sisyphus, who provides the model for a writer's life.

Maybe I should have lied about my own occupation: "What are you doing, Mummy?" "Studying to be a neurosurgeon." Or about their father's publishing career: "Where's Daddy?" "Operating a sky crane." Anything but the awful truth.

Maybe I should have shut up each time

I finished a chapter. My crows of delight, although infrequent, only inspired the girls to announce ecstatically to puzzled sandbox companions, "Mummy's finished Chapter Three!" and race off to crayon their entire books in a single afternoon. This only encouraged them to think that writing books was easy, kids' stuff. An maybe news of "Daddy's authors" should have been kept from children. As it happened, Daddy's successes only inspired more confusing sandbox conversation: "Daddy's books are number one on both the Biction *and* the Non-biction lists," they'd trumpet, only slightly inaccurately.

Maybe, as parents, we should have been secret readers, slinking unobtrusively off into closets with a flashlight to get our fix, without risking setting a bad example, or—horrors—creating a love of books, and those who write them. Maybe we should have resolutely plunked overselves down in front of the tube, watching "Dynasty" and "Dallas" until Johnny Carson came marching home again. We should have done this all for the sake of the children—non-literate, non-writing, non-author offspring.

Surely we shouldn't have asked for poems and stories instead of expensive store-bought items for birthday presents. Or oooed and ahhhed over every juvenile literary effort. And we should never, ever have let the kids help W.O. Mitchell open books to be signed at autographing sessions; or crawl under the dining room table to pluck at Alice Munro's shoes; or dance "the bare naked dance" to celebrate, in risqué fashion, Jack Batten's acceptance of the first copy of *Lawyers*. They should never have been allowed to listen to Andy Russell tell bear stories in his summer teepee; or to lead a foggy tour of Toronto Island with Vancouver Islander Jack Hodgins, who made an indelible mark on impressionable minds ("Zack Hozins?" one remarked months later, "He got curly hair.") Well, our list of sins could go on and on. Too late to undo all that now.

A new approach is called for. A harsh dose of reality. The writer's life is not all glamorous lunches at Fenton's, I will tell them. Come to think of it, I've never even been to Fenton's. Neither have my kids. O.K. Rephrase that statement to appeal to a wayward ten year old: the writer's life is not all glamorous lunches at Toby's Good Eats. Or triumphant cross-country book tours with stops at Expo 86, West Edmonton Mall and Canada's Wonderland.

No, not by a long-shot. And here I'll hit the budding authors with every conceivable drawback, indulging in hyperbole when necessary—which won't be often, since the facts of Canadian publishing can speak all too eloquently for themselves.

You *may* be successful, I'll begin reasonably. You may write wonderful, critically-acclaimed books. And you may become a household name in Canada. But, even if you do, you may still—like an eminent biographer and a Governor General's award-winning novelist not so long ago—find the taxman stomping on your doorstep, demanding back taxes. Why? Because, with the keen accounting eye but blurred cultural vision common to his condition, the taxman has judged you to be a "hobbyist" and therefore not eligible for various tax breaks. (Not the big buck tax shelters like apartment blocks and Canadian stocks which have been reserved over the years for people with *real* money. No, we're talking about pin money—or "pen money" —here. "Business expenses" like paper, typewriter ribbons, research costs, photocopying and other basic tools of the writer's trade.) Following a Canadian cultural Catch 22, our famous G.G. winner (like most other writers) was judged to have "no reasonable expectation of profit" from his so-called hobby (writing books of international renown) and therefore no right to deduct expenses. If this could happen to writers occupying the lofty heights, imagine what could happen to lesser literati scrambling uncertainly up the slippery slopes of Canadian publishing. That particular blooper has been changed, but who knows what might come next?

And, speaking of "profit": don't. There isn't likely to be any. The minimum wage looks good—very good—to most Canadian writers who scrounge around well (or badly) below the poverty line. And the fringe benefits. Talk about the fringe benefits. Well, on the upside, there are no time-clocks to punch (just walls). Coffee breaks and lunch breaks are free-floating and infinitely extendable. Digging the garden, stuffing a chicken and walking around the block can all be done while "working" (or, alternatively, *instead* of working). Seeing a byline or a name on a book jacket is definitely seductive (why do you think I'm writing this article?). But, children of my flesh, let me give you the low-downside. There is no sick pay; no maternity or paternity leave; no vacation pay; no over-time; no dental plan; no pension scheme. (This is getting discouraging and I'm probably losing my audience: when you're ten years old, maternity leaves and pension schemes do not loom large in your thinking.)

Not impressed by poverty? Well, how about rejection and humiliation? (Pay dirt! Any kid left out of recess games or uninvited to a birthday party knows about rejection and humiliation.) Even if your beloved book is published, there is no guarantee that you will ever see it in a bookstore. "Your book in stock? No, we don't want no more books until after year-end inventory." These immortal words, uttered off-handedly by the head of "Books" at a major department store during the critical pre-Christmas rush, still ring at my ears.

No, my children, I must protect you from such horrors. And if logic and pleading won't work, perhaps locking you in the dreaded Book Stocks will.

Through the Tunnel
Doris Lessing

Going to the shore on the first morning of the holiday, the young English boy stopped at the turning of the path and looked down at a wild and rocky bay, and then over to the crowded beach he knew so well from other years. His mother walked on in front of him, carrying a bright-striped bag in one hand. Her other arm, swinging loose, was very white in the sun. The boy watched that white, naked arm, and turned his eyes, which had a frown behind them, toward the bay and back again to his mother. When she felt he was not with her, she swung around. "Oh, there you are, Jerry!" she said. She looked impatient, then smiled, "Why darling, would you rather not come with me? Would you rather—" She frowned, conscientiously worrying over what amusements he might secretly be longing for which she had been too busy or too careless to imagine. He was very familiar with that anxious, apologetic smile. Contrition sent him running after her. And yet, as he ran, he looked back over his shoulder at the wild bay; and all morning, as he played on the safe beach, he was thinking of it.

Next morning, when it was time for the routine of swimming and sunbathing, his mother said, "Are you tired of the usual beach, Jerry? Would you like to go somewhere else?"

"Oh, no!" he said quickly, smiling at her out of that unfailing impulse of contrition—a sort of chivalry. Yet, walking down the path with her, he blurted out, "I'd like to go and have a look at those rocks down there."

She gave the idea her attention. It was a wild-looking place, and there was no one there, but she said, "Of course, Jerry. When you've had enough, come to the big beach. Or just go straight back to the villa, if you like." She walked away, that bare arm, now slightly reddened from yesterday's sun, swinging.

And he almost ran after her again, feeling it unbearable that she should go by herself, but he did not.

She was thinking, of course he's old enough to be safe without me. Have I been keeping him too close? He mustn't feel he ought to be with me. I must be careful.

He was an only child, eleven years old. She was a widow. She was determined to be neither possessive nor lacking in devotion. She went worrying off to her beach.

As for Jerry, once he saw that his mother had gained her beach, he began the steep descent to the bay. From where he was, high up among red-brown rocks, it was a scoop of moving bluish green fringed with white. As he went lower, he saw that it spread among small promontories and inlets of rough, sharp rock, and the crisping, lapping surface showed stains of purple and darker blue. Finally, as he ran sliding and scraping down the last few yards, he saw an edge of white surf, and the shallow, luminous movement of water over white sand, and, beyond that, a solid, heavy blue.

He ran straight into the water and began swimming. He was a good swimmer. He went out fast over the gleaming sand, over a middle region where rocks lay like discoloured monsters under the surface, and then he was in the real sea—a warm sea where irregular cold currents from the deep water shocked his limbs.

When he was so far out that he could look back not only on the little bay but past the promontory that was between it and the big beach, he floated on the buoyant surface and looked for his mother. There she was, a speck of yellow under an umbrella that looked like a slice of orange peel. He swam back to shore, relieved at being sure she was there, but all at once very lonely.

On the edge of a small cape that marked the side of the bay away from the promontory was a loose scatter of rocks. Above them, some boys were stripping off their clothes.

They came running, naked, down to the rocks. The English boy swam towards them, and kept his distance at a stone's throw. They were of that coast, all of them burned smooth dark brown, and speaking a language he did not understand. To be with them, of them, was a craving that filled his whole body. He swam a little closer; they turned and watched him with narrowed, alert dark eyes. Then one smiled and waved. It was enough. In a minute, he had swum in and was on the rocks beside them, smiling with a desperate, nervous supplication. They shouted cheerful greetings at him, and then, as he preserved his nervous, uncomprehending smile, they understood that he was a foreigner strayed from his own beach, and they proceeded to forget him. But he was happy. He was with them.

They began diving again and again from a high point into a well of blue sea between rough, pointed rocks. After they had dived and come up, they swam around, hauled themselves up, and waited their turn to dive again. They were big boys—men to Jerry. He dived, and they watched him, and when he swam around to take his place, they made way for him. He felt he was accepted, and he dived again, carefully, proud of himself.

Soon the biggest of the boys poised himself, shot down into the water, and did not come up. The others stood about, watching. Jerry, after waiting for the sleek brown head to appear, let out a yell of warning; they looked at him idly and turned their eyes back towards the water. After a long time, the boy came up on the other side of a big dark rock, letting the air out of his lungs in a sputtering gasp and a shout of triumph. Immediately, the rest of them dived in. One moment, the morning seemed full of chattering boys; the next, the air and the surface of the water were empty. But through the heavy blue, dark shapes could be seen moving and groping.

Jerry dived, shot past the school of underwater swimmers, saw a black wall of rock looming at him, touched it, and bobbed up at once to the surface, where the wall was a low barrier he could see across. There was no one visible; under him, in the water, the dim shapes of the swimmers had disappeared. Then one, and then another of the boys came up on the far side of the barrier of rock, and he understood that they had swum through some gap or hole in it. He plunged down again. He could see nothing through the stinging salt water but the blank rock. When he came up, the boys were all on the diving rock, preparing to attempt the feat again. And now, in a panic of failure, he yelled up, in English, "Look at me! Look!" and he began splashing and kicking in the water like a foolish dog.

They looked down gravely, frowning. He knew the frown. At moments of failure, when he clowned to claim his mother's attention, it was with just this grave, embarrassed inspection that she rewarded him. Through his hot shame, feeling the pleading grin on his face like a scar that he could never remove, he looked up at the group of big brown boys on the rock and shouted, *"Bonjour! Merci! Au revoir! Monsieur, monsieur!"* while he hooked his finger round his ears and waggled them.

Water surged into his mouth; he choked, sank, came up. The rock, lately weighed with boys, seemed to rear up out of the water as their weight was removed. They were flying down past him, now, into the water; the air was full of falling bodies. Then the rock was empty in the hot sunlight. He counted one, two, three. . . .

At fifty, he was terrified. They must all be drowning beneath him, in the watery caves of the rock! At a hundred, he stared around him at the empty hillside, wondering if he should yell for help. He counted faster, faster, to hurry them up, to bring them to the surface quickly, to drown them quickly—anything rather than the terror of counting on and on into the blue emptiness of the morning. And then, at a hundred and sixty, the water beyond the rock was full of boys blowing like brown whales. They swam back to the shore without a look at him.

He climbed back to the diving rock and sat down, feeling the hot roughness of it under his thighs. The boys were gathering up their bits of clothing and running off along the shore to another promontory. They were leaving to get away from him. He cried openly, fists in his eyes. There was no one to see him, and he cried himself out.

It seemed to him that a long time had passed, and he swam out to where he could see his mother. Yes, she was still there, a yellow spot under an orange umbrella. He swam back to the big rock, climbed up, and dived into the blue pool among the fanged and angry boulders. Down he went, until he touched the wall of rock again. But the salt was so painful in his eyes that he could not see.

He came to the surface, swam to shore and went back to the villa to wait for his mother. Soon she walked slowly up the path, swinging her striped bag, the flushed, naked arm dangling beside her. "I want some swimming goggles," he panted, defiant and beseeching.

She gave him a patient, inquisitive look as she said casually, "Well, of course, darling."

But now, now, now! He must have them this minute, and no other time. He nagged and pestered until she went with him to a shop. As soon as she had bought the goggles, he grabbed them from her hand as if she were going to claim them for herself, and was off, running down the steep path to the bay.

Jerry swam out to the big barrier rock, adjusted the goggles, and dived. The impact of the water broke the rubber-enclosed vacuum, and the goggles came loose. He understood that he must swim down to the base of the rock from the surface of the water. He fixed the goggles tight and firm, filled his lungs, and floated, face down, on the water. Now he could see. It was as if he had eyes of a different kind—fish-eyes that showed everything clear and delicate and wavering in the bright water.

Under him, six or seven feet down, was a floor of perfectly clean, shining white sand, rippled firm and hard by the tides. Two greyish shapes steered there, like long, rounded pieces of wood or slate. They were fish. He saw them nose towards each other, poise motionless, make a dart forward, swerve off, and come around again. It was like a water dance. A few inches above them, the water sparkled as if sequins were dropping through it. Fish again—myriads of minute fish, the length of his fingernail, were drifting through the water, and in a moment he could feel the innumerable tiny touches of them against his limbs. It was like swimming in flaked silver. The great rock the big boys had swum through rose sheer out of the white sand, black, tufted lightly with greenish weed. He could see no gap in it. He swam down to its base.

Again and again he rose, took a big chestful of air, and went down. Again and again he groped over the surface of the rock, feeling it, almost hugging it in the desperate need to find the entrance. And then, once, while he was clinging to the black wall, his knees came up and he shot his feet out forward and they met no obstacle. He had found the hole.

He gained the surface, clambered about the stones that littered the barrier rock until he found a big one, and, with this in his arms, let himself down over the side of the rock. He dropped, with the weight, straight to the sandy floor. Clinging tight to the anchor of stone, he lay on his side and looked in under the dark shelf at the place where his feet had gone. He could see the hole. It was an irregular, dark gap, but he could not see deep into it. He let go of his anchor, clung with his hands to the edges of the hole, and tried to push himself in.

He got his head in, found his shoulders jammed, moved them in sidewise, and was inside as far as his waist. He could see nothing ahead. Something soft and clammy touched his mouth, he saw a dark frond moving against the grayish rock, and panic filled him. He thought of octopuses, of clinging weed. He pushed himself out backward and caught a glimpse, as he retreated, of a harmless tentacle of seaweed drifting in the mouth of the tunnel. But it was enough. He reached the sunlight, swam to shore, and lay on the diving rock. He looked down into the blue well of water. He knew he must find his way through that cave, or hole, or tunnel, and out the other side.

First, he thought, he must learn to control his breathing. He let himself down into the water with another big stone in his arms, so that he could lie effortlessly on the bottom of the sea. He counted. One, two, three. He counted steadily. He could hear the movement of blood in his chest. Fifty-one, fifty-two. . . . His chest was hurting. He let go of the rock and went up into the air. He saw that the sun was low. He rushed to the villa and found his mother at her supper. She said only "Did you enjoy yourself?" and he said "Yes."

All night, the boy dreamed of the water-filled cave in the rock, and as soon as breakfast was over he went to the bay.

That night, his nose bled badly. For hours he had been underwater, learning to hold his breath, and now he felt weak and dizzy. His mother said, "I shouldn't overdo things, darling, if I were you."

That day and the next, Jerry exercised his lungs as if everything, the whole of his life, all that he would become, depended upon it. And again his nose bled at night, and his mother insisted on his coming with her the next day. It was a torment to him to waste a day of his careful self-training, but he stayed with her on that other beach, which now seemed a place for small children, a place where his mother might lie safe in the sun. It was not his beach.

He did not ask for permission, on the following day, to go to his beach. He went, before his mother could consider the complicated rights and wrongs of the matter. A day's rest, he discovered, had improved his count by ten. The big boys had made the passage while he counted to a hundred and sixty. He had been counting fast, in his fright. Probably now, if he tried, he could get through that long tunnel, but he was not going to try yet. A curious, most unchildlike persistence, a controlled impatience, made him wait. In the meantime, he lay underwater on the white sand, littered now by stones he had brought down from the upper air, and studied the entrance to the tunnel. He knew every jut and corner of it, as far as it was possible to see. It was as if he already felt its sharpness about his shoulders.

He sat by the clock in the villa, when his mother was not near, and checked his time. He was incredulous and then proud to find he could hold his breath without strain for two minutes. The words "two minutes," authorized by the clock, brought the adventure that was so necessary to him close.

In another four days, his mother said casually one morning, they must go home. On the day before they left, he would do it. He would do it if it killed him, he said defiantly to himself. But two days before they were to leave—a day of triumph when he increased his count by fifteen—his nose bled so badly that he turned dizzy and had to lie limply over the big rock like a bit of seaweed, watching the thick red blood flow on to the rock and trickly slowly down to the sea. He was frightened. Supposing he turned dizzy in the tunnel? Supposing he died there, trapped? Supposing—his head went around, in the hot sun, and he almost gave up. He thought he would return to the house and lie down, and next summer, perhaps, when he had another year's growth in him—*then* he would go through the hole.

But even after he had made the decision, or thought he had, he found himself up on the rock and looking down into the water, and he knew that now, this moment, when his nose had only just stopped bleeding, when his head was still sore and throbbing—this was the moment when he would try. If he did not do it now, he never would. He was trembling with fear that he would not go, and he was trembling with horror at that long, long tunnel under the rock, under the sea. Even in the open sunlight, the barrier rock seemed very wide and very heavy; tons of rock pressed down on where he would go. If he died there, he would lie until one day—perhaps not before next year—those big boys would swim into it and find it blocked.

He put on his goggles, fitted them tight, tested the vacuum. His hands were shaking. Then he chose the biggest stone he could carry and slipped over the edge of the rock until half of him was in the cool, enclosing water and half in the hot sun. He looked up once at the empty sky, filled his lungs once, twice, and then sank fast to the bottom with the stone. He let it go and began to count. He took the edges of the hole in his hands and drew himself into it, wriggling his shoulders in sidewise as he remembered he must, kicking himself along with his feet.

Soon he was clear inside. He was in a small rock-bound hole filled with yellowish-grey water. The water was pushing him up against the roof. The roof was sharp and pained his back. He pulled himself along with his hands—fast, fast—and used his legs as levers. His head knocked against something; a sharp pain dizzied him. Fifty, fifty-one, fifty-two. . . . He was without light, and the water seemed to press upon him with the weight of rock. Seventy-one, seventy-two. . . . There was no strain on his lungs. He felt like an inflated balloon, his lungs were so light and easy, but his head was pulsing.

He was being continually pressed against the sharp roof, which felt slimy as well as sharp. Again he thought of octopuses, and wondered if the tunnel might be filled with weed that could tangle him. He gave himself a panicky, convulsive kick forward, ducked his head, and swam. His feet and hands moved freely, as if in open water. The hole must have widened out. He thought he must be swimming fast, and he was frightened of banging his head if the tunnel narrowed.

A hundred, a hundred and one. . . . The

water paled. Victory filled him. His lungs were beginning to hurt. A few more strokes and he would be out. He was counting wildly; he said a hundred and fifteen, and then, a long time later, a hundred and fifteen again. The water was a clear jewel-green all around him. Then he saw, above his head, a crack running up through the rock. Sunlight was falling through it, showing the clean dark rock of the tunnel, a single mussel shell, and darkness ahead.

He was at the end of what he could do. He looked up at the crack as if it were filled with air and not water, as if he could put his mouth to it to draw in air. A hundred and fifteen, he heard himself say inside his head—but he had said that long ago. He must go on into the blackness ahead, or he would drown. His head was swelling, his lungs cracking. A hundred and fifteen, a hundred and fifteen pounded through his head, and he feebly clutched at rocks in the dark, pulling himself forward, leaving the brief space of sunlit water behind. He felt he was dying. He was no longer quite conscious. He struggled on in the darkness between lapses into unconsciousness. An immense, swelling pain filled his head, and then the darkness cracked with an explosion of green light. His hands, groping forward, met nothing, and his feet, kicking back, propelled him out into the open sea.

He drifted to the surface, his face turned up to the air. He was gasping like a fish. He felt he would sink now and drown; he could not swim the few feet back to the rock. Then he was clutching it and pulling himself up on to it. He lay face down, gasping. He could see nothing but a red-veined, clotted dark. His eyes must have burst, he thought, they were full of blood. He tore off his goggles and a gout of blood went into the sea. His nose was bleeding, and the blood had filled the goggles.

He scooped up handfuls of water from the cool, salty sea, to splash on his face, and did not know whether it was blood or salt water he tasted. After a time, his heart quieted, his eyes cleared, and he sat up. He could see the local boys diving and playing half a mile away. He did not want them. He wanted nothing but to get back home and lie down.

In a short while, Jerry swam to shore and climbed slowly up the path to the villa. He flung himself on his bed and slept, waking at the sound of feet on the path outside. His mother was coming back. He rushed to the bathroom, thinking she must not see his face with bloodstains, or tearstains, on it. He came out of the bathroom and met her as she walked into the villa, smiling, her eyes lighting up.

"Have a nice morning?" she asked, laying her head on his warm brown shoulder a moment.

"Oh, yes, thank you," he said.

"You look a bit pale." And then, sharp and anxious, "How did you bang your head?"

"Oh, just banged it," he told her.

She looked at him closely. He was strained. His eyes were glazed-looking. She was worried. And then she said to herself, "Oh, don't fuss! Nothing can happen. He can swim like a fish."

They sat down to lunch together.

"Mummy," he said, "I can stay under water for two minutes—three minutes, at least." It came bursting out of him.

"Can you darling?" she said. "Well, I shouldn't overdo it. I don't think you ought to swim any more today."

She was ready for a battle of wills, but he gave in at once. It was no longer of the least importance to go to the bay.

The Handbook of Non-Sexist Writing

Casey Miller
Kate Swift

At a deep level, changes in a language are threatening because they signal widespread changes in social mores. At a level closer to the surface they are exasperating. We learn certain rules of grammar and usage in school. When they are challenged it is as though we are also being challenged. Our native language is like a second skin, so much a part of us we resist the idea that it is constantly changing, constantly being renewed. Though we know intellectually that the English we speak today and the English of Shakespeare's time are very different, we tend to think of them as the same—static rather than dynamic. "Grammar," a nationally syndicated columnist wrote recently, "is as fixed in its way as geometry." . . .

What many people find hardest to accept is that a word which used to mean one thing now means another, and that continuing to use it in its former sense—no matter how impeccable its etymological credentials—can only invite misunderstanding. When the shift in meaning happened centuries ago, no problem lingers. One may be fully aware that *girl* once meant "a young person of either sex" and yet not feel compelled to invite misunderstanding by referring to a sexually mixed group of children as girls. When the change happens in one's lifetime, recognition and acceptance may be harder.

The word *intriguing* is such a case. Once understood to mean "conniving" or "deceitful" (like the verb *intrigue*, it comes—through the French *intriguer*, "to puzzle"—from the Latin *intricare*, "to entangle"), *intriguing* now means "engaging the interest to a marked degree," as *Webster's Third New International Dictionary* noted some two decades ago.

People still make statements like "They are an intriguing pair" with the intention of issuing a warning, but chances are the meaning conveyed is "They are a fascinating pair," because that is how a new generation of writers and speakers understands and uses the word. In one sense precision has been lost; in another it has only shifted. Today no one expects a 6-horsepower boat to be pulled by six horses.

The transformation of *man* over the past thousand years may be the most troublesome and significant change ever to overtake an English word. Once a synonym for "human being," *man* has gradually narrowed in meaning to become a synonym for "adult male human being" only. Put simply in the words of a popular dictionary for children, "A boy grows up to be a man. Father and Uncle George are both men." These are the meanings of *man* and *men* native speakers of English internalize because they are the meanings which from infancy on we hear applied in everyday speech. Though we may later acquire the information that *man* has another, "generic" meaning, we do not accept it with the same certainty we accept the children's dictionary definition and its counterparts: A girl does not grow up to be a man. Mother and Aunt Teresa are not men; they are women.

To go on using in its former sense a word whose meaning has changed is counterproductive. The point is not that we should recognize semantic change, but that in order to be precise, in order to be understood, we must. The difference is a fundamental one in any discussion of linguistic bias, for some writers think their freedom of expression and artistic integrity are being compromised when they are asked to avoid certain words or grammatical forms. Is it ever justifiable, for example, for publishers to expect their authors to stop using the words *forefathers*, *man*, and *he* as though they were sex-inclusive? Is this not unwarranted interference with an author's style? Even censorship?

The public counts on those who disseminate factual information—especially on people in the mass media and the publishers of textbooks and other forms of nonfiction—to be certain that what they tell us is as accurate as research and the conscientious use of language can make it. Only recently have we become aware that conventional English usage, including the generic use of masculine-gender words, often obscures the actions, the contributions, and sometimes the very presence of women. Turning our backs on that insight is an option, of course, but it is an option like teaching children the world is flat. In this respect, continuing to use English in ways that have become misleading is no different from misusing data, whether the misuse is inadvertent or planned.

The need today, as always, is to be in command of language, not used by it, and so the challenge is to find clear, convincing, graceful ways to say accurately what we want to say. That is what this book attempts to do, and it begins, appropriately, with more about *man*.

Consider the following title: "Development of the Uterus in Rats, Guinea Pigs, and Men." Generic terms, like *rats* and *guinea pigs*, are equally applicable to a class or group and to its individual members. Terms used of a class or group that are not applicable to all its members are false generics. The reason the research-report title quoted above sounds incongruous is that *men* in that context is a false generic. This was not always so.

Historical Background

Ercongota, the daughter of a seventh-century English king, is described in *The Anglo-Saxon Chronicle* as "a wonderful man." In Old English the word *man* meant "person" or "human being," and when used of an individual was equally applicable to either sex. It was parallel to the Latin *homo*, "a member of the human species," not *vir*, "an adult male of the species." English at the time of Ercongota had separate words to distinguish the sexes: *wer* (equivalent to the Latin *vir*) meant "adult male," and *wif* meant "adult female." The combined forms *waepman* and *wifman* meant, respectively, "adult male person" and "adult female person."

In the course of time *wifman* evolved into the modern word *woman*, and *wif* narrowed in meaning to become *wife* as we use that word today. *Man* eventually ceased to be used of individual women and replaced *wer* and *waepman* as a specific term distinguishing an adult male from an adult female. But *man* continued to be used in generalizations about both sexes. As long as most generalizations about people were made by men about men, the ambiguity nestling in this dual usage was either not noticed or thought not to matter.

By the eighteenth century the modern, narrow sense of *man* was firmly established as the predominant one. When Edmund Burke, writing of the French Revolution, used *men* in the old, inclusive way, he took pains to spell out his meaning: "Such a deplorable havoc is made in the minds of men (both sexes) in France . . ." Thomas Jefferson did not make the same distinction in declaring that "all men are created equal" and "governments are instituted among men, deriving their just powers from the consent of the governed." In a time when women, having no vote, could neither give nor withhold consent, Jefferson had to be using the word *men* in its principal sense of "males," and it probably never occurred to him that anyone would think otherwise.

Self

Peggy Rosenthal

If the word *self* were a stone and the sentences we hear or read or say were pathways, we'd probably be unable to get through an ordinary day without stumbling across all the stones in our way. The lines of best-sellers, popular magazines, and television talk shows are strewn with *self*: we're urged to fulfill ourselves, realize ourselves, know ourselves, be aware of (but not beware of) ourselves, love ourselves, create ourselves, feel good about ourselves, actualize ourselves, express ourselves, improve ourselves. Self-fulfillment therapy and self-improvement courses are booming businesses, run by alchemists who know how to turn the stones of *self* into gold. There is even in the city where I live an organization called The Self Center: a perfect title for our times, in which the self stands firmly in the center of our path, worshipped as our rock and our redeemer.

If we turn from the main roads of popular public discourse (and by discourse I mean all uses of verbal language, both written and spoken) into the areas of special-interest groups, we still stumble upon *self* almost wherever we go. "Women's self-knowledge," "self-fulfillment," and "self-identification" are proclaimed as goals of the Women's Movement. "Energy self-sufficiency" is our nation's goal, and "Palestinian self-determination" a goal for many in the Middle East.

Even on the narrower roads of academic disciplines, the ground remains familiar. We find *self* all over the place in the writings of philosophy: no surprise, since the self has been one of philosophy's prime subjects of

From *Words and Values: Some Leading Words and Where They Lead Us* by Peggy Rosenthal.
Reprinted by permission of Oxford University Press.

study ever since the Renaissance. Recent philosophical books like *The Nature of the Self*, then, follow a time-honored tradition. But in the profession of literary criticism the hundreds of recent articles and books taking *self* as their subject ("Saul Bellow's Idea of Self," "The Divided Self in the Fiction of Henry James," "The Flexibility of the Self in Renaissance Literature," *Imagining a Self*) are a relatively new development, and an unexpected one unless we realize that literary criticism is much more in touch with popular concerns than is usually granted.

When we come to psychology, *self* is no longer just a stone that we trip over, or pass by, or stoop to examine, on our way; it has swollen into a huge rock, even a cave, which we have to enter, explore, probe the depths of as we go through the discourse of the profession. And as we go through, we find ourselves coming full circle to where we began, since the cave of psychology opens onto the main road of popular discourse—even, we could say, spills onto it, considering the amount of best-seller material (*Games People Play; I'm OK, You're OK; Passages; Pulling Your Own Strings; Living, Loving, and Learning* is just some of it) that is the direct product of psychology.

Once we notice how often *self* turns up in our current public discourse, both popular and specialized, we can easily see why *self* is a main term in our private discourse as well, and even in our private thoughts. The going terms of an age tend to be, naturally, the ones we think with, talk to our family and friends with, figure out things with. So it's no surprise that we often think these days in terms of *self*, seeing *myself* as the unquestioned justification for almost any action and as the goal toward which everything else must lead. Adolescents choosing a career are counseled, for example, to study themselves and know themselves fully in order to figure out which career will be best (meaning most self-fulfilling). We don't question whether, in laying our heavily weighted *self* on people who are already at the most self-absorbed stage of life, we might be burdening them unfairly, even preventing them from moving at all. Nor do we question our own or our friends' divorces when they're justified, as they often are, in terms of *self* (self-fulfillment, self-realization, etc.); there's no doubt that without the word *self*, and the values and concepts it currently brings with it, the divorce rate would be considerably lower than it is. . . .

Though I don't want to get bogged down here in methodology, I have to make just one more distinction in order to be accurate about the way *self* pulls us: a distinction between the ways that a word's values, whether positive or negative, can be carried. Words lead complex lives and lead us along with them in complex ways; if we want to see how we're being led, rather than being led along blindly, we have to make an effort to follow our language with our eyes open to its subtle workings. What we see, then, when we look at how words carry their values, is that two different ways are possible. Some words carry their values inherently, in their very beings, so to speak: these are words whose referent* *is* a certain value, words like *good, pleasure, comfortable*, or, on the other side, *disgraceful, worthless, evil*. Many more words, though, carry their values not as inherent parts of themselves but *ad*herently, like labels stuck on their heads or behind their backs, or like little flags sticking up from them and bearing the imprint of a plus or a minus. These are words whose referent is not itself a value and which take on whatever attitude we have toward the referent at the time. Adherent values can therefore change over the years, as our attitudes do. For example, *simple*, which once carried the positive sense of "guileless" or "sincere" when applied to a person, now tends to carry the negative scornful implication of "simple-

minded" or "simpleton." Adherent values can vary not only over time but for different speakers at the same time: *car* spoken by the president of General Motors carries a proud plus, but in the mouth and mind of an environmentalist fighting air pollution, or of an energy conservationist, it carries a menacing minus, the sign of the skull and crossbones.

Self's positive value today is of the adherent and almost universal kind, like that of *sex*. Though critics of our self-concern have started speaking out in the past few years and so have begun to move *self* into the ambivalent category of *car*, *self* is still generally seen as an unquestionably good thing. But what's so good about it? What is there in *self* that we find so attractive? This is a question, really, about what *self* means to us. And it's a hard question to answer, not only because *self* has a variety of meanings, but also because *meaning* itself (and here another dual distinction is necessary) means at least two things. By *meaning* we mean the definition of a word: *jogging*, for example, means running at a slow, regular pace. But by *meaning* we also mean the concept or concepts carried by—or, as we usually say, "behind"— a word: *jogging* now carries the concept of good health, physical well-being, and even for some people mental well-being and peace of mind. Note that along with this concept of jogging as well-being (physical or mental) comes a positive value; the mere definition of jogging is neutral. Concepts often, as in this case, imply values: the attractiveness of jogging today seems to lie in the concepts behind it.

. . . .

* The object, concept, idea, or feeling a word names or to which it refers.

How to Write with Style

Kurt Vonnegut, Jr.

Newspaper reporters and technical writers are trained to reveal almost nothing about themselves in their writings. This makes them freaks in the world of writers, since almost all of the other ink-stained wretches in that world reveal a lot about themselves to readers. We call these revelations, accidental and intentional, elements of style.

These revelations tell us as readers what sort of person it is with whom we are spending time. Does the writer sound ignorant or informed, stupid or bright, crooked or honest, humorless or playful—? And on and on.

Why should you examine your writing style with the idea of improving it? Do so as a mark of respect for your readers, whatever you're writing. If you scribble your thoughts any which way, your readers will surely feel that you care nothing about them. They will mark you down as an egomaniac or a chowderhead—or, worse, they will stop reading you.

The most damning revelation you can make about yourself is that you do not know what is interesting and what is not. Don't you yourself like or dislike writers mainly for what they choose to show you or make you think about? Did you ever admire an empty-headed writer for his or her mastery of the language? No.

So your own winning style must begin with ideas in your head.

1. Find a Subject You Care About

Find a subject you care about and which you in your heart feel others should care about. It is this genuine caring, and not your games with language, which will be the most compelling and seductive element in your style.

I am not urging you to write a novel, by the way—although I would not be sorry if you wrote one, provided you genuinely cared about something. A petition to the mayor about a pothole in front of your house or a love letter to the girl next door will do.

2. Do Not Ramble, Though

I won't ramble on about that.

3. Keep It Simple

As for your use of language: Remember that two great masters of language, William Shakespeare and James Joyce, wrote sentences which were almost childlike when their subjects were most profound. "To be or not to be?" asks Shakespeare's Hamlet. The longest word is three letters long. Joyce, when he was frisky, could put together a sentence as intricate and as glittering as a necklace for Cleopatra, but my favorite sentence in his short story "Eveline" is this one: "She was tired." At that point in the story, no other words could break the heart of a reader as those three words do.

Simplicity of language is not only reputable, but perhaps even sacred. The *Bible* opens with a sentence well within the writing skills of a lively fourteen-year-old: "In the beginning God created the heaven and the earth."

4. Have the Guts to Cut

It may be that you, too, are capable of making necklaces for Cleopatra, so to speak. But your eloquence should be the servant of the ideas in your head. Your rule might be this: If a sentence, no matter how excellent, does not illuminate your subject in some new and useful way, scratch it out.

5. Sound Like Yourself

The writing style which is most natural for you is bound to echo the speech you heard when a child. English was the novelist Joseph Conrad's third language, and much that seems piquant in his use of English was no doubt colored by his first language, which was Polish. And lucky indeed is the writer who has grown up in Ireland, for the English spoken there is so amusing and musical. I myself grew up in Indianapolis, where common speech sounds like a band saw cutting galvanized tin and employs a vocabulary as unornamental as a monkey wrench.

In some of the more remote hollows of Appalachia, children still grow up hearing songs and locutions of Elizabethan times. Yes, and many Americans grow up hearing a language other than English, or an English dialect a majority of Americans cannot understand.

All these varieties of speech are beautiful, just as the varieties of butterflies are beautiful. No matter what your first language, you should treasure it all your life. If it happens not to be standard English, and if it shows itself when you write standard English, the result is usually delightful, like a very pretty girl with one eye that is green and one that is blue.

I myself find that I trust my own writing most, and others seem to trust it most, too, when I sound most like a person from Indianapolis, which is what I am. What alternatives do I have? The one most vehemently recommended by teachers has no doubt been pressed on you, as well: to write like cultivated Englishmen of a century or more ago.

6.   Say What You Mean to Say

I used to be exasperated by such teachers, but am no more. I understand now that all those antique essays and stories with which I was to compare my own work were not magnificent for their datedness or foreignness, but for saying precisely what their authors meant them to say. My teachers wished me to write accurately, always selecting the most effective words, and relating the words to one another unambiguously, rigidly, like parts of a machine. The teachers did not want to turn me into an Englishman after all. They hoped that I would become understandable—and therefore understood. And there went my dream of

doing with words what Pablo Picasso did with paint or what any number of jazz idols did with music. If I broke all the rules of punctuation, had words mean whatever I wanted them to mean, and strung them together higgledy-piggledy, I would simply not be understood. So you, too, had better avoid Picasso-style or jazz-style writing, if you have something worth saying and wish to be understood.

Readers want our pages to look very much like pages they have seen before. Why? This is because they themselves have a tough job to do, and they need all the help they can get from us.

7.   Pity the Readers

They have to identify thousands of little marks on paper, and make sense of them immediately. They have to *read*, an art so difficult that most people don't really master it even after having studied it all through grade school and high school—twelve long years.

So this discussion must finally acknowledge that our stylistic options as writers are neither numerous nor glamorous, since our readers are bound to be such imperfect artists. Our audience requires us to be sympathetic and patient teachers, ever willing to simplify and clarify—whereas we would rather soar high above the crowd, singing like nightingales. . . .

8.   For Really Detailed Advice

For a discussion of literary style in a narrower sense, in a more technical sense, I commend to your attention *The Elements of Style*, by William Strunk, Jr., and E.B. White. E.B. White is, of course, one of the most admirable literary stylists [the United States] has so far produced.

You should realize, too, that no one would care how well or badly Mr. White expressed himself, if he did not have perfectly enchanting things to say.

C H A P T E R
Three

Writing in Contemporary Styles

A.   FORE-WORDS

Warm up for the activities in this chapter by discussion and writing. These quotations and questions may help you begin.

Ernest Hemingway   "In stating as fully as I could how things really were . . . I wrote awkwardly and the awkwardness is what they called my style."

Louis Henri Sullivan   "Form ever follows function."

Robert Frost   "All the fun's in how you say a thing."

1.   In your Writer's Notebook, brainstorm a list of audiences with whom you will probably communicate this week. Explain how you will adjust your verbal style according to audience and purpose.

2.   What words characterize differences in musical style—for example, a military march and a sonata? Or ask the same question about art—for example, impressionist painting, such as that of Monet and Manet compared with works by O'Keefe, Carr, Bateman, or the Group of Seven.

3.   Listen to excerpts from taped speeches by individuals with strong rhetorical skills. Identify techniques of voice and diction which appeal to audiences.

B. FOUNDATIONS

In "Writing with Style," you worked on crafting a clear, concise style to express your writer's voice. This chapter focuses on Craig's concern, "What if we need more than one style?" You'll stretch to build a repertoire of writing styles for various purposes and audiences. As Robert Finch's "The Reticent Phrase" eloquently points out, this task is demanding but ultimately rewarding.

> Aptness shall come from whence, reticent phrase,
> to tinge precisely your pellucid wave?
> Not through the naked nonchalance of chance,
> like lightning down an uncontradicted sky.
>
> Aptness is folded underneath your candour,
> pooled in the polish of a reflective glare,
> wavers, dawdles, expands, a marine flower
> idling up fluid doldrums to the surface.
>
> The phrase, beating its music, preening its crest
> against a critical oar, draws at the secret
> till the day the oar rests as the wave sunders
> and the fastidious implication emerges
>
> a flower to pelt, an excalibur to wield.

If you completed question 1 of this chapter's Fore-words, you've already begun to explore the enormous scope in purpose and audience of your daily communication. The following samples highlight just a few possibilities. As you read, you'll notice similarities—an overlapping of purposes and styles. This demonstrates that *purposes and styles cannot be neatly boxed and labelled.* Writers write for many reasons, including combinations like the following: to argue or persuade, educate and inform, entertain and amuse, illuminate, express emotions, relate, describe, and define.

As you read these excerpts, reflect on commonalities and occasions when the styles may be of use to you.

Writing to Amuse and Persuade

Christie Blatchford

Many of the people I know regularly run in races. One man does marathons; you can always tell he's getting ready for one by the rapidly enlarging gap between his shirt collar and his neck. By marathon time a woman with slender arms could insert one of them in this gap, and even I can manage to squeeze in a hand. At least a half-dozen women of my acquaintance run ten-kilometer races a couple of times a year, and a good half of the people in my fitness class are also serious runners, and a few years back, one of my most unathletic friends actually took to the streets and slogged through a five-kilometer race. All of these people are adults and claim to do this voluntarily. I do not understand it. I think only very young children and dogs take naturally to running, and I am speaking from experience.

Writing to Amuse and Inform

Stephen Leacock

Until two weeks ago I might have taken my pen in hand to write about humour with the confident air of an acknowledged professional.

But that time is past. Such claim as I had has been taken from me. In fact I stand unmasked. An English reviewer writing in a literary journal, the very name of which is enough to put contradiction to sleep, has said of my writing: "What is there, after all, in Professor Leacock's humour but a rather ingenious mixture of hyperbole and meiosis?"

The man was right. How he stumbled upon this trade secret I do not know. But I am willing to admit, since the truth is out, that it has long been my custom in preparing an article of a humorous nature to go down to the cellar and mix up half a gallon of meiosis with a pint of hyperbole. If I want to give the article a decidedly literary character, I find it well to put in about half a pint of paresis. The whole thing is amazingly simple . . . .

But the deep background that lies behind and beyond what we call humour is revealed only to the few who, by instinct or by effort, have given thought to it. The world's humour, in its best and greatest sense, is perhaps the highest product of our civilization. One thinks here not of the mere spasmodic effects of the comic artist . . . but of the really great humour which, once or twice in a generation at best, illuminates and elevates our literature. It is no longer dependent upon the mere trick and quibble of words, or the odd and meaningless incongruities in things that strike us as "funny." Its basis lies in the deeper contrasts offered by life itself: the strange incongruity between our aspirations and our achievement, the eager and fretful anxieties of today that fade into nothingness tomorrow, the burning pain and the sharp sorrow that are sharpened in the retrospect of time, till as we look back on the course that has been traversed we pass in view the panorama of our lives, as people in old age may recall, with mingled tears and smiles, the angry quarrels of their childhood. And here, in its larger aspect, humour is blended with pathos till the two are one, and represent, as they have in every age, the mingled heritage of tears and laughter that is our lot on earth.

Writing to Amuse and Illuminate

Farley Mowat

One hot summer day I was meandering aimlessly beside a little local creek when I came upon a stagnant pool. In the bottom, and only just covered with green scum, three catfish lay gasping out their lives. They interested me. I dragged them up on the bank with a stick and waited expectantly for them to die; but this they refused to do. Just when I was convinced that they were quite dead, they would open their broad ugly jaws and give another gasp. I was so impressed by their stubborn refusal to accept their fate that I found a tin can, put them in it along with some scum, and took them home.

I had begun to like them, in an abstract sort of way, and wished to know them better. But the problem of where to keep them while our acquaintanceship ripened was a major one. There were no washtubs in Greenhedges. There *was* a bathtub, but the stopper did not fit and consequently it would not hold water for more than a few minutes. By bedtime, I had still not resolved the problem and, since I felt that even these doughty fish could hardly survive an entire night in the tin can, I was driven to the admittedly desperate expedient of finding temporary lodgings for them in the bowl of Granny's old-fashioned toilet.

I was too young at the time to appreciate the special problems which old age brings in its train. It was one of these problems which was directly responsible for the dramatic and unexpected encounter which took place between my grandmother and the catfish during the small hours of the ensuing night.

It was a traumatic experience for Granny, and for me, and probably for the catfish too. Throughout the rest of her life Granny refused to eat fish of any kind and always carried a high-powered flashlight with her during her nocturnal peregrinations. I cannot be certain about the effect on the catfish, for my unfeeling cousin—once the hooferaw had died down a little— callously flushed the toilet. As for myself, the effect was to engender in me a lasting affinity for the lesser beasts of the animal kingdom. In a word, the affair of the catfish marked the beginning of my career, first as a naturalist, and later as a biologist. I had started on my way to the wolf den.

Writing to Express and Illuminate

Janette Turner Hospital

I am lying about the night terror.

Every evening I silently implore the night nurse to douse me with sufficient sedative so that sleep will rush me on an express ride right through to morning, no stops. Yet I am too proud to ask her, to admit that I am afraid of the dark. And every night there is a derailment somewhere before sunrise.

The ward is black and still as death, and I try desperately not to look out of the window. I push my egg head back against the pillow, forbidding it to turn. But it turns against my will and sees the street where the street lamp burns like a coal against the sky, a devil's eye. My attention is riveted helplessly to it, I cannot turn away. Sheer terror rams through me at high voltage and my body begins to convulse, even the bed goes into spasms. It is impossible to breathe.

The night nurse comes running with medication.

In the morning Dr. Simon begs me once again to confide in him, but the street light is watching. Menacing. Mocking: See my innocuous daytime disguise? Who will believe you?

I am afraid of being thought crazy.

"I don't have night terrors," I tell Dr. Simon. "Only that dream I already told you about."

Erosion

It took the sea a thousand years,
A thousand years to trace
The granite features of this cliff
In crag and scarp and base.

It took the sea an hour one night,
An hour of storm to place
The sculpture of these granite seams
Upon a woman's face.

—E.J. Pratt

Writing to Inspire and Motivate

William Faulkner

I decline to accept the end of man. It is easy enough to say that man is immortal simply because he will endure; that when the last ding-dong of doom has clanged and faded from the last worthless rock hanging tideless in the last red and dying evening, that even then there will still be one more sound: that of his puny inexhaustible voice, still talking. I refuse to accept this. I believe that man will not merely endure: he will prevail. He is immortal, not because he alone among creatures has an inexhaustible voice, but because he has a soul, a spirit capable of compassion and sacrifice and endurance. The poet's, the writer's, duty is to write about these things. It is his privilege to help man endure by lifting his heart, by reminding him of courage and honor and hope and pride and compassion and pity and sacrifice which have been the glory of his past. The poet's voice need not merely be the record of man, it can be one of the props, the pillars to help him endure and prevail.

Writing to Inform and Interpret

Margaret Atwood

Poems which contain descriptions of landscapes and natural objects are often dismissed as being mere Nature poetry. But Nature poetry is seldom just about Nature; it is usually about the poet's *attitude* towards the external natural universe. That is, landscapes in poems are often interior landscapes; they are maps of a state of mind. Sometimes the poem conceals this fact and purports to be objective description, sometimes the poem acknowledges and explores the interior landscape it presents. The same tendencies can be present in the descriptive passages of novels or stories with natural settings. What we are looking at in this chapter is the types of landscape that prevail in Canadian literature and the kinds of attitude they mirror.

Writing to Inform and Explain

The McGraw-Hill Author's Book

The copy editor reads the manuscript for general sense and organization; corrects grammar, spelling, and punctuation; ensures consistency of usage; and typemarks the manuscript for the compositor. In some areas of publishing, "editing supervisor" and "copy editor" are the same person. In others, the copy editing is performed by highly qualified freelancers.

Human Ecology Foundation

People who are environmentally ill are no longer able to adapt to common exposures in their everyday environment. They may develop a variety of chronic or acute symptoms that are brought on by substances in the air, in food, or in water . . . Natural inhalants such as pollens, dusts and mould, and even natural foods may begin to affect people adversely. This aspect of the condition is referred to as allergy.

Writing to Inform and Persuade

John Kenneth Galbraith

Among the Social Sciences, and indeed among all reputable fields of learning, economics occupies a special place for reproach that is inspired by its language. The literate layman regularly proclaims his discontent with the way in which economists express themselves. Other scholars emerge from the eccentricities of their own terminology to condemn the economist for a special commitment to obscurity. If an economist writes a book or even an article in clear English, he need say nothing. He will be praised for avoiding jargon—and also for risking the rebuke of his professional colleagues in doing so. And economists themselves, in their frequent exercises of introspection, regularly wonder whether they are making themselves intelligible to students, politicians and the general public. Committees are occasionally impaneled to consider their communication with the world at large. Invariably they urge improvement.

How do these sample styles differ? How may they be of use to you now and in your post-secondary career? In Activity One, explore these questions. Then move on to Activities Two through Eight, which focus on "how-to's" of four useful style clusters.

Activity One   Identifying Styles and Your Writing Needs

Purpose

- to explore style variations

- to reflect on your present and future style needs

- to plan now to meet these needs

1.   After carefully examining one sample from each of the eight groups above, describe how the style of each differs from the others. Refer specifically to how the writer tailors language to purpose.

2.   Which styles will likely be of most use to these students?
a.   Kirsten plans a research career as a chemical engineer.
b.   Craig hopes to study investigative journalism and enter the broadcast industry.
c.   Sasha wants to manage a landscape architecture firm.
d.   Tarvo hopes to act in children's theatre.

3a.   Reflect on past occasions when you have written to inform and/or explain, inform and interpret, persuade, entertain, express emotions, or illuminate reality. Examples might be a debate for history class, valedictory speech, note of acknowledgement to a superior, and a journal or diary entry.
b.   How did your language differ for each occasion? Why?
c.   If you had multiple purposes, how did you decide which was most important?

4.   For which writing situations would each style be appropriate?

- Mowat's style—laboratory report, job advertisement, or friendly letter

- Atwood's style—sports column or scholarly essay
- Blatchford's style—personal diary or memorial speech.

Justify your answers by referring to the type and level of language.

5a.   Freewrite in your Writer's Notebook about writing style(s) you expect to use most often now and in the future. Explain.
b.   Set yourself one or more personal goals for working with styles. For example, Kirsten began with this statement:

> I expect to write a lot of lab reports and memos; therefore, I want to become more adept at writing in an informative, objective style.

An Overview of Four Style Clusters

Like Tarvo and his classmates, you've probably noted throughout Activity One the need to employ several styles from those listed below. As you complete Activities Two through Seven, keep in mind that the labels refer to a *cluster of characteristics*, not carved-in-stone, mutually exclusive "types":

Informative Styles

- *Purposes:*   to report or record without interpretation, bias, or opinion
- *Major Uses:*   reporting labs, recording minutes, explaining instructions or directions, defining terms, and reporting news
- *Language Characteristics:*   neutral, unadorned (most often formal, standard English)

Interpretive Styles

- *Purposes:*   to argue a case, inform, and persuade, according to the rules of evidence
- *Major Uses:*   scholarly and personal essays, debates, and contemporary interpretive journalism (profiles, feature articles, editorials)
- *Language Characteristics:*   blend of connotative and denotative (standard or non-standard, formal or informal)

Rhetorical and Poetic Styles

- *Purposes:*   to inspire, illuminate, and sometimes persuade, or express personal emotion
- *Major Uses:*   speeches, personal essays, and certain debates, as well as stories (fiction or non-fiction), poetry, and drama
- *Language Characteristics:*   blend of connotative and denotative language which appeals to the senses and emotions (standard or non-standard, formal or informal)

Stream of Consciousness and Interior Monologue Styles

- *Purposes:*   to illuminate, heighten verisimilitude, and express personal emotions

- *Major Uses:*   prose fiction and New Journalism

- *Language Characteristics:*   figurative/expressive language which appeals to the emotions and senses (most often blend of standard and non-standard informal English)

Informative Writing Styles

Unblemished informative styles are a challenge to write well. Before beginning Activity Two, speculate about reasons you might have difficulty reporting a school sports event or a rock concert in an informative style.

Activity Two   Recognizing and Writing Informative Styles

Purpose

- to recognize informative writing styles

- to practise finding and summarizing information

- to write in informative styles for more than one audience

1a.   Peruse the excerpts from the Human Ecology Foundation's "What Do You Know About Environmental Illness?" (page 115) and *The McGraw-Hill Author's Book* (page 115). Are they "pure" examples of informative styles? Does the following excerpt belong to the informative style cluster?

> Research on auditory-spatial perception in sighted and blind infants is reviewed in an attempt to understand the implications of this work for the blind infant's and child's use of sonar aids. A critical review of studies of sonar aid use by blind infants and children is provided. It is concluded that although there is some evidence that blind children can make use of sonar aids, a more complete evaluation of the impact of such sensory substitution on the development of blind children awaits further research. (Abstract, "Can Blind Children Use Sonar Sensory Aids?")

b.   List words which describe informative styles. Speculate about other likely sources of informative writing styles.

2.   Read the front and editorial pages in the *Globe and Mail* or another well-written newspaper for a week. With a partner, compare a front page report

with an editorial, considering which source meets the criteria of informative styles outlined above. An awareness of the following distinctions will help you complete this exercise:

- *Evaluative* words appraise subjectively (e.g., "It was a *good* thing you arrived on time").

- *Attributive* words imply or infer an attitude, opinion, or interpretation (e.g., "he claimed" implies disbelief).

- *Particularizing* diction reports without bias information perceived directly through the five senses (e.g., "he said").

3a.   In your Writer's Notebook, freewrite for 15 minutes a day in an informative style—that is, report, record, inform but do *not* judge, interpret, or assess. At the week's end, exchange samples with a partner and comment on each other's growth.

b.   Did you find this experiment difficult? Explain.

4.   Assume the role of a reporter. In an informative style, draft a front page story about the experience of reading the paper and working with your partner to complete question 3. Append an explanation of how the phrasing in this report differs from editorials you have read.

5.   In your Writer's Notebook, reflect on the potential role of informative writing in your post-secondary plans, and the value of this style for encouraging you to observe like a writer.

6.   As a class, compose a chart summarizing salient features of informative writing styles. Don't try to cover every eventuality. Consider characteristics, author involvement with text/voice, purposes, level of formality, tone, mood, and occasions for use in secondary and post-secondary institutions and the work world.

Chapter Five explores in more depth informative styles and journalistic writing. But now, let's consider a second grouping of major importance for your present and future success—the interpretive styles cluster.

Interpretive Writing Styles

Wrapped in a generous array of packaging, surface differences may obscure the three central features of strong interpretive styles. The writer

- adopts and argues a position (thesis)

- employs a careful balance of valid fact and opinion

- follows the rules of logical thinking.

Cameron Stewart's "The Illiterate Engineer—Truth or Consequences?" (page 152), is one form of interpretive writing to explore. As you read it, compare Stewart's language, its level of formality, connotative words, figurative language, and so on, with Blatchford's (page 111) and Galbraith's (page 115).

Activity Three   Examining Interpretive Writing
Purpose

- to analyze components of persuasive writing
- to listen for main ideas and supporting detail
- to identify the persuasive/emotive force of connotative words

1.   Paraphrase Stewart's argument. What types of evidence does he use to support his case? (*Tip:* Review techniques of showing on page 79.) Does personal opinion or bias appear?

2.   Cite words and phrases which create an invitational tone and encourage reader involvement. What suggests Stewart's expertise?

3a.   Keeping in mind purpose, audience, content, and level of formality, speculate about a publication—perhaps a newspaper, bulletin, or magazine— for which this essay would be appropriate.
b.   Compare Stewart's essay with "Nationalism and the Pacific Scandal" by A.A. Den Otter, published in the *Canadian Historical Review*. The excerpts are taken from the introductory and concluding sections of the essay. Consider

- statement and positioning of thesis
- level and type of language
- evidence of writer's voice.

Account for differences.

> This essay does not intend to debunk the CPR nation-building myth. Even if western settlement occurred a decade or more after the CPR was completed, the railway undoubtedly made the occupation of the Northwest feasible and it also provided practical access to British Columbia. Moreover, this paper will not unravel the intricacies of the Pacific Scandal of 1873. Instead, it will re-examine some of the events leading to the scandal in order to demonstrate that the Canadian Pacific Railway was primarily a co-operative business enterprise between Canadian and American capitalists, an alliance which enjoyed the active support of the Canadian government. It will also show that the opposition, which eventually scuttled the Canadian-American alliance, was inspired by international commercial and domestic political considerations rather than patriotic concerns. . . .

. . . As for Jay Cooke, his investments in railway projects were not inspired by annexationist ambitions. Instead, through various business decisions, Cooke became more and more involved in Northern Pacific concerns. He enmeshed himself gradually in the intense rivalry among the Atlantic seaboard cities for the lucrative traffic of the North American continent. He came to share the basic motivation of all nineteenth-century railway magnates—the primal drive to find traffic for their rail lines. Like his counterparts, Jay Cooke became an agent of railway technology's need to expand constantly in order to remain competitive and profitable. As the abortive history of the Canadian Pacific aptly demonstrates in this imperialistic fight for traffic, international boundaries are meaningless. North Americans built railways primarily for business rather than for nationalistic purposes.

4.   In your Writer's Notebook
a.   argue or support one idea
b.   compose an interview in which Forsythe queries Stewart. (See the interview, "Communicating with Style in the Workplace," on page 72.)

5a.   In your writing folder, draft an interpretive essay suitable for a specific publication.
b.   Hold a peer conference about the draft, using criteria derived from these quotations and the checklist on page 390:

Chekhov   "The art of writing is the art of abbreviation."

Strunk and White   "The approach to style is by way of plainness, simplicity, orderliness and sincerity."

6.   In a small group, co-write a formal version of Stewart's essay suitable for publication in a professional journal. Exchange work, and hold a conference with another group.

7.   In your Writer's Notebook, reflect on your present and future need for skillful interpretive writing. For example, Craig began with this statement: "As a journalist, I'll use interpretive writing in feature articles and editorials."

Activity Three focused on surface details of interpretive style. But to assess an author's argument or to advocate your own, you'll need a knowledge of logic and the rules of evidence. The distinctions between fact and opinion, and observation and inference are central to this process.

First, let's clarify the terms fact and opinion. A fact is information that may be

- perceived by the senses
- verified by objective *observation*
- presented independent of inference or interpretation.

For example, most people agree that this is a factual statement: *USSR is the largest country in the world.* It expresses a fact that may be *verified* through observation according to accepted standards of proof.

On the other hand, opinion is a personal interpretation or value judgement about information. Two reasonable people might, for example, agree on facts but not on the interpretation of facts. For example, consider this assertion: *As dark brown rugs show lint, you shouldn't buy one.* This is an opinion based on an inference about how someone should behave. Before moving on, come up with several examples which demonstrate your ability to distinguish between these concepts.

In Activity Four, practise working with these distinctions.

Activity Four   Distinguishing Between Fact and Opinion

Purpose

- to distinguish between *fact* and *opinion*

- to distinguish between observation and inference

- to practise speaking and writing with an effective balance of fact and opinion

1.   After your class arrives at working definitions of "fact" and "opinion," read the following statements:

- Red is a gorgeous colour.

- Red Lake is one of the ten most frigid places in Ontario during the month of January.

- All sane people can distinguish between fact and opinion.

- According to the authoritative *Canadian Encyclopedia,* Canada is the world's fourth largest exporter of iron ore.

- People with allergies should avoid cottages.

Which of the above is (or are):
a.   a wholly factual statement
b.   a statement containing evidence of opinion
c.   an observation
d.   a statement dependent on inference
e.   a statement expressing bias through connotative diction?

2.   Explain the value judgements in these quotations. Note the connotative diction which expresses these biases.

W.H. Auden   "Like all the sins except pride, anger is a perversion, caused by pride, of something in our nature which in itself is innocent. . . ."

Francis Bacon   "He that hath a wife and children hath given hostages to fortune for they are impediments to great enterprise, either of virtue or mischief."

Ethel Strainshamps   "Few people would care to take the negative side of the proposition that the women of the world are oppressed and scorned."

3a.   (Re)read the essays by Davies (page 45), Gibson (page 94), and Kome (page 54), *and* the excerpt below. Which work leaves the initial impression of relying more on fact than opinion? Does a close examination of the argument bear out this impression? Justify.

b.   Account for differences in level and type of language, documentation, and so on.

Rainy River Sturgeon

The majority of studies relating to native North American fisheries have focused on the marine coastal regions where anadromous species contributed greatly to subsistence and related activities of native peoples. Except by Rostuland (1952) and Cleland (1982), fishing among native peoples elsewhere in North America, particularly in the north-central interior, has been regarded as relatively unimportant. Indians living in the Canadian Shield and adjacent areas have been typically portrayed as big-game hunters; fishing has generally been considered important "only at those times of the year when big game were difficult to secure" (Rogers and Smith 1981, 133) or "when other resources failed" (Rogers 1983, 94; Steegman 1983, 255). According to some fisheries biologists (Schupp and Macins 1977, 1785), demands on the fisheries resources by Lake of the Woods and Rainy River Ojibway bands were "limited before the coming of white men."

   This view fails to recognize that many rivers and lakes in the region contained large-scale fisheries that were an important part of the seasonal round of resource activities for native peoples. One of these resources, the subject of this paper, is the Rainy River sturgeon fishery. It will be shown that sturgeon fishing was not undertaken only when big-game was scarce. Rather, it was an activity of great significance to Ojibway subsistence, commerce, society, and religion. The eventual severe depletion of this fishery at the end of the 19th century had a serious and lasting impact on the welfare of the local Ojibway peoples.

4.   In groups, compose statements to test your understanding of fact, opinion, observation, inference, bias, and slant.

5.   Select a topic about which you have strong opinions. Within five minutes, convince a partner your point of view is the right one. Tape your interaction.

a.   As you play the tape, distinguish between the fact and opinion in your argument. Repeat the process, changing roles.

b.   What did you and your partner learn about effective persuasion from this exercise?

6.   In your writing folder, draft an argumentative essay on a topic about which you have plenty of verifiable fact. Underline factual statements on the draft. If your writing partner queries any statements of fact, be prepared to substantiate them. (*Note*: To review writing with a thesis and other salient essay features, see Writer's Resource Five—Writing Essays on page 402.)

Of equal importance in interpretive writing is the ability to detect logical fallacies. An argument may *seem* logical but not meet the rules of logical reasoning. For example, propaganda often misuses logic to present a shiny veneer of legitimacy. Activity Five invites you to hone critical thinking powers and apply your learning to all forms of communication.

Activity Five   Detecting Logical Fallacies
Purpose

- to explore standards of logic required for argumentation

- to recognize and eliminate logical fallacies in writing interpretive styles

1a.   In conference with a partner, assess your essay from Activity Four, question 6. Use the three standards of logic for *advocating* a claim highlighted by Professor J. Anthony Blair of the University of Windsor in his presentation "Critical Thinking: The Role of Reason-Giving and Argumentation" at the Canadian Conference on Thinking:

Relevance:

- Is each piece of evidence relevant to the case?

- Does the truth of each piece of evidence bear directly on the truth of the case as a whole?

An argument based on irrelevant proof sounds like this: "James is an unlikeable person. Therefore, if he supports Mr. Singer and the Zings, they're an untalented group."

Acceptability:

- Is the proof reasonable, evident, and plausible?

- Is any statement given as evidence itself in need of proof?

An unacceptable argument sounds like this: "Janet shouldn't have lied to her boyfriend about the party because it's always wrong to tell an untruth."

Sufficiency:

- Does the evidence provide *sufficient* grounds for belief of the assertion? Is the evidence sufficient to persuade?

- Is the evidence of an *appropriate* sort?

An argument with insufficient proof sounds like this: "Eating carrots improves the eyesight in the dark. I know this because I've eaten six carrots a day for six weeks and see things in the dark I've never seen before."

b.   Make notes on revisions to undertake before moving on to question 2.

2a.   Working as a class or in small groups, compose examples of the logical fallacies outlined below. Note any overlapping between these fallacies and the tests set out by Professor Blair.

- An *ad hominem* argument attempts to discredit an individual in order to discredit his or her idea.

- An *association* encourages the audience to react emotionally to an issue or ideal by paralleling it with a strong positive or negative connotation.

- An *appeal to authority* argument attempts to transfer respect or adoration for a famous individual to support a conclusion about a subject on which the person has no expertise.

- A *begging the question* argument assumes as its premise the conclusion it intends to prove.

- An *equivocation* is an argument that misleads or deceives the listener through ambiguous use of (a) word(s).

- A *cause/temporal* or *post hoc* argument falsely assumes that one event causes another simply because it occurred earlier than the second.

- A *non-sequitur* is an argument in which the conclusion does not necessarily follow from the premises (initial statements and assumptions).

- A *false analogy* assumes that because two objects or people, for example, are similar in two respects, they are totally similar.

For examples of these and other logical fallacies, see a text such as *Introduction to Logic* by Irving M. Copi.

b.   In conference with a new partner, retest your draft and planned revisions for ambiguous or fallacious thinking.

3.   In your Writer's Notebook, reflect on how knowledge of logic and bias may enhance your ability to

- view television commercials or news reports with a discriminating eye

- draft a first-rate history essay, science lab, book report, or debate

- read a textbook

- prepare a debate or win a friendly argument

- assess newspaper editorials clipped in Activity Three.

4a.   Form debate teams of four. With your partner, co-write your speeches. Prior to the debate, invite someone from another team to check your work for faulty logic.

b.   Use the criteria checklist for debates (Glossary, page 406) and your knowledge of logic to assess each debating team.

5.   In your writing folder, revise your argumentative essay, eliminating ambiguous or fallacious reasoning. Or if you prefer, begin afresh; you might, for example, redraft your debate into an argumentative essay.

Rhetorical and Poetic Writing Styles

Imagine you're chairing a fund-raising campaign for a club or organization. The first draft of your speech to recruit support is a well-written piece of logical persuasion. But it lacks eloquence. What style will help you achieve your goals? Why do informative or interpretive writing styles not suffice?

Try a rhetorical style to inspire and illuminate, as well as persuade your audience. Rhetorical styles appeal to the senses through the kind of expressive language commonly associated with poetry. Metaphor, simile, repetition, rhythm, and sound and sight imagery tantalize and engage the non-rational mind. For example, review Faulkner's speech on page 114; phrases such as "the last ding-dong of doom" evoke a haunting emotional response. Or read Martin Luther King's rhetoric (page 151). Note delightful phrases and images that stick in your mind. Does connotative or denotative diction dominate?

Poetic writing styles also employ figurative or expressive language. But significant distinctions result from differing purposes and relationships with the audience. As rhetorical writing is intended for public consumption, the author keeps in mind audience reaction during the composing process. Poetic writing, whether verse or prose, is primarily expressive. The writer's main concern is personal illumination; audience response is secondary.

Reflect on language you enjoyed as a child. Chances are you recall verses with vivid language such as these:

> Elephants a-pilin' teak
> In the sludgy, squdgy creek,
> Where the silence 'ung that 'eavy you was 'arf
>   afraid to speak.
>
> —Rudyard Kipling

Here is a child, who clambers and scrambles,
All by himself, and gathering brambles.

—Robert Louis Stevenson

With your class, consider the appeal of phrasing such as "sludgy, squdgy," "clambers and scrambles," and "gathering brambles." Or ponder lines from Shakespeare—perhaps one of these famous quotations:

When shall we three meet again,
In thunder, lightning, or in rain?
. . . .
Fair is foul, and foul is fair.

—*Macbeth*

More sinned against than sinning.

—*King Lear*

What's in a name? That which we call a rose
By any other name would smell as sweet.

—*Romeo and Juliet*

In Activity Six, explore rhetorical and poetic language that delights the eye and ear.

Activity Six   Exploring Expressive or Figurative Language

Purpose

- to enjoy sound and sight in language
- to identify techniques of figurative language and their effects on audience response
- to write in poetic and rhetorical styles

1.   As volunteers read these passages, listen for phrasing that speaks to the senses—what you see, hear, feel, taste.

Tennessee Williams

It wasn't far. The walk soon ended and under their feet was the plushy coolness of earth. The moon flowed aqueously through the multitude of pointed oak leaves: the dirt road was also like moving water with its variations of light and shade. They came to a low wooden fence. The boy jumped over it. Then held out his arms. She stepped to the top rail and he lifted her down from it. On the other side his arms did not release her but held her closer.

"This is it," he told her, "the field of blue children."

She looked beyond his dark shoulder. And it was true. The whole field was covered with dancing blue flowers. There was a wind scudding through them and they broke before it in pale blue waves, sending up a soft whispering sound like the infinitely diminished crying of small children at play.

She thought of the view from her window at night, those nights when she cried bitterly without knowing why, the dome of the administration building like a white peak and the restless waves of moonlit branches and the stillness and the singing voices, mournfully remote, blocks away, coming closer, the tender, foolish ballads, and the smell of the white spirea at night, and the stars clear as lamps in the cloud-fretted sky, and she remembered the choking emotion that she did not understand and the dread of all this coming to its sudden, final conclusion in a few months or weeks or more.

Mark Twain

To be, or not to be; that is the bare bodkin
That makes calamity of so long life;
For who would fardels bear, till Birnham wood do come to Dunsinane,
But that the fear of something after death
Murders the innocent sleep,
Great nature's second course,
And makes us rather sling the arrows of outrageous fortune
Than fly to others that we know not of.
There's the respect must give us pause:
Wake Duncan with thy knocking! I would thou could'st;
For who would bear the whips and scorns of time,
The oppressor's wrong, the proud man's contumely,
The law's delay, and the quietus which his pangs might take,
In the dead waste and middle of the night, when church-yards yawn
In customary suits of black,
But that the undiscovered country from whose bourne no traveller returns,
Breathes forth contagion on the world,
And thus the native hue of resolution, like the poor cat i' the adage,
Is sicklied o'er with care,
And all the clouds that lowered o'er our housetops,
With this regard their currents turn awry,
And lose the name of action.
"Tis a consummation devoutly to be wished. But soft, the fair Ophelia:
Ope not thy ponderous and marble jaws,
But get thee to a nunnery—go!"

F. Scott Fitzgerald

We walked through a high hallway into a bright rosy-coloured space, fragilely bound into the house by French windows at either end. The windows were ajar and gleaming white against the fresh grass outside that seemed to grow a little way into the house. A breeze blew through the room, blew curtains in at one end and out the other like pale flags, twisting them up toward the frosted wedding-cake of the ceiling, and then rippled over the wine-coloured rug, making a shadow on it as wind does on the sea.

2.   In your Writer's Notebook freewrite about the appeal of the above passages.

a.   Reflect on your general response to each, which passage you prefer, and why.

b.   Record phrasing you enjoy. Speculate about the attraction of each; for example, does it intrigue the eye, the ear, or both? What other senses and associations come into play?

c.   Ponder the colours and shapes evoked by each passage and account for these reactions with specific words and phrases.

3.   Review figures of speech (page 408) and rhetorical techniques (page 126):

a.   Match literary terms with phrasing from your list of appealing diction (question 2a).

b.   With a partner, comment on three examples of effective figurative language.

4a.   With a partner, read aloud "Dark Pines Under Water" and "The Difference"; compare the poets' use of language with King's or Fitzgerald's. Consider:

· author's awareness of audience

· deliberate attempts to engage audience response

· types of expressive language or rhetoric.

Dark Pines Under Water

This land like a mirror turns you inward
And you become a forest in a furtive lake;
The dark pines of your mind reach downward,
You dream in the green of your time,
Your memory is a row of sinking pines.

Explorer, you tell yourself this is not what you came for
Although it is good here, and green;
You had meant to move with a kind of largeness,
You had planned a heavy grace, an anguished dream.

But the dark pines of your mind dip deeper
And you are sinking, sinking, sleeper
In an elementary world;
There is something down there and you want it told.

—Gwendolyn MacEwen

The Difference

Your way of loving is too slow for me.
For you, I think, must know a tree by heart
Four seasons through, and note each single leaf
With microscopic glance before it falls—
And after watching soberly the turn
Of autumn into winter and the slow
Awakening again, the rise of sap—
Then only will you cry: "I love this tree!"
As if the beauty of the thing could be

Made lovelier or marred by any mood
Of wind, or by the sun's caprice; as if
All beauty had not sprung up with the seed.—
With such slow ways you find no time to love
A falling flame, a flower's brevity.

—Dorothy Livesay

b.   With your partner, revise a paragraph from the King or Fitzgerald passages using verse form; keep the original phrasing intact. A word processor will facilitate your experimentation with line placement. Does verse enhance or detract from the meaning? Justify. Then co-write one stanza of verse by MacEwan or Livesay as prose. Exchange work with others and share responses.

5a.   In your writing folder, draft a speech or debate using appropriate rhetorical techniques.
b.   With a conference partner, compare your draft with the essay or debate you wrote in interpretive style (Activity Five, question 5.) What differences in style are apparent?

6.   In your Writer's Notebook, reflect on:
a.   future opportunities to experiment with these styles
b.   occasions for which these styles are inappropriate.

Stream of Consciousness and Interior Monologue Writing Styles

The final group of writing styles we'll examine appears not only in modern prose fiction but also in certain types of poetry, drama, and essays. Like poetic and rhetorical writing, these styles depend heavily on the power of emotionally laden words.

Stream of consciousness imitates the mind's natural internal dialogue. The best tool for understanding its subjective texture and shape is spontaneous writing. For the next fifteen minutes, freewrite in your Writer's Notebook about spontaneous thoughts and feelings. Try not to censor your expression or pause for punctuation. You are your only audience and will not be asked to share this passage.

Does the form of your writing look anything like this dream excerpt from Judith Guest's novel *Ordinary People*?

> *Shock. His mind egg-shaped gray loose tracings of paths over it rat scratchings white hospital gown gentle Leo helps him into it never hurries him old friends in the steel-and-white room greet him with smiles "Here he is just lie back and relax head on the pillow that's it" get him ready. . . .*

Or perhaps it sounds something like this passage from Blair Martin's short story, "Independence Day":

> The air, I can see the air. Taste the water. Sky's Navy blue—"I stood arrow straight, unencumbered by the weight. . ." So long Carolyn, be a good college girl. Good luck, friend. . . The air. Tastes like water. That tree, the brown, green, silver willow, I remember those summers, Scott and Andrew and Chris, Thomas and Adrienne, all day 'til Mom yelled out the door always when we'd found the perfect hiding place. And those forts we spent hours in the sun hammering and sawing forever, each piece just right and sit under a leaky roof and eat a box of cookies somebody stole from their mother and belch and laugh and read . . .

There's no *one* way your passage should look, but if it resembles a logically structured essay, you've probably edited your thoughts. For students such as Kirsten, who are highly skilled logical thinkers, privacy and practice may encourage experimentation with stream of consciousness styles. Your critic, the so-called left-brain function discussed in Chapter One, must let the right brain do its work.

Stream of consciousness writing is characterized by the features listed below. Which ones are evident in the passages by Guest and Martin?

- purposeful disregard of conventional grammar, punctuation and, perhaps, spelling

- focus on abstract images and impressions, emotions and associations

- apparent disregard of logic, sequence, and linear plot

- focus on personal reality conveyed in informal language
- preponderance of expressive language
- no acknowledgement of external audience
- outer reality important only as it affects the speaker.

A closely related style is interior monologue. It *differs* from stream of consciousness because an external audience is acknowledged. This is accomplished by references to time, sequence, and place, as well as judgements about or identification of characters or events. Examine the passages by Martin (page 131), Guest (page 131), Faulkner (page 144), and Joyce (page 150). Which of them acknowledges an audience, and how is this achieved?

In Activity Seven, enhance your ability to work in these styles.

Activity Seven   Writing Stream of Consciousness and Interior Monologue Styles

Purpose

- to practise writing and revising these styles
- to reflect on stylistic experimentation
- to consider appropriate occasions for use

1a.   As volunteers read excerpts from *The Sound and the Fury* (page 144) and *A Portrait of the Artist as a Young Man* (page 150), enjoy the poetic language.
b.   Reflect on initial responses in your Writer's Notebook. Rank passages in order of preference. Justify.

2.   Discuss these questions in small groups:
a.   Do people's reactions to these styles appear to mirror learning preferences?
b.   What personal qualities do you feel Faulkner or Joyce have revealed through their writer's voice? Justify your speculations with textual references.
c.   Pinpoint stylistic similarities in work by Guest, Faulkner, Joyce, and Martin, and samples of poetic and rhetorical styles.

3.   Rewrite a portion of one passage in verse. Reflect on whether the form suits the meaning.

4a.   Co-write two essays comparing Faulkner's and Joyce's styles. Consider rhythmic patterns, appeals to the senses through imagery, and overall realism. In the first essay, your purpose is to inform and educate. In the second, you are to persuade.

b.   Append an explanation of how you altered language and other writing variables to suit each purpose.

5.   In your writing folder, draft a passage in stream of consciousness style, perhaps as a diary entry. Then write the same passage using interior monologue style. Label techniques through which you acknowledge audience. Exchange work with a partner and offer constructive comments on rough drafts.

6.   In your Writer's Notebook, speculate on
a.   purposes and audiences for which these styles may be inappropriate
b.   occasions when a knowledge of these styles may enhance your reading and writing.

C.   AFTER-WORDS

Reading and Responding

1.   Label the style employed in the Amnesty International open letter by president Bob Goodfellow. Evaluate its appropriateness for the writer's purpose and audience.

Letter from Amnesty International

One of the most awful memories I have is of children screaming through the night.

—A lawyer speaking on the long-term
effects of ill-treatment and detention on children.

Dear Friend:
   With your past support Amnesty has accomplished a great deal. But one of the areas we were able to investigate in more depth last year has caused me great concern.
   I'd like to encourage you to renew your support to Amnesty today and help thousands of children who are imprisoned and subjected to state-sanctioned abuse. Many are tortured . . . some are executed . . . others just "disappear."

2.   William French's travel article, "Mr. Shaw Was Not at Home" (page 145), demonstrates an effective blend of poetic, rhetorical, and interpretive writing styles: he persuades, inspires, and illuminates in an engaging essay. Assess the validity of this comment, giving specific textual references.

3a.   What techniques of persuasion does Lady Macbeth use in the following speech? Is the style interpretive, rhetorical, poetic, or a blend of these?

> Was the hope drunk,
> Wherein you dress'd yourself? Hath it slept since?
> And wakes it now, to look so green and pale
> At what it did so freely? From this time,
> Such I account thy love. Art thou afeard
> To be the same in thine own act and valour
> As thou art in desire? Would'st thou have that
> Which thou esteem'st the ornament of life,
> And live a coward in thine own esteem?
> Letting "I dare not" wait upon "I would,"
> Like the poor cat i' th'adage?

b.   Does this speech from Lady Macbeth's sleepwalking scene exhibit the qualities of stream of consciousness or interior monologue?

> Out, damned spot! out, I say! One: two:
> why, then 'tis time to do't. Hell is murky. Fie,
> my Lord, fie! a soldier, and afeard? What need
> we fear who knows it, when none can call our power
> to accompt? Yet who would have thought the
> old man to have had so much blood in him?

4.   Study the following excerpt from the essay "Can Blind Children Use Sonar Aids?" reprinted from the *Canadian Journal of Psychology*. Which passage(s) in this chapter does the style most closely resemble? Consider purpose(s) and audience, level and type of language, statement and positioning of thesis, balance of fact and opinion, and so on.

The most accurate information about the distal world that is available to the blind[1] infant and child must come primarily from the auditory system. However, naturally occurring auditory information is very different from visual information, and such differences pose problems for the developing blind child. In this paper we discuss research on an auditory spatial sensor designed to give the blind infant and child some of the spatial information normally obtained through vision[2]. Because this device depends on the auditory modality, we first discuss the use of auditory information in guiding the activities of both blind and sighted infants and children. In the course of this discussion we also describe some of the important differences between visual and auditory information that contribute to problems faced by the developing blind child.

Notes:
1.   For the purposes of this paper, *blind* refers to the totally blind who make up about 10% of the population of those who are legally blind. Persons classified as legally blind may have useful vision.

2.   Although an appreciation of the possible problems in spatial perception and cognition in the blind is fundamental to understanding their development, other aspects of development including emotional, social, linguistic, and general cognitive development are obviously crucial in presenting a full description of the development of blind children. For further reading on these topics the reader is referred to the work of Fraiberg (1977) and the review of Warren (1984). The latter source, in particular, provides many references for further reading about development in blind children.

5.   Read "Canadian Spoken Here" by Walter S. Avis (page 138). Identify and comment on the effectiveness of:

a.   the thesis and types and quality of evidence

b.   the (blend of) style(s) employed

c.   the "fit" of the writing variables set out in Chapter Two (pages 81-84).

The Writing Folder

1.   Rewrite a draft from your writing folder or Writer's Notebook using a different style for a similar audience. For instance, revise a found poem in starker language. Or write two essays on the same controversial topic for two different purposes and audiences. Assess the merits of each, considering which is most suitable for your content, audience, and purpose.

2.   Illustrate your understanding of relationships between style in visual arts and language. For example, draw a comic strip or single frame in three distinct styles; tailor language to the visual depiction. Accompany cartoons with a statement of purpose, audience, and style adaptations.

3.   In a formal interpretive essay, demonstrate your understanding of stylistic similarities in writing and music. You might examine two musical styles and match each with its verbal partner.

4.   Compose two polished after-dinner speeches for a politician of your choice for two distinctly different audiences. Append a brief commentary on ways you've tailored language to audience.

5.   Compose a letter to the editor of a specific newspaper using appropriate techniques of interpretive and/or rhetorical style to convince your readers.

Independent Study

1.   Review your Writer's Notebook entries and/or unpolished pieces from your writing folder. Devise a topic which reflects and extends your learning about style.

2.   Use creative thinking strategies to stimulate ideas:

a.   List your associations with: sandpaper, tears, laughter, midnight blue, scalpel, politics, sports, and ice cream. Do your associations point to areas of interest?

b.   Follow a train of thought. For example, ponder what would happen if . . . you travelled around the world next year . . . or you learned to . . . ?

3.   Study the stylistic merits of two contemporary writers. Reflect your understanding of technique in an original short story, literary essay, or research paper. Suggestions:

- M.F.K. Fisher, *Two Towns in Provence* (Vintage)

- Nadine Gordimer, *A World of Strangers* (Penguin)

- Katherine Govier, *Fables of Brunswick Avenue* (Penguin)

- Graham Greene, *The Heart of the Matter* (Penguin)

- Janette Turner Hospital, *Dislocations* (McClelland and Stewart)

- Margaret Laurence, *The Stone Angel* (McClelland and Stewart)

- Adele Wiseman, *Memoirs of a Book-Molesting Childhood and Other Essays* (Oxford)

4.   Research reviewers' reactions to new writing styles. For example, examine the reception of work by James Joyce or Virginia Woolf, and base a short story, one-act play, or essay on your findings.

5.   Study emotional appeals in the language of speeches. Reflect your learning in several speeches which you write and tape. Append a brief analysis of stylistic techniques.

6.   Assess the success with which a film captures the original writer's style in a work first published as a short story, novel, essay, or narrative poem. Suggestions:

- E.M. Forster, *Room with a View*

- Alice Munro, "Thanks For the Ride"

- Earle Birney, "David"

- Jane Austen, *Pride and Prejudice*

- Emily Brontë, *Wuthering Heights*

- Henry James, *Daisy Miller*

- Paul Scott, The "Raj Quartet," including "The Jewel in the Crown"

The Writer's Notebook

1. Freewrite about your understanding of this chapter's key concepts.

2. Reflect on the growth of your writing process. Have you

- experimented with a new prewriting strategy

- become more skilled at producing a first draft

- progressed toward your style goals

- noted problem areas

- discussed personal progress with your instructor

- listened for your voice as you worked with each style?

3.   Speedwrite for fifteen minutes in response to one quotation; keep in mind the lessons of this chapter.

W.H. New and W.E. Messenger   "Subjectivity or objectivity is almost always a matter of degree; one is relatively subjective or objective at any given time. Even a camera can lie."

Ortega Y. Gassett   "The metaphor is probably the most fertile power we possess."

Lucy Maud Montgomery   "The point of good writing is knowing when to stop."

Edward Gibbon   "The style of an author should be the image of his mind, but the choice and command of language is the fruit of exercise."

READINGS 3

Canadian Spoken Here

Walter S. Avis

Fifteen years ago a writer in a Canadian magazine complained that the word *snye* was not defined in any dictionary in spite of the fact that the Canadian Board on Geographical Names had certified it as "a lawful and proper generic term." A few years later another writer, in another journal, complained that none of his dictionaries included the word *mukluk*. Nor have these been the only voices raised in frustration because so many terms met with in Canada were ignored by dictionaries. Until quite recently, however, all were voices crying in the wilderness; for few Canadians were interested enough in their speech to undertake the gigantic task of finding out about it. Consequently, there were no Canadian dictionaries worthy of the name; and our imported dictionaries virtually ignored Canadian usage. After all, British dictionaries are primarily intended for Britons and American dictionaries for Americans; no reputable editor claims anything more.

To say that British and American dictionaries do not reflect Canadian usage is to say that Canadian English is neither British nor American, that the English spoken in Canada is distinct in many ways from that spoken in the United Kingdom and from that spoken in the United States. It should be observed that this distinctive variety of speech is referred to as "Canadian English" and not as the "Canadian language," for Canadians share one language with Britons, Americans, and a host of other people both inside the Commonwealth and beyond it. To claim that there is a Canadian language, or, as many Americans do, an American language, is to distort the meaning of the word *language* for nationalistic purposes. On the other hand, it is a form of

blindness to insist, as many do, that "English is English" and that it is folly to dignify the "slang and dialect" of Canada by discussing it as if it merited serious attention.

Any Canadian who has spent some time in both the United Kingdom and the United States knows that his English is recognized as non-British by Britons and (perhaps less often) as non-American by Americans. While it is true that the uninformed in Britain may identify us with Americans and the uninformed in the United States may identify us with Englishmen, people in both countries who are familiar with Canadians recognize speech habits that are unlike their own. An American, for example, may point to our way of using *blind* where he would use *shade*, *tap* where he would use *faucet*, *serviette* where he would use *napkin*, *braces* where he would use *suspenders*, and *porridge* where he would use *oatmeal*; or he might point to our way of pronouncing *been* to rhyme with "bean" instead of "bin," *ration* to rhyme with "fashion" instead of "nation," *lever* to rhyme with "beaver" instead of "never," and Z to rhyme with "bed" instead of "knee." He will certainly notice that most of us pronounce *lout* with a different sounding vowel from that of *loud*. He will, in fact, wrongly insist that we pronounce *out* to rhyme with "shoot," just as speakers of Scots dialect do.

The Britisher, on the other hand, will observe that we pronounce *aunt*, *glass*, *path*, *clerk*, *war*, and *tomato* in a way quite different from his; he may also note that most of us make no distinction between the vowel of *caught* and that of *cot*, whereas for him the vowels are very different indeed. He observes, too, that many of the words he uses every day in England are simply not understood by his Canadian friends. Suppose he gets into a conversation about cars. Says he, "I think a car should have a roomy boot." Communication will come to a halt until someone rescues him by pointing out that Canadians call a *boot* a "trunk." Before this chat is over, he will learn that Canadians use *hood* for his *bonnet, muffler* for *silencer, bumper* for *fender,* and (egad, sir!) *fender* for *wing.* These few examples illustrate the point that Canadian patterns of speech are neither British nor American, though they are in some degree a blend of both.

Canadian English, then, is a dialect which resembles American English in some respects and British English in others and includes, at the same time, a great deal that is significantly Canadian. The explanation of this mixed character lies in the settlement history of the country. As the eastern regions of British North America were opened for settlement, before, during, and after the Revolutionary War, Americans were prominent among the settlers. New Englanders began moving into Nova Scotia several decades before the Revolution and the Loyalist influx of 1790 brought thousands more. Today, as in the days of Judge Haliburton's *Sam Slick, the Clockmaker,* the New England origin of large numbers of Bluenoses is evident in the speech and customs of the province. Both New Brunswick and the Eastern Townships of Quebec were first colonized by American Loyalists and, in both areas, post-Loyalist settlers added to the preponderance of American stock.

In Upper Canada the early influx of American settlers was especially significant, for Ontario was to become the populous heart of English-speaking Canada. By 1795 there were some 10,000 Loyalists settled around Kingston and Niagara, at the opposite ends of Lake Ontario. When the War of 1812 began, the population of Upper Canada had grown to some 50,000, almost entirely made up of former Americans, both Loyalist and post-Loyalist, none of whom were any less American in language and manners than their former compatriots to the south. This American preponderance is evident from the composition of the legislative assembly in 1828, there being four members born in Ireland, six in Scotland, seven in England,

three in other British colonies, thirteen in Canada, and fifteen in the United States.

In Ontario, there is no doubt, American speech habits have been entrenched from the beginning. The settlers from south of the line introduced their system of education along with their system of municipal government. The public elementary school was always the normal thing in Upper Canada, many of the textbooks being imported from the United States or adapted from American models. This state of affairs did not pass unnoticed, as is made clear in the following observations made by a British doctor travelling through the province in 1832:

> It is really melancholy to traverse the province and go into many of the common schools; you find a herd of children instructed by some anti-British adventurer, instilling into the young and tender mind sentiments hostile to the parent state [that is, American geography and history with a republican bias]; and American spelling books, dictionaries and grammars, teaching them anti-British dialect and idiom.

Later in the century the conditions which so irritated the doctor were somewhat moderated by the mildly pro-British reforms of Egerton Ryerson, a second-generation Loyalist from New York, who was superintendent of education in Ontario from 1844 to 1876. One of the reforms is alluded to in the following quotation from a contemporary issue of *The Voice of the Fugitive* (Oct. 23, 1851) published in Sandwich, Canada West:

> We are also in great need of reading books, slates, and some 6 or 7 dozen of Webster's spelling book (only American spelling book allowed in Government schools) for the use of poor scholars.

Ryerson's success in eliminating American influence from the schools was far from complete; yet his efforts and those of others with similar views have doubtless had a significant effect on the English of Canadians, for the practice of "teaching British" has a long history in this country. It must be remembered that the prestige of British English has always exerted a strong influence on Canadian patterns of speech, especially among the educated. Nevertheless, it seems clear that the American idiom was already implanted deep in Upper Canada when the great stream of British immigrants began to flow into the country during the later stages of settlement.

Population movements between the United States and Canada have never ceased to be an important factor in the settlement of the Dominion of the North. When hard times struck Upper Canada in the 1830's, many Canadians joined the American settlers, who, freed from the Indian menace in Illinois and Indiana, were moving into the Middle West. The exodus of Canadians to the States during this period brought about the opening up of the old Northwest. The transcontinental railway was undertaken by the Canadian government and attractive land grants were made available to prospective homesteaders. The forty-ninth parallel during this period was little more than a geographical abstraction; the tax collector was, as one historian has said, the only important indication that a boundary existed.

In the 1870's and the 1880's many farmers in Upper Canada contracted "Manitoba fever" and hastened to take advantage of the opportunities Manitoba had to offer. These settlers, many of them of Loyalist background, reached their new homes by way of the United States, being joined en route by many landhungry Americans. Immigrants from the Old Country were very much in the minority and generally settled in their own communities, as did the Red River Scots of Lord Selkirk.

Twenty years later, Saskatchewan and Alberta were opened up, at a time when the American Northwest had been largely settled. The C.P.R., completed in 1885, carried great numbers of eastern Canadians and some Britishers to the new territories. But the greatest number of settlers came from the south, where the frontier was fast disappearing, almost a million Americans entering southern Alberta and Saskatchewan from 1900 to 1915. Thus, the North American character of the English spoken on the Prairies was entrenched through the domination of Canadians (mostly Ontarians but a substantial number of Maritimers) and Americans among the English-speaking settlers. The thousands of non-English-speaking Scandinavians and central Europeans who immigrated to the Prairie Provinces learned the kind of English spoken by their neighbours, most of whom, as we have seen, spoke the North American variety. Latter-day American arrivals, particularly in oil-rich Alberta, have reinforced this North American pattern.

Fewer Americans were drawn to British Columbia, largely because the type of farming land was not to their liking. As a result, the Pacific-coast province was settled, in large measure, by emigrants from the British Isles, although Canadians from both Ontario and the Maritimes were well represented. This British predominance has had a noticeable but as yet undefined effect on the nature of British Columbia English, especially in certain areas —as the Okanagan Valley and southern Vancouver Island—and among people at the higher social levels, who traditionally send their children to private schools conducted more or less on the British pattern. On the other hand, British Columbia has strong lines of north-south communication with the United States, lines which have in many ways been more active than those running eastward through the Rockies. This close bond with the United States has also had its effect on the English of British Columbia, perhaps most noticeably in Vancouver and its areas of influence.

This summary of population movements, oversimplified as it obviously is, should serve to emphasize the significance of the American element in Canadian settlement history. Influence from the United States has been constant and strong from the beginning. Canadians are often taught from American textbooks; they listen to American radio programs, watch American television and movies, read American novels; in large numbers they are constantly moving back and forth across the border, as immigrants, as tourists, as students, and as bargain hunters. Finally, as a North American country, Canada quite naturally shares a large vocabulary with the United States, a vocabulary made up of words designating all manner of things indigenous to this continent. One need only leaf through the *Dictionary of Canadianisms* or the *Dictionary of Americanisms* to appreciate this fact. There is nothing very surprising about the closeness of Canadian and American English.

It must be understood that the United Kingdom has also made an enormous contribution to the settlement of English-speaking Canada. For more than a century an almost continuous stream of Britishers, speaking various dialects, have emigrated to Canada. In most communities, especially those along the Canada-United States border (where Canada's population is still concentrated), these newcomers came into contact with already established Canadians and, as might be expected, their children adopted the speech habits of the communities they settled in. Only in certain areas, where relatively homogeneous Old Country groups established themselves, did markedly British dialectal features survive through several generations. Such communities can be found in Newfoundland, northern Nova Scotia, the Ottawa Valley, the Red River region, and the parts of British Columbia already mentioned. It might be added that the English-speaking natives of Montreal and Quebec have an English and Scots heritage going back nearly two centuries, a fact that is often evident in their speech, which is, nevertheless, obviously Canadian. British immigrants have unquestionably made substantial contributions to every department of the language, none perhaps in greater degree than the Scots and Scots-Irish, who have from earliest times been prominent in Canada's affairs, the Scots schoolteacher, or dominie, being a part of the community scene in so many areas in colonial times. To a great extent, what is not American about Canadian English has been brought directly from the Old Country, such features often competing with American variants already current in Canada, and even gradually displacing them. Just such a process seems to be taking place at present with respect to the pronunciation of *schedule*: the British (shej ül), though apparently used by a minority, might well be displacing the characteristically American (skej ül), very probably influenced by the practice of CBC announcers.

With the passing years, the speech habits of educated Canadians have become remarkably homogeneous, though by no means free of regional variety. Taken as a whole, the language of this country is neither British nor American: it is distinctively Canadian. This distinctiveness is most easily demonstrated with reference to the vocabulary, for there are hundreds of words which are native to Canada or which have meaning peculiar to this country. All of these words, which may be called Canadianisms, and many more, are defined in Canadian dictionaries already available or soon to be published; many, indeed, will be found in Canadian editions of foreign dictionaries, especially of the larger size, for foreign dictionary-makers are at last aware that Canadians, who form an important part of their market, are nowadays expecting dictionaries to give information about Canadian words, pronunciations, and spellings.

There is a surprisingly large number of Canadianisms, some of national currency, others largely regional; still others are confined mainly to special fields of activity, such as logging, fishing, or athletics. Most are terms coined in this country from English-language resources, or words borrowed here from the several other-language groups encountered by English-speaking Canadians. Others are native English words which have taken on specialized or transferred meanings here in Canada.

Prominent among Canadianisms are proper nouns, such as names of regions: *French Shores, Cariboo*; of natives of certain regions: *Herring Chokers, Spud Islanders*; of things associated with persons or places: *Calgary redeye, Digby chicken*. Needless to say, many terms referring to things political are peculiarly Canadian: *Grit, Socred, reeve, rural municipality, police village*. Moreover, various institutions of a social character have Canadian names, most of them being Canadian institutions: *collegiate institute, separate school*. A great many words are loanwords from other languages: French, *aboideau, shanty*; Eskimo, *komatik, oomiak*; Amerindian languages, *chipmunk, pemmican*. Sometimes the origin of such loanwords is obscured in the process of adoption: *chowder, shanty, mush, shivaree, snye*, for example, are all borrowings from Canadian French, the original forms being *chaudière, chantier, marche, charivari*, and *chenail*.

Many Canadianisms seem more or less limited to certain regions: to Newfoundland, *jinkers, glitter*; Maritimes, *gaspereau, Cape Island Boat*; Ontario, *fire-reels, Aurora trout*; Prairies, *pothole trout, grid road*; British Columbia, *salt chuck, kokanee*; Northland, *cat-swing, cheechako*.

The field of sports has made its contributions as well, for hockey and lacrosse, and probably broomball, were born and developed here, while a native variety of rugby, that is, football, has developed among us. Furthermore, curling, introduced from Scotland, has flourished so remarkably in Canada that many of the terms our curlers use came into being in this country. From hockey and lacrosse we get *blueline, rover, spearing, crosse*; from rugby-football, *rouge, flying-wing*; from curling, *spieler, knockout game*. And in the area of sport, needless to say, numerous slang terms have made their appearance: *import,*

homebrew, rink rat, deke. In other areas, too, slang has been born: *suitcase farmer, screech, Spam medal, pogey*, although most slang heard in Canada is imported from south of the border.

Sometimes names for a commonly encountered thing will be numerous indeed. The perky little Canada jay, familiar to all who frequent the Canadian bush, has been called many names over the years and across the country; here are a number (28) that have been met with by readers for the *Dictionary of Canadianisms* (not all, of course, are in current use; some are highly regional; and a few may well have been used in error by early travellers unfamiliar with the country and its creatures): *blue pie, butcher bird, camp bird, camp robber, Canada jay, Canadian jay, Canadian wood jay, caribou bird, carrion bird, cinerous crow, grease bird, gray jay, Hudson Bay bird, Johnnie, Labrador jay, lumberjack, meat bird, meat hawk, meatjay, moose bird, moose jay, Oregon jay, Rocky Mountain jay, Rupert's bird, venison bird, whisky-jack, whisky-jay, whisky-john*.

The proliferation of names for the Canada jay is, obviously, an exceptional case; it is much more usual for a word to become popular and take on a wide range of meanings over a period of time, often in a relatively limited geographical region. Take for example, the word *Siwash*, which came into English from the Chinook Jargon, a once widely used trade-language on the Pacific Coast. In Chinook Jargon the word meant "Indian" and was derived from French *sauvage*, as Indians were called by the coureurs de bois and voyageurs in the days of exploration. Our earliest evidence of the word in a normal English context is in a trader's journal dated 1851 at Kamloops Fort. It may be that the word originally referred to the Salish Indians of southwestern British Columbia and adjacent parts of Washington, but in due course it came to mean any Indian. The term spread into the Yukon and the Northwest Territories during the late nineteenth century, probably by way of the fur traders and later by way of the sourdoughs, many of whom had worked in the Cariboo gold diggings before moving on to the Klondike. As the years passed, *Siwash* took on additional meanings, one of them being "any Indian language" and still another "the Chinook Jargon." Some persons appear to have used the word to mean "male Indian" only, using *klooch* or *kloochman* for "woman" or "wife"; still others used the word to refer to a person camping on the trail Indian-style, that is with no shelter other than that provided by nature. For the word had by now taken on verbal meanings, one of these being "to travel light, establishing *Siwash camps*" (an Indian-style camp using natural resources for protection from the elements). Another verbal meaning, this one at the slang level, is "prohibit from obtaining liquor; place on the Indian list," a meaning developing out of the fact that it was illegal in British Columbia and the Northwest (as in other provinces) to sell liquor or beer to Indians.

Although the word had no apparent derogatory connotations in the beginning, it certainly developed them in the nineteenth century, at least in the senses having to do with people. It first came to be used of Indians in a derogatory way, and later of any person as a term of contempt. It was a "fighting word," so to speak, and as such fell out of decent use. Indeed, such names as *Siwash sweater*, a long-established term for the warm pullover of gray, unbleached wool made by the native Indians of southern Vancouver Island, became unusable, being displaced in recent years by *Indian sweater* or *Cowichan sweater*. Thus when a word loses prestige in one area of its use, the unfavourable connotations invariably spread to other areas, causing an avoidance of the term by sensitive persons and creating a need for new words having favourable or neutral connotations.

This word *Siwash* has been especially prolific in compounds over the past century; in addition to *Siwash camp* and *Siwash sweater*,

already mentioned, the *Dictionary of Canadianisms* lists *Siwash berry* (the saskatoon), *Siwash blanket* (a low cloud ceiling), *Siwash dog* (a hybrid sled dog in the Northwest), *Siwash goose* (the western grebe), *Siwash house* (the Indian hall at a trading post), *Siwash logger* (a no-account beachcomber), *Siwash pudding* (a pudding made with saskatoon berries), *Siwash rhubarb* (a kind of plant; Indian rhubarb), *Siwash slipper* (a moccasin), *Siwash sock* (a puttee-like duffel sock worn inside moccasins), *Siwash tongue* (the Chinook Jargon), *Siwash wapatoo* (an edible tuber; Indian potato), *Siwash wind* (a brisk wind). When to this impressive list we add such derivatives as *Siwashing, Siwashdom, Siwash fashion,* and *Siwash style,* it can be seen that this term has been uncommonly productive.

Another word of great interest is *snye*, which comes into Canadian English from Canadian French, the source being the dialectal *chenail* (as opposed to Mod.F *chenal* channel). We encounter this word first in the 1820's during the building of the Rideau Canal between Ottawa (then Bytown) and Kingston. As among the voyageurs, it referred to a side-channel, especially one which by-passed a rapids or falls, creating a kind of island. Such snyes, often shallow and sometimes dry, were deepened and widened to serve as channels for the Ottawa lumbermen to run their timber rafts through in by-passing obstructions in the river. During the height of the lumbering period in this neck of the woods, *snye* was a widely used word, occurring in such compounds as *dry snye, snye dam,* and *timber snye,* and in numerous place names, as *Gloucester Snye* and *Mississippi Snye*. It is as a place name that the word is best known today in the Ottawa Valley.

Later in the century the word *snye* makes its appearance in the Northwest. Here too it was taken into English from the French of the voyageur, but here it has continued to flourish. In the Northwest *snye* refers primarily to a narrow, meandering, sluggish side-channel of a river, usually shallow and often coming to a dead end (also called a *blind snye* or *blind slough*). It does, however, seem to have developed some secondary meanings in recent years: (a) a stream connecting two rivers some distance away from their confluence, thus creating an island (a meaning apparently developing out of the familiarity many persons had with "the Snigh," a water-course of just this description at Fort McMurray on the Mackenzie River); (b) a channel, or other adequate stretch of water, utilized as a landing place for bush planes (also called a *landing snye*); and (c) any small tributary stream. Over the years this borrowing from Canadian French has had many spellings, including *schny, she-ny, shnay, snie,* and *snigh,* several of them revealing early stages in the process of anglicization, *sh* representing the pronunciation of French *ch.* The currently accepted pronunciation is (sni), although older (shni) is said to be heard in places still; the usual spelling is *snye,* the older *sny* also being met occasionally. The plural, it seems, may be either *snyes* or *snies.*

This process of borrowing and the continuing development of meanings within the language is one of the most intriguing aspects of English, or any other language, for that matter. Canadian English provides numerous examples of just such proliferation, as in the case of *bateau, cariole, cache, shanty,* and many more. Often words which are not themselves of Canadian origin develop meanings or become elements in compounds which are, and here we might cite such words as *beaver, bush, Indian, lumber, slough, timber,* and *wood.* Of course, many of the words which we call Canadian are now to be classed as "historical" or "obsolete." But the meanings of such no-longer-used words are important to people who read earlier writings for whatever reason and, of course, to those who read historical novels about the early days of life in Canada. For this reason as well as for their intrinsic interest, such terms as *York boat, Red River cart, Montreal canoe, buffalo runner,* *home-guard Indian, pork-eater, Eastmain, Rupert's Land, New Caledonia,* and a host of others have their claim to the attention of the student of Canadian English.

Of course, the field of Canadian English involves much more than the searching out and defining of words and expressions. One must be concerned with the study of regional speech, called "dialect geography," a thoroughly fascinating area of study; one must also be concerned with pronunciation patterns, not only from a regional point of view but from a social point of view as well. And, finally, although this is a rather special area of language that is purely visual, one must be concerned with practices of spelling, for here perhaps more than anywhere else inadequately informed critics of language focus their attention. Such problems can be understood only after an extensive and thorough examination of the language as it is spoken in Canada and after an intelligent assessment of the practices of educated Canadians in these matters. The worker in the vineyard is sometimes frustrated by the very complexity of the evidence, but the irritations are more than balanced by the utterly thrilling discoveries one makes and by the pleasure that comes with deepening one's knowledge of man's most precious possession—his language.

From The Sound and the Fury

William Faulkner

As soon as I turned off the light and tried to go to sleep it would begin to come into the room in waves building and building up until I would have to pant to get any air at all out of it until I would have to get up and feel my way like when I was a little boy *hands can see touching in the mind shaping unseen door Door now nothing hands can see* My nose could see gasoline, the vest on the table, the door. The corridor was still empty of all the feet in sad generations seeking water. *yet the eyes unseeing clenched like teeth not disbelieving doubting even the absence of pain shin ankle knee the long invisible flowing of the stair-railing where a misstep in the darkness filled with sleeping Mother Father Caddy Jason Maury door I am not afraid only Mother Father Caddy Jason Maury getting so far ahead sleeping I will sleep fast when I door Door door* It was empty too, the pipes, the porcelain, the stained quiet walls, the throne of contemplation. I had forgotten the glass, but I could *hands can see cooling fingers invisible swan-throat where less than Moses rod the glass touch tentative not to drumming lean cool throat drumming cooling the metal the glass full overfull cooling the glass the fingers flushing sleep leaving the taste of dampened sleep in the long silence of the throat* I returned up the corridor, waking the lost feet in whispering battalions in the silence, into the gasoline, the watch telling its furious lie on the dark table. Then the curtains breathing out of the dark upon my face, leaving the breathing upon my face. A quarter hour yet. And then I'll not be. The peacefullest words. Peacefullest words. *Non fui. Sum. Fui. Nom sum.* Somewhere I heard bells once. Mississippi or Massachusetts. I was. I am not. Massachusetts or Mississippi. Shreve has a bottle in his trunk. *Aren't you even going to open it* Mr and Mrs Jason Richmond Compson announce the *Three times. Days. Aren't you even going to open it* marriage of their daughter Candace *that liquor teaches you to confuse the means with the end.* I am. Drink. I was not. Let us sell Benjy's pasture so that Quentin may go to Harvard and I may knock my bones together and together. I will be dead in. Was it one year Caddy said. Shreve has a bottle in his trunk. Sir I will not need Shreve's I have sold Benjy's pasture and I can be dead in Harvard Caddy said in the caverns and the grottoes of the sea tumbling peacefully to the wavering tides because Harvard is such a fine sound forty acres is no high price for a fine sound. A fine dead sound we will swap Benjy's pasture for a fine dead sound. It will last him a long time because he cannot hear it unless he can smell it *as soon as she came in the door he began to*

cry I thought all the time it was just one of those town squirts that Father was always teasing her about until. I didnt notice him any more than any other stranger drummer or what thought they were army shirts until all of a sudden I knew he wasn't thinking of me at all as a potential source of harm, but was thinking of her when he looked at me was looking at me through her like through a piece of coloured glass *why must you meddle with me dont you know it wont do any good I thought you'd have left that for Mother and Jason.*

Mr. Shaw Was Not at Home

William French

It takes a certain God-given talent to get lost three times in the 30 kilometres between Rudyard Kipling and Vita Sackville-West, but I modestly admit I qualify. In my defence, I can only argue that the secondary roads of Kent, in southeast England, are as labyrinthine as the minds of some authors, and I was driving alone, without navigator or medium. And getting lost, after all, can turn up unexpected delights, such as antique stores with names like My Aunty Had One But She Threw It Away, and pubs with real ale, real British pub food and comely barmaids.

A couple of days before my search for the elusive Vita, I *had* displayed some navigational skill. I traversed the 455 kilometres between William Wordsworth and Dylan Thomas without once losing track of where the polestar would have been if it hadn't been raining, as usual. But that was mostly motorway driving, from the Lake District to South Wales. Britain's motorways are a hedonistic delight for the time-pressed literary explorer, as they are for thousands of truck drivers who all try to pass each other at the same time and care not a whit for the welfare of those in search of Jane Austen or Thomas Hardy.

My mission, when I started out from Cambridge, was to visit as many literary sites in Britain as I could manage in 10 days, I made some arbitrary omissions; it would be possible to spend the entire 10 days in London or Edinburgh or Dublin, visiting the local haunts and houses of famous authors. I ruled out the obvious, including Stratford, in favor of an itinerary that combined the chance to see something of the English countryside and places associated with famous authors.

My basic reference was *The Oxford Illustrated Literary Guide to Great Britain and Ireland*, a worthy tome whose heft equals the grandeur of its subject. As compelling evidence of the richness of Britain's literary heritage, it contains 1,231 entries on places and notes on 913 authors. Those are just the *dead* authors, since living writers don't appreciate tourists peering in their windows to see whether they're working or just lazing about. I devised a kind of counterclockwise route from Cambridge—based partly on homage, partly on curiosity—that included most of the highlights and ended close enough to London for a graceful exit from Heathrow Airport.

At the end of my 2,500-kilometre odyssey, I was ready to offer this advice: don't try to do the trip in 10 days. Too much time is spent driving and not enough in contemplation of Wordsworth's "host of golden daffodils." But it could be done comfortably in two weeks, or the itinerary could be used as an ad-lib, pick-and-choose guide for whatever part of Britain a tourist happens to be in.

Among the exotic objects I viewed en route were Charlotte Brontë's nightcap (the one she wore to bed, not the final drink of the day), William Wordsworth's ice skates, Thomas Hardy's shaving mug, Rudyard Kipling's 1928 Rolls-Royce, the original Hogarth Press on which Leonard and Virginia Woolf printed T.S. Eliot's *The Waste Land* and the starched collar Charles Dickens was wearing when he suffered his fatal collapse. I gazed into the very mirror that Jane Austen used and watched the graceful herons Dylan Thomas wrote about at his retreat in Wales. I could have bought souvenirs such as a D.H. Lawrence tie, a Brontë mug or a Jane Austen

Puzzle and Quiz Book had I been so inclined. I prowled through graveyards at twilight, explored echoing country churches and generally confirmed my belief that a country's level of civilization can be measured by the respect it accords its writers. Britain, by that standard, is exceedingly civilized. . . .

My next stop, Shaw's Corner, at Ayot St. Lawrence, about 50 kilometres north of London, provided a timely lesson. The village in which George Bernard Shaw lived from 1906 until his death in 1950 is beginning to be drawn into the London commuter belt but still retains its rural charm. It's reached by narrow country lanes, flanked by high hedges, on which two spavined horses would have difficulty passing. If two cars meet, one of them must back up to the nearest lay-by. Thus it was with a certain sense of triumph that I navigated the lanes, found the house, rang the bell—and discovered Mr. Shaw was not at home, nor indeed was anyone else.

The place was closed, locked up, drapes drawn to prevent even a free peek. I learned later that the National Trust, which administers Shaw's Corner, closed the house every Friday and Saturday, normally two of the busiest days of the week, to save wear and tear. (I arrived on a Friday.) If the trustees really want to prevent heavy traffic, they should open the house only between midnight and 7 a.m., but obviously they haven't thought of that yet. The lesson is worth noting: some museums keep eccentric hours, and guidebooks occasionally have the wrong information, so it's wise to phone ahead and confirm schedules.

Unwilling to admit defeat at Shaw's Corner, I pushed through a gate marked No Entry into the back garden, where Shaw's ashes were scattered. By following a meandering path through the woods I unexpectedly discovered Shaw's summer workhouse, where he did much of his writing in the last 44 years of his life. It's appropriately spartan—wicker chair, wooden table, pen stand, fold-down cot. On the way back to the car park I encountered the gardener and chatted her up. She didn't know much about the inside of the house but explained all about the herbaceous beds, the vegetable garden—a priority with Shaw, since he was vegetarian—and the beehives, although they aren't Shaw's originals.

Heading north to Eastwood, the town near Nottingham where D.H. Lawrence was born, I caught sight of a sign that flashed by as the highway crossed a bridge. River Ouse, it said—the river in which Virginia Woolf drowned herself in 1941. Unexpected references like that keep popping up all over Britain. Eastwood, about 15 kilometres west of Nottingham, is not hard to find, but the house in which Lawrence was born in 1885 is a challenge. I drove right by it the first time, failing to notice the small plaque, and ended up in a restaurant called The Phoenix. It turned out to have a Lawrence connection; until 1920, it was the building in which the Mechanics' Institute was located, with its library of a thousand books. Lawrence, being a miner's son, spent much of his leisure time there and referred to it in *Sons and Lovers*. On the spot where he devoured books, the locals now devour scampi and chips, play video games and listen to the Beach Boys.

The house in which Lawrence was born is just around the corner from The Phoenix. It's a modest row house and a modest museum. Lawrence lived there for only the first two years of his life, but it's similar to other houses the family occupied in Eastwood. It's furnished in the style of the period, and the repressive Victorian atmosphere from which Lawrence fled has been preserved. (*Watch and Pray*, exhorts an embroidered motto on the wall.) One of the upstairs bedrooms has been set aside for an imaginative video depiction of Lawrence's life in Eastwood. For most of my visit on a rainy Saturday I was the only one in the house, except for the shy curator. The town is clearly not inclined to exploit the fame of its most notorious son.

The situation is altogether different at the Brontë Parsonage Museum in Haworth, 13.5 kilometres east of Bradford in the rolling countryside of the Yorkshire moors. Tourism is the principal industry in the town, and the Brontës are the star attraction. There's an Emily Cafe, a Rochester Restaurant, a Brontë Hotel, and a Heathcliffe apartment block. The parsonage itself, built in 1778, is tidy almost to the point of sterility, but there's an abundance of Brontë memorabilia involving Charlotte, Emily, Anne and Branwell and original furniture, including the sofa on which Emily died. The main rooms are roped off to prevent complete access, which makes viewing something of a problem when crowds are large.

The nearby church, which the Brontës attended and in which Charlotte and Emily were buried, was demolished in 1879 to make way for the larger, new church, into which the original tower was incorporated. The grave sites were left undisturbed and can still be visited in the church. But the most memorable feature of the neighborhood is the graveyard, which overflows the space between church and parsonage. It's moss-covered, crumbling, decidedly spooky and helps explain the atmosphere in which *Jane Eyre* and *Wuthering Heights* were created. New burials have been prohibited in the graveyard since 1850 when it was closed for health reasons after the town's water supply was found to be contaminated.

Grasmere, where William Wordsworth completed some of his most important work between 1799 and 1808, is a busy tourist village too, but not only because of the poet. The Lake District is one of the most scenic areas in Britain, an ideal base for hiking in the nearby hills. The area is a bit like Ontario's Muskoka district with a Yorkshire accent.

Dove Cottage, where Wordsworth lived with his sister, Dorothy, (and with his bride, after 1802) is in many ways a model of what a literary site should be. Visitors knock at the door for admittance, and a guide takes them through the house room by room. Our guide, a young man, was witty and informative, although he didn't venture an opinion on the nature of the relationship between Wordsworth and his sister, a matter of some speculation among scholars. One of the items he pointed out was the window through which the visiting Sir Walter Scott, tired of the Wordsworths' spartan fare, escaped one morning to find a decent English breakfast. Samuel Taylor Coleridge and Thomas De Quincey were other frequent visitors; De Quincey in fact moved in after the Wordsworths left and lived there 25 years, lost in his laudanum dreams. He averaged eight glasses a day, our guide informed us, explaining that laudanum is wine to which opium has been added. He didn't say whether De Quincey favored red or white wine.

Dove Cottage was built as an inn in the seventeenth century, and it has the cosiness associated with congenial drinking places. Part of its charm is that it's not cluttered with exhibits but looks much as it did when Wordsworth lived there. Nearby, a former barn has been converted into the Grasmere and Wordsworth Museum, which has abundant memorabilia not only of Wordsworth but of all the poets of the Lake District. The exhibits are tastefully displaced, and it's possible to put on a headset and hear some of Wordsworth's poetry recited in the style of a BBC announcer. A very good restaurant is nearby, operated by the Wordsworth Trust. Wordsworth's modest grave is easily found in the local churchyard.

The long drive from Grasmere to South Wales links two cultures. Swansea, where Dylan Thomas was born (1914) and grew up, is in a different country with different traditions. The town is ringed now with oil refineries, docks and power plants; after driving through, I kept right on going and found a hotel in Mumbles, a quaint seaside town across the bay. Swansea looks better from that distance, and it's pleasant to watch the city at twilight as the lights come on and to speculate about the events described in *A Child's Christmas in Wales* that took place there.

There's a plaque on the house where Thomas was born and another in the nearby Cwmdonkin Park where he played as a child, but the main point of interest is Laugharne, 60 kilometres west along the coast. Thomas spent various periods there as a young poet and finally settled permanently in 1949, with his wife, Caitlin, in a cottage above the shore, The Boathouse. He left from there on his last, fatal trip to the United States. Laugharne is of course the Llareggub of Thomas's play for voices, *Under Milk Wood*, but it wears its fame lightly. The Rose and Crown Pub calls itself Dylan's Diner, but it can't compete with Brown's Hotel, the centre of the Thomases' social life. It's still possible to get a decent pub lunch in the room where Dylan and Caitlin usually drank more than they needed. The same furniture is still in use, as the historic photos on the wall testify.

The Boathouse is located halfway between the top of a steep cliff and the shoreline. Gazing out the window at the ever-changing estuary below, it's easy to see why Thomas loved the place. Down a path is the small hut where he did his writing, and it has the same view of the sea, the same haunting counterpoint of seabirds' cries. The hut is locked, but a window offers a view of table, chair, bookshelves and old newspaper clippings on the wall. The parlor is the only room kept as it was when the Thomases lived there, with the same furniture. It's a comfortable room, and Dylan's memorable voice reading his poems is a constant presence, channelled through an old wireless set from a tape machine in the reception area. I doubted whether the two china dogs on the mantel were from the Thomas era; it seemed unlikely they could have survived the rough-and-tumble arguments and the drunken threshings that Caitlin, by her own admission, gave Dylan. As it turns out, however, they *are* from that time.

The other rooms are used to display photos and memorabilia; watercolors of the area by local artists can be purchased, as well as Dylan's books. There's no reference to his burial place, but if you ask, the curator will provide directions to the churchyard half a kilometre away and explain how to find the simple white cross. In the nearby church, St. Martin's, there's a replica of the plaque in Poets' Corner in Westminster Abbey, with Dylan's lines "Time held me green and dying/Though I sang in my chains like the sea."

Again the landscape changes dramatically between South Wales and the Wessex country of Thomas Hardy's novels, centred on Dorset. Hardy was strongly influenced by the gentle, pastoral landscape of his native heath, as his novels attest. Two sites offer the opportunity to pay him tribute—the museum in Dorchester and Hardy's Cottage, in which he was born (1840), in Higher Bockhampton, five kilometres northeast, where he wrote *Under the Greenwood Tree* and *Far From the Madding Crowd.*

The elegant Hardy Room in the museum contains furniture from Hardy's final home, Max Gate, and personal belongings. But the showpiece is his study at Max Gate, reconstructed as it was about 1900—a rather formal and tidy room for a writer. For some reason the room is behind a glass viewing wall, and reflections on the glass make it difficult to see details.

The first thing a visitor to Hardy's Cottage at Higher Bockhampton sees is a sign: Thieves Operate in This Car Park. You Are at Risk. The parking lot is a kilometre or so away from the house, and the path leads through a dense grove of trees. The lush gardens around the house are open to all comers, but the house itself can usually be seen only by appointment. The day I visited, there were no prior appointments, so the house was open to anyone with the admission price, £1.20.

It's a sturdy place, built by Hardy's great-grandfather in 1800, but none of Hardy's possessions remain—they are all housed in the Hardy Room in the Dorchester Museum. The parlor and one other ground-floor room are open, as well as three bedrooms upstairs,

including the one in which Hardy was born and wrote the two novels. A visit to Higher Bockhampton could be considered a nature ramble with literary overtones. (It was a slow day for thieves too; nothing was stolen from my car.)

Jane Austen's house in Chawton, about 130 kilometres from Dorchester, remains much as it was when she lived there from 1809 until her death in 1817. Her writing table is still in the drawing room, where she had little privacy. Her family knew she was a writer, but during the gestation period of a story, she wanted to keep it a secret. A squeaking door warned her to hide the evidence when someone approached. The door is still there, but only squeaks when it's damp; the floors more than make up for it, however. Despite the interruptions, she was able to write or rewrite her six major novels there. The house is cheerful, with lots of white paint and Laura Ashley wallpaper. It's a browser's delight, with abundant memorabilia.

Rudyard Kipling bought Bateman's, near Burwash, in 1902 for £9,200. The residence, built in 1634, looks like a manor house and was certainly suitable for one of the most eminent and affluent authors of his day. The elegance of Bateman's was enhanced when Kipling furnished it in seventeenth-century style, with the occasional piece from India for exotic interest. One of the curiosities is the wallpaper in the dining room; it's leather, embossed with birds, trees and flowers. All the rooms still have Kipling's furniture, including the vast desk on which he wrote, flanked by a metre-high Canadian silver dollar, mounted on a wooden block, which was given to him during a lecture tour of Canada. There are paintings and a bust, his knife and pocket watch and his Nobel Prize citation from 1907. Outdoors, the gardens are immaculate, and in the middle distance is Pook's Hill.

Kipling was fascinated by cars and owned many, but he never learned to drive: he was always able to afford a chauffeur. Obviously his kind of literary sentimentality and patriotism paid handsome dividends. Incidentally, his 1928 Rolls Royce, in mint condition, suffers from the same handicap as Hardy's study: it's behind glass, and reflections make it difficult to see and impossible to photograph. . . .

My last stop was the coastal resort of Broadstairs, a favorite of Charles Dickens's. The main attraction is Bleak House (originally called Fort House), so designated because it's not where he wrote that novel. There's also Dickens' House, so called because he never lived in it.

Broadstairs, with its long history of smuggling, is a raffish kind of place, full of the cheerful vulgarity of English seaside resorts. Bleak House reflects the mood; it's a somewhat tacky museum that mixes genuine Dickens memorabilia with cases of seashells and The World's Biggest Moth, a hodgepodge of Victorian bric-a-brac. But the Dickens connection is legitimate; he completed *David Copperfield* at Bleak House and, after a violent North Sea gale battered the house, got the idea for the novel after which the house is now named.

Dickens in fact dominates the town—there's a Fagin's Pub, a souvenir shop called What The Dickens, a pub called Barnaby Rudge and, naturally, The Old Curiosity Shop. It's hard to escape him; I discovered he wrote *Nicholas Nickleby* in the hotel I stayed in, the Royal Albion. He wrote part of *The Pickwick Papers* at 12 High Street, now demolished, and *The Old Curiosity Shop* and *Barnaby Rudge* while staying at Archway House, which still spans the walk leading to Bleak House.

I drank to his memory in the pub of the Royal Albion and headed for Heathrow, notebooks stuffed with the kind of ephemera that help bring literature and its creators to life.

On the plane home I pondered a similar odyssey to literary sites in Canada. It could start with Lucy Maud Montgomery's birthplace in Prince Edward Island and Thomas Chandler Haliburton's house in Windsor, Nova Scotia, then jump to the Stephen Leacock summer home in Old Brewery Bay in Ontario and Robert Service's cabin in Dawson City . . . and then? There *are* a few more literary sites open to the public, but perhaps a Canadian tour, to be as rewarding as a British pilgrimage, should be delayed a while. Say a century or so.

From A Portrait of the Artist as a Young Man

James Joyce

Once upon a time and a very good time it was there was a moocow, coming down along the road and this moocow that was coming down along the road met a nicens little boy named baby tuckoo. . . .

His father told him that story: his father looked at him through a glass: he had a hairy face.

He was baby tuckoo. The moocow came down the road where Betty Byrne lived: she sold lemon platt.

> O, the wild rose blossoms
> On the little green place.

He sang that song. That was his song.

> O, the green wothe botheth.

When you wet the bed first it is warm then it gets cold. His mother put on the oilsheet. That had the queer smell.

His mother had a nicer smell than his father. She played on the piano the sailor's hornpipe for him to dance. He danced:

> Tralala lala
> Tralala tralaladdy
> Tralala lala
> Tralala lala.

Uncle Charles and Dante clapped. They were older than his father and mother but uncle Charles was older than Dante.

Dante had two brushes in her press. The brush with the maroon velvet back was for Michael Davitt and the brush with the green velvet back was for Parnell. Dante gave him a cachou every time he brought her a piece of tissue paper.

The Vances lived in number seven. They had a different father and mother. They were Eileen's father and mother. When they were grown up he was going to marry Eileen. He hid under the table. His mother said:

—O, Stephen will apologise.

Dante said:

—O, if not, the eagles will come and pull out his eyes.

> Pull out his eyes,
> Apologise,
> Apologise,
> Pull out his eyes.
>
> Apologise,
> Pull out his eyes,
> Pull out his eyes,
> Apologise.

A Christmas Sermon on Peace

Martin Luther King

Peace on Earth . . .

This Christmas season finds us a rather bewildered human race. We neither have peace within nor peace without. Everywhere, paralyzing fears harrow people by day and haunt them by night. Our world is sick with war; everywhere we turn we see its ominous possibilities. And yet, my friends, the Christmas hope for peace and good will toward all men can no longer be dismissed as a kind of pious dream of some utopian. If we don't have good will toward men in this world, we will destroy ourselves by the misuse of our own instruments and our own power. Wisdom born of experience should tell us that war is obsolete. There may have been a time when war served as a negative good by preventing the spread and growth of an evil force, but the very destructive power of modern weapons of warfare eliminates even the possibility that war may any longer serve as a negative good. And so, if we assume that life is worth living, if we assume that mankind has a right to survive, then we must find an alternative to war—and so let us this morning explore the conditions for peace. Let us this morning think anew on the meaning of that Christmas hope: Peace on Earth, Good Will toward Men. And as we explore these conditions, I would like to suggest that modern man really go all out to study the meaning of non-violence, its philosophy and its strategy. . . .

I have a dream that one day men will rise up and come to see that they are made to live together as brothers. I still have a dream this morning that one day every Negro in this country, every colored person in the world, will be judged on the basis of the content of his character, rather than the color of his skin, and every man will respect the dignity and worth of human personality. I still have a dream to-day, that one day the idle industries of Appalachia will be revitalized, and empty stomachs of Mississippi will be filled, and brotherhood will be more than a few words at the end of a prayer but rather the first order of business on every legislative agenda. I still have a dream to-day, that one day justice will roll down like water, and righteousness like a mighty stream. I still have a dream to-day, that in all of our state houses and city halls, men will be elected to go there who will do justly and love mercy and walk humbly with their God. I still have a dream to-day, that one day war will come to an end, that men will beat their swords into plowshares and their spears into pruning hooks, that nations will no longer rise up against nations, neither will they study war any more. I still have a dream to-day, that one day the lamb and the lion will lie down together and every man will sit under his own vine and fig tree and none shall be afraid. I still have a dream to-day, that one day every valley shall be exalted and every mountain and hill will be made low, the rough places will be made plain and the crooked places straight, and the glory of the Lord shall be revealed, and all flesh shall see it together. I still have a dream, that with this faith we will be able to adjourn the councils of despair and bring new light into the dark chambers of pessimism. With this faith we will be able to speed up the day when there will be peace on earth, and good will toward men. It will be a glorious day, the morning stars will sing together, and the sons of God will shout for joy.

The Illiterate Engineer—Truth or Consequences?

Cameron Stewart

What do engineers and computers have in common? No, it's not a riddle. The question came to mind as I listened to one of my professors lament his students' communications problems.

Engineers and computers have a symbiotic relationship based on numbers. Computers spit them out in vast quantities, and engineers analyze them. A match made in heaven, you say? Perhaps. But the bond holds fast only if the glue is high-quality. And the glue is words.

As my professor noted, engineers who can't communicate their analyses are as useful as a computer without a screen or printer. You can set a computer to task for days on end, but if a human being can't clearly formulate the results into words, the work is meaningless —just "bits hanging in mid-air."

"Techno-twerps"—computer worshippers of the engineering world—interact brilliantly with their computers, but no one else. How can we benefit from their findings if they are locked inside a cage of impenetrable verbiage?

What does my professor mean when he talks about the need to graduate literate engineers? My feeling is it encompasses more than spelling, punctuation, and slapping together sentences in some semblance of order.

Literacy implies being able to summarize the methods and thinking that went into, say, designing a computer chip. This might be accomplished by writing a report or giving an oral presentation with meticulous tables and diagrams. One way or other, you'll wind up justifying your work to the boss. Your input will help to determine whether the project goes ahead.

But not every engineer reports to a boss; many become consultants. In your own business, success hinges on client satisfaction. To inspire confidence in your engineering ability you'll need words to communicate proposals. "But what I really meant was. . . ." satisfies neither party and may lead to embarrassing misunderstandings.

Personal experience impressed upon me the importance of clearly stated expectations. Several summers ago, my job as a consultant on a geophysical survey in northern Ontario was jeopardized by verbal vagueness. When a friend had to pull out of a contract at the last minute, I took over.

But my impression of job requirements turned out to be quite different from the client's. Since I hadn't nailed down the specifics myself, I had no way out. For two months, I worked in dense, black-fly infested woods, doing twice the job I had expected. Although the report was successful, a lot of aggravation could have been avoided if we'd clearly communicated the details in advance.

The productive lifespan of today's engineer is five years; that's how quickly changing technologies make knowledge obsolete. Engineers booted upstairs to management may initially be jubilant. But the techno-twerp's celebration gives way to despair if strong communications skills are lacking. To relate well to the new environment and a broad spectrum of coworkers, written and oral skills are the key.

If you're looking for suggestions to build skills now, you're on the right track. Take advantage of high-school writing workshops or technical writing courses in the Extension Divison of a local community college or night school. Or practise producing high-quality diagrams through computer software packages or yearbook layouts. Oral presentations may make you a bit uncomfortable; but better to acquire the poise and confidence that comes from practice than squirm somewhere down the road.

If you're adopting a "wait and see" attitude, don't. Unfortunately, the university environment may not offer necessary support. Often content-laden courses leave professors with little time to correct basic writing problems. And some courses give little opportunity to practise written and oral skills.

That's why some engineering students get past first year without language proficiency. Just recently, a fellow teaching assistant—an East Indian graduate student in mechanical engineering who emigrated to Canada at age eleven—lamented: "Sometimes when I'm marking," he said, "I can't tell whether the students or I have taken English as a second language."

As tomorrow's engineer, be ready to meet challenges of your technical know-how and literacy. Whether it's writing reports or persuading the boss a design will work better "next time," an engineer needs numbers *and* words to "glue" them together.

P A R T
B

Branching Out

CHAPTER
Four

Writing the Elements of Narrative— and More

A. FORE-WORDS

Warm up for activities in this chapter with discussion and writing. The quotations and questions below may help you begin.

Thomas Hardy   "We are storytellers all . . ."

W.S. Maugham   "[Plot] is a direct line to the reader's interest."

H. Percy   "Narrative voice tells the writer, 'This is the way I want to be written.' "

1.   After sharing a favourite childhood story, reflect on the memories it evokes.

2.   Enjoy a storytelling performance. Through what dramatic techniques does the professional storyteller captivate the audience?

3.   "Decode" the story told by a photograph, poster, painting, or other still visual.

B. FOUNDATIONS

Imagine yourself and a few friends tucked away in a sailboat, eagerly anticipating an adventure. As sailors who've shared many outings, you relax in each other's company. But you're becalmed. There's no outboard motor, no radio, no television, no newspapers. The wind won't change until dawn. How will you wile away the hours?

If a storyteller is on board, you're all set. One famous spinner of tales, Joseph Conrad, opens *Heart of Darkness* just this way. Sitting cross-legged aboard the *Nellie*, Marlow, the narrator, begins, "And this also . . . has been one of the dark places of the earth." Suddenly his friends are alert; Marlow's off on one of his stories. "I was thinking of very old times, when the Romans first came here. . . ." Some eighty pages later Marlow finishes the tale, and they set sail enriched by narrative recollections.

Even if you're not on board ship or huddled round a campfire, stories are all around you. Listen in the cafeteria, at work, or around the family dinner table. Chances are you'll hear stories. They're different from Marlow's. You may call them jokes or tall tales or gossip, but they captivate the Tarvos, Kirstens, Craigs, and Sashas among us. Indeed, if you'd been visiting the Royal Ontario Museum, you might have overheard David Suzuki telling his daughters "A Grim Fairy Tale." Enjoy the story, which is reprinted on page 198, before reading on.

"Story" *loosely* describes narrative forms we encounter in daily life. As with Suzuki's piece, narrative may be spoken and/or written. It may be presented in verse or in prose. If narrative grows from the imagination, we call it fiction—novels, short stories, fairy tales, and so on. When narrative is based on reality or fact, it is labelled non-fiction and found in personal essays, newspaper and magazine features, profiles, memoirs, biography, and television documentaries. However, "A Grim Fairy Tale"—a fable within an article or essay—illustrates that fact and fiction may be inexorably blended to defy neat labels of genre.

Moving on, we should define anecdotes, stories, and plots. An *anecdote* is a very short tale of a single incident based on a true event. It has a beginning, middle, and end. A *story* is marked by a sense of completeness built around a change; something has happened for better or worse. Finally, if the storyteller or writer artfully resequences the story's incidents to dramatize cause and effect, then the story has a *plot*; it is a "plotted story." As E.M. Forster explained, " 'The King died and then the Queen died' is a story. 'The King died and then the Queen died of grief' is a plot." The reason, Forster explains, is that the latter example emphasizes causality. He adds, speaking of the death of the Queen, "If it is in a story, we say 'and then?' If it is in a plot, we ask '*why?*' "

Human beings have long been attracted to story. As listeners or creators, we are integrated and unified. Canadian writer Rudy Wiebe explains:

> The impulse to make story needs no defence. Where it arises, who knows. It simply is, like the impulse to sing, to dance, to play games. It would seem, however, that storymaking is the uniquely human of these impulses for, though many animals sing, dance and play games, perform intricate and beautiful dances, it still remains to be discovered whether any make stories .... I can imagine that story has existed as long as humanity and language (perhaps longer than language: story can be mimed) and I further imagine that the early forms of it developed from ... dreaming how we wish things were; recounting what happened; explaining why things are as they are; instructing ourselves and our children; making an imitation.

Powerful narrative is a product of meticulous preparation and spontaneity. Analytical faculties lay the groundwork for intuitive insight from your creative self. In this chapter, you'll sharpen narrative writing as well as other forms of communication. Let's begin by letting story speak for itself. As volunteers read these passages, decide whether each is an anecdote, plot, story, or none of these. The sources appear in the "Sources and Credits" list at the end of this book. Titles for each passage have been added.

The Mosquito and the Thunder

Once the Mosquito paid a visit to the Thunder. The latter, seeing that the Mosquito was gorged with blood, asked him where he obtained it, and told him that he had been wishing to get some for a long time, but did not know where to obtain it. The Mosquito answered, "I got the blood from somewhere." The Thunder was annoyed at this evasive answer, and said, "Why do you answer me thus? Don't you know that I can shoot you and kill you?" The Mosquito, being afraid, then said, "I suck it from the tree-tops."

By this lie the Mosquito saved the people, and that is the reason that the Thunder strikes the tree-tops to the present day. If the Mosquito had told the truth, then the Thunder would now shoot people and animals instead of trees.

On Milton Acorn

Around this time (spring, 1960), a poetry conference was going on at Queen's University. Milton [Acorn] obviously wanted to go, and I urged him to do so. "I haven't got any good clothes," he said. "Doesn't matter ... ; all poets are poor," I rebutted. And he went, hitchhiking to Kingston.

Milton didn't show up back at Roblin Lake for two days, looking bedraggled and bearded when he did appear. "How was the conference?" I wanted to know. Milton didn't want to talk about it, but I pressed him severely. It turned out he hadn't attended the literary gathering at all—had been too shy to speak to any of the poets. He'd seen them going inside the hall, had recognized James Reaney and others, but something shy in his personality had prevented him joining them.

Where did he sleep in Kingston? On a park bench near Lake Ontario. What did he eat? The few sandwiches he'd taken with him couldn't have lasted long. I don't know how much money he had, but I really don't think he'd eaten anything but sandwiches during those two days.

For What It's Worth

During the Depression Babe Ruth, asked to take a cut in salary, held out for his $80,000 contract. A club official protested, "But that's more money than Hoover got for being President last year."

"I know," said Babe, "but I had a better year."

Salt Cod, Anyone?

In Saskatchewan during the Depression, the farm families on relief were given salt cod from Newfoundland. The fillets were a good size—big enough for a boy's behind. The kids took them, flat and frozen, complete with a tail for grip, and tobogganed down the hills.

A Matter of Dress

[Stephen Leacock], this most popular and prolific of Canadian writers, was also by all accounts one of the worst dressed. Around McGill University, where he taught for thirty-three years, he was a familiar figure even at a distance, owing to his tattered academic gown, which was often bedecked with ashes from his pipe, or his moth-eaten raccoon coat, which went on year after year lacking several of its buttons. These outer garments, however, hid even greater eccentricity beneath, much of it apparently due to Leacock's absence of mind.

Not only was the watch-chain stretched across the waistcoat mended with one or more safety pins, it often supported his latchkey, so that he would not forget to carry it and thus lock himself out of his home. Once, after he had been interrupted midway through dressing for dinner, he descended the stairs half in formal dress and half in loud checks. His mother-in-law suggested that there should be no fear of embarrassment should Leacock lose his trousers in some accident since he was likely to be wearing a second pair under the first. But her theory was never tested because when Leacock could not immediately locate a belt he would take the precautions of using a necktie or even a piece of rope to hold up his trousers. Also, he was known frequently to wear two hats at the same time, one jammed inside the other.

Sir Arthur Currie, the principal of McGill, was the host of an important dinner party to which Leacock arrived very late and not in a complete state of dress. "Lady Currie," he asked the hostess, "would you tie my tie? My niece, Barbara, [was] out." Lady Currie did as requested and, turning, introduced him to the guest of honour, Lord Bessborough, the governor general.

As a class, consider which storytellers most successfully "hooked" and held your interest. In Activity One, continue to explore the magic of story which enriches our daily lives.

Activity One   Discovering the Impulse to Make Story

Purpose

- to raise awareness of story's social role

- to recognize and practise techniques of storytelling

- to review the elements of story

1.   After viewing a filmed legend, folktale, or children's story, freewrite in your Writer's Notebook about the impulse to "make story," as Rudy Wiebe describes it. You might respond to this statement: "You're never too old for a good story." Or draft an informal reflective essay for your writing folder about the role of story(telling) in your childhood.

2.   Invite a storyteller into your class or attend a local storytelling session. Identify techniques by which performers attract and hold your attention. (*Tip:* Excellent storytellers may be found in your own family or neighbourhood.)

3.   As you share anecdotes in small groups, reflect on the ingredients of effective storytelling. Tarvo's "Tips for Storytellers" may help you hone these talents.

- Use a conversational tone of voice.

- Vary sentence length, pacing, and dramatic gestures to build tension and suspense; don't be afraid of silence.

- Focus on key chunks or scenes; "hang" them on memorable diction from the original.

- Practise performance techniques with a tape recorder, including the Adam's Apple Test suggested by Beverly Inman-Ebel of the Communication Clinics in Chattanooga, Tennessee, who says that if your middle finger vibrates when placed on the Adam's apple, you're on pitch and that natural pitch is the "huh" of "Uh-huh."

- Weave listeners' responses into the story as you create it, suggests Hildy Stollery of the Institute of Child Study.

- Store outlines, chunks, key phrasing, and ideas for "next time" on a computer disk or index cards. If you're working with a modem, exchange local folklore with students in other areas.

4.   In small groups:

a.   Tell a circle story—a person begins a tale, and everyone adds to it; you might retell the myth of "The Mosquito and the Thunder" or the anecdote about Leacock. Or begin with one of these openings:

- I just couldn't believe my ears.
- I never meant for anyone to get hurt.
- I was down to my last dime when she walked through the door.

b.   Share individual stories—perhaps a childhood memory or bedtime story. Or nine students divide into three subgroups; Group A mimes action and characterization, as B provides narrative, and C fills in dialogue.

5.   Draft a formal persuasive essay about the value of storytelling in the senior English classroom. Your aim might be to convince a skeptical parent or school board official.

6a.   In pairs, experiment with practical applications of storytelling:

- Retell in story form a small chunk of history you're having difficulty remembering. Focus on a key person. (*Tip:* To study a master at work, view a film narrated by Pierre Berton such as "City of Gold," National Film Board, 1957.)
- In story form, third person, tell about a school subject with which you're having difficulty. A second group member offers a solution in story form, third person.
- Compose a nonsense verse to help recall a factual detail. Perhaps you already know several, such as "i" before "e" except after "c."

b.   In your Writer's Notebook, note specific ways you could enhance performance in other subject areas using your learning about narrative.

An Overview of the Elements of Narrative

Why study character, plot and conflict, dialogue, and point of view? Like Kirsten and Sasha, you may be wondering how narrative fits in with your present interests and future goals. In Activities Two through Eight, you'll build practical strategies to modify and apply narrative techniques that may enhance many forms of oral and written communication.

But first, review key concepts of story by reading Deborah Hecht's "Lessons from the Kitchen Table" (page 186).

A passage from Margaret Laurence's *The Stone Angel*, reprinted below, succinctly models narrative elements Hecht discusses. As you work through the components in each activity, keep in mind the beauty of the whole, which defies logical analysis. (*Note:* The narrator, Hagar Shipley, is a crusty ninety-year-old who lives with her son, Marvin, and Doris, his wife.)

Doris is a good enough cook—I'll give her that. Even when she and Marvin were first married, she could turn out a decent meal. Of course, she always had to prepare meals, even when she was quite young. A big family, she came from, with nothing to speak of. I learned to cook after I was married. As a child I spent hours in our huge warm green-cupboarded kitchen, but only to watch and nibble. Watching Auntie Doll slap and pat at the pastry or pare an apple all in one long curled ribbon of peeling, I used to think how sad to spend one's life in caring for the houses of others. I never had any premonition, and I felt myself to be—oh, quite different from Auntie Doll, amicable but different, a different sort entirely.

Doris baked yesterday. Lemon slice, with browned coconut on top, and chocolate strip with walnuts. Good, she's iced it. I like it so much better this way. She's made cheese bread, as well—aren't we grand today? I do believe she has spread butter on it, not that disgusting margarine she buys for economy. I settle snugly, and sip and taste, taste and sip.

Doris pours more tea. We are comfortable. Marvin is hairy in shirtsleeves, elbows on the table. High day or holiday or Judgment Day—no difference to Marvin. He would have put his elbows on the table if he'd been an apostle at the Last Supper.

"Care for a little more lemon slice, Mother?"

Why is he so attentive? I watch their faces. Does a questioning look pass between them or do I only fancy it is so?

"No, thank you, Marvin." Aloof. Alert. Not to be taken in.

He blinks his pallid eyes and grimaces his face into a puzzled frown, wanting to speak something but unable to begin. He has never had a facility with words. I grow more suspicious by the minute, and regret now the tea and my own partaking. *What is it? What is it?* I want to shout the question impatiently at his face. Instead I fold my hands, as I am meant to do, over my silk lilac belly, and wait.

"The house seems kind of empty now that Tina's not here," he says at last, "and Steven doesn't get home very often."

"She's been gone a month or more," I remind him tartly, somehow delighted that it is I who am reminding him of a thing.

"It's too big, that's what Marv means," Doris puts in. "It's too big, with neither of the kids here now except holidays and that."

"Big?" Why should I take it so keenly? "I wouldn't call it big, as houses go."

"Well, you couldn't compare it to the big new split-levels and those," Doris says. "But it's a four-bedroom house and that's big enough for these days."

"Four bedrooms big? The Currie house had six. Even the old Shipley place had five."

Doris lifts brown rayon shoulders, looks expectantly at Marvin. *Say something*, her eyes spell, *your turn now*.

"We thought," Marvin speaks as he thinks, slowly, "we got to thinking, Doris and me, it might be a good idea to sell this house, Mother. Get an apartment. Smaller, easier to keep, no stairs."

I cannot speak, for the pain under my ribs returns now, all of a stab. Lungs, is it? Heart? This pain is hot, hot as August rain or the tears of children. Now I see the reason for the spread table. Am I a calf, to be fattened? Oh, had I known I would not have eaten a bite of her damnable walnuts and icing.

"You'll never sell this house, Marvin. It's my house. It's my house, Doris. Mine."

Building the People of Narrative

Why begin with the concept of characterization? As Laurence's passage demonstrates, narrative's lure lies with people. You read on to discover more about Hagar. Examine Hagar's words, thoughts, actions, and reactions. What do you know about her from less than three hundred words? What entices you to find out more? The fascination with the inner workings of others' lives— whether fictional or real—corroborates Alexander Pope's sentiment, "The proper study of mankind is man."*

If you're in doubt, just consider the popularity of soap operas, and magazines such as *People*, the *National Enquirer*, and *Rolling Stone*. What draws you to one film or book and not another? More often than not, the character of real or imaginary people is the answer.

The real and imaginary individuals of literature are a motley crew. But despite their differences, you've probably observed key similarities. Generally, the individuals you read about or view on film or stage are:

- special or unique, yet realistic

- worth caring about—sympathetic or empathetic

- learning, growing, changing—often through emotional upheavals or other significant experiences.

According to novelist Gail Godwin, contemporary protagonists enlist emotional support because of what "they are able to make out of what they are given." They do not win every battle; rather, readers are attracted to them because they see them grow through personal conflicts and admire their ability to draw meaningful "connections" between present and past experiences.

---

* Pope's generic use of *mankind* is typical of his era.

Readers follow their stories in search of their own—to "Make sense of [personal] circumstances," to enrich the sense of the possible; through shared experience the reader grows too.

Real people depicted in non-fiction "stories"—biographical sketches, anecdotes, memoirs, feature articles, profiles—are intriguing for similar reasons. The audience is drawn into real-life drama because the writer artfully *selects* and *orders* the individual's "presentation" in a colourful, forceful manner. As with fiction, the writer is a "stage manager"; each detail—in this case, factual detail—contributes to the portrayal of the whole person. Barbara Wade Rose's portrait of Jean Little in "Play It Again, Sam" (page 172) or Farley Mowat's tale about the catfish (page 113) exemplify dramatic non-fiction that piques the reader's curiosity.

You'll practise techniques of memorable characterization for fiction and non-fiction in Activity Two.

Activity Two   Creating Memorable Characterization
Purpose

• to recognize and employ characterization strategies

• to compare techniques of characterizing real and imaginary individuals

• to refine knowledge of "show, don't tell" devices

1.   After freewriting in your Writer's Notebook about interesting people, build a class list of approximately twelve fascinating characters and/or people from stage, screen, and print. Beside each name, indicate memorable qualities or traits.

2.   With a partner, select one real or imaginary individual to become better acquainted with.
a.   In your Writer's Notebook, "build" the individual using *hunches, intuition,* and *imagination*. To begin, speculate about X's views on a controversial topic, or favourite people, foods, travel, music, movies, books, and clothes. Or compose Twenty Questions and answer them.
b.   After outlining qualities you'd emphasize in an anecdote about this individual, draft a character sketch.
c.   Draft a 350–400 word anecdote about the character in your writing folder assignment. Check to see you've applied your knowledge of style, and used appropriate devices for showing.

3.   Identify examples of how character is revealed through dialogue (what the individual says, what others say about the individual), as well as through actions and reactions in the passages below. See also the non-fiction excerpt from an article by William Broyles on page 175 and Farley Mowat's account of grandma and the catfish on page 113.

Judith Guest

"Did you call him?"

"Yeah, he's up."

She sighs. "I hate to play golf when it's cold. Why doesn't anybody in this league know enough to quit when the season's over? Leaves on all the fairways, your hands frozen—it's ridiculous."

He leans toward her; gives her a kiss on the neck. "I love you."

"I love you." She is looking at him in the mirror. "Will you talk to him this morning? About the clothes? He's got a closet full of decent things and he goes off every day looking like a bum, Cal."

"That's the style. Decency is out, chaos is in—" As her brows lift, he nods. "Okay, I'll talk to him."

John Updike

We eat meat, meat I wrestled warm from the raw hands of the hamburger girl in the diner a mile away, a ferocious place, slick with savagery, wild with chrome.... I wielded my wallet, and won my way back. The fat brown bag of buns was warm beside me in the cold car; the smaller bag holding the two tiny cartons of French-fries emitted an even more urgent heat. Back through the black winter air to the fire, the intimate cave, where halloos and hurrahs greeted me ...

F. Scott Fitzgerald

The only completely stationary object in the room was an enormous couch on which two young women were buoyed up as though upon an anchored balloon. They were both in white, and their dresses were rippling and fluttering as if they had just been blown back in after a short flight around the house. I must have stood for a few moments listening to the whip and snap of the curtains and the groan of the picture on the wall. Then there was a boom as Tom Buchanan shut the rear windows and the caught wind died out about the room, and the curtains and the rugs and the two young women ballooned slowly to the floor.

The younger of the two was a stranger to me. She was extended full length at her end of the divan, completely motionless, and with her chin raised a little, as if she were balancing something on it which was quite likely to fall....

The other girl, Daisy, made an attempt to rise—she leaned slightly forward with a conscientious expression—then she laughed, an absurd, charming little laugh, and I laughed too and came forward into the room.

"I'm p-paralyzed with happiness."

4. Working with a partner, generalize about "character" portrayal in literature.

a. Draw up tentative guidelines about building the people of fiction and non-fiction.

b.   Test your ideas against well-designed characters.

5a.   Read Craig's Writer's Notebook entry about question 2c:

> I just reread my anecdote about Marilyn. It's too obvious and talky.
> I remember what Blythe and Sweet, the English professors who
> "collaborwrite," said: "Too much telling is risky business." Must apply their
> ideas noted from *Writer's Digest*. To *show* character, they advise planting a
> suggestion, appealing to sight as well as sound, and tagging the individual
> with a characteristic gesture which reveals a central trait. So instead of my
> line *saying*, " 'You're lying,' she said *angrily*," I'll try this: "She threw the
> plate to the floor [suggestion of anger]. 'You're lying,' she said. [terse
> dialogue] As the curry seeped into the white pile, she turned on her heel and
> flounced out" [suggestion of impulsive nature]. Also, remember to clarify
> her motivation—more on that later.

b.   Could your anecdote from question 2c. benefit from the type of change
Craig made? Get a partner's views. Revise.

6.   In your writing folder, draft an essay, scenario, or vignette about
characterization. These statements may help you begin:

• You can't just "figure out" a memorable fictional character the way you
  develop anecdotes about real people.

• It's harder to create characters of the opposite sex.

• It's important to identify with your character.

• Effective characters are people in whom we see a little of ourselves.

If you have had difficulty "finding" a character to work with, Craig's ideas,
listed below, may be a welcome resource for future activities.

• Build on an anecdote—real or imaginary. Morley Callaghan observes
  that "A writer is very lucky when someone tells him a little story that is
  half complete. What has been given to him in this way seems to set his
  imagination off, and almost at once he finds himself completing the
  story in his mind."

• "Elaborate" on a real person. Eudora Welty reported her first decent
  short story "began spontaneously" from a neighbour's comment.
  Lawrence Block, author of *Writer's Digest* magazine's monthly "Fiction"
  column, also suggests beginning with a real person. Next time you're on
  public transit, invent "facts" about a person you observe: ". . . jot down
  a slew of one-liners loaded with data about the person's . . . life." Let
  your imagination play before sketching your character.

• Scour newspapers and news magazines. Journalist Jon Franklin suggests
  beginning where newspaper accounts end. Profiles, want-ads, personals,
  quotes of the day, captions, cartoons, births and deaths, and profiles of

entrepreneurs and scientists are fertile sources. In fiction, adapt the character to suit your needs.

- Keep a receptive mind. In an interview, Jane Rule suggested that characters may "find" you.

- Collect vivid phrasing about characters and people; a computer file is a handy medium.

- Write yourself a letter or make a journal entry. Begin and end anywhere, letting your mind play. Listen to music or doodle.

- Read the classics; keep them by your writing station for leisurely browsing.

Now we'll move beyond character into the action or movement of narrative.

Constructing Narrative Plan: Plot and Conflict

An effective narrative plan—*how* you tell the story—captures your audience's attention. Whether the tale is a true account of a single event, or a complex interplay of imaginary forces, each sentence should *propel* the audience toward its destination—the end or resolution.

In writing about plot, three well-known authors emphasize *motion toward a goal*. Hugh Hood describes "an action or thrust, a movement towards a revelation of some sort." Elizabeth Bowen writes of "the knowing of destination," and Gustave Flaubert of "unfolding" a tale.

To study this concept in action, review *The Stone Angel* excerpt. As a class, discuss how Laurence moves the reader closer to Hagar's realization of Marvin and Doris's intention of sending her to a nursing home. Or reread Mowat's account of the catfish. How does he build suspense and entice you to read on?

Now, let's suppose you're planning a story about *your* grandmother. Through Activity Two you've set out her character as you want to show it. Is there a plot formula? There's no one right way to build a character; you'll need to experiment with narrative plans. The best ideas will likely spring from collaborative efforts of rational and imaginative powers. Graham Greene relies on his unconscious if faced with a seemingly unsolvable plot problem. Before bed, he'll reread his draft. On awakening, the path is clear.

Writer John Metcalf describes the beginning of a story as "pictures or words," repeatedly passing through his mind. He explains the story's conception by comparing his mind to an inflated balloon decorated with a picture and contained within a box. As a story grows, the balloon tries to break free. But Metcalf writes only when he can "guess at the general shape and form of the whole picture." He "translates" the picture into words. What causes the balloon to blow up? A desire to "celebrate," to "chart the past."

If you're wondering where to find this balloon, look around you. Perhaps all the stories have been told, but you're searching for a *new twist*—a vision which reinterprets and individualizes human experience. The old favourites—the search for love, fear of rejection, sibling rivalry, the journey from innocence to experience—still make the best stories.

Reflect on personal experiences which illuminate these classic themes. How would grandma—or an imaginary character—be affected by a specific problem you've confronted? Return for a moment to Craig's character, Marilyn. What motivated Marilyn's flash of temper? Suppose Craig answers "fear of rejection." Did this fear initiate her conflicts? The smashed plate dramatized fear. What were her choices? How did she try to surmount the obstacle? What do her choices show about her? And most important, how does she change or grow through experience?

In Activity Three, you'll review elements of plot before setting a character in motion. As you work through the steps, keep these two questions in mind:

- What incidents and actions will portray my character's tale?

- How can my character be most vividly portrayed through narrative (straight *telling*) and/or scene (*showing* through dialogue, interior monologue, or stream of consciousness)?

Activity Three   Making Choices About Narrative Plan

Purpose

- to recognize and use key plot elements
- to embellish plot with detail
- to write both narrative and scene

1a.   What has this description of Munro Leaf's *The Story of Ferdinand* (Puffin Books) lost in the summary?

> Once upon a time in Spain there lived a bull named Ferdinand. He was different from other bulls. He didn't like to fight. Ferdinand just liked to lie in the meadow and smell the flowers. As he grew, Ferdinand watched other bulls proving their war-like nature, vying to fight the matador. One day, men from the city came in search of ferocious bulls for the bullring. Ferdinand accidentally sat on a bee. Mistaking his crashing and thumping for a bellicose nature, the men took Ferdinand off to the bullring. But Ferdinand spied rainbowed flowers on hats in the crowd. He was so happy he just sat down in the corner and smelled the flowers. And that is Ferdinand's story.

b.   This version is pure narrative. Co-write an improved version. Use:

- at least one piece of dialogue

- vivid verbs and forceful nouns

- a style more appropriate to the content and purpose.

2.   In your writing folder, rewrite a children's classic in three versions, using only scene (i.e., dialogue) in the first; only narrative (i.e., telling) in the second, and a balance of scene and narrative in the third. Then, assess the merits of each version in your Writer's Notebook.

OR

Rewrite either Purdy's anecdote about Milton Acorn (page 160), using only dialogue or a combination of dialogue and narrative, or the tale of Mosquito and Thunder (page 160) in pure dialogue. What you've learned in Chapter Three will help you select an appropriate style.

3.   In your Writer's Notebook, reflect on writing scene and narrative. One of these statements may help you begin:

- Scene is more difficult to write well than narrative.

- The main function of narrative is to enrich scene: to show passage of time or change of place, or to identify the speaker.

4a.   "Expand" an anecdote from your writing folder (Activity Two, question 2c.) into a plot map—a visual representation of the individual's journey. Include starting point, junctures for choice/decisions, paths taken, climax, and conclusion. Students with graphics programs may enjoy devising a computer map.
b.   With a writing partner, assess the quality of your plot map according to these criteria and consider any necessary revisions:

- Are the starting point and goal clearly established?

- Does the connecting path *zig-zag* to represent obstacles?

(*Test:* Join the starting point and goal. A straight line reflects a dearth of conflict. Replot.)

5a.   In your writing folder, draft one or more conflict scenes derived from the plot outline. Don't worry yet about links.
b.   Ask a partner to assess the success of each.

6.   Reflect in your Writer's Notebook about the experience of plotting a story. Were you working with an imaginary character drawn largely from within, a real person portrayed as real, or a combination of the two? How did these factors affect your composing process?

Developing Dialogue

Are you the type of reader who skips through narrative in search of passages like this?

Louisa May Alcott

"Christmas won't be Christmas without any presents," grumbled Jo, lying on the rug.

"It's so dreadful to be poor!" sighed Meg, looking down at her old dress.

"I don't think it's fair for some girls to have plenty of pretty things, and other girls nothing at all," added little Amy, with an injured sniff.

"We've got a mother and father and each other," said Beth, contentedly from her corner.

Colette

The light from the setting sun touched the curtains, shone through the drawing room from end to end, and Irene's friends cried out in admiration.

"It's like a fairyland!"

"And the Seine's on fire!"

"The sky's going pink . . ."

Jean Little

"Can I come, too?" Sarah asked. Jeremy jumped. The dreamy look left his eyes. Lost in his thoughts, he had not known that she was there until she spoke. Now he looked up at her standing on the dock above him.

"No," he said.

"I have my life jacket on."

"No," he repeated, his voice hard.

He gave her no reason for his decision. He knew better. Give Sarah any excuse for an argument and you were asking for trouble. She was like a bull-dog; she never gave up. Now, instead of going away, she stayed right where she was and drooped with disappointment. She looked so sad and small that he wanted to hit her.

"You heard me," he told her, stung into speech by her waiting silence. "I said 'No' and I meant it. Do me a favour and scram."

If you prefer dialogue to narrative, you probably included more scene than narrative in your writing from Activities One, Two, and Three. Dialogue is an effective technique of showing. The best contemporary dialogue is lean and economical and propels the story along at a neat clip. Although it sounds natural, it is not natural speech. Speculate on the results of an experiment such as this:

> You practise active listening in the cafeteria, on the job, in a restaurant. For a week, you log observations in your Writer's Notebook about how people talk in everyday life, listening for junk words ("uh," "um," "ah"), differences in pace and tone, sentence fragments, type of diction, and interjections.

If you transcribed these conversations word for word, would they constitute dialogue? Justify in class discussion.

In Activity Four you'll refine your ability to write dialogue. Before you begin, reread the excerpt from *The Stone Angel*. What does the dialogue *show* about Hagar's character? How does each passage advance the mounting tension?

Activity Four   Writing Effective Dialogue
Purpose

- to reflect on effective dialogue
- to advance plot through conflict dialogue
- to tailor dialogue to audience and purpose

1a.   In pairs, create dialogue through role playing, recording your interaction for later scrutiny. You may wish to dramatize one of these conflict situations or create your own. Within three minutes, raise the situation to a high point of tension and resolve it. Before beginning, clarify your character's *motivation*.

- A teenager with low grades is denied use of the family car.
- A sixteen-year-old wants a higher allowance.
- A teenager argues with a parent about placing a grandparent in a nursing home.
- A boss fires a part-time student employee.
- A recent high-school graduate prepares for a job interview by role playing with a friend.
- Parents dispute a teenager's plans for an out-of-town weekend with friends.
- A young couple tries to decide where to go on a date.
- A sixteen-year-old urges parents to leave him at home alone while they vacation in Florida.
- Siblings argue about "personal space."

b.   As you listen to the tape, consider if you:

- showed personality and motivation
- escalated conflict by confronting one or more obstacles
- used appropriate diction and sentence length
- avoided a clichéd happy ending?

If not, don't be surprised. Why may spontaneous speech not achieve these goals—especially within a time limit?

2a.   In your writing folder, draft a skit of your role playing topic for a specific audience and purpose. Use dialogue to meet goals from question 1b.
b.   With a partner, assess the skit against a class checklist.

3.   What can be perceived about a television show with the picture off? Compare messages conveyed verbally and visually in programs such as a prime-time drama versus "Sesame Street."

4.   Examine conflict scenes from Activity Three, question 5. Have you used dialogue as an effective tool of showing?

5a.   With a partner, discuss techniques of showing through dialogue which would strengthen your essays and book reviews.
b.   Examine a piece of work from another subject, considering whether it could be improved through dialogue or quotation(s).

Point of View

Visualize this scenario: You're looking after your four- and six-year-old cousins on a rainy weekend. You've run out of games and television and fairy tales. For a new slant, change the point of view from which you tell a story. Perhaps the children can help. How would Cinderella tell her own story? How did Sleeping Beauty *really* feel about the prince? Invite the children to draw what they "see" as they pretend to be Cinderella, or the prince, or Jack-and-the-Beanstalk.

How might "reseeing" stories enhance your understanding of a history text, a novel, or a newspaper report about an international trade conference? Speculate on these questions as you work through this section.

Point of view or perspective focuses and unifies your tale. A writer or speaker produces a work, but it may unfold through the eyes of a narrator. In short stories, novels, narrative poetry, and certain forms of non-fiction, a narrator filters and interprets reality for the audience. Most contemporary drama, on the other hand, is presented directly.

As senior students you're familiar with first person ("I") and third person ("he" or "she") distinctions. A limited narrator who disappears inside a character cannot penetrate the minds and hearts of others. On the other hand, an omniscient narrator knows all, and may share perceptions with the audience. Review these concepts as you read the passages below. How would each sound be rewritten from an altered viewpoint?

Charlotte Brontë

There was no possibility of taking a walk that day. We had been wandering, indeed, in the leafless shrubbery an hour in the morning; but since dinner

(Mrs. Reed, when there was no company, dined early) the cold winter wind had brought with it clouds so sombre, and a rain so penetrating that further out-door exercise was now out of the question.

Kate Chopin

Knowing that Mrs. Mallard was afflicted with a heart trouble, great care was taken to break to her as gently as possible the news of her husband's death.

It was her sister Josephine who told her, in broken sentences, veiled hints that revealed in half concealing. Her husband's friend Richards was there, too, near her. It was he who had been in the newspaper office when intelligence of the railroad disaster was received, with Brently Mallard's name leading the list of "killed." He had only taken the time to assure himself of its truth by a second telegram, and had hastened to forestall any less careful, less tender friend in bearing the sad message.

William Broyles

I am hanging by my fingertips from a rock ledge 7000 metres above sea level. My foot, searching for a dimple in the rock to push from, finally catches on a tiny protrusion. I take eight breaths, then push. My hand goes up to another rock, finds a hold.

Somewhere above me is the summit of Aconcagua, at 7021 metres the tallest mountain in the Western Hemisphere. Storm clouds are gathering. It is past five in the afternoon, and soon the temperature will fall to almost 30 below zero. For three days I have been unable to eat. I am dehydrated. My brain, starved for oxygen, has all but ceased to function. In the snow on the summit is the body of an Argentinean who froze to death after reaching the top a few days ago. Four other climbers have died on the mountain in the past month.

I have never climbed a mountain in my life. In fact, I am afraid of heights. *What am I doing here?*

When selecting a "teller" in fiction or non-fiction, consider whether the narrator or perspective is appropriate for purpose and audience. Is the individual sufficiently intelligent, sensitive, and reliable for the audience to trust? Suppose you're a reporter preparing a feature on families who've lost their homes to fire. To draw your readers into the emotion, you may want the intimacy of first-person narration. However, you'd be wise not to elect the families' two-year-old twins to recount their memories; you must work within the strengths and limitations of the narrator. If the narrator cannot tell your story, select a more appropriate candidate.

Before beginning Activity Five, study the point of view used in *The Stone Angel* excerpt (page 164). Why is first-person narration effective? Recast the opening using third person; how does this change the story's impact? Or retell the passage from Doris's or Marvin's points of view, considering how perceptions may alter a story.

Activity Five   Selecting Point of View or Narrative Perspective

Purpose

- to determine appropriate point of view for various purposes and audiences

- to experiment with point of view and appropriate diction

- to use knowledge of point of view to enhance reading skills and analysis of literature

1a.   In groups, rewrite a short newspaper report from the perspectives of two people mentioned or quoted in the original. Use an informative or interpretive style. How do focus, diction, emphasis, and characters' perceptions alter a story? (*Tip:* A sports feature or report on a concert would work well for this exercise.) Justify changes in emphasis and focus to a partner.

b.   Predict how "reseeing" may improve the way you interpret news stories. How may this strategy inform your essays and book reviews in disciplines such as history, family studies, politics, and economics? Discuss specific examples as a class.

2.   Working with a partner, recount details of a real-life controversial event—a sports match, concert, accident, date, or examination—from two different points of view. Your purpose and audience should remain constant. Comment on the experiment in your Writer's Notebook.

3.   In your writing folder, draft accounts of an imaginary event from two perspectives. Select a style from the poetic/rhetorical cluster or experiment with stream of consciousness/interior monologue. One of these ideas may help you begin:

- a grandmother and teenager attend an opera, ballet, or sports event

- a blind date or first date

- a marriage proposal

- an engaged couple plan furniture purchases or their wedding

- a brother and sister watch television or paint the house.

4.   Rewrite one of the following passages in your Writer's Notebook, using a style appropriate for purpose, audience, and subject matter. Or co-write this assignment on a word processor.

- "The Mosquito and the Thunder" from Thunder's perspective
- Mowat's story about grandma and the catfish from the latter's perspective
- Doris's or Marvin's viewpoint in *The Stone Angel* scene.

5.   In your writing folder, rewrite one conflict scene from your "expanded anecdote" from previous activities.

6.   Freewrite about point of view for fifteen minutes. You might begin with one of these ideas:

a.   I like to write in the first/third person because . . .
b.   First-person writing is difficult unless you learn to . . .
c.   Establishing intimacy is easiest in the first person . . .
d.   My favourite novel/movie retold from a different point of view would be delightful/horrendous . . .

Setting and Theme

Some things are best left understated: when it comes to building setting and theme, this approach is worth remembering.

Your story's "when and where"—the setting of the narrative—may emerge spontaneously, woven in among other details. For example, Thomas Hardy opens *Tess of the d'Urbervilles* this way:

> On an evening in the latter part of May a middle-aged man was walking homeward from Shaston to the village of Marlott, in the adjoining Vale of Blakemore or Blackmoor. The pair of legs that carried him were rickety, and there was a bias in his gait which inclined him somewhat to the left of a straight line. He occasionally gave a smart nod, as if in confirmation of some opinion, though he was not thinking of anything in particular. An empty egg-basket was slung upon his arm, the nap of his hat was ruffled, a patch being worn away at its brim where his thumb came in taking it off. Presently he was met by an elderly parson astride on a gray mare, who, as he rode, hummed a wandering tune.

Margaret Laurence begins *The Stone Angel* this way:

> Above the town, on the hill brow, the stone angel used to stand. I wonder if she stands there yet, in memory of her who relinquished her feeble ghost as I gained my stubborn one, my mother's angel that my father bought in pride to mark her bones and proclaim his dynasty, as he fancied, forever and a day.

Discuss what you know about the setting of these novels and how you know each detail.

Before investigating setting further in Activity Six, let's review the concept of theme. Perhaps you're wondering why we didn't begin with theme. After all, most stories—fictional or factual—are "about" something. In most well-told contemporary narratives, theme or focusing vision emerges naturally from speech (dialogue, quotation, monologue), conflicts, and characterization or other methods of showing. Meaning is dramatized or shown. In exposition, the writer clearly states the thesis or main idea.

But writers of narrative undermine their relationship with modern audiences if the story's "meaning" is spelled out didactically. The magical interaction between storyteller and audience thrives on an ambiguous quality which defies definition. If you're familiar with *The Great Gatsby*, you'll notice how the excerpt on page 167 contributes indirectly to Fitzgerald's themes. Or if you know *The Stone Angel*, consider theme in relation to the novel. You'll examine theme further in Activity Six.

Activity Six   Building Setting and Theme
Purpose

- to examine techniques of revealing setting in fiction and non-fiction

- to explore how setting builds atmosphere

- to note how theme emerges spontaneously

1a.   In groups, study how Broyles (page 175), Mowat (page 113), and two other writers establish setting in their work.
b.   Read aloud from *The Great Gatsby* (page 167). How does Fitzgerald evoke atmosphere and blend it with setting to help us envision his characters?

2a.   Read the excerpt from Sandra Birdsell's account of life in the Red River Valley (page 178). Note examples of phrasing and imagery which enliven it. Compose a found poem with Birdsell's phrases. Or draft a paragraph about the Red River Valley from the perspective of an inhabitant who dislikes it.

Why do I live here?
I ask a friend. Grasshoppers and crickets sing from either side of the dirt road. It's not quite a full moon but bright enough for long shadows. Perfect night to play Dracula. It's my turn to wear the cape. The question eats at me, interferes with the game. On the horizon Winnipeg shimmers pink and still. You live here, he says, because you're short. You're close to the ground and if a big wind should come along you'd be safe. And yet you feel tall. Naw, that's not it, my daughter says. We've got a curved sky and living here is like living inside a bubble. A small town inside a bubble, she says, jabbing the air with her sharp fingernail.
It's Sunday and the question rankles as I make my weekly trip through the forest where thick, dark trees wrestle the granite boulders for soil. I push the speed limit to get to the lake before all the others and finally I find my

spot, huddle down into the sand, and stare out across the water. I think: Why do I live here? Eureka! The answer comes to me. It's not the curved sky or the horizon or because I'm short. It's because when I live in the Red River Valley I'm living at the bottom of a lake. When you live at the bottom of a lake you get cracks in your basement walls, especially in River Heights where they can afford cracks and underpinning and new basements. I like the cracks. The wind whistles through them, loosens the lids on my preserves, makes the syrup ferment, and the mice get tipsy. In the potato bin sprouts grow on wrinkled skin, translucent, cool sprouts. They climb up the basement walls, push their way through air vents, and up the windows in my kitchen. I don't have to bother about hanging curtains.

And time is different here. The days piled on top of lake sediment shift after a good storm so that yesterday slips out from beneath today. Or even last Friday with all its voices will bob up from the bottom and it's possible to lose track of tomorrow. You can just [ignore] tomorrow and go out and play Dracula.

b.   In your writing folder, draft several paragraphs in a rhetorical style; evoke the atmosphere of a place you know well. Use mainly narrative telling as Birdsell does. Then if you wish, add scene (dialogue) and compare the results of the two ways of writing.

3.   In your Writer's Notebook, argue one statement using an interpretive style:
a.   Setting is often disclosed indirectly through conflict and characterization.
b.   The "when" and "where" of non-fiction may be as important a backdrop for characterization and atmosphere as in fiction.

4.   In conference with a partner, identify how you've established the "when" and "where" of your story or "expanded anecdote" from previous activities. What atmosphere have you created? Redraft your work if you wish, refining techniques that convey setting.

5.   (Re)read Doris Lessing's "Through the Tunnel" (page 96). With a partner
a.   Note details which establish setting and atmosphere.
b.   Determine themes and how they are unfolded for the audience.

Looking Beyond Narrative

Hands-on experience with narrative's mechanics has expanded your repertoire of communication skills. In previous activities, you've paused briefly to reflect on ways your knowledge may enhance other coursework. In Activity Seven, draw these ideas together.

Activity Seven   Looking at Narrative and Beyond
Purpose

- to enhance oral and written communication through narrative techniques

- to strengthen skills of search and active reading

- to reinforce group writing and computer skills

Complete questions 1, 2, 3b., and 4 in small groups.

1.   After reading the following statements, discuss the applicability of each to your work.

Tarvo: By creating my own stories, I've found out what to look for in others' work. On the exam I *knew* how to "show that King Lear's character is revealed through a series of dramatic conflicts with himself."

Sasha: Playing with pieces of the puzzle made me feel more confident when I wrote my history book report. I saw the writer's bias about the Quiet Revolution.

Kirsten: Storytelling techniques like using effective voice and gesture and key phrasing helped my history seminar; instead of just reading Champlain's letters to his wife, I turned them into a story.

Craig: I unified an art history essay with anecdotes about Emily Carr. It livened up the analysis and drew the whole piece together.

2a.   Review recent writing assignments for other classes. In your Writer's Notebook, speculate on how learning about narrative techniques may benefit these or other written and oral work. Or complete this exercise in chart form at the computer.

b.   How may learning about narrative enhance your ability to handle post-secondary challenges? Students with graphics computer programs may enjoy brainstorming ideas, using mapping or clustering techniques (see page 387).

3a.   If your school belongs to a computer network, draft a persuasive letter to a correspondent explaining how narrative may enhance analytical and critical work. Invite a response.

b.   Initiate a database of references for anecdotes and quotations to enliven essays and reports in other subject areas.

4.   Enhance your skills of search and active reading. In the time allotted by your instructor, locate a narrative work of your choice in the resource centre and read it, using the Active Reading checklist on page 393.

5.   Prepare a chart, computer exercise, or set of overhead transparencies which instruct grade 9 or 10 students in using narrative techniques to enrich oral and written work.

C. AFTER-WORDS

Responding to Reading

1.   Read "On the Role of Story and the Storyteller" (page 185) from a speech by Morley Callaghan. Argue or support one idea.

2.   Tell a story derived from an idea in one reading.

3.   After reading Damon Knight's "It All Begins With Characters" (page 188) and Charlotte Brontë's comments on morality and character (page 185), role play *one* of these situations with a partner:
a.   A conversation between Knight and Callaghan about their approaches to writing.
b.   Debate with Brontë her concern that it may be ethically wrong to create certain types of characters; you might refer to one or more controversial characters on television, rock video, or other media.

4a.   As a class, compose a master list of "how-to" tips for writing narrative, keeping in mind advice from the readings, as well as personal experience.
b.   In conference with a partner, assess the strengths of your "expanded anecdote," using these how-to tips.

5.   Refresh your knowledge of style and structure by (re)reading essays in this chapter and completing the following:
a.   Identify styles used by Knight and Callaghan. Justify with textual references.
b.   Evaluate the aptness of each style to its purpose, audience, and content.
c.   Compare essays by Callaghan, Hecht, and Suzuki, considering:

•   clarity and placement of thesis

•   types and quality of evidence or illustration

•   type and level of language

•   use of transitions and other devices to enhance unity and coherence

•   organization of material.

The Writing Folder

1.   Write an anecdote or excerpt from a science-fiction story dramatizing Callaghan's argument in "The Role of the Storyteller."

2.   What questions might a talk-show interviewer pose to Callaghan and Suzuki on the same program? Identify a common theme or interest; then compose a selection of queries and answer several.

3.   Compose a humorous anecdote, skit, or story based on fact or fiction about a child's first encounter with a storyteller in a bookstore, classroom, or library program.

4.   Revise and polish your "expanded anecdote" begun in Activity Two, question 2c.

5.   Write a dialogue between yourself and one of your imaginary characters, dramatizing your feelings about your relationship with this character.

6.   Write a formal essay about the art and craft of composing narrative. Use an interpretive style. You may wish to illustrate the essay with examples from your "expanded anecdote," showing how you revised and strengthened it.

7.   Draft an essay, vignette, or anecdote based on strategies you've devised to cope with writer's block. This idea may help you begin: Aldous Huxley reportedly solved writer's block by flipping through "almost anything"; ideas came in "driblets."

Independent Study

1.   Plan a Writers-in-Libraries or storytelling program for your school board's elementary and/or secondary schools. Preliminary research should include an investigation of current provincial or city-sponsored programs.
a.   Compose a report which includes goals, strategies, financing, and resources. (See *Quill & Quire*, "Library News," Martin Dowding, July/86.)
b.   Or write a short story, one-act play, or feature article based on this experience.

2.   As a class project, compose an annotated "Classics for Canadian Students" recommended reading list for ages three to eighteen. Balance genres, past and present literature written by males and females, and Canadian and non-Canadian authors. During the course, each student contributes at least two titles of full-length works, plus an annotation for each; these titles may be part of an individual independent study project. Post the list in the library. Or ask volunteers to give book talks to junior students at your high school, or at an elementary school or local library.

3.   Research the narrative tradition in oral culture. Devise an essay about storytelling—its evolution or techniques—with your teacher. The oral component may include a storytelling session.

4.   Research anecdotes, songs, and jokes about local folklore. Reflect your learning in an imaginative form—perhaps a one-act play, an analysis of themes, or a short story. For your oral presentation, recount anecdotes, jokes, and or play songs for the class.

5. Read novels, plays, or collected short stories by a well-known author. Analyze narrative techniques (e.g., portrayal of characterization or use of scene and narrative) in the works.

The Writer's Notebook

1. Freewrite about key concepts of narrative and your experience with them.

2. Freewrite about the growth of your personal writing process; don't forget to comment on your utilization of word processing facilities.

3a. Comment on one quotation in light of personal experience writing narrative:

Anthony Trollope   "The ordinary talk of ordinary people is carried on in short, sharp, expressive sentences which . . . frequently are never completed—the language of which . . . is often incorrect."

Gustave Flaubert   This writer's inner identification with his character, Emma Bovary, was so strong he reportedly said, "I *am* Madame Bovary."

Robert Frost   "Everything written is as good as it is dramatic."

William Styron   "Sometimes I feel that the characters I've created are not much more than . . . projected facets of myself."

b. If you wish, exchange reflections with a partner and respond in writing to one idea your partner expressed that "says" something to you.

4a. Respond in essay form to this question: How do you go about the process of writing?
b. Compare your experience with those recounted below by two students from Hearst, Ontario.

Courtney Walker

I write the piece in my head before I actually pick up a pen and write it on paper. I like to *see* how it looks and how it will turn out before I actually write it. It's difficult to do because what I conjure up in my mind never turns out to look as wonderful on paper. Somewhere between the creative side and the pen controlled by the analytical side of my brain, the heart of my brilliant vision usually dies. [Now] I'm finding out how to control this. . . . The most difficult part is the self-assessment. I find it hard to criticize my work. I think it's because I'm afraid of being too hard on myself, but then it ends up that I'm not nearly as hard as I should be.

Reprinted by permission of U.F.S., Inc.

Debra Woods

How do I go about the process of writing? Almost like a kid having a temper tantrum. . . .

Thinking is especially hard. I get really frustrated because I want the best idea. I tear up sheets and storm out, leaving the thinking process for a while. When I've pondered long enough, I get myself into a no-nonsense mood. I hype myself up. The next idea I get I will write about. . . . Sometimes when I feel I'm taking the plot up a back alley, I start over. . . . It's important to write no matter how silly the words may seem. From a jumble of words comes an idea, a plot, a storyline.

Over the past few months, I've learned that peer-assessing and editing are very important . . . I agree with Farley Mowat when he says that [writing] "is a trade and the only way to acquire the expertise is to practise that trade for as long as it takes to become a good workman."

c.   If your school belongs to a computer network, you may wish to exchange reflections about your experiments with writing.

5.   Speedwrite about how you measure your own growth as a writer. Hemingway, for example, kept a chart nearby on which he posted his daily progress to keep himself honest. Or plan a skit which satirizes a writer's obsession with the notions of growth and progress.

6.   Reflect on the development or evolution of your criteria for good writing over the past several months.

READINGS 4

From The Editor's Preface to *Wuthering Heights*

Charlotte Brontë

Whether it is right or advisable to create beings like Heathcliff, I do not know; I scarcely think it is. But this I know: the writer who possesses the creative gift owns something of which he is not always master—something that, at times, strangely wills and works for itself. He may lay down rules and devise principles, and to rules and principles it will perhaps for years lie in subjection; and then, haply without any warning of revolt, there comes a time when it will no longer consent to 'harrow the valleys, or be bound with a band in the furrow'—when it 'laughs at the multitude of the city, and regards not the crying of the driver'—when, refusing absolutely to make ropes out of sea-sand any longer, it sets to work on statue-hewing, and you have a Pluto or a Jove, a Tisiphone or a Psyche, a Mermaid or a Madonna, as Fate or Inspiration direct. Be the work grim or glorious, dread or divine, you have little choice left but quiescent adoption. As for you—the nominal artist—your share in it has been to work passively under dictates you neither delivered nor could question—that would not be uttered at your prayer, nor suppressed nor changed at your caprice. If the result be attractive, the World will praise you; if it be repulsive, the same World will blame you, who almost as little deserve blame.

On the Role of the Story and the Storyteller

Morley Callaghan

A country may have great corporations, but if it has no literature it is a country that has no soul. It is a shop keeper's society. The new nationalists, it seems to me, are concerned only with who is minding the store.

Yet I hear of busy men, saying in the newspapers, "I have no time for novels." Or if they are critics of a certain sophistication they say, "The story form is exhausted. Narrative is dead. It's a technological age. What we want is information. Useful information."

A long time ago Jesus of Nazareth told stories, baffling parables that go on haunting men. But I'm sure there was some businesslike Pharisee in the listening crowd who muttered, "Why doesn't he give us the facts? Why the mystery? Why doesn't he give us some real information?"

Information! Instead of the knowledge, the intuitions of imagination. It is the bedeviling fantasy of our time. We are stuffed with information. It pours in on us from a thousand machines until life has no meaning at all.

Well, I like to think that the Bay of Pigs operation was the end product of a deluge of unconsidered, undigested, confusing information—handled without imagination. It gets worse, too. I understand that the avenues of information to the great intelligence agencies are so heavy, that the directors never really know what is going on from one day to another. What a wild, fascinating and mysterious period to live in.

But it is a time of comedy, too. Parents, grown men, stuffed with facts about life, ask their kids, "What is the matter with our lives? Teach us how to live." And they wonder why the kids look down on them. A time when there are no great new temples, no gods and no tombs, because there is no sense of eternity.

Just information. Just technology. Outer space and inner despair. Yet it is the artist in words, or in paint or sculpture or in music who has a sense of form; in the glory of form is a sense of eternity. In short, it is the artist alone in this wild babble of information who tries to give some meaning to life. . . .

Yes, I firmly believe that the young, more and more, will be driven out of dreadful necessity to the story teller, the mythmaker; for now there is a world we are all in that now belongs to him alone. It is the private world, the domain of secret private relationships, the dead of night in a man's heart that drives us all to alcohol or drugs or suicide.

Technology may triumphantly take a man to the moon, but the man takes all his despairing questions and his secret loneliness with him, no matter how far away he flies. Since all art has to do with the relationship of things, the great writer deals with man's relationship in his lonely inner world.

Unlike the psychoanalyst, he gives it form and meaning; he places it against eternity; he takes you with him into this world that is really your own, though you hide from it. He lifts you out of it in contemplation.

Loneliness! I don't mean the kind of romantic loneliness that has been fascinating students in the work of the German writer, Herman Hesse, *Steppenwolf*. Yes, the lone wolf exulting in his loneliness loping across the steppes. No, that's not it. That was nineteenth century German romanticism.

I mean the desperate real loneliness we suffer in our relationship with other people. A few weeks ago the beautiful, rich and successful young actress, Inger Stevens, committed suicide. Her friends said she felt lonely. The long loneliness of the inner world. The domain left now to the imaginative writer, whispering to the reader about it in this private world.

Lessons from the Kitchen Table

Deborah C. Hecht

Sometimes it seems everything I know about storytelling came straight from my grand-mother's kitchen table. After dinner, Grand-ma, my mother, and my aunts tidied the kitchen, then sat around the table. That is when the stories began.

"Remember the Thanksgiving when Ben and Rebecca had such a fight that she threw her engagement ring in the street?"

"It wasn't her ring—it was his mother's brooch, and she threw it down the stairs."

There was a pause, while the storyteller gathered strength, and when she began to speak again her tone of voice had changed. I sat at the far end of the table, wondering whether it was the ring or the brooch, eager to hear what happened next. I sat as quietly as possible, trying to make myself even smaller than I was, because if I was noticed then the entire story would be told in Yiddish and I'd miss the best parts.

Why did the stories so influence me? The storytelling voice was incantation and correction, endless debate over details. The women sat at the kitchen table, their voices rising and falling with passion and secrecy. There was a power in their stories which I sensed, but did not understand.

The stories were rich with emotion, with history and details that mattered. They were the opposite of minimalism—around the kitchen table, they were stories in which actions had consequences that touched the future. The stories had a point, and often ended with the warning, "So let that be a lesson to you !" Events of the past could guard us in the future and there were, indeed, lessons to be learned.

Each story began with vivid characters in conflict with each other and their world, a world that was filled with infinite possibilities as well as infinite dangers. Each character had a reason for his behavior, a motive for his actions; he either wanted or feared something, and the question was *what*, followed closely by *why*. Nothing happened without a reason: even an event that seemed random later fit into a larger pattern than first met the eye.

Details were so hotly debated that sometimes I was frightened by the intensity of emotion. Charges and countercharges were hurled across the table. Details were important because changing even one could shift the entire focus of a story. If Rebecca threw her engagement ring into the street, the quarrel was only between two lovers. But if she threw her future mother-in-law's brooch, a future that included endless conflict with the older woman was a certainty.

The passion involved in the storytelling came from the women's involvement in the story itself, from their caring, from their conviction about the characters and the events that confronted them, and from their interest in how it all turned out. The sense of secrecy came from the belief that mysteries were being revealed, and revealed with a delicacy that only increased my fascination. Nothing taught me as much about love as a look and a shrug exchanged between my mother and her sister when they were arguing the story of Ben and Rebecca.

"He was a saint," my aunt said, tapping her fingernails on the oilcloth.

"Love," my mother said. "Go figure it. Remember how he came home from work, so eager to see her, to hear any little detail about her day?"

The two sisters gave each other a look and a shrug, and then my aunt cleared her throat and took out a linen handkerchief. "No man ever loves you for a clean kitchen floor," my aunt said. She looked at me, acknowledging my presence for the first time since I had crept into the room. "So let that be a lesson to you, young lady!"

I did learn lessons. They are in the stories I write, stories firmly grounded in characters and their conflicts. I need to know what each character wants or fears, and why. And when I'm puzzled, I think back to specific stories I heard at that table. Recently, when I was revising a love story, I needed additional details to illustrate a deep but undeclared love shared by the central characters, Glory and Timothy. That's when I remembered the story of Ben and Rebecca.

As I struggled with the revisions, I remembered how deeply my mother and her sisters valued having someone with whom to share details of everyday life. So, in describing her relationship with Timothy, Glory tells a friend: "Who else listened to every detail of my day? Who else ever took me to see the dinosaurs?" And then, later in the story, Timothy says, "I want to meet everyone in your life. Your family, your friends . . . everyone. Even your *kindergarten* teacher."

Still not satisfied with the revisions, I remembered the impact of gestures in telling that story: my mother and her sisters, just like characters in a story, often said the most important things with gestures instead of words. What gesture would show Timothy's feelings vividly enough to convince even my mother and my aunts that this was a man in love? For this story, I needed more than a look or a shrug—positive action was required. So when Glory, who was getting over a cold, coughs as they're out walking, Timothy leads her into a drugstore.

> Inside the drugstore, he piled half a dozen different kinds of cough drops and a box of tissues on the counter. He chose a vaporizer and cough syrup, then went back for a bottle of chest rub that she remembered from her childhood.
> "What's all this?" she asked.
> He looked at her as if he were surprised. "Love," he said. "This is love."

The story of Glory and Timothy would have been incomplete without my kitchen-table memories. I need to write as if my stories were being shared with those demanding, passionate storytellers—women who cared about defining a past, with its richness of detail and resonance of meanings, in order to protect the future.

It All Begins With Characters

Damon Knight

Stories are about people; there are no exceptions. In the visual arts, you can use human figures or not, as you please, but that is not true of fiction. Even if the original germ of your story is something else—a gadget, a background, a situation—there is no story until the moment you add characters.

Characters are not merely an essential element in fiction, they are central to it: they pull all the other elements together. They respond to background and setting, they react to situation, they use or abuse the gadget. You may have thought of the greatest background or situation or gadget in the world, and yet if your characters are lackluster, the story will fail.

Let's say you have an uneasy feeling that there is something wrong with the characters in your stories. You can hardly remember them yourself; they are like blobs of ectoplasm, bloodless and half-transparent.

Other people seem to be able to create strong, opaque, memorable characters. There must be a secret. What is it?

I am going to tell you the truth. You may not like it at first, but you will in a minute. Writers who create strong characters *don't know* how they do it. It happens. They don't need to use any of the tricks I'm going to teach you—but some of them did once.

A word of explanation before I begin the tricks: Please remember that you can't create characters with your conscious mind; that job, along with all the other important work in writing, belongs to the unconscious mind.

I hate that term, by the way, for all kinds of reasons—it's too long, it's a misnomer, it drips with Viennese connotations. But you do have two minds: the conscious mind and the other one. I like to call the other one Fred.

Now, then, the first thing you have to know about Fred is that he is *not* unconscious: he knows everything you know and think and feel, along with a lot of other stuff you are not aware of and that he has trouble telling you about. Fred is your major asset, but he probably was not born knowing how to create characters. Your job is to help him learn. That's what the tricks are for. Once he has learned, you won't need the tricks again.

All right, are you ready? Here we go.

1. Write a biographical sketch. Very early in my career I realized that I didn't know *anything* about my characters. They were just names and job descriptions: "Jacobson, the blackbearded engineer." There could be a million engineers with black beards: which one was this? I had no idea.

So I wrote a biographical sketch of Jacobson. I forced myself to decide where he went to school, who his parents were, how many brothers and sisters he had. Was he married, or had he been? Any children? It helped, because now I was thinking about him as a person. The story was still junk, because I was a very young writer then, but at least I was focusing on the problem, and eventually that made all the difference.

The interesting thing is that I only had to do this once: after that, Fred got the idea and began to flesh out the characters by himself.

2. Write a personality profile. Can a computer program help you create characters? Maybe so. There is a program called Mind Prober that asks you to say which of about a hundred adjectives apply to the person you want to analyze. They are words like these:

achieving	responsible
adventuresome	rigid
ambitious	sarcastic
apprehensive	secretive
carefree	striving
meticulous	suspicious
nurturing	talkative
optimistic	trusting

passive   unconventional
quiet   wary

When you have said yes or no to all the adjectives, the computer prints out a personality profile of that person, telling you how she is likely to behave at work, in personal relationships, and so on. At the least, saying yes or no to these adjectives, whether you use the program or not, will draw your attention to the astonishing variety of ways in which people can be different from each other.

3. Put your character in a setting. There is no such thing as a character apart from setting, background and situation. Imagine a character floating in space all by himself. He has no parents, no friends, no acquaintances; he has no memories and no expectations. This is not a character but a vegetable.

Who is your character? You can't answer that without answering other questions as well. Where is she? When? What is her situation? What pressures does she have to respond to right now?

C.S. Forester said that there are two kinds of writers—those who invent a character and then think of something for him to do, and those who invent a situation and then think of somebody to put in it. Whichever kind of writer you are, sooner or later you must bring the two things together and make them an organic whole. This sounds like a burden, but it isn't; it's a heaven-sent opportunity. The situation develops and exposes character; through stress, you find out who your character really is.

4. Work against the stereotype. If your characters are thin and unbelievable, it may be partly because you're copying them from other characters. The remedy for this is to recognize the stereotype and deliberately work against it.

Here is a lovely example from my book *Creating Short Fiction.* I can praise it without immodesty because the example isn't mine—I borrowed it from my wife, novelist Kate Wilhelm.

Let's say your character is a police sergeant with almost 20 years' experience. He need not be a wrestling fan, a beer drinker, or a Republican. He may be a Marxist and a Transcendental Meditation student who breeds dahlias and has a child bride.

Now you see that your policeman is no longer a stereotype, and therefore he has become more believable and much more interesting, because the things he does and says will not be stereotyped either.

5. Watch people. One Saturday morning in summer, on a city bus in Eugene, Oregon, I sat across the aisle from a large black man wearing a T-shirt with a picture of Donald Duck's nephews, Huey, Dewey and Louie. His skin was the color of milk chocolate, and so was theirs. He had a paperback with a racy cover in his hand, but he wasn't reading it; he was leaning back, having a conversation with a young white man two rows away. They were talking about their plans for tomorrow. "You'll be singing hymns," said the black man with a chuckle, "and I'll be sleeping in my bed."

I was struck by his good humor, the statement he was making with his T-shirt, and his easy relationship with his white friend. I didn't just watch him, I tried to memorize him, and it worked. Now, five years later, I still have him sharp and clear; I can see him and hear his voice. If I ever need him, there he'll be.

Real people are indispensable ingredients. Watch the way they move; listen to what they say and the way they say it; try to figure out what they are telling you about themselves. If you observe them closely, real people reveal themselves in just the way that good characters do. Even their evasions and concealments tell you something.

6. Try third person. Do you habitually write in first person? That may be one of the reasons your characters are thin. Try third. For most beginning writers, first person is not the easiest way to establish character, as they imagine, but the hardest. To begin with, the "I" of the character tends to get all tangled up with the writer's "I." Second, the character may not be able to tell the reader what she's like because she doesn't understand herself very well, and third, unlike the writer, she doesn't have to tell the truth.

Here's a hint that I will throw in for nothing: First person is great when you want to distance the character from the reader or allow him to conceal something important about himself.

Years ago I read a story by Joel Townsley Rogers, told in the first person by an artistic young man married to a rich older woman. The young man wanted to be a playwright, and he was always thinking about his scenarios. Only toward the end of the story did I realize that the "scenarios" were plots to kill his wife.

In a third-person story this would have been cheating. The writer can't lie, but a first-person narrator can.

7. Get inside the character. I don't mean anything mystical by this. I just mean that if you are always looking at your characters as if they were actors on a proscenium stage, you are wasting half your talents. You are the director, that's true, but you are also the actors—you can't hire anybody else for the job. Imagine yourself inside the character's body, seeing with his eyes, feeling what he feels. This is a potent technique for bringing a character to life by exposing the setting through his senses.

Here is an example from my novel *The Other Foot* (published by Berkley as *Mind Switch*, I'm sorry to say).

The dim gray light of early morning flooded the outer rooms, illuminating everything but emphasizing nothing. For some reason—the biped had noticed it before—it made you see the undersides of things more than usual, the loose dingy cloth hanging under the seat of a chair, the grime and dust in corners, the ordinarily inconspicuous streaks, smears, scratches.

My character is a biped from another planet who has grown up in a zoo in Hamburg. In this chapter, he has just been transferred to another zoo in Berlin, and his perceptions are colored by the fact that he is alone on his first morning in a strange place. (And he notices the underside of things partly because he feels small and insignificant.)

Remind yourself to perform this exercise not just with the central character, but with *all* the important characters. You will probably find that some of them won't do what you meant them to. Then you will have to let them do something that makes sense.

8. Get outside the character. This is the opposite of the last one, and it's just as important. In every vivid characterization is an implicit comment: the author is looking at the character from the outside, with sympathy or amusement or both; you know not only what the character is like but also what the author thinks about him.

Here is an example I discuss in *Creating Short Fiction*:

James Morton Maxwell opened a wrought-iron gate, stepped inside and closed it behind him. He was a man in his 40s, red-faced and stout, with a ragged blond mustache. His yellow hair, badly trimmed, stood out in moist spikes under the brim of his Panama hat. The lapels of his seersucker jacket were wrinkled. From where he stood, a flagstone path led between tall mock orange bushes, heavy with blooms, to the entrance of a gray stone house. The blinds were shut.

Maxwell stood in a listening attitude. There was no sound except for the *wheep, wheep* of a lawn sprinkler somewhere off to his right. In Maxwell's protuberant eyes as he looked up at the house there was something indecisive, perhaps a touch of fear. He moistened his lips, started heavily up the walk.

Your character can't see himself from the outside, but other characters can. If you're having trouble getting outside, write a scene (whether or not you will use it in the story) in which we see your character through the eyes of another person. You may find out some things that will surprise you.

9. Say "I know your secret." In a novel called *Big Money*, by P.G. Wodehouse, there is a character who believes he can extract money from any stranger by sidling up and whispering, "I know your secret." His theory is that *everybody* has a secret, and he is right. What is your character's secret? What is it that she thinks about often but never talks about? Once you know that, you will understand the character a lot better than you do now.

Don't imagine that the secret has to be something dire and bloody: it may be merely embarrassing. Here is the passage with which I introduced a major character in my novel *CV*:

> Dr. Wallace McNulty, at the age of 49, had had a singular notoriety thrust upon him. A garbled newspaper item about his being elected president of the Santa Barbara County Medical Society, shortly after the death of his wife of 20 years, had been published in *The New Yorker*, in one of those little quotes they ran at the ends of columns. Instead of just saying that he had graduated from the University of California, the item had gone on to list a whole lot of other states, as if he had graduated from all of them, too. Dr. McNulty carried the clipping around in his wallet awhile and showed it to friends, feeling embarrassed but thinking he ought to be a good sport; he found, however, that one out of every three people would read the clipping and then blink at him and say, "Did you really—?" Then he would have to explain that it was a joke, a mistake. He threw the clipping away after

a week or two, but whenever he introduced himself to people, there was always a moment when he was waiting for them to say, "Dr. Wallace McNulty? Aren't you the one who—?"

You can probably tell that I liked McNulty when I wrote that; I liked him better and better as I got to know him. I didn't *plan* him—he walked onto the page, and so did all the other characters. All I did was send out a casting call. That's what I was doing when I was a young writer, too, but it wasn't working.

10. Forget about misery. If you are a student, or a young person recently shoehorned into the work force, you probably have a lot of experience of misery, despair, boredom and lethargy. And you remember that somebody once told you, "Write about what you know." So you write about a character who is just barely managing to breathe. Wrong.

Your reader already *knows* about misery, despair, etc.; she doesn't need you to tell her that life is a bummer. The characters who will command her attention are people who are living *intensely*.

Tolstoy may have been right when he said, "All happy families resemble one another; every unhappy family is unhappy in its own fashion"; but people who are functioning are all different; people who can't function are all alike, and they are very boring.

Is this unfair? All right, it's unfair. But if the characters you write about depress *your* heartbeat and make *your* eyes glaze over, what exactly are you selling?

Self-pity is a destructive emotion, particularly for you as a writer, because it makes you incapable of feeling pity for anybody else. If you are chronically sorry for yourself, please go and read *One Day in the Life of Ivan Denisovich*, by Alexander Solzhenitsyn.

11. Express character in action and dialogue. This is another way of saying "Show, don't tell"—good advice (most of the time), because we tend to believe what we see and hear for ourselves.

12. Love. Now I am going to tell you the last and most important secret of all. I am afraid it will sound mushy. The secret is love.

You can put traits together like Tinkertoys until kingdom come, but if you don't love your character, forgive his faults, and want him to succeed just as if he were a real person, he will be a tailor's dummy. The whole point, after all, is to make your reader care. First you must care.

You say you can't love your characters because they are made of straw? OK, but that's where we started. Try learning a few new tricks.

The Secrets of Writing Powerful Dialogue

Gary Provost

"Janet," I said to one of my seminar students, "what do you do for a living?"

"I'm a waitress," she said.

"That's nice," I said.

Thirty other people were in the room, listening to this conversation. They were bored.

"Janet," I said again, "what do you do for a living?"

"I'm a waitress," she said again.

"A waitress?" I said. "Don't you think that's a pretty moronic way to make a living?"

"Well, well no," she said. "I like it."

"You like it? You're sitting there seriously telling me that you actually like lugging hamburgers around for a bunch of idiots who don't know how to cook?"

By now all the people in the seminar were leaning in the direction of the conversation. They wondered what Janet would say next, and what I would say after that. They cared about the conversation. I had their attention.

I carry on conversations like this once at every seminar to point out one of the common mistakes writers make in using dialogue in fiction and nonfiction. It is one of six dialogue mistakes I have found over and over again during a year of reading and critiquing manuscripts, and I will tell you about it after we've discussed the other five.

When was the last time you had a conversation like this?

"Hi Randy, how you doing?"

"Oh, I'm fine, Gail. I see you've got a new dog."

"Yes, Randy, a cocker spaniel."

"That's a nice looking dog, Gail."

Probably never. Occasionally when we speak to someone, we use his name. Usually it's an expression of affection. And many times parents use a name when they are angry, as in "Jamey Murphy, you get out of that trash barrel right this instant." But that's about it. In real life we rarely use the name of the person we are speaking to, and the listener's name should occur just as infrequently in your dialogue. New writers have a habit of using it constantly. It's awkward, it's artificial, and it marks the writer as an amateur.

Can you hear the awkwardness, the intrusive quality of the direct references in the exchange between Randy and Gail? The dialogue is like a stream and the *Randys* and *Gails* are like boulders interrupting the flow. Now read the dialogue without the *Gails* and *Randys* and you'll hear the dialogue flow more smoothly.

Using direct reference is just a bad habit, and you can break it easily. If you glance at a page and see that you have one character using the other's name ten times, cross out at least eight of them. Then read the dialogue without the other two. You probably don't even need them.

If you are making this mistake because you think the reader won't know who is speaking to whom, don't worry about it. The reader has a number of clues. The change in paragraphs signals a new speaker. The attribution (*he said, she said,* etc.) shows who is speaking. The style of speech often tells the reader who is speaking. And, of course, the content of the dialogue tells the reader who is speaking. If we know that Gail owns the dog, there's no doubt about who Randy is speaking to when he says, "Your miserable mutt nearly chewed my leg off and I'm going to sue you for every cent you have."

The only time you should use direct address is when you are getting something in return for it, such as characterization or story value. The word *Gail* in "Well, Gail, I see you have a new dog," doesn't do any work. But if you wrote, "Well, honey, I see that you have a new dog" or "Well, jerko, I see you have a new dog," the direct address tells the reader how the speaker feels about the person he is speaking to, and it communicates the tone of the conversation.

Writers often are insecure about their dialogue because they aren't sure the reader can hear the tone of voice, understand the implication. They try to solve the problem by describing the dialogue. The character says something, then the writer tells you *how* he said it. The tools the writer most often uses to make this mistake are verbs and adverbs. With verbs it looks like this.

"I'm not afraid of you," I announced.
"Oh," Joel snarled, "what are you going to do, scare me off with a song?"
"Maybe," I shot back.
"Or maybe you're going to hit me with a karate chop," he chided.

In this case the variety of verbs (*announced, snarled, chided,* etc.) is distracting, silly and unnecessary. When we know the characters and the situation, we can hear the tone of voice without the writer interrupting the dialogue to tell us.

Here is how the same mistake would look with adverbs.

"I'm not afraid of you," I said quickly.
"Oh," Joel said, sarcastically, "what are you going to do, scare me off with a song?"
"Maybe," I replied weakly.
"Or maybe you're going to hit me with a karate chop," he said defensively.

The writer in this case thinks he's improving the dialogue by writing *sarcastically, derisively,* etc. In fact, he is robbing the dialogue of its impact and its spontaneity by constantly interrupting to explain how something was said. That dialogue is from *Popcorn* (Bradbury Press), a children's novel my wife and I wrote. But when we wrote the dialogue, we didn't use any adverbs, or any verbs, except *said,* a word so common and so easily understood that it sails right by without interrupting the dialogue.

Use *said* or no verb at all most of the time. Rarely use adverbs to describe dialogue, and only when necessary. Remember that 90% of your dialogue should contain its own tone of voice, and not require explaining. Your reader is no dummy. If you have given him a clear sense of who your character is and what he is experiencing, the reader will hear the tone of voice without your explaining.

Much will depend on the characterization you have done in other parts of the story, but one key to getting tone of voice into dialogue is to do what professional actors do when they work on lines. For each character, ask the questions, "What is my motivation?" and "What am I feeling as I speak these lines?" Often a writer throws lines of dialogue down on paper without really thinking about the emotions of the character. So, get inside the character's skin. Is he angry? Scared? Is he offended by what was just said? Amused? Is he trying to be clever, or is he trying to hurt someone's feelings, or make her laugh, or manipulate her? What is he trying to accomplish with these words that he is speaking? If you can feel what your character feels, your reader will probably hear what you hear.

Heavy-handed dialogue occurs when the reader can see the writer at work, loading the dialogue with a lot of information that just wouldn't come out in normal conversation. Most of the manuscripts I read were loaded with heavy-handed dialogue. Here's an example.

> "You and I stole ten thousand dollars, Sam. We embezzled it from the Valentine Corporation, and when Jervis inspects the books on June fifth he's going to know it. Your brother Warren is a lawyer and he's married to Valentine's sister. I say we tell him," Tony said.
>
> "We can't tell anybody. You're already on probation for beating up that guy at the Rainbow Lounge last summer, and how long do you think I would last as a cashier at Rockingham Race Track if they knew I stole ten thousand bucks on my last job?"

It's obvious that the dialogue is there not to inform the characters but because the writer wants to communicate it to the reader. The reader is annoyed, just as he would be if he could see how the magician was palming the cards.

Dialogue should be lean, and to the point. It should not be weighted down with details and background information.

There are two ways to solve the heavy-handed dialogue problem. One is to be direct, not devious. For example:

> Sam's brother was a lawyer and he was married to Valentine's sister.
>
> "We've got to tell your brother," Tony said. "He's the only one who can help us."

This doesn't disturb the reader because it implies what Tony was thinking. We will believe Tony was thinking about the fact that Sam's brother is a lawyer married to Valentine's sister. We won't believe that Tony would tell Sam things Sam obviously knows.

The other way to repair this heavy-handed dialogue is to be devious, but not direct.

You can get information across to readers in dialogue smoothly if you make the reader believe the character would say that. A speaker can believably repeat information the listener knows if the information answers a question, or requires emphasis. For example:

> "Ten thousand bucks, Sam, that's what we stole and I don't think the Valentine Corporation is going to overlook it when they find out."
>
> "How are they going to find out?"
>
> "Jervis is checking the books on June fifth. He'll spot it. We've got to tell your brother."
>
> "What the hell has my brother got to do with this?"
>
> "He's a lawyer, isn't he? He's married to Valentine's sister. He can get us off the hook."
>
> "No. We can't tell anybody."
>
> "Why not?"
>
> "You're already on probation for that fiasco at the Rainbow Lounge."
>
> "Look, I never beat that guy up. I was framed."
>
> "Doesn't matter. The court says you did it. And what about me? You think the Rockingham Race Track is going to be thrilled to find out one of their cashiers stole ten thousand dollars from his last employer?"

If a speaker is giving a listener information the listener doesn't *need*, then the speaker must have a *need* of his own. In my last example, Tony *needs* to convince Sam to tell Sam's brother. Sam *needs* to convince Tony to keep their secret. The important thing is that each speaker is speaking out of *his own need, not the need of his listener*. The dialogue becomes heavy-handed when the speaker starts throwing in known information that can't serve his need. For example, "Doesn't matter. The court says you did it. And what about me? Do you think Roz Bagley, my boss at the Rockingham Race Track in Salem, is going to be thrilled when she finds out that one her cashiers, along with you, stole ten thousand dollars last June from the Valentine Corporation?"

So when you hunt for heavy-handed dialogue to cut from your manuscript, ask yourself, "Is this information known to the listener?" If the answer is yes, ask, "Is repeating this information serving some need of my speaker?" If the answer is no, get rid of it, or rewrite it so that it does serve some need of your speaker.

Dialogue has a number of legitimate jobs. It moves the story forward. It characterizes people in the story. It provides information. But dialogue should never be used to fill up space on the page, to create scenes that could be replaced with a simple transition, or to cover ground that could be covered more quickly or more effectively with simple narrative. That's unnecessary dialogue.

One of the most common examples is dialogue in introductions.

> "Beverly, I'd like you to meet William Warner," Angie said. I reached out and shook Mr. Warner's hand.
>
> "Hi Beverly," he said, smiling.
>
> "And this young lady is Mr. Warner's secretary, Deanna Frost," Angie said, "Deanna, this is Beverly Conti."
>
> We shook hands. "Hi Deanna."
>
> "Hi," she said. "Nice to meet you."

Some writers do this every time one character is introduced to another throughout a novel. It's boring. Just write: "Angie introduced me to Mr. Warner and Deanna Frost, his secretary." Then get on with it.

Also don't have characters saying things if you can say them better yourself. To use an example from nonfiction, my book *Fatal Dosage* has Anne Capute, defendant in a murder trial, coming to the courthouse for the first time. I could have created dialogue like this:

> "The courthouse is kind of scary, isn't it?" she said to Pat. "It looks like a big granite monster that's going to gobble me up."

> "I suppose," Pat said, "but at a time like this everything is frightening."
>
> "Yes," she said, "even you. You look like you're on your way to accept an award. With your three-piece suit and your brief case, you're really one of them, aren't you?"
>
> "What do you think is in this brief case, Anne? The secrets of the bomb?"

I could have gone on like this and created an acceptable dialogue scene. But I wanted to create a sense of Anne's aloneness, her isolation even from her own lawyer, and I knew I could do it better than my characters could. So the dialogue was unnecessary. I wrote the scene this way:

> As Anne followed Pat Piscitelli along the courthouse path that sunny morning she trembled inside. She felt as if the courthouse were a huge granite monster waiting to gobble her up. The building was frightening. But then, she thought, everything is frightening. Even Pat, walking ahead of her in lively steps as if he were on his way to accept an award. He wore an expensive three-piece suit, and a brief case hung from his hand. He seemed to be one of "them" and that's what frightened her. The brief case reminded Anne of the man who follows the President around, carrying a brief case handcuffed to his wrist. The secrets of the bomb are in Pat's brief case, she thought, and she wondered who would win the war.

So, dialogue is unnecessary when it's used to do work that could be done by a simple sentence like, "Marie introduced me to her parents"; when it does work you could do more effectively another way; when it doesn't reveal character or move the story forward; and when there is no tension present in the scene, which I'll explain later.

When I first became a newspaper reporter, I had a bad habit of stating something, and then repeating it in quotes. Typically, I would write something like this:

Mayor Ferguson told the City council last night that he will not support the bond issue for a new recreation center.

"I've decided not to support the bond issue for the new recreation center," he told the packed council chambers.

Of course, I was getting paid by the column inch, so maybe my redundancy was making me richer. But that kind of redundancy in your dialogue, another common mistake, will only make you poorer. Here's an example from one of the manuscripts I read.

Holly had quit her job as a secretary to form her own company, Colorwear. She would take common sweatshirts and T-shirts and, with an airbrush and immense talent, turn them into works of art.

And then, a few pages later.

"I quit my secretary job to form my own company. It's called Colorwear."

"What do you do?" Paul asked.

"I do airbrush paintings on sweatshirts and T-shirts, that sort of thing."

One of those sections must go. Which one? It depends. If you just want to get some information across, some foundation for future story events, a few direct sentences of narrative will work best. If you're trying to show some conflict, some tension, some character, or something developing in a relationship, the dialogue will work best. The dialogue, of course, can accomplish both jobs, but it usually takes up more space. If you spend more words, you should get more work done. But remember, dialogue that only repeats information is doing no work at all.

Do you remember my conversations with Janet the waitress that opened this article? The first was boring and the second was not, because the first had no tension. I asked Janet what she did for a living, she told me and I said, "That's nice." There were no unanswered questions, nothing more for her to say, and no resulting conflict between us.

In the second conversation, I ridiculed her job. She had to defend herself. I had to support my previous statements. Eventually she would have had to criticize me. I would have had to insult her, and maybe we would have started throwing punches at each other. That's tension. What will she say to that? What will he answer? Will they slug each other? Tension makes the reader ask questions, and it makes him continue reading for the answers.

Whenever you write dialogue, tension should be present. It doesn't have to be two people on the verge of a fight. It could be two people in love, each trying to get the other to say it. It could be two people cracking a safe. It could be two people talking about almost anything, but an element of tension must be present in the scene for the dialogue to hold the reader.

Many writers write dialogue that has information, but no tension. Here's an example.

"I'm glad you made it," Ellen said when her mother arrived at the door. "I was getting worried."

Marge came in and dropped her bags on the floor. "I got tied up in traffic on the Connecticut Turnpike. It's a real mess today."

"Did you stop to eat?"

"Yes. I stopped at Burger King for one of those, what do you call them?"

"Whoppers," Ellen said. "They call them Whoppers."

The dialogue is believable, but it's not exciting. It doesn't fascinate the reader because it doesn't create questions in his mind. It doesn't make him worry or wonder about what happens next. Tension could be added to this scene in a variety of ways. You could put tension directly into the spoken words. For example:

"Well, you finally made it," Ellen said when her mother arrived at the door. "I was getting worried. I wish you had at least called."

"Called? How I am going to call when I'm stuck in the middle of the Connecticut Turnpike? It's murder out there."

"Well, I hope you at least had enough sense to stop and eat. You know how your blood sugar is."

"I ate, I ate."

"Where, Ma, where did you eat?"

"I stopped at Burger King. I had one of those Big Macs."

"Whoppers, Ma, Whoppers, that's what they call them. Big Macs are at McDonald's."

"OK, so I had a Whopper."

In that example, the tension is between the characters and it comes out in the words they speak, the dialogue. However, tension in a dialogue scene doesn't have to be in the dialogue. In this next example I will leave the dialogue just as it was originally but I will increase reader interest by adding tension between the lines of dialogue. Also, I will change the source of the tension to show you that the two characters don't have to be antagonistic toward each other.

"I'm glad you made it," Ellen said when her mother arrived at the door. "I was getting worried."

Marge came in and dropped her bags on the floor. She stood by the counter as if she needed it to hold herself up and she took deep breaths. For the first time she looked old, frail. The light had gone from her eyes. Ellen's heart pounded.

"I got tied up in traffic on the Connecticut Turnpike. It's a real mess today," Marge said when she finally caught her breath.

"Did you stop to eat?"

"Yes, I stopped at Burger King for one of those, what do you call them?"

"Whoppers," Ellen said impatiently. "They call them Whoppers." Tonight she would cook, she thought, cook her mother a good healthful meal, and then everything would be all right.

So tension is that quality of "something else going on" during the dialogue. It's what makes the reader concerned enough to keep reading even when the actual spoken words are mundane. Remember, if the reader doesn't care what happens next, the dialogue is not working.

There's no absolute rule about when you use dialogue and when you shouldn't, but here's a good generalization: If a stranger were nearby, would he try to eavesdrop on the conversation? If the answer is no, don't use the dialogue. If the answer is yes, use it. And you can quote me on that.

The Set Up
Rita Schepok

Situation: A grandmother has set up her teenaged granddaughter with a neighbour's son. After the date, the girl describes the boy to her mother. A short time afterward, the grandmother telephones to give her impression of the boy to the girl's mother.

Mom, I'm never going to let grandma set me up with someone again. I should have known it was a risk in the first place. You should have seen the guy. Seriously mom, he was an absolute wimp. He actually wore a hideous, outdated three piece suit to go to McDonald's. I was so embarrassed. The entire time I prayed that nobody I knew would come in. What a klutz. After dropping one milkshake on the floor, he dribbled the other down his disgusting orange tie. You couldn't tell though, because it blended in with the polka dots. He wore those thick glasses too, you know, the kind that look like telescopes. All he talked about was chess, the math league, and the theory of relativity. Boring! What a twit. After we ate, he asked me if I wanted to go to his house to examine the rat he was in the process of dissecting. I almost threw up but he beat me to it. Yeah mom, he actually gagged and threw up right on the sidewalk. I'm not surprised because he ate like a complete swine. I wondered how a lanky guy like him could eat so much. He attempted to kiss me goodbye but I was repulsed by the piece of lettuce between his front teeth so I refused. Yuck. I don't want to talk about it anymore. It's an experience I'd rather forget. I never want to see him again.

[*And now for the subsequent call from grand-ma . . .*]

Oh, he's a wonderful boy. He dresses very nicely and is quite intelligent. I knew the two of them would have a terrific time. He is such a gentleman, as well. I had him for dinner once and he behaved perfectly. That boy has wonderful manners and he is extremely polite. He eats rather moderately though, quite odd for a boy his age. He is quite a conversationalist and I could speak with him for hours without losing interest. He is a nice looking boy with a nice build. He does wear glasses but they make him look extremely debonair and intellectual. He is involved in many exciting school leagues. That boy has such spirit! I also understand he is interested in biology and is working on complicated projects at home. Nothing pleases me more than a neat young man with intelligence. I would love to see him going steady with my only grandchild. It would make me so proud. They had such an enjoyable afternoon that I arranged another date for next Saturday. Remember though, it can't be too late because he is expected home when the streetlights turn on. Such a responsible boy. Well dear, make sure you let her know he'll be by on his scooter-board at approximately 1:00. Bye now!

The Opera Experience

Beth Singleton

A "cultured" grandmother takes her young teen-age grandson to the opera. They confide in their mother/daughter about their reactions.

Son: Mother, I'm never going to another opera in my entire life. It was the most boring experience I have ever had. The people had huge mouths that belted out these agonizing moans. It was torture, mum. It was disgusting. I mean, the audience's hair was flying back from the force of those groans. It was awful. How can Grandma find it entertaining? Really mum, it sounded like a sacrifice of wailing pigs. And they looked like pigs, too! They must have had to really reinforce the stage because the moaners were so fat. And grandma complains about the lyrics in *my* songs. It sounded to me like they were making up the words as they went along, until the lady behind us started singing, too. It was bad enough having the performers belt out that noise but when the moaner behind us started going at it, it was the ultimate. I ended up going to the bathroom about a hundred times because I couldn't wait to get out. When we finally left, my ears were ringing and I had a really major headache. I can't ever go again. Please tell Grandma for me.

Grandmother: Oh dear, that was the most dynamic rendition of that opera I've ever heard. I'm so glad that I brought Kevin. The singers had such a flare; such stage presence. Kevin seemed so overwhelmed at points that he would put his head back, close his eyes and try to absorb the atmosphere. He seems destined to be in the opera. He certainly appreciated the performers' artistic talents. I was so surprised because I wasn't sure if he would enjoy himself. And the lady behind us had such a gift. She was humming to the music with such fine intonation that it was almost as though she were one of the performers. The opera is so different from what he usually listens to, but I'm sure he'd enjoy going again. I know it's been a while since the family has had season's tickets but this year I'm sure it will be worth it. Oh, I'm so anxious to take Kevin again. It gives me such a thrill to see my grandson interested in the finer activities. I hope there is another opera soon.

A Grim Fairy Tale

David Suzuki

My daughters love the Royal Ontario Museum in Toronto. Fortunately, their dad never tires of it either. Our favourite displays, of course, are the dinosaurs and other prehistoric animals. The other day as we approached the awesome display of *Megaceros giganteus*, the long-extinct Irish elk with its spectacular antlers, Severn marvelled at their size and asked what happened to them. Taking a bit of paleontological liberty, I told her the following story.

Thousands of years ago, one gargantuan bull elk ruled all of the others of his species throughout Europe. He was the most magnificent elk ever known, with an immense set of antlers, a powerful bellowing voice and a majestic muscular body. And as he strode across the vast plains, the ground shook and all the other elks trembled with fear and envy. With his strength and antlers, he was invincible, overwhelming any who dared challenge his power. Those who shared his territory accepted his authority. Each day, he surveyed a different part of the vast expanse of his range.

One day, he ventured further than he had ever gone, beyond his own terrain. But he was confident in his might; after all, his antlers were the greatest weapons ever developed. Presently, he spotted another elk in the distance. "Who could be so impudent to encroach on my turf?" he wondered and hurried toward the figure. He recognized him as a stranger by the colour of his fur. The foreigner was every bit as big and carried a set of antlers as impressive as his own. Trembling with fear and rage, he ran at the stranger and bellowed with all his might, "This is my territory! *I* rule it! Submit, back away or be destroyed!" He was shocked to hear a reply that rang through the air, "No, this is *my* land and *you* are trespassing! *I* am the commander here!" Pawing the ground and shaking their antlers, the two giants stood facing each other, threatening and yelling all day while the smaller elks caught between them cringed in fear of being crushed by these superb animals. When night fell, the two bulls retreated to their respective camps and called for their scientists and engineers.

"I have met a mighty force," each told his respective minions, "and I need reinforcements, an advantage to overcome my enemy's strength. Do everything you can or else he will overwhelm me and subjugate you in slavery." And so a great effort was made. One had many long, sharp spines added to his antlers to stab his opponent, while the other had a large, heavy club placed up front to deliver a knockout blow. The next day the two stags hurried back to the border only to discover the ingenious changes added to each other's antlers overnight. Once again, they stood shaking and roaring but each fearing the other's possible advantage. When night fell, they rushed back for additional reinforcements and defences against the enemy's clever inventions. Antlers were armoured with flat surfaces to blunt the other's blows and embellishments were added at the edges to probe other weaknesses in the defensive shield.

And so it continued day after day. Each night, the bulls required more help and demanded that those under their control contribute more resources, muscle power and imagination, for victory by the other male brought terrifying possibilities. But each new addition to those giant antlers had other repercussions. The weight of the racks was so great that the bulls' necks had to be shored up with muscle and bone. But now they couldn't turn their heads as quickly and so they needed other elk to provide an early warning of danger and possibly even absorb the first blow. Legs had to be increased in diameter to support the massive weight and to generate the driving power to wield the antlers. Their bodies were increased in girth to provide more lung power and stomach volume to fuel the muscles. More and more material, effort and creativity went into supporting those magnificent antlers.

Inevitably, rumbles of discontent spread from the lower ranks of elk. "Those antlers are draining resources from everything else," they grumbled. "Wouldn't it be better to sit down and discuss a way to co-exist, perhaps share space, and maybe even co-operate?" some suggested. But the two males bellowed at such treachery. "How dare you consider co-existence with a tyrant? The best protection is a superior offensive capacity and an invincible defence. We have to develop cleverer ways to gain an advantage." And when one asked, "Is it worth the expense?" both of the great elks replied, "Of course it is! There will be enormous spin-offs. You'll have more shade from my antlers on hot days and birds will find greater space to perch on." And so it went. Each new development led inevitably to more complex and contrived inventions. Those antlers were an obsession to the two bulls and came to dominate every other elk's life.

"And then what happened, daddy?" asked Sarika, my three-year-old.

"Well, dear," I replied, "eventually the smaller elks realized that the two opponents had put all their faith in massive antlers that looked impressive but were completely unreliable and impractical. So they simply left the two giants alone to roar and threaten each other. Eventually the sheer weight and cost of those antlers broke their backs and both of them died. The other elk were grateful that they hadn't developed such useless structures —their antlers were quite big enough. So they lived together in herds and turned their attention to the important business of living."

"Oh," said Severn, "and that's why Canada shouldn't get involved in Star Wars?"

"Yes, sweetheart," I said. Even a six-year-old can see the obvious.

CHAPTER
Five

Writing Non-Fiction Prose

A. FORE-WORDS

Warm up for the activities in this chapter by discussion and writing. These quotations and questions may help you begin.

Pierre Berton   "I'm an old newspaper man. . . . By the time I get to the typewriter, the book has written itself in my head."

Rudyard Kipling   "I keep six honest serving men/(They taught me all I knew)/Their names are What and Why and When/And How and Where and Who."

William Zinsser   "People and places are the twin pillars on which most non-fiction is built."

1.   In your Writer's Notebook, freewrite about your past experience with non-fiction.

2.   Brainstorm types of non-fiction you'd find in a search of your home.

3.   Recount a true family story that you consider newsworthy.

B. FOUNDATIONS

Learning to write contemporary non-fiction makes good sense. The essay is the genre you're most likely to encounter in post-secondary experience—at university or college, on the job, or in day-to-day living. And it doesn't have to be like eating liver—good for you, but not your favourite fare.

If non-fiction conjures up images of stuffy analysis and dry reports, take a closer look. Chances are you encounter lively non-fiction every day; media news broadcasts, daily sports, magazine interviews with favourite groups and personalities—all are popular non-fiction. As you probably discovered in Chapter Four, captivating stories are often about real people and events.

In this chapter, you'll prepare non-fiction suitable for publication in a newspaper or newsmagazine. With this practical focus, you'll refine skills required to compose standard academic essays, reviews, and reports *and* enjoy the challenges of teamwork. You'll practise writing both objectively and persuasively—writing to inform, amuse, persuade, reflect, and illuminate. And you'll create an imaginative product as well.

From time to time, Tarvo, Kirsten, Sasha, and Craig will recount their experiences publishing a school newspaper. You may follow a similar process or adapt ideas to your requirements. For instance, if teamwork is inappropriate or publication facilities unavailable, create a personal mini-publication, or simply complete activities, omitting the publication step.

Tarvo and the other students got started with a little community assistance. Here's what happened.

Setting: A career planning assembly. The communications officer from a local media firm explains her company's new Adopt-a-School program. Students are encouraged to consult employees about skills needed for their positions. In some cases, on-the-job experience and class speakers may be arranged. Students are leaving the assembly . . .

Craig: Great idea, you know. I'd sure like to see a newsroom.
Sasha: Maybe we could all go.
Tarvo: I bet she'd give us some leads for our publishing project.
Kirsten: Let's hope so. We need some advice on getting started.
Sasha: Maybe we could talk to a couple of the students on this *Fresh Perspective* newspaper Tarvo found. Look at this . . . . [See page 204]

After consultation, the students decided to publish a school newspaper, along with other classmates. They prepared a proposal form specifying details such as audience, editorial policy, departments, and staffing for their instructor's approval.

Be A

Fresh Perspective INTERN

When you enroll in the *Fresh Perspective* Internship Program, you get meaningful, practical training and experience in basic reporting. You get:
- an intensive, six-day journalism training program!
- a practical, three-day photography course!
- a personal mentor—a professional working in our area of interest—to give you advice and guidance!
- a chance to be a *Fresh Perspective* Section Editor or Co-Editor!

The training's FREE—but you must make a commitment:
- to work on *Fresh Perspective* for the 1987-88 school year
- to attend weekly editorial meetings
- to meet deadlines and follow through on commitments

JOURNALISM INTERNS
Course runs Oct. 27 to Nov. 5; Tues., Wed., and Thurs., 4:30 p.m. to 7:30 p.m.

PHOTOGRAPHY INTERNS
Two sessions: Nov. 10, 11 & 12, 4:30 p.m. to 7:30 p.m.
Nov. 17, 18 & 19, 4:30 p.m. to 7:30 p.m.
Each session is limited to four persons.

ADVERTISING INTERNS
A course has not been established. You will be trained by youth advertising sales staff and a personal mentor. Call 592-9003 for an interview. This is considered a part-time job.

TO REGISTER, CALL PAT AT 592-9003.
Bring a lunch to evening classes.
All classes held at
Youth Communication / Toronto, 312 Adelaide St. W., Suite 205A,
Toronto M5V 1R2

By permission of *Fresh Perspective* (October, 1987)

Like these students, you'll need to make basic decisions. Are you planning a newsmagazine, a newspaper, or a hybrid? If the student body is your audience, how will you adapt material to meet varied needs and interests? You'll answer these and related questions as you complete preliminary activities.

Before you begin, this excerpt from George Crabbe's "The Newspaper," written in the early nineteenth century, may set the mood for your exploration.

> I sing of news and all those vapid sheets
> The rattling hawker vends through gaping streets;
> Whate'er their name, whate'er the time they fly,
> Damp from the press, to charm the reader's eye:

Activity One   Making Decisions About Non-Fiction
Purpose

- to compare periodicals' language, audience, and content

- to decide on a class/group publication (optional)

- to begin housekeeping details

1.   Discuss favourite newspapers and magazines. Predict which newspaper sells most widely in your community. Consider the implications of these questions for a class publishing venture.

2.   Imagine you are an entrepreneur publishing a new periodical in today's competitive market. In your Writer's Notebook, reflect on necessary decisions (e.g., audience, content). Exchange ideas in class discussion.

3.   In pairs or small groups, familiarize yourself with newspapers and news-magazines available in your community.
a.   How do periodicals differ in purpose, target audience, content, visual appeal, advertising, format, and language?
b.   In your Writer's Notebook, freewrite about the appeal of specific publications.
c.   Prepare a composite portrait of one publication's typical reader, focusing on education, interests, age, income, and marital status.

4.   What philosophical and practical issues do the following statements raise about your venture? Jot points in your notebook.

Albert Camus   "A free press can, of course, be good or bad, but most certainly, without freedom it will never be anything but bad . . . "

Thomas Fuller   "Even doubtful accusations leave a stain behind them."

Allan J. Lerner   "Men die but an idea does not."

John Locke   "New opinions are always suspected, and usually opposed, without any other reason but because they are not already common."

Henry David Thoreau   "Any man more right than his neighbours constitutes a majority of one."

Oscar Wilde   "There is no such thing as a moral or immoral book. Books are well written or badly written."

5a.   Co-write a (publishing) proposal in an informative style. Ask your instructor for guidelines. (*Tip:* Students with word processing facilities may wish to organize their files according to the categories set out in the proposal.)
b.   Freewrite about the experience of staffing your press, noting problems in need of attention. Speculate on solutions.

Before moving on to the peculiarities of journalism, refresh your knowledge about key concerns highlighted in the questions below. You may also wish to consult Workshop Supplement Writer's Resource Five, and Chapters Two and Three.

SASHA'S QUESTION   *How can we build smooth transitions?*

Use transitional devices to

- clarify the relationship between paragraphs

- show the reader logical connections

Techniques

- Refer to information in your preceding paragraph. For example, in paragraph one, explain that you "tinker" with old cars; then begin paragraph two like this, "An interesting aspect of tinkering with old cars . . ."

- Repeat at the beginning of a paragraph a word used at or near the end of the preceding one. For example, the last sentence in paragraph one reads " . . . in all old German cars" and the first sentence in the next paragraph begins "Antique German cars . . ."

- Use connectives. Examples are, *similarly, in contrast, otherwise, for example, as discussed, also, in addition, nevertheless, meanwhile, at the same time, consequently, for this reason, first, second.*

KIRSTEN'S QUESTION   *When should I use quotations?*

Use quotations to

- show support for your idea or provide another reason

- disagree with someone and go on to make your opposing argument

- unify your work
- reinforce the ending
- build a strong title.

TARVO'S QUESTIONS Does the thesis or main idea always appear in paragraph one? When can I use a one-sentence paragraph?

That depends on the type of non-fiction you're writing. The thesis generally appears in paragraph one of scholarly essays and reviews, though not always. Paragraph length is also determined by the type of non-fiction you are writing. Formal or scholarly essays exhibit longer paragraphs than the average news story.

CRAIG'S QUESTION In what types of non-fiction are narrative techniques appropriate?

You're usually free to experiment with techniques such as dialogue, anecdotes, and characterization in informal writing. In formal scholarly essays, which demand objectivity and detachment, these techniques are usually inappropriate. Quotations from authorities and your own crisp style are always suitable, however.

KIRSTEN'S QUESTION Where can I find a sample of a serious essay which is not stiff sounding or ponderous?

What follows is a reflective essay by writer's craft student Blair Martin. It is an example of the kind of essay Kirsten is requesting. Listen for tone and transitions, and assess its overall effectiveness.

Le Piste

If I have given you delight
By aught that I have done,
Let me lie quiet in that night
Which shall be yours anon.

And for the little, little span
The dead are borne in mind,
Seek not to question other than
The books I leave behind.

Rudyard Kipling left behind the epitaph quoted above to his life and work, the thousands of pages and hours of thought. It is both the gift and the curse of those addicted to the command, "Write!" Slaves to ourselves, we must hammer and scratch with pens until we can say, "It's almost right." A small pile of plain paper and ink sits before us. But if we can coax life and emotion out of those sheets then we will have succeeded. At least until the desire comes to collect again. The experience can be both a source of pride and painful frustration. My career as a high-school poet has been, like most writers', a manic depression of elation and inadequacy.

Writing thrives on discipline. It requires patience and a commitment never to leave a page blank. Often I've stared at my pen, willing the ink to run of its own accord. Strangely, it never seems to work. Although it is always easier to write only when the pen is alive, mediocre work during a dry spell is infinitely more productive than naked pages. Not only does this speed up the process (which is especially important the night before your essay is due) but it also builds a rhythm for you, a pattern to slip into the next time.

My own rhythm rarely changes. To begin, I concentrate all my thoughts on one idea until the faint traces of sentences touch the edges of my mind. A particular word or phrase which appeals to me will form the nucleus of my sentence. I then weave others around it, incorporating them all into a paragraph. Sustaining a high level of intensity throughout the work is perhaps the hardest challenge, impossible on the first draft. Teachers repeatedly scrawl "revise" on my writing. The encouragement to slave for this refined quality can only be burned into your work if you have a need to write in your blood, too hot to ignore.

Canadian author Farley Mowat has written, "read and write, like one possessed. And don't bother at all unless you've got the fire in your gut." You must have a voice inside, kicking and screaming above the thunder of normalcy. I was ten when I began to hear. Hiding under the covers with a flashlight, I read a 1928 copy of *All Quiet on the Western Front*. The yellowed pages were alive, physical, pushing me into my other self. I knew. I knew that I had been captured by those misty faces hovering just behind those old pages. Since then, I have read, scouring books for elements of style that attracted me and packaging them off to the dusty recesses of my mind for later use. I have learned it is not a sin to walk on someone else's path; read and learn from their success.

Writing, good writing, is one of the most difficult tasks we can set for ourselves. It demands a thorough knowledge of the mechanics of English as well as natural flair and desire. This desire is the curse of the writer, the back-breaking self-destruction that is never satisfied or satiated. But if you accept the loneliness and the revelations that writing brings, then you will reap the rewards only writing can give. And you will not be forgotten.

Before beginning Activity Two, read the excerpt from Catherine Bauer's "The Essay Is Alive and Well" printed below. Then work through the exercises which reinforce knowledge of essay style and structure.

. . . Today, over three hundred years [after Montaigne created the essay form], the essay is alive and well. Montaigne's intimate personal essays became the model for the informal familiar essay.

Continuing in the essay tradition today are Joan Didion, Lewis Thomas, Edward Hoagland, Nora Ephron, and Lewis Lapham, all with books in print. As well, personal essays appear in many current periodicals, and many syndicated columns are essays.

The informal conversational style of a personal essay is highly individualized and reflects the fact that all people are different. The essay's contents reveal the author's likes and dislikes, whims and prejudices to the extent that the reader feels he has met and chatted with the writer.

An essay may be the prose of a mood; always it is an act of personal disclosure. E.B. White, one of the best and most widely read essayists of our time, has said, "One thing an essayist cannot do, he cannot indulge himself in deceit or concealment, for he will be found out in no time." He notes that Montaigne possessed the gift of natural candor, and regards it as a primary contributing factor to that writer's popularity.

A personal essay can deal with situations, events, places, or things which are amusing, annoying, pleasing, dangerous, or ridiculous. It may be satirical, serious, provocative, controversial, humorous, philosophical, or a combination of these things. Usually an essay has a light touch; often it has a captivating rhythm. . . .

Scrutinize your environment to find situations, attitudes, institutions, events, and people. Then select a topic and examine your attitudes toward it. Don't be surprised if you discover new topics as your write. . . .

Style is the life of the essay and style reflects your unique perception of the topic. Be original in expressing yourself: use good figures of speech acquired from your own observation of life. Strong, striking imagery coloured with emotion, rather than big words, gives effectiveness and power to your writing.

Make comparisons, both literal and figurative; writers who use comparisons increase . . . vividness. Use anecdotes and dialogue. Set aside fear and conformity as you employ the spontaneous natural language of conversation.

Finally, shape your presentation. An essay has structure; it shouldn't just ramble. It should have an intriguing opening, build to a climax, and be carried smoothly to a convincing conclusion.

Activity Two   Reviewing Essay Style and Structure
Purpose

- to review the essay—format, style, and structure

- to refine thesis-writing skills

- to review the continuum of formal-informal writing

1a.   After reviewing guidelines on page 390, précis Bauer's advice in approximately 150 words.

b.   In conference with a partner, assess the précis using criteria from page 390 or those developed by your class.

2.   Working with a partner:

a.   Read aloud the excerpt from June Callwood's informal article, "Summer Musings on the Abuses of the Lowly Toe," printed below. Which two of the normal structural components of the essay have been omitted? Co-write the two missing paragraphs.

b.   Do Martin's and Callwood's essays follow Bauer's advice, as well as expressing the writers' voices? Justify with textual references.

Summer Musings on the Abuses of the Lowly Toe

Despite their frivolous look, toes are highly functional. By a miracle of balance, the upright human being stands on narrow tripods extending from the heel to the great and next-to-great toes. When a person is erect, the toes carry between 5 and 10 percent of the forefoot load on the metatarsal heads and extend the weight-bearing area of the foot by a helpful inch or two. Toes are most useful, however, when involved in the kinetic chain of movement which produces walking. At the point of highest flex, when the pedestrian's weight has rolled from the heel to the flat stance position and is heaving forward to the ball of the foot, the toes assist in the springy action of the push-off and take one-third of the person's load.

Toes are also essential for maintaining balance. If someone is lightly pushed from behind, toes reflexively will tighten to brace the foot. They absorb one-quarter of the body weight that suddenly has shifted to the front of the foot and thereby help save the person from toppling.

Toes are only beginning to gain the respect they merit. Orthopedic training programs tend to dismiss foot pathology with two or three lectures, though orthopedists spend one-fifth of their time looking at feet. Complaining of this singular lack of preparation, Dr. Melvin Jahas of Mount Sinai Hospital in New York wrote scathingly that the skin of the foot is made up of a thick layer of dermis and epidermis "and an even thicker layer of orthopedic ignorance."

In the past, orthopedic surgeons had the imperial inclination to solve foot problems by cutting off any toe that offended. A common treatment for persistent corns on the lesser or baby toe was to amputate or fillet the toe. While the surgery was an unqualified success at removing corns, patients complained that they were tippy afterwards. Eventually doctors realized that even the absurd baby toe has a serious role in maintaining balance. People who have more than one toe amputated must substitute a prosthesis in their shoe to compensate for the loss.

Toenails are another matter. They are the vestigial remains of the human being's intrepid ancestors who needed nails to forage for food, defend themselves and climb trees. Their present purpose is unclear. One theory holds that nails offer protection for the precious sense of touch. Nails are composed of keratin, water, and minute quantities of other ingredients, including a dash of arsenic. They grow more quickly in summer than in winter, grow at an uneven rate (the middle digit being the most energetic) and account for most visits to foot specialists. One survey of 12,000 patients of podiatrists found that 7,402 of them had nail disorders.

Old people have particular problems with toenails because they aren't supple enough to reach their toes easily. Their toenails tend to thicken, the extreme manifestation of which is called ram's horn. Trimming toenails is especially difficult for arthritic hands, which is why one of the exquisite pleasures of old age is the gift of a warm footbath and a pedicure.

The names of the ailments to which toes are vulnerable are graphic: hammertoes, claw toes, curly toes and overlapping toes. Few of these deformities are genetic; they are acquired by adults wearing too-tight shoes or too-short socks or hose made of artificial fibre. All feet change size during a tiring day, becoming puffy and wider toward evening, but few shoes accommodate this alteration. At day's end, the unhappy toes are bunched together in miserable disarray that can ossify if it is continuous. Sometimes surgery is required to restore order.

Toes are a feminist issue. Shoes with high heels and pointed toes are arousing to men, but it is significant that few men wear them. The damage high heels cause to toes fills foot clinics, making them almost sororities. High heels displace body weight and cause the wearying foot to slide to the front of the shoe, with the woman's entire weight pressing on the toes. Doctors and podiatrists agree that high heels are a major cause of toenail disorders and painful corns.

Female babies develop their toes more rapidly in the womb than do male babies, possibly in response to some sense of alarm at what lies ahead. A baby boy's littlest piggy doesn't have a bone in it until he is 7 months old. Humans are more interested in their toes when they are 6 months old than they ever will be again.

Ingrown toenails are caused by rounding off the corners of the nail prettily instead of cutting it straight across. Everyone knows this, but people round their toenails anyway because to do otherwise snags socks and inflicts serious wounds on bed-partners. Don't doze off; this is important stuff. Dr. Leslie Kenerman, an English orthopedic surgeon, cleared up much of the confusion about the clandestine activities of toes when he wrote penetratingly that "the movement of toes lies in dorsiflexion rather than plantarflexion."

Toes are smarter than they look. People who are armless learn to handle a knife and fork with their toes and also use them to write, paint a landscape and knit a hat.

3a.   Draft an informal interpretive essay for your writing folder. In conference with a partner, assess your work using a class criteria checklist or the one on page 389. Scrutinize the thesis with special care. Does it pass the tests of significance and clarity set out in Writer's Resource Five? For additional practice with thesis construction, complete parts b. and c. with a partner.

b.   Rate each of the following statements on a scale of 1 (low) to 7 (high) for its effectiveness as a thesis. Justify each rating. The statements are answers to the question, "What career is most suited to your interests and abilities?"

- Engineering is a field which meets my needs.

- I'd really like to be an engineer because my sister is one and she's very successful.

- A career in chemical engineering research is ideally suited to my academic strengths and personal interests; I'm mathematically inclined and enjoy nothing more than problem-solving through experimentation.

- Why do I want to be an engineer? Let me tell you.

c.   For three of the questions listed below, draft thesis statements for informal essays. Exchange work with a partner and assess the quality of each thesis statement, using the 1-7 scale. Justify each rating to the writer. Revise if necessary and/or invite a second response.

- What personal qualities help an athlete succeed?

- What steps could a junior student take to plan career goals?

- How do you ready yourself to compose?

- According to what criteria can a book or film be assessed?

- How can educational institutions encourage independence of mind and habit among the student body?

4a.   What clues suggest "The Creative Approach" (page 249) is a more formal essay than Martin's or Callwood's? Identify techniques the writer has used to keep the essay "light" without undermining its serious intent.
b.   Does this essay follow Bauer's advice?

5a.   Draft a formal interpretive essay for your writing folder, employing sound techniques of structure and style.
b.   Repeat steps outlined in question 3a.

6a.   In conference with a partner, reflect on the development of your essay writing skills over the past several years. Summarize your discussion in your Writer's Notebook.
b.   Students with word processing facilities may wish to create a database of criteria checklists suitable for measuring the growth of junior writers' essay skills.

Now let's move on to the next step in your non-fiction project—documenting your experience.

Recording Your Venture

You may wish to record your publishing venture, and perhaps print journal excerpts. Tom Parkin's journal entries, quoted in his article, "An Outdoor Journal" (page 248), concern a completely different type of adventure but may spark your enthusiasm.

Regardless of whether you decide to chronicle your experiences, you'll need a grounding in fundamentals of journalism. Following the steps of Tarvo and his classmates will get you started.

First, they explored a variety of structures in contemporary journalism and compared them to the classic essay format. They observed that scholarly essays often resemble the structure of a hamburger. The sliced bun represents the introduction (including a thesis statement) and the conclusion, which hold together the "meat" or body of the essay.

On the other hand, standard news story form generally resembles an inverted pyramid. At the top (the widest part of the triangle) stands the *lead*— the opening sentence reporting key facts. The lead answers one or more of the story's who, what, when, where, why, and how. In fact, the lead *is* the story in condensed form. Subsequent sentences add supporting facts and interesting, but non-essential, details. Finally, peripheral details end the story. This format grew up at the turn of the century for reasons of space; the rewrite editor "clipped," starting with the final paragraph.

Other aspects of journalistic format were also born of practical considerations. The newspaper reader can quickly skim the lead, digest the story's gist, and move on to another piece. Short paragraphs also facilitate skim-reading.

However, not all news stories assume the standard form. Interpretive and expansive pieces—feature articles, columns, reviews, editorials—usually blend elements from classic or academic essay forms with inverted pyramid form. And news magazine articles, often written at a more leisurely pace than daily newspaper reports, diverge as well. In this modified pyramid, the lead "sets up" the storyline; then the story doubles back, narrating the chronology throughout the body. If the lead is too bulky for one sentence, the writer may extend introductory facts—perhaps through more than one paragraph.

You'll notice the lead is a constant in journalism. It grabs the reader's attention, functioning like a short story's narrative hook. Lyn Hancock, author of popular non-fiction stories about animals and travel, offered the following ideas for types of leads when she served as Writer-in-Residence. A lead may be a

- question, anecdote, or piece of dialogue

- quotation, exclamation, or an unusual twist

- shocking or contrasting statement, exaggeration, or arresting language (pun or alliteration)

- definition or explanation.

Parody, epigram, addressing the reader directly ("you"), or literary allusion may also work well.

Leads may also be classified according to the information conveyed. In *Mass Media Journalism*, Moynes and White suggest these classifications: that the *major lead* give only the most important fact of the report; that the *summary* lead blend information of equal importance; that a combination or feature summary lead begin the sentence with the major idea but then elaborate with other facts.

As a class, discuss how the lead's form and content influence audience reaction. When is one approach most valuable? In Activity Three, refine your understanding of leads. But first, consider these tips and tidbits from other journalists.

- Jack Sampson, author of *Successful Outdoor Writing*, favours the use of the active voice and vivid, forceful verbs: ". . . put the 'angle' or substance of the news into the main clause," not in a subordinate clause.

- J.N. Hook, author of *Writing Creatively*, notes that a good headline summarizes a news story in the form of a statement and contains a verb (sometimes only implied).

"News" for a school paper, according to Hook, should meet these criteria:

- Is it *appropriate*—interesting and relevant—for the readers?

- Is it *timely*? (Old news may be dead news.)

- Is it *important* to the readers' lives?

Now, extend and apply these fundamentals of journalism in Activity Three.

Activity Three   Sharpening Tools of the Trade
Purpose

- to write a variety of lead forms and headlines

- to examine and apply the inverted pyramid form

- to recognize "news" in school, community, and society

1.   For each lead sentence or paragraph identify the technique(s) used, label its "Six Honest Serving Men" (5W's and the H), and assess its effectiveness as a narrative hook.

- "On Monday, at 1:05 pm, a slightly stooping, apparently serene Klaus Barbie stepped into the dock of the Rhône Criminal Court in Lyons."

- "Puffs of smoke rise from a surgical opening in the head of a patient stretched out on the operating table."

- "Adolescence is a little like cooking with a new recipe."

- "Science provides a unique way of describing the world around us. Its basic methodology is to focus on one aspect of nature, isolating it from all else, controlling everything impinging on it and measuring everything that happens."

- "Rock 'n' roll. It was pioneered by the likes of Elvis Presley, Little Richard, and Jerry Lee Lewis. They sang about and for youth. They gave youth a voice and parents didn't like it. It was loud, noisy garbage, they said, that made their kids rowdy and rebellious."

2.   Practise composing leads. You may wish to work with articles in today's newspaper, an essay in your writing folder, anecdotes from Chapter Four, or freewriting from your Writer's Notebook.

3a.   Examine headlines in a recent newspaper. How many contain verbs or "and" "a," "an," and "the"?
b.   Practise writing headlines for the leads composed in question 2.

4.   How do the formats, or structures, of front page stories, features, columns, reviews, and editorials differ from one another?

5a.   Identify a dozen newsworthy events of interest to your classmates. Test your predictions by surveying peers' reactions.
b.   Draft a 350-word inverted pyramid report for the front page of a school paper or a publication of your choice. Use a neutral informative style. You might report on:

- an event at school (e.g., a sports meet, dance, concert, debate, speaker, or birthday celebration in the cafeteria)

- a historical event

- a community event.

Label the who, when, why, where (page 213) and the type of lead employed.

6a.   Working with a partner, comment on each other's drafts, noting evidence of showing, not telling, and detached, objective reporting.
b.   Write several new leads for each other's reports. How does each lead alter the reports' impact? Which do you prefer? Why?

You may wish to read "Making Your Article Leads Sparkle" (page 235) before moving on to the next step—a review of the concept of impartiality or objectivity raised in Chapter Two.

Completing Activity Three may raise problems such as those dramatized below.

Kirsten: I didn't use a value judgement. There's not one opinion.
Craig: Come on. You wrote, "she said with glee"—you're indicating an attitude. Say "she laughed."
Sasha: Craig, by not reporting a tornado, *you're* distorting why everyone stayed home from the dance. By omission you're implying . . .
Craig: —Okay, okay . . . we need to work on this, I guess.

By "this" Craig means objectivity and the difficulty of achieving it. Frank Luther Mott in *News in America* makes the following comments about this problem:

The term [objectivity] is doubtless unfortunate. It means, of course, reports which are written or broadcast without any bias or influence from the opinions of the reporter or editor, as opposed to subjective news, which would be controlled and presumably distorted by the ideas and views of the reporter and editor.
    The trouble is that complete objectivity, in this sense, would never be possible, even for a robot to achieve, for there must be some mind behind the creation of the robot. News is gathered, written, edited, and distributed by human beings, all of whom have certain ideas, feelings, attitudes, opinions and prejudices . . .

Nonetheless, in a basic news story, the reporter strives for impartiality. In Activity Four, you'll explore common pitfalls of writing "front page" news objectively and compare it with persuasive writing. Before you begin, read "Is Objectivity Possible?" (page 257).

Activity Four   Reporting Versus Persuading and Interpreting

Purpose

- to review the concepts of impartial and subjective writing
- to distinguish between evaluative, attributive, and particularizing diction in written and oral delivery

Note: This Activity builds on Chapter Three, Activities Three and Four, and on this chapter's Activity Three.

1.   In conference with a partner, review diction in your draft from Activity Three, question 5b., labelling instances of evaluative, attributive, and particu-

larizing diction (page 119). If necessary, revise to include only the facts.

2.   How does "Covering Refugees with Figures of Speech" by Karim H. Karim (page 247) underscore the importance of reportorial objectivity?

3.   Debate resolutions about media objectivity. You might consider ideas such as these:

• Objectivity in a pure sense is impossible in the hectic world of day-to-day reporting.

• A free press is an unbiased press.

• Learning about attributive, evaluative, and particularizing language can enhance expository and argumentative essays and laboratory reports.

4a.   Working with a partner, read aloud the following debate column from *Chatelaine*, which illustrates one form of persuasive writing.

Integrated Sports: A Question of Fair Play?

When 10-year-old Torontonian Justine Blainey lost patience with the short playing season and limited ice time in her all-girls hockey league in 1983, she tried out and qualified for a boys' team. Sport officials cried foul, citing regulations that bar female players from boys' leagues unless there is no girls' league available to them. In 1985, Blainey, charging sex discrimination, began a two-year legal battle for her right to play.

Last December [1987], a board of inquiry appointed under the Ontario Human Rights Code ruled in Blainey's favor, but similar cases may follow in other provinces. Does equality in sport demand full integration? Or do biological differences mean second-class status for girls who join the boys?

Pro   Helen Lenskyj is a member of the Canadian Association for the Advancement of Women and Sports, which backs Blainey.

Introduction   The sign on the boys' clubhouse reads, "No girls allowed." Boys play street hockey while girls watch. Male athletes in the locker room act like 10-year-olds when female reporters appear. This is the world of sport: masculinity and machismo. Why would any girl or woman want to join it? Why not play on the girls' team instead?

Conclusion   Your daughter might have a Gloria Steinem coaching her team, or she might have a Margaret Thatcher. The key lies in the value system, not the gender, of the sports leader. And if that sports leader is genuinely concerned about your daughter's right to equal opportunity in sport, he or she will support the option of playing on an integrated team.

Con   Fran Rider is the president of the Ontario Women's Hockey Association (O.W.H.A.), one of Blainey's most vocal opponents.

Introduction   Full integration for all ages in all sports will mean drastically reduced opportunities for female athletes. With controlled emigration of girls to boys' teams, girls' teams will fold, and many girls unwilling or unable to compete with boys will have no chance to play. This is equality?

Conclusion   If we really want more opportunities for female athletes, then let's start giving girls more funding, facilities, media coverage, corporate sponsorships and elite opportunities. And let's stop demeaning female teams with cheap talk about integration. We need not defeat men in head-to-head combat on the playing field to prove we're their equals.

b.   List persuasive techniques employed. What characteristics of interpretive and rhetorical styles can you identify? Which introduction and conclusion do you find most convincing? Why?
c.   Does the preamble reveal editorial preferences? Justify your response.

5.   Compare the samples of persuasion used in question 4 with the newspaper editorial, "Tackling Illiteracy" (page 244), as well as a standard news story. Consider language, tone, distance between writer and audience, rhetorical devices, leads, paragraphs, and structure.

6a.   Debate these generalizations in light of your learning:

- The more controversial a topic, the more reliance should be placed on fact.

- Formal persuasive writing relies primarily on logic; informal pieces tend to permit emotive language.

b.   As a group, compose criteria for appropriate use of fact and opinion and methods of persuasion in your publication.

7a.   Co-write a basic news story, *reporting* your publication's editorial policy.
b.   Draft individual editorials for your writing folder, convincing your audience the policy is sound, or survey students in the cafeteria about their views on a topical school issue. Draft an editorial of interest to them.

The General and Special Interest Column

Tarvo and Sasha are drawn to another form of persuasive writing—the general interest column. Publications often feature regular columnists, some syndicated across North America and Britain (see cartoon on opposite page). Share names of favourites with classmates.

You've read a sample of June Callwood's general interest column in Activity Two (page 210). Whether her topic is famine in Ethiopia, mental hospitals in Canada, or the "lowly toe," Callwood informs, interprets, persuades—and sometimes cajoles, delights, and amuses. So consistent is her voice, regular readers may feel personally acquainted, just as you may "know" your favourite DJ.

Reprinted by permission: Tribune Media Services.

A closely related form is the special interest column. While Tarvo's group was discussing plans, a touchy language issue arose—the proliferation of jargon or language peculiar to a group, profession, or activity.

Kirsten: I'm thinking about doing a science column.
Sasha: The last science article I read was full of terms that didn't really make sense. Anyway, I'm more interested in sports.
Tarvo: Okay. But you should be wise to sports talk, too. And Craig—you're sitting on a minefield—with your computer stuff.
Craig: You should see the examples Safire collects. Stock market writers talk about *blips* for fluctuation and *spike* for a sharp up-down motion, and economists have *price freezes*. Political reports use *glitch* and *damage control* as euphemisms for blunders. It's like referring to used cars as *pre-owned vehicles* . . . so . . . *pseudo*.
Kirsten: Hah! There's another one—pseudo is just trendy talk for "fake" in fashion magazines. And there's *faux* pearls and *integrity* of a garment.

This dialogue highlights a concern for all writers, particularly in special interest columns. Although you and your readers share interests and tastes, language should be clear, concise, and precise. Skilled specialty writers occasionally devise innovative phrasing or words which effectively communicate their intent, though it's non-standard English. Poet Leigh Hunt advised: "learn the right of coining words in the quick mint of joy." And language columnist William Safire suggests coining words is "no big deal" *if* a new word is really required. But think twice before peppering your article with clever new words. Are you enhancing your work or merely trying to sound authoritative—a member of an "in" group? Don't let the column's informality fool you; readers will turn the page to greener pastures if meaning is obscure.

Before completing Activity Five on language usage in non-fiction, read "I'm Sorry I Don't Speak the Language" (on page 243) from the OP ED page* of the *Globe and Mail*.

Activity Five   Language for General and Special Interests

Purpose

- to recognize techniques which appeal to readers
- to identify suitable material for columns in your publication
- to focus on appropriate language usage

1.   List features of form, language, and tone exhibited in general interest columns. Compare columns with editorials and front-page reports.

2a.   What information about the "average reader" would help determine whether Safire's "Bizbuzz" (page 253), which appeared in the *New York Times*, meets the criteria of general interest?
b.   Identify your publication's "average reader." In your Writer's Notebook, speedwrite about attractive topics for this clientele.

3.   Draft a general interest column for your publication. If you're preparing a school newspaper or magazine, you might highlight inexpensive vacation spots, satirize cafeteria food, or give advice about getting along with siblings.

4a.   Survey sports columns, identifying examples of jargon and non-standard usage that enrich or frustrate. Rephrase in standard English.
b.   Which of the problems Bill Ward identifies in "Sportswriting Pitfalls" (page 259) did you encounter in your survey?
c.   Collect amusing examples of jargon. Use them to create a found poem or a nonsense verse for your publication. The following excerpt from John Leo's "Journalese for the Lay Reader" is a good place to begin.

---

* This term refers to the page OPposite the EDitorial page.

Journalese, the native tongue of newsgatherers and pundits, retains a faint similarity to English but is actually closer to Latin. Like Latin, it is primarily a written language, prized for its incantatory powers, and is best learned early, while the mind is still supple. . . .

Every so often, an inexperienced reporter attempts to describe a dwelling as "attractive" or "impressive." This is incorrect. In journalese, all homes are either modest or stately. When confronted with a truly ramshackle fixer-upper, knowing scribes will deflect attention to the surrounding area, describing the residence as "off the beaten track" or "in a developing area," that is, a slum. Distaste for the suburbs is conveyed by mentioning "trimmed lawns and neat flower beds," thus artfully suggesting both compulsiveness and a high level of intolerance for life in its hearty, untrimmed state.

Journalese is rich in mystic nouns: gentrification, quichification, greenmail, dealignment, watershed elections and apron strings (the political coattails of a female candidate). But students of the language agree that adjectives do most of the work, smuggling in actual information under the guise of normal journalism. Thus the use of soft-spoken (mousy), loyal (dumb), high-minded (inept), hardworking (plodding), self-made (crooked) and pragmatic (totally immoral). A person who is dangerous as well as immoral can be described as a fierce competitor or gut fighter, and a meddler who cannot leave his subordinates alone is a hands-on executive. When strung together properly, apparently innocent modifiers can acquire megaton force. For instance, a journalist may write, "A private, deliberate man, Frobisher dislikes small talk, but can be charming when he wants to." In translation this means, "An antisocial, sullen plodder, Frobisher is obnoxious and about as articulate as a canteloupe." The familiar phrase "can be charming" is as central to good journalese as "affordable" is to automobile ads and "excellence" is to education reports. It indicates that Frobisher's charm production is a rare result of mighty exertion, yet it manages to end the revelation about his dismal character on an upbeat note.

5a.   In an interpretive or rhetorical style, draft a letter to the editor, an editorial, or a special interest column for your publication; give your views about specialized language or jargon. Or use jargon to parody its abuse in a special interest column or editorial for your publication.
b.   Explain which style you selected and account for your choice.

6.   Draft a special interest column on a topic of your choice. Next, write a letter to the editor arguing that the publication should purchase your column. Ask a partner to check for jargon, euphemisms, or slang, which detract from clear communication. Plan revisions.

7.   Work with your writing group to raise awareness of words. You might:

- establish a database of "Trendy Words" and invite contributions from other classes and their teachers

- hold a "Wonderful Words" contest; students submit suggestions for the word they like best (announce criteria—the most unusual or most frequently mentioned—at the outset)

- write a column, editorial, or news report about the "Trendy Words" database or "Wonderful Words" contest.

Features: Focus on New Journalism

Next, the team investigated feature articles, working with this description composed by Sasha and Tarvo:

> ... The feature article allows considerable scope for the writer's creativity and personal voice. Often an in-depth treatment, the feature may assume the shape of a spool (like the essay): the introduction and conclusion form approximately one-fifth each and the body composes the remaining three-fifths. Also like an essay, the feature is unified through more than standard reportorial slant. The lead suggests an angle or focus which builds into a theme of sorts to unify the article.
>
> Like columns, feature stories deal with virtually any topic. Human interest stories, "how-to" pieces, and celebrity interviews are popular. The talented investigative reporter ferrets out the story's *why*, building the foundation for the cause-and-effect plotted story [see Chapter Four]. Indeed, features may be as entertaining as fiction.

French's "Mr. Shaw Was Not at Home" (page 145) exemplifies a feature travel article. You may wish to discuss it before continuing.

In the midst of a library search for collected feature stories, Tarvo and Sasha stumbled across a puzzling form.

Tarvo: [holding Hugh Hood's *Flying a Red Kite*] Seems these are short stories—but I don't know. . . . Listen to this: "In the spring of 1952, six weeks after I finished my M.A. courses and involved myself in further graduate studies. . . ." You know, this sounds true. . . . He went to graduate school about then. And look, in the introduction he says it's an essay "in the genre Thurber created." But the sub-title of this book is *The Collected Stories: I.*
Sasha: [perusing the volume] . . . they're kind of neat. . . .
Tarvo: Yeah. It sounds like *In Cold Blood*—that novel we read last year.
Sasha: Come on, Tarvo . . . that wasn't a novel. Remember? Capote based it on factual research. It's like the stuff we did on narrative . . . I even saw a contest for this announced in *Canadian Author & Bookman*—"Creative Non-Fiction" they called it. . . .

---

* American humourist James Thurber.

Sasha's right. The group had unearthed New Journalism, also called Literary Journalism, a popular form of dramatic non-fiction which employs narrative techniques to enliven actual events. Because talented investigative reporters often write New Journalism, we'll examine it in conjunction with feature-writing.

The introduction to *The New Literary Journalists* by Norman Sims is a good place to begin:

> Today, scraps of information don't satisfy the reader's desire to learn about people doing things. Readers deal in their private lives with psychological explanations for events around them. They may live in a complex social world, amid advanced technologies, where "the facts" only begin to explain what's happening. The everyday stories that bring us inside the lives of our neighbours used to be found in the realm of the fiction writer, while non-fiction reporters brought us the news from far-off centers of power that hardly touched our lives.
>
> Literary journalists unite the two forms. Reporting on the lives of people at work, in love, going about the normal rounds of life, they confirm that the crucial moments of everyday life contain great drama and substance. Rather than hanging around the edges of powerful institutions, literary journalists attempt to penetrate the cultures that make institutions work.
>
> Literary journalists follow their own set of rules. Unlike standard journalism, literary journalism demands immersion in complex, difficult subjects. The voice of the writer surfaces to show readers that an author is at work. Authority shows through. . . . The dramatic details yield only to persistent, competent, sympathetic reporters. Voice brings the authors into our world. . . . Unlike fiction writers, literary journalists must be accurate. Characters in literary journalism need to be brought to life on paper, just as in fiction, but their feelings and dramatic moments contain a special power because we know the stories to be true. The literary quality of these works comes from the collision of worlds, from a confrontation with the symbols of another real culture. Literary journalism draws on immersion, voice, accuracy, and symbolism as essential forces.

In Activity Six, you'll focus on these dramatic techniques of modern journalism.

Activity Six   Writing Features and New Journalism
Purpose

- to listen for story in non-fiction
- to examine techniques of New Journalism
- to write a New Journalism feature for your publication

1. Bring to class samples of New Journalism you admire. (*Tip:* If your library's catalogue doesn't list this subject, look up these names: Joan Didion, Tom Wolfe, Sara Davidson, and Harry Bruce.)

a. Take turns reading aloud from several short pieces, listening closely for elements of story (Chapter Four).

b. Exchange samples and compare them with a literary essay, a news report, a column, and a fictional short story; consider style, structure, content, and strength of voice.

c. Role play a conflict situation from one article; try not to exceed the reporter's information.

2. In your Writer's Notebook, freewrite about the likely appeal of New Journalism in your publication. Brainstorm topics.

3. Co-write creative openings (first paragraphs) for several feature articles. Topics may include:

*   a Student Council election, first dates, blind dates

*   eating lunch in the school cafeteria

*   trying a new sport or a new school

*   collaborative writing in the computer lab

*   homework, habits, teenage trends, the job market.

Note dramatic devices of "showing."

4. Draft a feature article for your publication, using techniques of New Journalism to dramatize your subject. Keep in mind what Peter C. Newman, one of Canada's leading journalists and historians, has said about creative non-fiction:

> [In traditional terms] novels entertain and non-fiction informs. In the age of television ... you have to entertain as well as inform. This is what creative non-fiction is: you apply fictional techniques to non-fiction. For instance, I use many metaphors when I write. Some people say I use too many, but I don't apologize.

If, like Kirsten, you have trouble with this style, review the following ideas for opening up your creativity.

*   Ask yourself, "What are some possible ways of doing this task?" rather than focusing on "one right way."

*   Ponder this: advances occur when people try something new.

*   Compose half a dozen metaphors about objects in the room you are in or similes about forms of reportorial writing you've studied. For example, "The editorial is like a . . ."

- Read cartoons or jokes such as the *Globe and Mail's* "Your Morning Smile." (Tarvo likes puns such as this one: "Beware of backslappers. They're usually trying to make you cough something up.")

- Daydream about a pleasant day last summer.

- Speedwrite about occasions when you felt creative or the last time someone complimented you on a job well done.

- Mentally follow an unlikely train of thought; see where it takes you. For example, "What if I were to . . . ?"

- Visualize yourself as a successful reporter pounding out a dramatic story; imagine what you are feeling.

The Review, Profile, and Interview

Other popular forms of non-fiction journalism are investigated in Activity Seven. Before beginning, familiarize yourself with these definitions:

- The *review* is a form of persuasive essay, offering a personal interpretation or assessment of just about anything—an event, book, or record album, for example. Reputable reviewers provide readers with valid evidence for their judgements.

- The *profile* appears in a variety of forms. Also labelled the biographical sketch, it is generally an informal, third-person snapshot of a noteworthy individual.

- The *interview* quotes the direct speech of its subject. It resembles the format of a play script, as the interviewer and subject take turns speaking. Occasionally, a writer weaves quotations from the subject into the article's narrative and exposition.

Activity Seven   Exploring the Interview, Review, and Profile

Purpose

- to explore variations in structure and style of the profile, interview, or review

- to write in one or more of these forms for your publication

- to practise skills of search

1.   Peruse interviews in a variety of publications from your resource centre. *Rolling Stone, Canadian Author & Bookman, Books in Canada, Quill & Quire,* and *People* are good places to begin. Compare the style, structure, and content of sample interviews for several audiences; account for differences.

2a.   What tips about the form or structure of interviews may be gleaned from those with Mordecai Richler (page 359), Robert Frost (page 346), the Interview Organizer (page 399), or from "Setting a Good Example" (page 239)?

b.   Write a character sketch of the persona conveyed in one interview; give traits supported by textual evidence.

c.   Working with a partner, practise interviewing each other. A tape of the interaction will help identify your strengths and those areas in need of further work. Or role play an interview, taking turns as the interviewer and a noteworthy subject.

3a.   To what type of reader is "The Authors Behind the Back-Cover Blurbs" (page 238) tailored? What language or content might frustrate the "average reader" of *your* publication?

b.   With a partner, brainstorm ideas for suitable reviews; a school variety show or art exhibition, or a popular film may be of interest. Devise imaginative introductions for several pieces.

c.   Draft a review for your publication. (*Note:* You may wish to begin by reading "How to Write Book Reviews" by Kevin Anderson (page 234).

d.   Read "Setting a Good Example" (page 239). In conference with a partner, determine whether you've used examples to their best advantage in your review. Consider revisions.

4.   Read "Winning Writing Contest Changed Mistry's Life" (page 233). In chart form, compare it with several profiles about contemporary figures of public interest in other fields. Consider specific techniques of showing which bring subjects to life, such as anecdote, analogy and other figures of speech, dialogue, and so on. Does each inform accurately through vivid images and a clear angle or focus?

5a.   Interview a profile subject, following guidelines established by your instructor and the Interview Organizer.

b.   After drafting the profile, exchange work with a partner. Compose a character sketch about your partner's subject, giving evidence from the draft. Discuss whether your impressions are compatible with those your partner intended to convey.

c.   Ask your subject to approve the final draft before publication.

6.   In your Writer's Notebook, freewrite about effective techniques of showing in reviews, interviews, and profiles.

Advertising Copy

Will your publication include advertising? If so, you'll need to examine copywriting—a special form of persuasive writing. Whether the approach is "hard-sell" or subtle, advertising aims to influence audience behaviour. Copywriting skills must be honed just as any other specialty writing. Indeed, practitioners say the craft may require special talent; notable writers such as Hemingway, Shaw, and (Stephen Vincent) Benet apparently were unsuccessful at creating memorable copy.

In print advertising, words and images often work together, although the graphics and text are usually created by different people. Taking a team approach, Craig and Sasha pooled their talents to devise the following "Tips on Preparing Advertising Copy" for the class.

> We compiled hints from practising professionals and from our own analyses of appealing ads. Our quotations are from *The Art of Writing Advertising: Conversations with Masters of the Craft.*

- William Bernbach says "every word, every graphic symbol, every shadow" should enhance the point.
- David Ogilvy suggests building ads around "action and pictures."
- Use succinct, fresh, colourful language, not clichés.
- Research your audience's interests, motivations, goals.
- Leo Burnett suggests keeping a "corny language" file—vivid phrasing that intrigues your ear. When composing an ad, review the file, attending to the associations these words trigger.
- Dick Wasserman advises keeping in mind the three parts to ad copy: the "bridge" between the headline and the main body, the body that sells the product, and the "call to action"—the urge to buy.
- Use simple, declarative sentences.
- Write as if you're speaking to one person.
- Avoid parenthetical phrases and dependent clauses. They tend to slow things down.
- Read your copy aloud to ensure a natural flow.

In Activity Eight, practise writing advertising.

Activity Eight   Advertising Language
Purpose

- to write the language of advertising
- to devise appropriate guidelines for your publication's advertising copy
- to compare techniques of advertising and propaganda

Note: You may wish to review connotative language, and rhetorical and poetic styles before beginning (see the Glossary).

1.   Bring to class several magazines containing a variety of advertisements.
a.   With your group, consider visual and verbal techniques of persuasion, and their suitability for your type of publication.
b.   Focus on diction—emotive language, appeals to the senses, poetic or rhetorical language. Compose generalizations about your findings.
c.   Define the concept of "good taste" in advertising. Do any selections exceed these bounds? Justify.
d.   Are any products of hazardous or dubious quality?

2.   Keeping in mind your explorations in question 1:
a.   Compose criteria for your publication's advertising copy
b.   Freewrite in your Writer's Notebook about effective advertisements and list guidelines for ethical, tasteful advertising. Before starting, you may wish to read Samuel Johnson's essay, "The Abuses of Advertising" (page 245), written in 1759, and the following advice from Richard Hoggart:

> There is, of course, good persuasion as well as bad persuasion; and advertisers keep the debate murkier than it should be by sliding between the two types. In one sense, any good book is an act of persuasion. But the gap between that and the persuasion of advertisers is so large as to make virtually a difference of kind. Good persuasion, whether in dispassionate argument or in a powerfully moving novel, has two root qualities: respect for the reality of the subject, and respect for the listener's right to judge for himself his attitude to the subject. This definition does not rule out emotional engagement; any important commitment is a mixture of emotion and intellect. But it insists on emotional relevance—that the emotion, in both its nature and its intensity, fits the theme.
>   Naturally, the line between this and illicit emotional persuasion is a continuous one, and it is difficult to decide just where the watershed comes.

3a.   Read "What Can I Do?" (page 229). Compare its audience, purpose and types of persuasion, and language usage with readings from question 3. Account for similarities and differences.
b.   Brainstorm associations with the words *advertising* and *propaganda*. Distinguish between the terms, referring to several dictionary definitions. Does either term describe "What Can I Do?"
c.   Could the writer's tone and/or approach undermine the purpose of the piece in contemporary society?

4.   Read the quotations on Michele Landsberg's *Women and Children First* (which appeared on the front and back covers of the book's Penguin edition) printed below and "Be a *Fresh Perspective* Intern" (page 204). How does each attempt to influence the reader's behaviour? Account for differences in level and type of language.

Margaret Atwood   "This is a non-fiction book that reads like fiction—warm, rich in incident and detail, compassionate, funny. It's rare to read a book by a feminist that can be pro-women, pro-men and pro-family. Michele Landsberg is in favour of fully human beings, and she is a delight to read."

Pierre Berton   "It is not possible for anyone to read Michele Landsberg without examining his or her own attitudes to the male-female relationship. For eloquence, literary skill and sheer humanity she has few peers among columnists."

June Callwood   "Simply the best book about the lives of women that I have ever read."

"BRAVE MEN

SHALL NOT DIE

BECAUSE *I* FALTERED"

What can I do?

THERE is one job you *alone* can do. It concerns the man you love. He has a terrific task ahead of him—a task that will get more irksome as the days go by, until this war is won —or until we shall lie vanquished at Hitler's feet.

So we ask you to help him keep fit and happy for his job, whether it be on the production line or the firing line; in the factory or in the office; producing munitions of war or maintaining essential war services.

More and more will be expected of him as the days go on. He will be tired . . . at times depressed with the seemingly endless cry for more and still more of his time and energy.

Be thoughtful of him. When he spends more hours at his desk or with his tools than in the past, he is not being intentionally neglectful of you. Those evenings you have enjoyed at the movies or at social gatherings may become fewer and fewer, because his hours of sleep are so important to him and to those who are dependent on him for supplies.

Make it your duty to keep him fit and happy for his job. Be sympathetic, patient and understanding when he is tired and fretful. Encourage him in his sacrifice by showing your pride in his achievements. Give him the happy smile when problems you may not be able to share cast their shadow on his face.

This is the responsibility of every woman who cherishes the love of a man and deserves his esteem.

—This message is issued by the Department of Munitions and Supply for Canada.

Peter Gzowski   "I always suspected that Michele Landsberg was the smartest and wisest person writing about this kind of issue in Canada. This book confirms that suspicion . . . "

Margaret Laurence   "Every woman will see something of herself in this book. Every man could learn from it."

5a.   In a small group, assume the role of employees in an advertising agency designing a print campaign for a specific client. Brainstorm imaginative ideas for presentation—language and layout. Draft more than one approach in keeping with your client's guidelines.
b.   Role play a meeting with your client in which you present your proposals. Your task is to convince the client to accept your agency's ideas over those of a competitor.

6.   After revising or adapting your client's favourite advertisement, exchange work with another group for comments.

C. AFTER-WORDS

Responding to Reading

1.   What considerations does the following passage from *Othello* bring to mind regarding issues to resolve before publishing your periodical?

> Good name in man and woman, dear my lord,
> Is the immediate jewel of their souls:
> Who steals my purse steals trash; 'tis something, nothing;
> 'Twas mine, 'tis his, and has been slave to thousands;
> But he that filches from me my good name
> Robs me of that which not enriches him,
> And makes me poor indeed.

2a.   Locate one exemplary interview, profile, and review. For each, compose several "responding to reading" questions.
b.   Exchange material with a partner and complete the questions about each form.

3.   After reading the articles and excerpts listed below, estimate the success with which each embodies Duquin's advice in "Setting a Good Example" (page 239). Justify with textual references.

- John Allemang, "Winning Writing Contest Changed Mistry's Life" (page 233)

- Michael J. Bugeja, "Making Your Article Leads Sparkle" (page 235)

- David C. Burrows, "The Language of Finance" (page 238)

4.   Study the opening paragraphs of the selections listed below. For each one that contains a lead, classify it according to type.

- Robina Salter, "Write Science Stories Simply" (page 255)
- Diana Stout, "Recapture Your Feelings" (page 257)
- "Tackling Illiteracy" (page 244)

5.   Speculate on the audience for which the readings listed in questions 3 and 4 were originally written. Consider language, subject matter, and so on.

The Writing Folder

1.   Revise and polish one or more pieces of writing from the activities in this chapter. Submit them to your editorial board for publication, according to the terms of your proposal.

2.   Prepare a "how-to" article about writing one form of non-fiction. Or write a "how-to" article and a model of that form. Contribute your work to the class database or the library's "Student Samples" file.

3.   Prepare two editorials, front-page news reports, personal essays, or special interest columns on the same subject for publications with very different target audiences. Append a brief analysis showing how you've tailored each to its audience.

4.   Dramatize your publishing experience in a one-act play, narrative poem, or short story, using fragments from your journal.

5.   Rewrite an article for a different type of publication.

6.   Research and write a variation on one of the non-fiction forms you've studied. You might consider the photo essay or a science article, for example.

Independent Study

1.   Investigate in more depth one form or style of non-fiction; devise a specific topic for your teacher's approval.

2.   Initiate and publish a small newsletter at your place of work, a club, community centre, or neighbourhood residents' association. For example, if your part-time employer hires many students, management may be interested in funding a small newsletter to communicate with this group.

3.   Locate a work-study placement with a publication such as *Fresh Perspective* (see page 204), a community newspaper, or a newsmagazine. Or investigate an after-school placement with a community agency or charitable foundation; many organizations need help with their bulletins, newsletters, or fund-raising literature. Arrange specific terms for credit with your teacher.

4.   If your school belongs to a computer network, you may wish to initiate and contribute to a "Network News" publication for subscribers. Arrange details with your teacher.

5.   Research memoirs or biography by famous figures in a field of special interest. You might read works by or about entrepreneurs or political, cultural, or sports figures. One of these suggestions may be of interest:
a.   Collaborate with an elderly member of your family or a community figure in the preparation of his or her memoirs.
b.   Collaborate with several individuals and prepare an anthology of memoirs such as *A Scottish Childhood* (compiled and edited by Antony Kamm and Anne Lean; Collins in Association with The Save the Children Fund, 1985).

6.   Interview several print or broadcast journalists about a specific aspect of their work that interests you. Devise a project with your teacher.

7.   Study the work of an outstanding non-fiction writer such as Pierre Berton, June Callwood, Jon Franklin, Michele Landsberg, Peter C. Newman, David Suzuki, or William Zinsser. Devise a specific focus with the assistance of your instructor.

The Writer's Notebook

1.   Freewrite about your learning of key concepts in this chapter.

2.   Reflect on the growth of your personal writing process during this publishing venture. One of these questions may help you begin:

- Do you agree with T.S. Eliot that "an editor should tell the author that his writing is better than it is. Not a whole lot better, a little better"?

- What qualities would an ideal writing partner possess?

- Has your getting-ready-to-write process recently changed?

- Do you agree with Donald Murray that "writers need to write before writing"? How do you engage in this process?

- How do you know when you're ready to write?

3.   If you have kept a journal, study it for clues about your responses to teamwork on long-term projects. Speculate on the implications for post-secondary plans.

4.   Update your Writer's Portrait.

READINGS 5

Winning Writing Contest Changed Mistry's Life

John Allemang

Rohinton Mistry has not had a lot to do with the world of writers, apart from publishing one of the past year's finest books. He has had little to do with the lecture circuit and is no master of the publicity game, so even if he wins the Governor-General's Award for fiction, you won't see him swilling champagne on the evening news. When the winners are announced today in Calgary, the 35-year-old Mistry will be far away from the Olympian heights in his adopted home of Brampton, working steadily and seriously as always.

Brampton is better known as a punchline in former Ontario premier William Davis's speeches than as a town that has nurtured one of Canada's finest young writers. But it is here in quintessential suburbia, in a large new house on a street named after a Canadian prime minister, that Mistry has crafted the loving tales of his native India. *Tales From Firozsha Baag*, the account of the little universe contained within a Bombay apartment block, is almost impossible to find in Brampton, and has probably not been much read in Toronto, even as a pretty Penguin paperback, but it has garnered for its young author glowing reviews in both his countries.

The applause from India is no surprise. Writing in the tradition of Narayan and Naipaul, Mistry has recreated a corner of Parsi community down to the smallest detail. But the praise he has won in Canada surprises him. "When I saw that the book was so readily appreciated," he says, "I could never quite decide whether it was because, one, multiculturalism is in fashion, or, two, it was a case of let's encourage this poor guy from India or, three, because the writing is good."

The "ethnic" tag disturbs him no end, not least because when he looked the word up in Webster's, he discovered that one of its meanings was "heathen." (He likes the sound of this word, especially as it applies to a man who, small, thoughtful, gentle, is clearly far away from the usual notion of heathen.) But he comes round to the more comforting idea that the warm reception for his book was because the writing is "quite decent."

This quality of his writing, however he understates it, was there from the start, which was only five years ago. Brought up to love reading (Enid Blyton and the Biggles adventure books were his early favorites), Mistry had never written more than school essays when his wife showed him an ad for a literary competition at the University of Toronto. The two of them were attending night school there, Mistry to get away from his job at the Canadian Imperial Bank of Commerce, his wife to make the shift from secretary to high school teacher. He entered ("I probably wouldn't be a writer if it weren't for that contest") and won in 1983, sent off a few stories over the next year to Canadian literary magazines, and won the U of T competition again in 1984, when Mavis Gallant was the judge.

By 1985, Mistry had quit the bank (which he, unlike T.S. Eliot, found very uncongenial) and became a fulltime writer. He keeps as low a profile as is humanly possible, avoiding the temptations and distractions posed by the big cities.

That isn't quite true. About 18 months ago, he and his wife (who is also a Parsi from Bombay), went to Los Angeles where she taught and he wrote. But he saw nothing there to make him think he wasn't better off in Brampton, and Canada. "It wasn't an inner-city school, it had enrichment programs and yet the school was appalling. It had a 20-foot wall around it, and you had to check in at security going in and out. And a good thing, too. My wife lost two students to guns in her first three months."

But the trip gave him some interesting material, didn't it? "That's the sad thing," he answers after a moment's thought. "The most appalling things in life are the most promising things for a writer."

How to Write Book Reviews

Kevin J. Anderson

Okay, so how do you go about writing a book review in the first place? First you have to read the book. I don't mean sit down on the bus and skim a chapter or two—you must actually *read* the thing all the way through. Some reviewers don't operate this way, preferring to rely on their own first impressions, choosing to read the plot summary, the promotional literature, then browsing over a few passages in order to get a feel for the author's style.

This is, generally, how people *buy* books; but I don't think reviewing them by this method is fair to the author. Somebody spent a good deal of time writing the book you're holding in your hands, and you should give the author a fair chance right up to the very end. After all, you wouldn't want somebody basing judgement of *your* book on only a plot summary and some skimmed passages, would you?

Be aware of such features as foreshadowing, characterization, and plot (when dealing with fiction), or format, interest-level, and readability (when dealing with nonfiction). Take careful notes, and keep a record of your thoughts as you go along. It's important to write down all your first impressions because they form the outlook you have on the book. For example, if the cover art offends you, you may subconsciously dislike the book all the way through.

In a sense you are reviewing the publisher's product as much as you are the author's work, and publishers read reviews, too. You may base a part of your judgement on whether you would *buy* the book as it is. Look at the printing, the cover art, the price, the paper quality, the plot summary or the promotional blurbs on the cover. Does it interest you? Would you pry open your wallet for this book? If it is a children's book, how do you think it will stand up to abuse and repeated readings?

Finally, as you are reading, be conscious of the *writing* itself. Look at the writing style and the clarity of prose—is everything understandable? Is it full of clichés? Does the author have a fresh outlook? Is everything organized in a serviceable fashion? Many reviewers include a quotation from the book, so watch for flashes of genius, or a particularly terrible sentence if you have to give a bad review. Quoting the author lends credence to your case—it's as if the author is personally giving you evidence to support your opinion.

When you type your final copy, state all the necessary facts about the book at the top of the review. List the title, the author, the publisher (possibly the publisher's address), the year of publication, the page count, the price, and some magazines need the ISBN (International Standard Book Number) that is listed on the inside of the book. And of course, your own name as reviewer. . . .

Avoid plot summaries. One or two sentences should be enough to let the reader know the essence of the book and the basic idea behind it. Instead you should concentrate on the writing, the characterization, the technique, etc.

As with any type of writing, you must *grab attention fast*. Readers usually have a limited amount of time to devote to any magazine, and your review is competing against the other articles in the publication for their attention.

Avoid reviewing books in fields that don't interest you in the first place—for example, don't pan a book because it is science fiction, or mystery, or romance if you don't like those genres, or if you are not familiar enough with them to provide new insights.

Finally, sometimes the most difficult part of any review, you must come to a conclusion about the book. Was it good, or not? A good measuring stick is to see how successful the author was at what he or she intended. Look at the book and try to pin down exactly what worked and what didn't. What would you have done differently? You can turn the reviewing experience into a method to improve your own writing. Look at the author at hand—he or she did something right, otherwise the book wouldn't have been published in the first place. What can you and other writers learn from this book?

Making Your Article Leads Sparkle

Michael J. Bugeja

The writer, like the salesperson, has only so much time to close a deal. So if you want to peddle your prose to an editor, you had better make your pitch fast—in the lead of your article.

The pitch delivers the first impression of you and your work, and if yours is wordy or trite, the editor will react as you might to a gabby salesperson: *sorry.* . . .

To sidestep that, you must recognize several varieties of lead problems. The no-frills newspaper-like lead is a good device to show common weaknesses and the ways to overcome them. Hang all the ornaments and accessories you need on that basic frame, and your feature or nonfiction lead will succeed.

The lead is the eye-catcher of an article. In it, you present your best piece of information in the "hot spot"—the first ten words.

Begin your lead with a proper noun, and you bore the reader:

> The Department of Game, Fish and
> Parks report that winterkill has spoiled

what some anglers hoped would be a banner year for bass at area lakes. But a little help from hatcheries can ease the problem this spring.

When you put the news in the hot spot, the lead thaws:

> Winterkill at area lakes has spoiled what some anglers hoped would be a banner year for bass. But a little help from hatcheries can ease the problem this spring.
> The Department of Game, Fish and Parks. . . .

A salesperson would not make a pitch by defining the product—"A vacuum is a device to clean carpets"—and neither should you. The typical "definition" lead is as exciting as a dictionary:

> The American Agriculture Movement is an organization of hundreds of family farmers who want to have a say in US farm policy.

Such methods belittle the reader because the leads begin at square one. Worse, they don't inform. The reader takes note when you perk your lead with news.

> Farmers who recently returned from protests in Washington are bouncing atop tractors again at harvest, but woe to the politician who tries to take them for a ride.

Akin to the definition lead is the "background precede": information that's timely and factual but too weak to lead into a feature. Too much emphasis on the time element can kill a story, especially if it is intended for a magazine:

> Vocational Education Week, Feb. 12-18, is being recognized by the three vo-tech facilities that serve county students.

When you rewrite or edit such a lead, look to the second through fifth paragraphs in the body of the story for lead material. Put the background precede high in the article, but obscure the time element:

> Students who do poorly in the classroom but who work well with their hands often gain confidence in their potential at area vo-tech schools, county educators say.
> Vocational Education Week was recognized this winter by the three area vo-tech facilities.

In each of these revisions, the writer wants to keep us reading just as a salesperson wants to keep us listening. Dull material is excised from the hot spot.

Sometimes, however, an otherwise saleable story may arrive in unattractive wrapping. . . .

The "say-nothing" lead is as alluring as a plain brown wrapper. This type of lead promises much but delivers little, usually only the topic of the story:

> The reorganization of the telephone company has caused some interesting rate changes in long-distance calling.

To test if you have a say-nothing lead, read the first paragraph aloud as a broadcaster might and then stop (a tactic Chevy Chase often used for laughs on the mock news segment of the old "Saturday Night Live"). A say-nothing lead will sound humorous because it is woefully incomplete. Usually, the real lead will emerge in the second or third paragraph of the original story. Adapt it for a lead:

> The best times to call long distance are listed by the telephone company in the current directories. Yet that information actually may increase your monthly bill because rates have been affected by the recent reorganization.

More incomplete than the "say-nothing" is the "label" lead, usually one word. Manufacturers cut costs when they tag generic labels on their products, and writers cut corners when they resort to this type of lead:

> Violence.
> A problem that affects nearly 20% of dating couples, says a nationally known sociologist.

Writing one-word leads is easy because the reader does the brainwork, imagining the range of possible meanings. Typically, a label lead produces another fragment that the reader must connect with other information for meaning. To correct this problem, make the fragment an appositive and look lower in the story for more material to complete the sentence:

> Violence, a problem that affects nearly 20% of dating couples, ranges from shouting to rape.
> Dr. Brenda McKinley, a nationally known sociologist, . . .

Sometimes the wrapper is so colorful that we question the quality of the product. Simply, the claims on the label are too amazing for belief. This occurs with leads that overreach:

> Oklahomans are eating so much these days—and dying because of it—that soon nobody will be around to do the cooking, doctors say.

Apart from being clever, this lead exaggerates fact. The writer who misleads his reader is as crooked as a salesperson who bilks his customer. No lead, no matter how astounding, will salvage a story. Play it straight:

> Too many Oklahomans are fat and unhealthy, no longer dying from old age as their pioneer forefathers, but from heart attack and stroke, doctors say.

Keep the reader in mind and you will overcome problems with boredom, brainwork and misinformation. You will also succeed by avoiding clichés and tired expressions, which no writer should pitch to an audience. The weary salesperson wastes our time. So does the writer weary of his topic. Nobody would read an article that begins:

Well, it's done.

At a gathering in the local Holiday Inn, Sister Mary Teresa won the million-dollar lottery that everyone has been making such a fuss about.

Such leads tell us more about the writer than the topic. Moreover, they do not convey truth—what it felt like for the person who experienced an event. Leads that focus on human interest capture our attention:

Sister Mary Teresa considered it gambling, but she kept the lottery ticket her father gave her last summer. Now she's a millionaire who plans to give her winnings to Catholic charities.

Readers anticipate the next word in a sentence, the next turn of phrase. If you surprise them—exceed their expectations—they become excited about the topic. But if you express ideas in customary ways, readers say: "I've heard it all before." Editors who see "question" leads have heard them all before:

What do you do if one day the federal government tells you it intends to confiscate the land your family has farmed for five generations so it can build a lake?

The question begs a silly answer: "Bury toxic waste in your fields." The reader anticipates a punchline, which eliminates the element of surprise. You are forced to switch from the second person to the third person in the body of the story. To fix this, combine the best elements of the question and punchline. Keep the lead in the third person:

When the government evicted Tom Hadley to build a lake on land his family farmed for five generations, he went to court—not to keep the acreage but to haggle for a price.

Occasionally, the writing itself is the stumbling block of a lead.

You must sell the subject of your story quickly and creatively. You can't afford to back into the lead:

He's known by many names: "The Hunting Hero," "Mr. Deer," "Joe Williams."

If he isn't the finest hunter in Oklahoma, then he is as close as one can get. . . .

This is a man who only recently held a rifle for the first time.

If you seem to be backing into your lead, resist the urge to create a new topic and scan the second through fifth paragraphs of your story. Often you will find sharp sentences you can combine for a lead:

If he isn't the finest hunter in Oklahoma, then he is as close as one can get. Not bad for a man who until recently never held a rifle.

When writers try hard for a creative lead, they usually rely on metaphors. When they rely too heavily on metaphors, they usually mix them:

Would-be tycoons made thousands of requests this year to drill oil wells in the state, each hoping to sprout a gusher-producing derrick but no one struck gold.

You can't compare one object—oil derrick —to two others—plants and gold mines—in your lead. If you must use metaphor to create your lead, be consistent. Use words in keeping with the idea you are trying to sell to an editor:

Drillers hoping their wells would spout gushers made thousands of requests this year for state permits, but each bid came up dry.

Sometimes experienced writers pitch leads so well that they (and even copy editors!) take them for granted. Here's a lead that contains strong verbs typical of good writing, but nevertheless could use some final touches:

Earthen scars concealing ten miles of new waterline now snake through a Cherokee village south of Oklahoma City. Creeping along, it sidles up and bumps to a stop at the house where Sarah Walkingstick lives with her daughter's family.

In the above example, an "earthen scar" cannot snake, creep, sidle, and bump without mixing metaphors. Also there is subject-pronoun disagreement. All, however, are relatively easy to touch up:

An earthen scar concealing ten miles of new waterline snakes through a Cherokee village south of Oklahoma City. It coils to a stop at the house where Sarah Walkingstick lives with her daughter's family.

After you rewrite your lead, make sure the rest of your story is as polished and lively. A good lead cannot guarantee a sale, but a bad lead can lose one.

The Language of Finance
David C. Burrows

When you buy stock, you're "going long", to use Bay Street parlance. Holding a long position means you buy stocks you hope will appreciate so you can sell them later at a profit.

There is another way to "invest" in stocks—the opposite way. You can "go short" by selling a stock you don't own from funds borrowed by your broker, in anticipation of a price decline. If the price falls, you buy other shares at a lower price and pocket the difference, which is your profit.

Short selling is riskier than buying stocks because, theoretically, your loss can be unlimited if the stock goes up instead of down. After all, there's no ceiling on how high a stock can go. However, in the real world, you can stop your loss at almost any point. All you have to do is instruct your investment execu-tive to buy the stock back if the price increases by a certain percentage (perhaps 10 or 15 per cent) over the price at which you sold short. So you can get out of a losing transaction quickly and keep most of your capital intact.

When does it make sense to sell short? Mainly in bear markets, when more stocks are falling than rising week after week and month after month. In such a market it's unrealistic to assume that you can consistently manage to find the very few stocks that will buck the downward market trend. It's much easier to go with the trend, hoping that stocks will keep falling. Periods of market volatility also pro-vide good short selling opportunities, but pri-marily for aggressive investors who want to try to capitalize on sudden market correc-tions.

The stock exchanges in Canada have two rules which apply to short selling. The first is the necessity of declaring a short sale when the shares are sold. The second is the "last sale rule" whereby short sales are permitted at a price not below the price of the last sale of the shorted security. (The Vancouver Stock Exchange rule is slightly different.) Short sales must be identified as such so these rules can be observed.

There is an alternative to short selling that has a similar effect—buying a "put" option. This gives you the right (but not the obliga-tion) to sell 100 shares at a certain price by a certain date. The advantage of a put is that if the stock advances, instead of declines, all you can lose is the price of the put (called the premium), which normally is a small percent-age of the market price of the stock.

The Authors Behind the Back-Cover Blurbs
Marc Côté

Perhaps the most difficult effort in the world of contemporary writing is that made to remain clear of any particular school of writers or writing theory. Peter O'Brien and the interviewers from the journal *Rubicon,* where all these reviews were previously published, managed to make this effort and achieve a valuable end in *So To Speak.*

The writers included in the collection are Josef Skvorecky, Roo Borson, Rudy Wiebe, Peter Van Toorn, Nicole Brossard, Christopher Dewdney, Margaret Atwood, Jack Hodgins, Erin Mouré, Mavis Gallant and Leon Rooke. Almost all the interviewers were at one time students at McGill University.

In his introduction, O'Brien states that *So To Speak* is neither inclusive nor exclusive. While some famous writers are missing—Timothy Findley and Alice Munro among them—other writers who are not well known are included alongside the better-known names of Atwood, Hodgins and Gallant. This mix of the familiar with the unfamiliar makes for interesting and informative reading.

An interview serves several purposes. One, according to Leon Edel on the back cover of the book, is to "answer a modern need to add document to creation." This is an academic end, and rightly so; the interviewers were all active in academia. But as Vehicle is not an academic publisher its aim must be to publish books of interest to the general public. This is the second purpose for interviews: to give readers a guided glimpse of the minds and personalities behind *The Handmaid's Tale, The Resurrection Of Joseph Bourne* and *Home Truths.*

Although a writer's personality should not be confused with the works produced, readers are curious and want to know something beyond the short biographical blurbs on back covers. It is in this that the *Rubicon* interviewers are most successful.

The best interview of the lot is Debra Martens' with Mavis Gallant. It is clear in the interview that Gallant does not particularly want to be questioned: she won't talk about her friends, she won't discuss her work, she won't comment on her past. Gently, though, Martens proves to be a dextrous interviewer,

rephrasing her questions, adjusting them to help Gallant feel more able to answer directly. Gallant, through Martens' work, comes across as a nicer, cleverer and more talkative woman; she is as charming in print as in person—something other interviews have not been able to communicate.

In some cases, though, the interviews are a little awkward: the questioner persists along a line the author does not seem interested in. Or worse, bad technique is revealed when the interviewer ignores an interesting point raised by the author in favor of what reads like the next question on the list. In other cases, specifically the interview with Christopher Dewdney, the author is compelled to say, over and over, how he is amazed and impressed by the research performed before the interview. Such obscure points brought into the discussion make it hard for the reader to appreciate the interview.

Setting a Good Example
Lorene Hanley Duquin

When you learned to add, a teacher probably wrote $1 + 1 = 2$ on the blackboard and then showed you that 1 apple plus 1 more apple equals 2 apples. The teacher was using apples as an example to make an abstract concept seem real and interesting. It was better than just telling you $1 + 1 = 2$. It was showing you.

You use this same powerful tool when you incorporate examples into your work. Examples answer the questions: *How? Why? When is that the case?* They create pictures in readers' minds.

Good examples can be analogies, real-life anecdotes, or fictional scenes. They also can be a specific sample of something that explains or elaborates on what you're trying to say.

Let me give you some examples.

An *analogy* likens one thing to another, which helps the reader understand your point.

For instance, when you create an analogy to explain the human heart, you could say the heart is like a pump. I used an analogy in an article for *Mother's Today* to show how a baby-sitting co-op works:

> A babysitting club can work like a savings account. But instead of money, members deposit the number of hours they spend babysitting and they withdraw hours when another member babysits for them.

An *anecdote* is a short, real-life narrative, which illustrates the point you're trying to make. I used the following anecdote in an article for *Modern Bride* to illustrate my point that men and women can have strong personal preferences on something as mundane as bath towels:

> Sheila and Bill had to compromise on their bath towels, for instance. He liked a slightly rough, textured towel that stimulates the skin, while she preferred the soft, terry velour towels.

A *fictional scene* is a short, made-up narrative that illustrates your point. It is usually written in the second person, and places the reader in a "let's suppose" situation. I created this scene in an article for *Campaigns & Elections* as an example of how endorsements can hurt a candidate:

> For example, if you are endorsed by the local senior citizen's lobby in a race for a school board seat, your opponent might go to the PTA and say, "This man's endorsed by the very people who consistently vote against school budgets."

A *sample* can be one or more aspects of something that will elaborate your point. In an article for *Seventeen* on how to run for class office and win, I used the following sample to show the kinds of high-contrast colors that work best on campaign posters:

> For example, black lettering on a pale-pink background has higher contrast than yellow lettering on a white background.

Lively Writing

In addition to helping your readers understand, good examples can make your writing come alive. Several years ago, I wrote a dramatic narrative for *McCall's* about a little girl named Shanda Baldwin, who slipped into a deep coma after she had been accidentally poisoned with carbon monoxide. The doctors couldn't predict when or if she would wake up. The family had to wait and see. In my rough outline of the story, I wrote:

> Shanda's grandfather didn't like the idea of just waiting to see what would happen. He thought the family should talk to Shanda and try to wake her up.

When I went back to the transcript of my interview with Shanda's grandfather, I found that this former dairy farmer had used a powerful example of how he had dealt with sick animals on the farm when he talked about trying to wake Shanda up. Look at the difference adding Warner's example makes:

> The uncertainty bothered Shanda's grandfather. A former dairy farmer, Albert Warner remembered when his animals were sick and he had to nurse them back to health. "A sick calf can't tell you what's wrong, but you don't give up trying," he told Linda, "and you don't give up trying to comfort it. I think we should talk to Shanda and try to wake her up."

Finding Examples

There are two ways to find examples—from first-hand sources and from second-hand sources.

First-hand sources are the people you interview. Whether you're talking to an expert, a public relations person, a victim or a friend, look for colorful descriptions, anecdotes and analogies that will enliven your writing.

Second-hand sources are books and newspapers, television and radio programs, public relations information, and magazines and newsletters.

First-hand sources are *always* preferred.

Chances are you'll never get the opportunity to listen to a professional writer conduct an interview. If you could, you'd find that the writer constantly asks for examples throughout the interview.

Here is an excerpt from an interview I conducted with psychologist Warren Keller for an article I was researching for *Working Mother* on why it's important to get to know the parents of your children's friends.

> **Keller:** I feel very strongly that it's important to know the parents of your children's friends because there's a strong tendency in children to adopt the value system of their parents. The strategy of getting to know the other parents will depend on the age of the children.
>
> **LHD:** Can you give me some examples for working mothers who have young children?
>
> **Keller:** Working mothers. It can be more of a problem for working mothers because they're not home as much and probably don't have as much opportunity to meet the parents. It does take time to get to know the parents of your kids' friends, and everyone's short of time but I think there are some very simple things a parent could do. For example, if you're home on a Saturday, you can invite parents in when they drop their kids off or you can stay for a few minutes to talk when you drop your child at a playmate's house. You can also seek out other parents when you attend school or community functions. Even introducing yourself over the phone is better than no contact at all.
>
> **LHD:** Can you think of anything else working parents could do?
>
> **Keller:** Well, they could take their child's friend along with them on a family outing. Spending that time with your child's friend is going to tell you a lot about what that child is allowed to do and how things operate at his house. The child

> has probably adopted the value system of his parents.
>
> **LHD:** Adopted the value system of his parents? Can you point to an instance where that would be a problem?
>
> **Keller:** Well, it's going to be a problem if you have a different set of rules for your child than the friend's family has. Or you might suspect a problem such as an alcoholic parent and you might decide you don't want your child to play at that friend's house. Or maybe you find the kids aren't being properly supervised. There's nothing wrong with exerting some control over your child's relationships.

Get the idea? If I hadn't probed for examples, I would have had little to tell my readers. The next time you hear a radio or television talk show host interview someone, listen for the way they probe. They're after the same thing you are—good examples.

But sometimes even the best interviewer will come up empty-handed. At that point, you must turn to secondary sources.

That happened to me when I was working on an article for *Weight Watchers Magazine* on what to do when you lose weight and your clothes are too big. I interviewed a professional seamstress who advised checking each garment for good quality and construction before going to the trouble of having it altered. Writing the article, I realized that I needed some concrete samples of "good quality." I found just what I needed in several sewing books. My final draft read:

> Now examine the quality and the construction of each item in your closet. Everyone's definition of quality differs, but if the garment was expensive, is made from high-quality fabric, or has a designer label, chances are it'll be worth altering. Here are some other examples of high-quality construction:
>   • Straight, even machine top-stitching with no broken threads.
>   • Finished seams to prevent raveling.
>   • Good-quality buttons and well-made buttonholes.

• Pattern designs, plaids and stripes matched up at the seams.
• Reinforced stitching in the arms, sleeves and crotch.
• Zippers that work well and lie smooth.

Newsletters are another good source of examples. In an article I was writing on head injury for *Kiwanis* magazine, I found some perfect examples of different types of head injury in a newsletter that was published by a rehabilitation center. If I hadn't found what I was looking for in the newsletter, I would have called the newsletter editor or a public relations person for the hospital. Such people can be a big help in finding examples because they're familiar with the subject.

Radio and television are also good secondary sources. If I know that an interview show or news segment will be aired on a subject that I'm writing about, I tape it. Often such programs will contain the examples I need to flesh out my article.

But sometimes, even secondary sources won't give you a perfect example. When that happens, you must make up your own. It requires some thought and a lot of imagination. In an article I was writing for *Mature Outlook* on how lonely people can get ripped off by dating services, my interviews turned up several anecdotes from senior citizens who had had bad experiences with professional matchmakers. But I needed a concrete example that would tie everything together.

To find that example, I did a little brainstorming. I came up with the idea that someone who joins a dating service is lonely and willing to take a risk, a gamble. The idea began to take shape. In my example, I showed the readers that dating services exist for the same reason Las Vegas casinos do: Everyone knows that most people will lose, but lots of people are willing to gamble that they'll be one of the few lucky winners.

It's OK to make up an example if, as in the above, you're drawing an analogy. It's *not* OK

to make up an anecdote and lead readers to believe that the incident really happened. If you really need an anecdote and can't find one, turn it into a fictional scene by using the second person.

For example, suppose you're writing an article about auto breakdowns and you want to give the reader some examples of cars that don't start. You're tempted to write:

For instance, Jane Montgomery turned the key in the ignition and nothing happened. Not even an *r-r-r-r*.

Don't do it. Just change that example from the third person to the second person.

For instance, you put the key in the ignition and nothing happens. Not even an *r-r-r-r*.

Now you've created the same effect. But by using the second person, you are not deceiving readers.

Writing the Example

Whenever I begin to write an example, I think of an Irishman I know named Tom Flynn. He is a master joke-teller. His jokes are concise. He doesn't waste a lot of words leading up to the punch line. The words he uses all create emphasis and expectation. In the end, he makes a point.

A good example is just like that.

Each time I write an example, I ask myself:

• Is this example necessary?
• Is it overstated?
• Could I tell this more simply and still make a point?

Suppose you're trying to explain that in some cases, collision insurance for your car might not be necessary. You need an example to show the reader when the extra coverage isn't necessary. You could write:

Sometimes, collision insurance isn't necessary. For example, if your car is more than five years old and in bad condition with many rust spots and several dents, you probably don't need collision insurance because if you were in an accident the cost of repairing the car or replacing it would probably cost less than what you'd pay for the insurance.

Not a bad example. But lousy writing. Tighten it:

> Sometimes, collision insurance isn't necessary. Suppose your car is more than five years old and in bad condition. If you're involved in an accident, the cost of repairing the car or replacing it would probably be less than what you'd pay for insurance.

Did you notice that in tightening the paragraph, I eliminated the phrase, *For example?* There are a number of ways to lead into an example. When I write my first draft, I usually start every example with a *for instance* or a *for example.* But then I look to see if that phrase is necessary. In many cases, it's not. The context of the example will tell the reader its function. Many of the examples in this article aren't specifically identified as such. And that last sentence is an example of an example that isn't identified as such.

An example can be introduced simply with a colon: like this.

In other cases, I still need a lead-in, but I can alter the position of the phrase in the sentence. It doesn't always have to go first, for example. I can also change the phrase for variety or to better fit the rhythm and tone of the article. Instead, I might use: "Here are some examples:" or "Let me give you an example."

A Never-Ending Process

Finding examples and fitting them into your article is a continuing process. It's not something that becomes automatic. You must think about it every time you write an article. But sometimes, even professional writers miss: Last week an editor from *Childbirth Educator* called. "I like your article on how to produce a

slide show," she told me. "But there are a couple of places where I'd like to see some more examples."

No better example of my point: good examples often make the difference between an article that sells and one that doesn't.

I'm Sorry, I Don't Speak the Language

"Let me make one thing perfectly clear," President Richard Nixon used to say as he prepared to plunge relentlessly into the linguistic fog. It never really lifted, but from time to time another figure would materialize on the podium—that of White House spokesman Ron Ziegler, who said, at the height of the Watergate scandal, "My previous statements are inoperative."

The golden rule for those within hearing distance of any political utterance is never to begin by sifting the words for meaning. That way lies certain confusion, if not madness. Priority must be given to discerning the *effect* the speaker hoped to achieve by his words. The real import of those words should then fall into place.

Obfuscation in public utterance is by no means peculiar to English, although Canadians who have listened to Throne Speeches might have gained the impression that we have a stranglehold on the art of elliptical language. In fact, alongside some other cultures, we are glittering examples of clarity and directness.

We take you now to Japan, a land of exquisite politeness, where it is often considered coarse to deliver a blunt yes or no. There are, after all, so many ways to couch the meaning in gentler terms, up to—and including—total inversion. Thus, when action is requested, the response might be *"Eii doryoku shimasu,"* which literally means "We shall make efforts," but which actually means "We shall do nothing."

Similarly, when a minister in the Japanese government assures members of the Diet that he will respond to a request with *"kakyuteki sumiyaka"* (the greatest expedition possible), he is making it clear to those who really understand the language that it will not be a rush job.

Mexicans are another people who prize politeness above candor. The visitor who asks direction in the street may come across someone who is so embarrassed at not knowing the answer that he will avoid admitting it, settling instead for the wildest guesses. ("Just keep going until you reach the outskirts of the city. You can't miss it.")

In the cultures of several Southern African states there is a reluctance to admit sluggish responses. This has given rise to a system of graded alacrity. The job may be done "now" (don't hold your breath), "just now" (marginally faster) or in the top gear of "now-now," which could mean tomorrow.

But let's go back to more familiar territory, once described by satirical lyricist Dave Frishberg (with a refreshing lack of circumlocution) as "a blizzard of lies." This would include such wonderful gems of insincerity as "let's do lunch sometime," "your cheque is in the mail," "I'll get back to you," and, usually from secretaries, "He's at a meeting/out of his office/in conference."

There are mysteries here to baffle the Japanese, who may not know that "How are you today?" is not an inquiry after the state of your health. Then there's "Pleased to meet you," "Tomorrow without fail" and "Your secret is safe with me." On picking up the telephone, which of us has not been greeted with the news, "Congratulations, you have been chosen ..."? And is there anyone so out of touch with Western culture that the assurance "We'll keep your name on file" does not inspire utter despair?

We keep a special range of phrases with which to deflect childish demands. Maybe

some of these are still familiar: "Maybe tomorrow," "We'll see" and "This won't hurt a bit."

So, as you go about your business, be on guard against humbug and shallow affectation. And have a nice day.

Tackling Illiteracy

By the turn of the century, more than one billion people worldwide will be unable to read or write the words and numbers crucial to their daily lives. This represents a doubling of the number of illiterates in only 50 years, and paints a chilling picture of the world in the twenty-first century.

While the increasing number of those learning basic reading and writing skills is encouraging, it is not keeping pace with soaring birth rates and the need to deal with advancing technologies. Worse, the learning gap between men and women is widening, and already two-thirds of the world's illiterates are women.

A full 98 per cent of illiterates eke out a living at subsistence farming or in the shantytowns of the Third World. It is possible to admire them for their cunning, inventiveness and tenacity, but there is nothing to envy in their lives of poverty and hopelessness, deprived of the fundamental tools to forge a better life.

A literate population is more productive, healthier and less likely to be exploited; its members can learn of the latest farming techniques and health-care improvements and be apprised of their basic human rights. One UNICEF study demonstrated that infant mortality could be reduced by 10 per cent if parents could read simple phrases pertaining to inoculation, oral rehydration therapy and the importance of breast-feeding (as opposed to the improper use of baby formula).

Despite decades of effort by the United Nations and member countries, graveyards of failed literacy programs dot the world. This failure is not for lack of good intentions, but rather because of too grand a vision and a lack of practicality.

Non-governmental organizations such as the Canadian Organization for Development Through Education are world leaders in developing successful Third World education programs because they have taken a practical approach. CODE has recognized that malnutrition, ill health and illiteracy form a triple scourge for developing nations. Rather than pour millions of dollars into Western-style educational programs, they have targeted the slum-dwellers and rural poor with "teaching for survival," a technique that will benefit generations to come.

In Tanzania, farmers learn that reading can teach them better grain storage methods which, in turn, will put more food in the bellies of their children. In India, rickshaw pullers quickly appreciate that the ability to write numbers can prevent greedy moneylenders from taking advantage of them. In essence, the message is that literacy programs will work only if they help people help themselves.

While the attitude of donor nations is slowly falling into line with this approach, a stronger commitment is required. The Canadian International Development Agency, for example, spends a paltry $2.5-million of its $2-billion annual budget on literacy.

Western aid groups should work with developing nations to create long-term strategies to teach reading and writing. In addition, they should follow through by building the infrastructure to permit life-long learning, including adult education, rural libraries and community newspapers.

Canada can also put its unique strengths to work in the Third World, by exploiting a multicultural base to prepare texts for diverse cultures and supplying newsprint—a rare commodity in many nations—to permit the printing of books, pamphlets and newspapers.

The Abuses of Advertising

Samuel Johnson

The practice of appending to the narratives of public transactions, more minute and domestic intelligence, and filling the news-papers with advertisements, has grown up by slow degrees to its present state.

Genius is shewn only by invention. The man who first took advantage of the general curiosity that was excited by a siege or battle, to betray the readers of news into the knowledge of the shop where the best puffs and powder were to be sold, was undoubtedly a man of great sagacity, and profound skill in the nature of man. But when he had once shewn the way, it was easy to follow him; and every man now knows a ready method of informing the publick of all that he desires to buy or sell, whether his wares be material or intellectual; whether he makes cloaths, or teaches the mathematics; whether he be a tutor that wants a pupil, or a pupil that wants a tutor.

Whatever is common is despised. Advertisements are now so numerous that they are very negligently perused, and it is therefore become necessary to gain attention by magnificence of promises, and by eloquence sometimes sublime and sometimes pathetic.

Promise, large promise, is the soul of an advertisement. I remember a "wash-ball" that had a quality truly wonderful, it gave "an exquisite edge to the razor." And there are now to be sold "for ready money only," some "duvets for bed-coverings, of down, beyond comparison superior to what is called otter down," and indeed such, that its "many excellencies cannot be here set forth." With one excellence we are made acquainted, "it is warmer than four or five blankets, and lighter than one."

There are some, however, that know the prejudice of mankind in favour of modest sincerity. The vendor of the "Beautifying Fluid" sells a lotion that repels pimples, washes away freckles, smooths the skin, and plumps the flesh; and yet, with a generous abhorrence of ostentation, confesses, that it will not "restore the bloom of fifteen to a lady of fifty."

The true pathos of advertisements must have sunk deep into the heart of every man that remembers the zeal shewn by the seller of the anodyne necklace, for the ease and safety "of poor toothing infants," and the affection with which he warned every mother, that "she would never forgive herself" if her infant should perish without a necklace.

I cannot but remark to the celebrated author who gave, in his notifications of the camel and dromedary, so many specimens of the genuine sublime, that there is now arrived another subject yet more worthy of his pen. "A famous Mohawk Indian warrior, who took Dieskaw the French general prisoner, dressed in the same manner with the native Indians when they go to war, with his face and body painted, with his scalping knife, tom-ax, and all other implements of war: a sight worthy the curiosity of every true Briton!" This is a very powerful description; but a critic of great refinement would say that it conveys rather "horror" than "terror." An Indian, dressed as he goes to war, may bring company together; but if he carries the scalping knife and tom-ax, there are many true Britons that will never be persuaded to see him but through a grate.

It has been remarked by the severer judges, that the salutary sorrow of tragick scenes is too soon effaced by the merriment of the epilogue; the same inconvenience arises from the improper disposition of advertisements. The noblest objects may be so associated as to be nade ridiculous. The camel and dromedary themselves might have lost much of their dignity between "The True Flower of Mustard" and "The Original Daffy's Elixir"; and I could not but feel some indignation when I found this illustrious Indian warrior immediately succeeded by "A Fresh Parcel of Dublin Butter."

The trade of advertising is now so near to perfection, that it is not easy to propose any improvement. But as every art ought to be exercised in due subordination to the publick good, I cannot but propose it as a moral question to these masters of the publick ear, whether they do not sometimes play too wantonly with our passions, as when the register of lottery tickets invites us to his shop by an account of the prize which he sold last year; and whether the advertising controvertists do not indulge asperity of language without any adequate provocation; as in the dispute about "straps for razors," now happily subsided, and in the altercation which at present subsists concerning *Eau de Luce*.

In an advertisement it is allowed to every man to speak well of himself, but I know not why he should assume the privilege of censuring his neighbour. He may proclaim his own virtue or skill, but ought not to exclude others from the same pretensions.

Every man that advertises his own excellence, should write with some consciousness of a character which dares to call the attention of the publick. He should remember that his name is to stand in the same paper with those of the King of Prussia, and the Emperor of Germany, and endeavour to make himself worthy of such association.

Some regard is likewise to be paid to posterity. There are men of diligence and curiosity who treasure up the papers of the day merely because others neglect them, and in time they will be scarce. When these collections shall be read in another century, how will numberless contradictions be reconciled, and how shall fame be possibly distributed among the tailors and boddicemakers of the present age.

Surely these things deserve consideration. It is enough for me to have hinted my desire that these abuses may be rectified; but such is the state of nature, that what all have the right of doing, many will attempt without sufficient care or due qualifications.

Covering Refugees with Figures of Speech

Karim H. Karim

While statistics often are quoted to support contrary arguments, figures of speech—being less precise than their numerical counterparts—have even greater potential for misuse. The connotative nature of words can, consciously or unconsciously, create an undertone in prose that on the surface appears neutral. Thus, while such verbal devices as metaphors are deemed essential to good writing, the systematic attachment of negative or positive imagery to individuals, groups, or situations does not make for fair or balanced journalism.

Barrie Zwicker, second editor and publisher of *content*, did an article on stereotyping in an early issue of the magazine. He asked: "Can we do without stereotypes, without generalizations? Perhaps not. They are an economy, shortcuts we substitute for endless inquiry. What matters is the character of the stereotypes, who is using them and why, what attitudes they enforce. In our writing we must recognize them for the coarse and heavy-handed language tools they are, the broadaxes of language. We also need to see that each person employs a *pattern* of stereotypes which is not neutral."

When a consistent pattern of hackneyed descriptions is combined with slanted statistics, the supposed neutrality of reporting is diminished further. And at the point where the truth is barely discernible under layers of words and numbers, covering the story becomes precisely that.

Reporting on the arrival of refugee-claimants in Montreal a year ago was characterized by inflated and ambiguous numbers buttressed by imagery that was predominantly aqueous. The groups of newcomers were described almost invariably as vast quantities

of water rushing in to inundate Canada. The primary image of "flood" was elevated practically to the status of an epithet as newspapers communicated a level of apocalyptic hydrophobia probably not experienced since Noah's time.

Weather-watchers at the Montreal *Gazette* broke the story Dec. 30, 1986, with: "Refugee applicants flood Mirabel airport." The following day, a Canadian Press article in the *Globe and Mail* said: "One of the hundreds of Turkish refugees who have recently flooded into Canada. . . ."

Growing stronger with daily use, the image had entrenched itself as the standard—almost natural—characterization of the situation by the second week of coverage. The *Gazette*'s Jan. 6, 1987, editorial stated that "Federal, provincial and voluntary resources are being strained by this flood of newcomers" and "the imposition of visa requirements helped stem a similar flood of 'refugees' from Portugal." It suggested that "Ottawa should take exceptionally energetic measures to stop the flood."

The following day, the *Toronto Star* reported on Immigration Minister Benoit Bouchard "responding to a public uproar over the arrival of a flood of foreigners—many of them Turks." Joining the chorus, the weekly *Montreal Downtowner* carried a front-page piece Jan. 7 which said that "Refugees, most of them Turks from Germany, are flooding Montreal."

An elaborate network of related metaphors emerged to support the image of "flood"—including trickle, stream, flow, pour, awash, tide, wave, swamp, and deluge. The *Downtowner* mixed metaphors with "this is just the tip of the iceberg in terms of the steady 'deluge' of refugees" in its Jan. 7 issue. Finally, two weeks after it had first sounded the "flood" warning, the *Gazette* signalled the all-clear with a Jan. 13 headline announcing that the "Flood of refugee claimants dries up."

The *Globe and Mail*'s choice of words insisted even more urgently that the country was soon to be completely overwhelmed. On Dec. 31, it wrote of "the wave of more than 700 refugees [that] swept into Montreal" and the "head of a Montreal social support group, [who] said that the group had been swamped." The Jan. 7 issue said "the system is very near the bursting point." A Jan. 5 editorial spoke of "a world awash with 11 million refugees" and that "the pipeline is full of Portuguese and Turkish applicants."

But perhaps the paper's most vivid and disturbing image was drawn by the conclusion of its Dec. 31 editorial which, in asking for stringent refugee restrictions, warned that junior minister Gerry Weiner "cannot simply play the Dutch boy who sticks his finger in the dike." The message seemed to be that if immigration barriers were not immediately reinforced with legislative steel, the unwashed millions will wash over Canada.

Figures of speech such as those used to report the refugee situation have become integral to contemporary writing, but the repetitious and consistent application of negative, inanimate metaphors to specific persons or groups can result gradually in their dehumanization. The individuality of refugee-claimants was being effaced by the unremitting barrage of imagery, making them seem instead as masses of alien matter that was forcibly attempting to penetrate our domain.

An air of authenticity was lent the coverage by the liberal peppering of statistics which, however, were grossly exaggerated when compared with actual figures. Working in tandem, the aqueous metaphors and the inflated numbers created a threatening image of a massive, faceless invasion of our territory.

One would conclude that usual journalistic standards were suspended once it became clear that many of the newcomers were not what they claimed to be. The existence of a closely-related set of metaphors and framing of the situation in many papers reveals either a lack of imagination or the uniform regurgitation of the language, definitions, and perspectives originating from dominant sources.

In his piece on stereotyping, Zwicker quoted from George Orwell's essay *Politics and the English Language*. A writer, said Orwell, can shirk his duty and "let the ready-made phrases come crowding in." These words and phrases "will construct your sentences for you—even think your thoughts for you, to a certain extent—and at need they will perform the important service of partially concealing your meaning even from yourself. It is at this point that the special connection between politics and the debasement of writing becomes clear."

An Outdoor Journal

Tom W. Parkin

For all the interest in Canada's outdoors, there is still an art of the explorers that modern recreationists have not revived. It is writing—the keeping of a daily log or journal. From factors, adventurers and surveyors we have detailed accounts of life on the frontier. They wrote about the weather, the country, the people they dealt with; whatever seemed of importance that day. Many of those early journals were subsequently published because they were entertaining reading and revealed exciting information about the New World.

Nowadays the wilderness is old hat; keeping journals is considered old-fashioned. Recorded observations are left to naturalists or researchers. I admit I wouldn't add pen and book to a heavy pack. But I do enjoy keeping a written record of back country canoe trips. Here weight and space are not a restriction.

Paddling seems to make me reflective. The intensity of the experience is often so strong that writing it down is a way of digesting it or ensuring the smaller pieces aren't forgotten:

September 10, 1982
The river is fast and smooth and very dirty.
It hisses sand along the canoe bottom. I can tell
my rate of travel by the sound it makes. On low
gradients the water can't carry the particles and
the hiss diminishes. Upwellings bring larger
grains with more force, and the noise is almost
like a small leak spurting under my gear.

As an outdoor writer that kind of observation is often useful to set a mood in an article I might write later. But writing a journal is strictly for yourself. Don't be critical of how you express your thoughts. It's the process of writing, not thinking, that will bring later insights. Just get down whatever you feel is important. It might be as simple as a joke:

August 10, 1984
Tonight Paul introduced us to Sock, a
mysterious mixture of hot chocolate and the
contents of a sock. It turned out to be white
rum. The wool prevented bruising of the bottle
and concealed the contents from the uninitiated.

For some people the act of writing about themselves is as difficult as speaking in public. What helps to overcome this is to write at a specific time or place each day. The routine breeds familiarity. I like to retreat to the tent after supper, but before it's too dark to read.

If all this sounds like extra work for little reward, remember that a journal can have very practical uses. You may be looking at pictures later and forget where some were taken. Or years from now a friend might be planning the same trip. Could you give that friend a description of where the portages were? How about the name of the lake with such good fishing in front of the campsite? Or a journal might simply refresh a favorite memory. Here's how we concluded one wilderness journey:

August 17, 1984
We crowded into a roadside cafe for the last
supper, happy to be out of the rain. Deb and
Joan had been the last canoe all afternoon, and

now announced that they had been devising the
trip awards.
Wilf was presented with a box of waterproof
matches as he always rose early to be the
campfire lighter. He soon became known for his
explosive gasoline starts. No scouting technique
for that pyromaniac—Wilf's into high tech.
Philosopher-of-the-trip award went to
MaryAnn, whose pronouncement "So!" became
a byword during silent moments of conversation.
She was presented with a sewing kit.
Rob liked to play in the rapids with his boat,
and make us wait for him at every boulder and
backwater. He received a stone marked with an
endless eddy turn so that he might practise them
even in his bathtub.

That was the funniest trip of my life. Looking back through my journal, I see that it wasn't wilderness that we explored so much as ourselves. In a way, that's the only exploration left to us.

Perhaps this is why journals have fallen out of favor. We fail to see our own discovery of the outdoors as important. What an error. As wilderness diminishes, it becomes increasingly important that we validate our experience and communicate the wild to others.

The Creative Approach
The Royal Bank Letter

The notion of creativity is so new in the historical scheme of things that it was not until well into the present century that the word began to show up in dictionaries. Writers and philosophers in the past have had a great deal to say about talent, imagination and inspiration, but only in relatively recent times have these been wrapped together into the phenomenon we call creativity.

The oversight can be traced back to old-fashioned snobbery of the kind that took for granted that the common man was incapable of "creating" anything. The sages of history believed almost unanimously that the universe functioned according to a cosmic pattern in which everything and everybody had a place, with themselves near the top. The place of ordinary souls in the natural order was decidedly not to bring new ideas and works into being. It was to stick to the labours assigned to them in the eternal plan.

The closest traditional thinkers ever came to the modern concept of creativity was their concept of genius, which was strongly influenced by snobbery and determinism. The word "genius" derives from the term for the presiding spirits which were supposed to have dwelt within people in ancient Rome. The individuals known as geniuses were thought to be endowed by the gods with transcendental intellectual and/or artistic powers. Like gentlemen, geniuses were born, not made.

If the occasional prodigy like Michelangelo was thrown up out of the masses, the anomaly was conveniently explained by the theory that he was divinely inspired. Otherwise men (almost always men; hardly ever women) of genius came from the dominant class. This was hardly surprising, because they were the only members of society with the education and leisure to make the most of their talents. The bulk of the people had neither the time nor the opportunity to exercise whatever creative ability they might have had.

The prospect that there might be a vast untapped mine of talent and intelligence in the population at large was scarcely considered. Neither was much thought given to the possibility that talent might come in degrees, so that people of lesser abilities might be capable of making valuable contributions to the quality of life.

The advent of public education in the western nations in the latter part of the 19th century did little to change this attitude. The method of teaching by rote was not conducive to encouraging youngsters to use their imaginations. The idea that creativity in childhood should be actively nurtured would have been considered next to heresy in the age of "spare the rod and spoil the child."

It took the pioneers of psychology to see the plain fact that one did not have to be divinely endowed to conceive original works of art or inventions. William James was moving in the direction of our present conception of creativity when he wrote in his *The Principles of Psychology* in 1890: "Genius, in truth, means little more than the faculty of perceiving in an unhabitual way."

Carl Jung spoke of the "creative man" in his essays in the 1920s and '30s, though he remained somewhat mesmerized by the mystical theory of genius. Nevertheless, he and other writers on psychology helped to refine the concept of creativity we have today.

That concept, as it is usually understood, is that the potential for originality exists to a greater or lesser degree in every human. It is like a sixth sense, as inherent in the organism as the other five. If it cannot exactly be taught, it can be cultivated by training, example, and habituation. And it can be brought to bear on work of any scale or nature: An office manager who comes up with a bright new scheme for handling paperwork is being as creative in her field as a novelist is in hers.

Though all this might seem clear enough, the question of what constitutes creativity remains beset by misconceptions. The most basic of these is that it is confined to the arts, an impression which artists themselves do little to correct. It is in the arts that creativity has become a rather derisive term. Critics and professional practitioners cringe at the thought of all the incomprehensible poetry, the graceless sculptures and truly primitive paintings produced in the name of letting the creative juices flow.

The opportunity to be creative has been interpreted by some as an opportunity to look and behave like an artist without going to the trouble of actually being one. This leads to another misconception of creativity, which is that it is sufficient unto itself.

It is, of course, associated with freedom— the freedom to let the spirit rove in the undiscovered reaches of the imagination. But what Matthew Arnold said about opinions is equally pertinent to creative endeavours: "It is a very great thing to be able to think as you like; but, after all, an important question remains: *what* you think."

Reporting on his experiences preparing a television series on the subject a few years ago, journalist Bill Moyers wrote: "Two things are implied in the word 'creativity' as I have come to understand it: novelty and significance. What is created is new, and the new opens up paths that expand human possibilities." Without the element of significance, creative efforts amount to no more than self-indulgence. As Ralph Waldo Emerson so nicely put it, "Talent for talent's sake is a bauble and a show."

Among the definitions of "creative" in the Oxford English Dictionary is "showing imagination as well as routine skill." The reference to skill is essential to the meaning. A man could compose music in his head like another Mozart, but without the skill to play it or to set in down in musical notation, his artistry would be lost to the world.

Sir Joshua Reynolds insisted that he would never have become known as a painter of genius if he had not acquired the requisite technique to take advantage of the artistic breakthroughs made before him. New heights, he said, are reached through a knowledge of what has already been done and a knowledge of how to build on it. "It is by being conversant with the inventions of others that we learn to invent; as by reading the thoughts of others, we learn to think."

The assumption that there is a mystical element in the creation of great works, he said, arises from an ignorance of the process. "The untaught mind finds a vast gulf between its own powers, and those of works of complicated art, which it is unutterably unable to fathom; and it supposes that such a void can only be passed by supernatural powers."

Reynolds did not deny that nature gives some people more capacity than others, but he nonetheless believed that strenuous effort is needed to make the best of whatever ability is present. "If you have great talents, industry will improve them; if you have but moderate abilities, industry will supply their deficiency."

Some of the most brilliant figures in history had to toil long and hard to give birth to their masterpieces. Beethoven's musical notebook bears all the scars of agonized creation. Dr. Samuel Johnson, by his own account, wrote "doggedly." The Nobel Prize-winning novelist Sinclair Lewis described the writing process as "painful." As a general rule, creation is "10 per cent inspiration and 90 per cent perspiration," as Thomas Edison said.

Discoveries in science and technology are thought by "untaught minds" to come in blinding flashes or as the result of dramatic accidents. Sir Alexander Fleming did not, as legend would have it, look at the mould on a piece of cheese and get the idea for penicillin there and then. He experimented with anti-bacterial substances for nine years before he made his discovery. Inventions and innovations almost always come out of laborious trial and error. Innovation is like hockey: Even the best players miss the net and have their shots blocked much more frequently than they score.

The point is that the players who score most are the ones who take the most shots on the net—and so it goes with innovation in any field of activity. The prime difference between innovators and others is one of approach. Everybody gets ideas, but innovators work consciously on theirs, and they follow them through until they prove practicable or otherwise. They never reject any thought that comes into their heads as outlandish. What ordinary people see as fanciful abstractions, professional innovators see as solid possibilities.

"Creative thinking may mean simply the realization that there's no particular virtue in doing things the way they have always been done," wrote Rudolph Flesch, the language guru. This accounts for our reaction to deceptively simple innovations like plastic garbage bags and suitcases on wheels that make life more convenient: "How come nobody thought of that before?"

Creativity does not demand absolute originality. It often takes the form of throwing an old ball with a new twist. A concert pianist may play a composition written three centuries ago note-for-note and still find unsuspected values in it. An engineer may devise a fresh application of a principle first propounded by Archimedes.

The creative approach begins with the proposition that nothing is as it appears. Innovators will not accept that there is only one way to do anything. Faced with getting from A to B, the average person will automatically set out on the best-known and apparently simplest routing. The innovator will search for alternate courses which may prove easier in the long run and are bound to be more interesting and challenging even if they lead to dead ends.

Highly creative individuals really do march to a different drummer. A study directed by J.P. Guilford, ex-president of the American Psychological Association, found that humans go about thinking in two ways. The most common way is convergent thinking, which spirals inward towards the centre looking for answers. The other is divergent thinking, which radiates out from the centre, opening up new lines of inquiry. Everybody thinks both ways from time to time, but particularly creative people are in the habit, whether natural or acquired, of thinking divergently.

Small children are divergent thinkers, always liable to take off on a tangent. Any thoughtful adult watching a group of them playing "let's pretend" will be humbled by their sheer creativity. Some psychologists, in fact, try to draw out the creative strain in adults by having them play like children. The practice recognizes the truth in Carl Jung's

statement that "the dynamic principle of fantasy is play, which also belongs to the child, and as such . . . appears to be inconsistent with serious work. But without this playing at fantasy, no creative work ever yet came to birth."

The poet and essayist Samuel Taylor Coleridge said that genius resides in a combination of a child's sense of magic and an adult's trained mentality. Unfortunately, most children start to suppress their wonderment and adventurousness even before they reach their teens. This happens because of pressure from their peers to conform to group standards. Originality begins to falter as soon as children conceive the fear of looking like fools.

In later life, especially within organizations, the people with the greatest mental openness and the most original slants on questions are often regarded as office clowns, whose far-out ideas are good-naturedly laughed out of meetings. Often, too, they settle into the role their colleagues have assigned to them. It is easier to play the eccentric than to fight for one's ideas.

Highly creative people *are* eccentric in the literal sense of the word. They have less respect for precedent and more willingness to take risks than others. They are less likely to be motivated by money or career advancement than by the inner satisfaction of hatching and carrying out ideas. In conventional corporate circles, such traits can look quite eccentric indeed.

But while there is an identifiable creative personality which follows these lines, testing has shown that very few people, if any, are without the instinct to be creative. One point on which all the experts are agreed is that many people are not as creative as they could be simply because they tell themselves that they are not the creative type. To act creatively, you must first give yourself permission to try.

Everybody, the saying goes, is a genius once a year; the certified geniuses merely have their bright ideas closer together. It might be added that everybody is a genius while asleep. "Dreaming is an act of pure imagination, attesting in all men a creative power, which, if it were available in waking, would make every man a Dante or a Shakespeare," wrote Frederick Henry Hodge, a founder of the transcendental school of philosophy.

Though some rare types are capable of re-capturing their dreams, most of us are left with only fragments or vague impressions of our unconscious wanderings. The nearest we can get to the perfectly free state of dreaming is to day-dream, which our culture tells us is not a fit thing for an adult to do.

In addition to the social misapprobation attached to day-dreaming, modern society makes it somehow anti-social to engage in silent contemplation. It is ironic that, in an age when people have more leisure time than ever before, they spend less time than ever ex-ploring their own imaginations. We always have to be *doing* something, if only watching television. Consciously creative persons do not feel uncomfortable "doing nothing." They allow for plenty of quiet time in which to spin fantasies and toy with ideas.

Because creativity is a habit of mind, creative people deliberately cultivate the habit. They train themselves to take a playful approach, thinking up metaphors and similes, playing imaginary roles, and conjuring up scenarios.

Physical age is not a factor. "No matter how old you get, if you can keep the desire to be creative, you are keeping the man-child alive," as actor John Cassavetes said.

In fact, young-minded people have an advantage over people who are merely young: they have years of learning behind them. "The real key to being creative lies in what to do with your knowledge," says creativity consultant Roger Von Oech. "Creative think-ing requires an attitude or outlook which allows you to search for ideas and manipulate your knowledge and experience."

Van Oech and others in his field see a serious need to develop the latent creativity in ordinary human beings. On the private level, an inability to express themselves causes some people emotional difficulties and even mental illness. On the public level, the exploi-tation of the creative resources within the population is essential to improving the lot of mankind.

At a time when we are using up our other natural resources at a perilously rapid rate, creativity is the chief renewable resource left to us in treating global problems. If we human beings are wise, we will work to remove the social and institutional barriers to exercising creativity everywhere. We should keep in mind that creation is the opposite of destruc-tion. Creativity offers the hope of new solu-tions to old problems. By making creativity a way of life at work, at home and at play, we can not only fulfil ourselves personally, but contribute to the building of a better world.

Bizbuzz

William Safire

Nobody can apply for a job these days—or interface with a personnel recruiter in the hopes of impacting on his bottom line—without a degree in "bizbuzz," the jargon that prioritizes the career path of the rising young ballpark figurer.

I have already flunked. The figures of speech used in the preceding paragraph are already business archaisms that might as well have been the patois of Commodore Vander-bilt or Andrew Carnegie.

"The biggest 'bad' corporate word," opines Walter Kiechel 3d, associate editor of *Fortune* magazine, "is *impact* as a verb." The former noun has been used so often in its verb form in board rooms that *impact on* has lost its punch, and rising executives are now testing the effect of *affect*.

"*Interface* is a dying word in management," adds John F. Lubin, professor of management at the University of Pennsylvania's Wharton

School. "It was taken from systems engineering, where it meant the juncture between two pieces. For a while, *system* was taking over the language of management, but this, too, is dying."

Bottom line is still kicking around, but too many outsiders have been using it, and in jargon, freshness is all. "The *bottom line* originally referred to earnings figures," reports Timothy B. Blodgett of the *Harvard Business Review*. "Bottom-line responsibility is responsibility for the economic welfare of a division or subsidiary that is supposed to turn a profit. However, the phrase has expanded to include more than just earnings and profits; it can mean, 'The onus is on us' for just about anything." Mr. Blodgett is a senior editor; he has a *straight-line responsibility* to the editor in chief, and a *dotted-line responsibility* to a bunch of other editors. Life follows chart. While we're entangled in lines, Professor Michael Porter at the Harvard Business School defines *dotted-line responsibility* as "when two people consult with or interact with each other, but one does not report to the other." In olden times, the "dotted line" was where the customer signed; now it is where the responsibility is diffused, and even that expression is fading fast.

Ballpark figure is developing a paunch, too. This derivation of "in the ballpark," an indication of proximity (in contrast to a ball hit clear out of the stadium), is being replaced by one of the new triple hyphenations that make up adjectival phrases dear to bizbuzz: *back-of-the-envelope*. There is a quickly figured difference in meaning, however: "A *ballpark figure* is a rough estimate," explains lexicographer Sol Steinmetz, "while a *back-of-the-envelope sum* is one simply or easily arrived at without the need of a pocket calculator."

Another example of the triple hyphenator is *top-of-the-line*, a compound adjective launched in the late 1960's by auto manufacturers to describe their most expensive models. The British equivalent is *top-of-the-market*, and the phrase is not considered run-down or ram-shackle by bizbuzz linguists on top of the state of the art, which is the bottom line on *top-of-the-line*.

Now that we know what is out, what is in?

If you are sad about the loss of *impact on*, try the new *abstract away*. "This means to dwindle into nothing," says the *H.B.R.'s* Blodgett. "If something *abstracts away*, it has ceased to be definable." Nice phrase; to move from the concrete to the abstract and then to vanish, like the Cheshire cat, leaving only the grin.

Hands-on, a compound adjective with one measly hyphen, has a stranglehold on the throats of businesspeople today. (I almost wrote "businessmen." Somebody must be getting to me.) The original meaning was "vocational," and the first citation in the Barnhart files is "hands-on instruction" for vocational schools, and was a play on "hands off," or so theoretical that it abstracted away. Now it means "practical"; nobody with hands-on experience, in a job interview, would claim anything as outdated as "practical experience." A synonym is *line* experience; this time, the metaphor is probably not from accounting, as in *bottom line*, but from the military, which contrasts *line* (from "front line") and *staff* (or headquarters) experience.

When in need of a modern mystifier, and tired of systems and the same old interfaces, reach for the favorite new management noun: *matrix*. "This came out of organizational behavior," says Professor Lubin, "and was used to describe orthogonal relationships." Asked to put that on a dotted-line basis, Professor Lubin explained: "That's when you have two bosses, or when responsibility is shared between divisions. Came from mathematics, and it's overused." He can hands-on that again. In the Wharton 1980 catalogue, a course in matrix management is advertised in this way: "The unique problem of changing, implementing and fine-tuning matrix forms will be highlighted." According to J.M. Rosenberg's *Dictionary of Business and Management*, "a matrix organization exists when organizational members have a dual allegiance— to a particular assignment or task and also to their department." O.K.: two bosses, a matrix and (soon to come) a patrix.

Students of bizbuzz (not to be confused with jargon scholars, who are in buzzbiz) search for optical combining forms. For a generation, combination-oriented linguists were studying the use of *-wise*, while formwise lexicographers were collecting the usages of *-oriented*. You could be *job-oriented*, *leisure-oriented*, or even *Occident-oriented*; similarly, languagewise, you could be *advertisingwise*, *careerwise*, or even *smartswise*.

Forget all that. The new combining forms are *-wide* and *-intensive*. According to Judy Uhl, senior editor of the division of research for the Harvard Business School, about whose dotted-line responsibilities I have not inquired: "A very common thing is to add *-wide* at the end of things to mean 'a totality,' such as *corporate-wide*, *industry-wide*. This can also be done without a hyphen, as in *personnelwide*."

On the *-intensive* front, the earliest entries were *labor-intensive* and *capital-intensive*, but Steinmetz has pockets bulging with citations for *profit-intensive*, *energy-intensive*, *people-intensive*, *assets-intensive*, and *technology-intensive*. His work is neologism-intensive, and applies dictionarywide.

Vision is a hot word in executive aeries, usually defined as "the ability to see around corners," rather than off into the distance. *Style* is equally sought after, and what *manager style* a corporation prefers determines its character. *Fortune's* Kiechel points to the popular *earthquake style*, "which is when a manager comes in and shakes everything up."

Bailout has replaced *rescue* in bizbuzz: A dispute is raging among etymologists about its derivation. One school holds that it is from the act of a pilot donning a parachute and leaping out of a falling airplane; another points to the frenzied activity of a fisherman bailing out a boat that is taking in water.

If a bailout fails, a company no longer goes bankrupt; it goes *belly up*, also a fishing meta-

phor, perhaps influenced by "belly up to the bar." At *Forbes* magazine, such a term is frowned upon. Geoffrey Smith, an assistant managing editor, who has a wavy-line responsibility to Malcolm Forbes, points to a memo directing writers to stay away from such bizbuzz as *clobber*, *plummet*, and *soar* (trite descriptions of earnings, gains or losses), along with *on stream*, *game plan*, *shortfall*, and *upscale*.

My top-of-the-line model has just intersected with my bottom-line judgment, forming a dotted-line responsibility to all those who want to bellow at bizbuzz and outplace all its speakers. That's earthquake style.

Write Science Stories Simply
Robina Salter

Science writers build bridges between laboratories and living rooms. Their news may enlighten, amuse, discourage, but it often gives us clues to having better health, greater energy, and maybe even longer life. A good science story intrigues the reader, opening a window onto the puzzle the scientist is piecing together on our behalf.

Basically science reporters write two kinds of stories: "spot news" and feature articles. Spot news happens one day and may appear in print by the afternoon or the next morning. One example of this kind of story comes from the University of Alberta where a professor has announced he can produce special radioactive solutions to check for signs of disease within the human body.

The feature story, moving at a more leisurely pace, gives the reader a broad picture of the research and more details of how the "findings" will affect our lives. For the latter type of story, "doing one's homework" ensures a more productive interview.

If I need more information than my science files offer, the scientist's secretary will often provide reprints describing the research. Major reference libraries in university centres hold a rich vein of data ensuring an informed interview.

Even when I think I know the answer to the question, I will ask it anyway so I can use the researcher's direct quotation. This provides a level of authenticity and a change of pace for the reader.

Whenever I begin to gather information for an article, I jot down the telling phrase, the spontaneous metaphor, the unsolicited simile, all of which are hard to come by when I am faced with a blank page and an imminent deadline.

When time permits, I tell the scientist at the outset that I shall read the first draft of the article to him or her by telephone. This assurance fosters trust from the moment I say, "Tell me about. . . ." The interview flows with an easy accord and accuracy is assured.

Before putting together the science story that goes to press, you need to consider the differences between academic writing style and the way your article must be phrased so your reader can complete the journey from living room to laboratory satisfactorily.

As you read technical material you will come upon a certain amount of gobbledygook, a mix of circumlocution and jargon obscuring meaning and often ending in "izing" or "ize." Beware of the trap whereby the suffix "ize" creates such monsters as "priorize," "normalize," and "legitimize," the stereotypes of the "in" jargon.

Resist the temptation to use the subjunctive mood to float false promises of "breakthroughs," and specious "cures" on such words as may, perhaps, maybe. Let's share all the news we are entitled to, but never promise more than the scientist can deliver.

Scientific texts are often bloated with the passive voice obscuring the source and boring the reader. When someone writes that "It was found that some of the DNA was isolated from the locus of the gene . . ." it suggests that some disembodied spirit, rather than a flesh-and-blood scientist did the experiment.

The passive voice does, however, vary the structure of the sentence and provides relief from the rhythm of subject-verb-object. But the active voice helps to keep the sentences crisp and clear. It calls for a specific subject and makes a forthright statement telling who is doing what in as few words as possible.

Some editors suggest sentences be kept to fifteen or sixteen words in length. An example they quote is that of the executive who once said that his children wrote model sentences of brevity and precision. The letters read, "I passed." Or, "I need money." Or simply, "I'm moving back home."

Another quality vital to science writing is clarity. To achieve clarity we must select effective nouns and verbs; the more apt the sentence's nouns and verbs, the fewer modifiers we need. Whenever possible use livelier verbs than "to have" and "to be." A sentence where "is" is the verb is dull indeed!

Often we render verbs impotent by locking them up in nouns as happens in the expression "in the creation of mutant genes. . . ." Change it to "in creating mutant genes . . ." and we have a stronger sentence whose meaning is clearer.

In the same vein we must also resist turning verbs into nouns. Have you ever heard a scientist or reporter say that he or she will "access the information" or that minority groups hope to "impact on legislation"?

Other language abuses to avoid include using the word "preventative" for preventive and "orientate" for orient. And the word "parameter" rightly belongs to the mathematician. (My prize for word abuse goes to the speaker who told his audience about the optimality of the personalogical parameters.)

Scientific literature abounds with "noun clusters," those strings of nouns strung together as in "health care physician manpower studies." Nevertheless, science reporters need not tie up their meanings in such devices.

Many people depend upon newspapers and

magazines for nearly all their news in science and medicine. Therefore such stories must speak clearly, overcoming jargon and other stylistic tics that obstruct the reader's understanding.

Is Objectivity Possible?

Paul Sheenan

Journalists are told by their editors to be objective in their news presentations—to report all facts without distortion, prejudice, or personal feelings. They are also advised by their editors to gather and present news which will stimulate and involve readers. Sometimes these two demands seem to conflict. If news stories are presented without personal involvement and interest readers may become bored; if news presentations express personal feelings readers might think they are biased and unreliable. And if news presentations are written as though by a robot, the words used would convey some feeling to the readers—if the readers were robots.

Though newswriters are reasonably sure of the distinction between fact and opinion when writing a news story, they are often not quite so confident in their choice of words for their story. Editors and reporters, being very sensitive to the power of language, realize that certain words in news copy can create positive or negative feelings. For example, does a student group "demand" or "request" a change in the school dress code? If the writer presenting a story on this subject uses "demand" he must be sure that the student group proposing the change is really "demanding" and not just "requesting" a change, because some readers might react negatively to student "protest" but positively to student "participation." To avoid taking sides in any dispute and spreading propaganda for any cause through their use of language, journalists take great pains in writing a story, deleting any words or sentences which will misrepresent a person or event.

A newspaper's job is to clarify issues and events, not to confuse them. To do this, journalists must decide *how* to report an event. Newspaper coverage of the foreign and domestic policies of the government differ in part from one newspaper to another because different publishers have different viewpoints about government activities. For example, a newspaper in favor of capital punishment might feature a series on "The Death Sentence—A Crime Deterrent" while a newspaper favoring abolition of the death sentence might provide front-page space for an article titled "Reforming the Penal System." Individual newspapers usually cannot avoid taking a position on the issue facing the public (during election campaigns newspapers openly support their candidates in their editorials), though the best newspapers try to prevent prejudice in their news reporting.

Recapture Your Feelings

Diana Stout

. . . Merely keeping a journal puts you on the road to becoming a better writer. The more you practice the better you become at whatever you attempt, whether it's playing the piano, woodworking or writing. The more you write, the more professional your writing will become.

Like the runner who uses a starting block to get off the line quickly in a race, you can use your journal as a starting block. Writing in your journal gets the words flowing from head to pen in small easy exercises much like the sprinter doing his warm-up exercises. How hard is it to write about yesterday's events or thoughts? Not hard at all. But how much more difficult is it to sit down and begin a story or article and have the words flowing as soon as you pick up your pen? It's not nearly the same exercise at all—it's like asking a runner to run a marathon without any warm-up exercises. Midway through the race, he's apt to cramp up and never see the finish line. Midway through your story or article you could hit a block and find yourself unable to finish your manuscript. Would you be able to get back on track or would you need to go back to the beginning and do those warm-up exercises to get your thoughts together so that your manuscript is clean and single-minded from beginning to end?

There are some authors who have no problem in getting started, but they are a rare and well-trained breed. There are many more of us who use our journals as stepping stones to our writing. While some writers write letters, make out grocery lists or whatever—keeping a journal is more beneficial. Think of the journal as a letter to yourself. What things do you want to remember?

Do you record bits and pieces of conversation you've heard? What struck you most about those conversations? Was it the accent, the truism, the humor, or was it something you wish you had said? Instead of wishing *you* had said it, use it. Characters and plots have been built on less than snatches of overheard conversations.

Did you record how angry you were with that certain someone and how you would have changed the conversation had you to do it all over again? Use those feelings of anger and attach them to one of your characters. Let the character feel the way that your heart pounded, the way that your palms turned sweaty, and the heat you could feel rising above your collar. Use your conversations. Have one character using his anger the way you think you did and have the other character smarter, responding the way you wish you had.

Did you record your last love affair—the Everest of joy you felt when you first fell in love and the Death Valley low of desertion, betrayal and resentment when you broke up? Record the feelings, emotions, and sensations you felt not only inside you but around you as well. Colors, conversations, even chores you

hate to do are different when you first fall in love than later on when you are in the depths of despair over a breakup.

The same is true of your depressions as you trod through the valleys and peaks of work, health, vacations, and day-to-day stresses. Record not only what happens to you and how you feel, but also how others felt and acted. Try to understand why certain things happen.

By learning the how's and why's, you can give your characters better motives for their actions, mistakes, and the failings they'll have.

Are you a people watcher? Most writers are. Record what you see. How do people dress? What little idiosyncrasies do you notice? What do people do when they think they're not being watched? How do they act when with a parent as compared to a friend or sibling?

Are there childhood events that are dear to your heart or events that can still make you angry or upset? Use your journal and write about them. Record everything you can remember. After some time has passed, go back and reread your entries. Did you write them as a child still gripped in emotion, or did you write about them as an adult looking back? Analyze what you wrote from different angles. Not only can you use those events in a book, but you might also be able to write a self-help or how-to article as I did.

For instance, there was a time when I hated Christmas. It wasn't until I "went back" about five years and started rereading my journal entries that I learned the reasons why. Using clues taken from my journal, I was able to make changes. Now Christmas has become one of my favorite holidays. I was also able to write several articles showing others how they could have a hassle-free Christmas, a fun holiday, a time to cherish and enjoy. Without my journal I would still be in my Christmas rut, and I wouldn't have made the article sales that I did.

Dreams and nightmares should also be recorded in your journal. The unconscious mind works best while you are sleeping. An answer to that plot problem you've been having could be revealed in one of your dreams. The crisis you need to finish your story could be a nightmare you had.

I always keep paper and pencil beside my bed. Many times I have awakened from a dream long enough to jot down a word or two in the dark.

Sometimes I don't remember having written anything, but seeing those scribbly marks the next day brings back the whole dream and sometimes a story or article to write as a result.

As a writer, develop the habit of keeping paper and pencil in those special places where you spend time. For me, it's the kitchen, my favorite chair, in the car and in the bathroom. Later those notes and jottings can be transferred into your journal, where you can expound and reflect upon them.

Writer's block is another common problem for writers. I have to admit that in all the years I have been writing, it has never been a problem for me. I may be working on a piece and get stuck at some point, but leaving it and working on something else usually gives me time to see that piece in a fresh light. Reading through my journal may give me new ideas and new angles. I believe writers can burn themselves out occasionally, but to run out of ideas—never! A journal is a fountain of ideas, full of the little things that happen day to day. It is those little things from which articles and stories are written.

A journal is the best piece of literature you can take with you when vacationing. The emotions and experiences one has when traveling are so vast that it is a loss to writers who don't pack their journals. How can you recapture your feelings the very first time you felt the airplane take off and you wondered how such a massive piece of equipment could get off the ground? How do you recapture the sound of the paddlewheels of the boat as it churns its way down the Mississippi?

The only way to really capture those moments, feelings and events is to write them down when they are happening or shortly thereafter. Don't wait until a week later when you'll be home, enclosed in your office, the pen flapping between your fingers, and you're stuck not knowing where to start.

A journal is the best way to relive and experience life as you've lived it, smelled it, heard it and watched it. A photograph can't begin to compare with the words you can write or the magic you can recreate through your pen.

Your journal is your own private gold mine. It can bring forth joy, sadness, excitement, dreams and memories of the past. . . .

Sportswriting Pitfalls

Bill Ward

1. *Writing in sports jargon*—Outlaw all sports language; write in clearcut language understood by the nonfan. Avoid such tangled construction as "The hurler unlimbered a blazer which the sticker cracked into the outer pasture for a one-bagger. The left gardener gloved it on the hop and sizzled it to the keystone snacker." One bit of sports slang is one bit too many.

2. *Organizing a game summary in chronological order*—Unless the kickoff is your most newsworthy element, organize the story with the most interesting details at the start. It is easy to tell a story chronologically; it usually is also dull.

3. *Narrating play-by-play*—This is dull, flat, routine, unimaginative, hard for the reader to follow, and stimulates few mental images. "Jones smacked the middle for six yards to the 18. Then Smith fired a pass to Smyth who took it on the 15 and ran to the 12. After two incompleted passes, Jones snaked to the 9. Funkle was thrown for a two-yard loss." Ad

. . . .

infinitum. Who cares? If you must include a play-by-play sequence, clip it short. Be sure it's important.

4. *Becoming a critic*—Your job is to report a game, not to coach a team. Frustrated athletes who become sports writers are the bane of coaches. Sports writers know very little about the techniques of the game; they know even less about the subtle problems that coaches and athletes encounter behind the scenes. I recall a metropolitan sports writer who criticized a collegiate halfback for loafing and losing. In truth, the halfback was badly crippled, a fact which had been hidden from the press and from the opposition before, during, and after the game.

5. *Failing to get specific, detailed facts*—Lazy, indifferent, unknowing? Whatever the reason, it's inexcusable. A sports writer must systematically dig, day by day, for any facts he may need for a story.

6. *Writing with too many adjectives and adverbs*—I have never visualized a "low fly-ball," so why a high one? There are also too many "vicious tackles, smoking slides, diving catches, smashing drives, blistering line-drives." Save your modifiers for moments of true impact.

7. *Including too many statistics*—Not many fans can tell what Biff McNasty hit in 1906; most don't care. Statistics are not sports, but merely a side-product. Thus, you must write about the action and the human interest. Don't turn a sports event into a bookkeeper's nightmare. "Tonight the Beaneaters (8 wins, 5 losses), averaging 6-2 in height and 195 pounds, meet for the second time the Yellow Sox (10 wins, 3 losses), averaging 6-1 and 184. The Beaneaters with a .321 shooting average came into the game with a 3-game winning streak (the longest in the conference this year thus far) after snapping a 5-game losing streak. . . ."

C H A P T E R
Six

Writing Short Stories, Drama, and Poetry

A. FORE-WORDS

Warm up for activities in this chapter by discussion and writing. These quotations and questions may help you begin.

Plutarch   "Painting is silent poetry, and poetry, painting that speaks."

Isaac Bashevis Singer   "When I was a little boy they called me a liar, but now that I am grown up they call me a writer."

F. Scott Fitzgerald   "I've asked an awful lot of my imagination."

1.   Share a favourite short story or poem with your writing group.

2.   Listen to a radio drama, noting how the experience differs from viewing a performance.

3.   Compare pacing and narrative techniques in your favourite situation comedy and an educational television theatre presentation. Account for variations.

B. FOUNDATIONS

Why do ye call the poet lonely,
Because he dreams in lonely places?
He is not desolate, but only
Sees, where ye cannot, hidden faces.

—Archibald Lampman

Do you daydream about writing a best-selling work of fiction or hit lyrics? Or perhaps you secretly long to be a screenwriter. In earlier chapters, you've built a strong foundation; now it's time to take the plunge. But where do you begin?

What if you were to write for a school literary magazine? In this chapter you'll explore possibilities and decide with your instructor which to pursue. As with the news project, publication is a bonus which focuses your writing and allows you to share your creativity with a real audience. But whether you publish a group or individual anthology, or just complete a selection of activities, you'll be challenged to write in a variety of imaginative forms. The process is enjoyable, and practical as well; writing poems, plays, and other forms of prose fiction enhances your ability to analyze literature.

Before commencing to write specific literary forms, you may wish to survey the territory as Tarvo and his group did. Their working definition had three parts. Literature is material

- written in verse or prose

- characterized by excellence of form, expression, artistic skill, and creative imagination

- of universal or enduring interest or importance.

The students visited libraries and bookstores, researching samples and talking to staff. Let's play selected scenes from a videotape made by two media students who chronicled highlights of their experience. (*Tip:* The videotape was an independent learning project donated by producers to the school's library of "how-to" material.)

Scene: Friday at 3:00. Tarvo, Kirsten, Craig, and Sasha are surrounded by heaps of magazines and books on the library floor.

Kirsten: Let's clean up. I'm late for work.
Tarvo: Me too. But have we defined "literary magazine"?

Sasha: There's so much stuff called "literature."
Kirsten: It's not just stories. We should organize departments.
Craig: What if we list the types we found and then weed some out?
Tarvo: Yeah. A "what if" list. Hey! Let's call our magazine WHAT IF?
Sasha: Let's include things for the whole family; it's more fun that way.

The following announcement summarizes the group's decisions about their second publishing venture.

WHAT IF?

An experimental literary magazine
prepared by students
for students and their families

GUIDELINES   We welcome submissions of tasteful material under 950 words. Sorry, we cannot return manuscripts. Typed submissions due by _____ .

DEPARTMENTS

Script It . . . . short drama
Big Kids, Little Kids . . . . verse and prose for kids and would-be kids (art welcome)
Spotlight on Local Literati . . interviews and profiles with school and community writers or local personalities
Our Story-Makers . . . . dramatic non-fiction and fiction
The Poetry Corner . . . . verse
The Jester . . . . humorous prose and verse

---

Before moving on to your own start-up exercises in Activity One, sample the following literary fare:

Elizabeth Barrett Browning

How do I love thee? Let me count the ways.
I love thee to the depth and breadth and height
My soul can reach, when feeling out of sight
For the ends of Being and Ideal Grace.

I love thee to the level of every day's
Most quiet need, by sun and candlelight.
I love thee freely, as men strive for Right;
I love thee purely, as they turn from Praise.

I love thee with the passion put to use
In my old griefs, and with my childhood's faith.

I love thee with a love I seemed to lose
With my lost saints—I love thee with the breath,
Smiles, tears, of all my life!—and, if God choose,
I shall but love thee better after death.

Farley Mowat

What makes a writer? In a nutshell: *writing* makes a writer. That is the first and most important dictum. There are few others.

Good writing requires a compulsion. You have to want desperately to impart something to your readers—something you believe to be of enormous importance. Anything less and you will be a mere dilettante; a hobbyist fooling around with words.

Another requirement is an intense intimacy with, and a love of, words. To be anything like an effective writer you must also be an omnivorous and voracious reader. Let words, and their uses, soak into every fibre of your being. Read everything that comes to hand, good, bad and indifferent. Reading should be an uncontrollable addiction.

These things are important, but as I said at the beginning, only writing can make a writer. So you write. And throw away. And write. And throw away. . . . I estimate that three quarters of what I've written has gone out with the garbage. Maybe more should have gone that route. Rarely, if ever, is the writer's skill a God-given talent. It is a trade, and the only way to acquire expertise is to practise that trade for as long as it takes to become a good workman.

That's how I see it. Read, and write, like one possessed. And don't bother at all unless you've got a fire in your gut.

Tanya Kanigan

Sun
so hot

I
smell

the dust
settling
on

the venetian blinds.

Shel Silverstein

I shot an arrow toward the sky,
I hit a white cloud floating by.
The cloud fell dying to the shore,
I don't shoot arrows anymore.

Activity One   Setting Up Your Literary Magazine
Purpose

- to review literary forms
- to set individual and/or group goals
- to make initial decisions

1a.   Freewrite in your Writer's Notebook about the piece you most enjoyed. Would it interest readers of a school literary magazine? Justify.
b.   What past experiences may help you write and perhaps publish literary forms? What snags do you anticipate?

2.   In small groups, survey several literary magazines. Your library may subscribe to some, such as *Writers' Magazine* and *Canadian Forum*, and may have previous class publications and yearbooks containing literary fare in its collection. Approach schools in your computer network about exchanging samples. How do literary and mass-circulation magazines differ?

3.   With your instructor, determine your publication's preliminary set-up, staffing, departments, work assignments, audience, due dates, and editorial policy. Your instructor may request a formal proposal.

4a.   In your Writer's Notebook, set personal goals for this project—or for writing literary forms—noting the importance of each for your future.
b.   Share reflections with a partner.

5.   In small groups, review major characteristics of the four style clusters treated in Chapter Three (page 117). Which style clusters are likely to be most valuable for writing poetry? Which are most pertinent for drama and which for prose fiction? Justify.

6.   In small groups, explore samples of literary forms with which you have not yet experimented in your writing program. Estimate the suitability of each for your literary magazine. *Tip:* Consult a source such as Booth and Skinner's *The ABC's of Creative Writing* (Globe/Modern Curriculum Press) for forms such as the chronicle, epilogue, eulogy, fairy tale, melodrama, and the yarn.

Now, set the wheels in motion. If possible, begin with advice from someone who has experience publishing a literary magazine. Activities Two through

Eight explore how to write selected forms of stories, drama, and poetry. We'll focus on forms chosen by Tarvo's group, but you aren't bound by their decisions. Whether you're preparing a class literary magazine or pursuing an independent program, adapt activities to your needs.

Our Story-Makers

"Show, don't tell" is advice often voiced by writing practitioners. It's sound policy. As you recall from earlier work, the best writers of fiction and dramatic non-fiction *show through people*—their dialogue, conflict, action, and reaction. In building an anecdote in Chapter Four, you honed techniques of showing in narrative writing. Now you'll focus on assembling the parts into a unified whole.

First, let's consider openings. Read "To Begin, To Begin" (page 297), and reflect on whether a story you've recently studied manifests Clark Blaise's advice.

Activity Two   Summing Up the Short Story
Purpose

- to focus on effective beginnings
- to examine structure
- to review narrative style
- to write a short story

1.   As a class, discuss strategies through which Atwood, Martin, and Richler entice you to read on.

Margaret Atwood

A long time ago Christine was walking through the park. She was still wearing her tennis dress; she hadn't had time to shower and change, and her hair was held back with an elastic band. Her chunky reddish face, exposed with no softening fringe, looked like a Russian peasant's, but without the elastic band the hair got in her eyes. The afternoon was too hot for April; the indoor courts had been steaming, her skin felt poached.

Blair Martin

All through August you can feel the tar-steaming sun out on the interstate. A Nebraska summer'll strike you like the hand of God. Even the kids home from school are quiet, tense. They say the heat does strange things to people who live out there in the cornfields. They say it can turn a god-fearing farmer into one of the Devil's own. But that's just talk.

I wasn't born here so I guess I don't have to stay. But somehow the sun just burns up your feet until you don't care anymore. Besides, I'm an old man now. I can't afford to see anything new. I came back in '32, when the Depression was tearing at every man's heart. My father sold cars back in Detroit before we left. No one was buying cars anymore so he packed up Mama and me and put us on one of those trains that were hauling half the people in the country somewhere, anywhere from where they were. Mama never said a word to my father, she just held my hand and told me to hope for the best. We drifted across the country for two years before the wind blew us into Sterling House. "Sterling House," my father smiled at the fields. "Why, this town must be made of pure silver." He worked his hands in the dirt for twenty years and all he ever dug up was roots.

Mordecai Richler

I wasn't quite eight years old when I first got into trouble over a girl. Her name was Charna, she lived upstairs from me, and we played together without incident for years. Then, one spring afternoon, it seemed to me I'd had enough of marbles and one-two-three-Red LIGHT!

2a.   "The opening paragraphs of Alice Munro's 'Thanks for the Ride' vividly model strategies to establish setting, atmosphere, and characterization, as well as 'hook' the reader and build tension." After reading the following excerpt with a partner, assess the validity of this quotation, providing specific textual references. Or, prepare an interpretive-style essay for your writing folder.

My cousin George and I were sitting in a restaurant called Pop's Cafe, in a little town close to the Lake. It was getting dark in there, and they had not turned the lights on, but you could still read the signs plastered against the mirror between the fly-speckled and slightly yellowed cutouts of strawberry sundaes and tomato sandwiches.

"Don't ask for information," George read. "If we knew anything we wouldn't be here" and "If you've got nothing to do, you picked a . . . good place to do it in." George always read everything out loud—posters, billboards, Burma-Shave signs. "Mission Creek. Population 1700. Gateway to the Bruce. We love our children."

I was wondering whose sense of humour provided us with the signs. I thought it would be the man behind the cash register. Pop? Chewing on a match, looking out at the street, not watching for anything except for somebody to trip over a crack in the sidewalk or have a blowout or make a fool of himself in some way that Pop, rooted behind the cash register, huge and cynical and incurious, was never likely to do. Maybe not even that; maybe just by walking up and down, driving up and down, going places, the rest of the world proved its absurdity. You see that judgement on the faces of people looking out of windows, sitting on front steps in some little towns; so deeply, deeply uncaring they are, as if they had sources of disillusionment which they would keep, with some satisfaction, in the dark.

There was only one waitress, a pudgy girl who leaned over the counter and scraped at the polish on her fingernails. When she had flaked most of the polish off her thumbnail she put the thumb against her teeth and rubbed the nail back and forth absorbedly. We asked her what her name was and she didn't answer. Two or three minutes later the thumb came out of her mouth and she said, inspecting it: "That's for me to know and you to find out."

You may also wish to (re)read Birdsell's vivid depiction of setting and atmosphere in "Red River Valley" (page 178).
b.   In your Writer's Notebook, speculate about the narrator's character and imagine how the plot develops through several conflicts to a conclusion.

3a.   In a small group, assess the effectiveness of the openings to "Through the Tunnel" by Lessing (page 96) and "A Tree. A Rock. A Cloud" by McCullers (page 310). Justify your responses with textual references.
b.   Draft a new beginning for two of the short stories listed above. Imitate the author's style as closely as possible.
c.   In conference with a partner, compare the original and revised versions. Does your version "sound" like the original author's voice?

4.   With a partner, review the expanded anecdote from your writing folder (Chapter Four). Does the piece

• open well

• build into a unified whole from which a theme naturally emerges?

5a.   Read Flannery O'Connor's "Writing Short Stories" (page 315) and Morley Callaghan's commentary to "All the Years of Her Life" (page 303). Note the most valuable tips in your Writer's Notebook.
b.   Revise your expanded anecdote from Chapter Four into a tightly structured short story. Or, if you prefer, begin fresh with a new idea more suitable for your literary magazine.
c.   With your partner, assess the on-going progress of your story, using appropriate criteria checklists such as those from the Workshop Supplement.

Script It

Drama is a literary work written for performance; the story unfolds through characters' dialogue and conflicts. In a sense, drama is the ultimate form of "show, don't tell." Narrative—stage directions and preliminary comments for the director and actors—plays a minimal role.

A drama department had been planned for *WHAT IF?* but how to squeeze in a play was a concern. The cameraperson captured this problem-solving in action.

Tarvo: Come on, Kirsten, we need a drama department.
Kirsten: Plays are too long—anyway, I don't like drama.
Sasha: Then how come you watch so much TV? That's drama.
Tarvo: We could use one-act plays or just scenes and vignettes and anecdotes in play form—skits. They don't *have* to be long.
Craig: Yeah. Who said we had to print full-length pieces?
Tarvo: We can use excerpts—especially suspenseful ones. You know, dialogues and monologues might be good. Remember that monologue by Joanna Glass we auditioned with last year in dramatic arts? I'll bet I remember what Lily Agnes says in *Artichoke*:

A young girl's room is a very private place. It's where I keep my personal belongings. It's where I have my private thoughts. And even though we're not religious here, my room is, for me, almost like a chapel. Grampa and I adore each other—but that doesn't mean we could share a room. Nearly every night I sing myself to sleep. And it was Grampa who said, "Lily, you have an interesting voice, but it is—untrained." And you must remember that Grampa snores and sometimes smells medicinal. In my old book of Emily Post she says that nothing must be spared the guest. She says he should have a good mattress and both a soft and firm pillow. He should have a brand new cake of soap, mouthwash and a good clothes brush. He should have a light at the head of his bed and two or three books should be provided. These books should be chosen more to *divert* than to *strain* the reader's attention. He should have an ashtray, a calendar, and a clock that works. In August, even though there are screens, he should have a fly swatter.

Those things require a generosity of self. I could manage them, with grace, for two or three days. I could manage them with a chip on my shoulder for a week. I can't manage them at all for the whole summer. (*Pause*) If there's any way to prevent it, I'd rather not leave my room.

Sasha: What a ham! . . . Kirsten, you could do a TV script. A commercial is a script, too.

As you experiment with drama, you'll discover your knowledge of narrative techniques provides a strong foundation. Dialogue, characters, point of view, setting, and theme are all dramatic elements. But since drama is direct storytelling by "scene," dialogue and conflict are in the spotlight.

Drama entertains, amuses, and persuades through action and reaction of characters enacting their "business." In fact, for dramatists "business" holds special meaning; it refers to the details of characters' movements and gestures which are woven into dialogue or provided as stage directions.

Tarvo and Sasha collected tips about writing drama from personal experience and the advice of professional playwrights. They compiled Activity Three which guides you through one approach to play building. A small group could construct this drama together, using linked word processors to "collaborwrite."

Activity Three   Building Drama
Purpose

- to examine effective dramatic elements
- to practise writing conflict dialogue
- to build a short one-act play

1a.   Take parts reading at least one short play. Josephine Tey's "The Pen of My Aunt" (page 317) provides an instructive review of dramatic elements. Or consult your library's resources for the following collections which offer engaging sample scenes:

- Richard Goldstone and Abraham H. Lass, *The Mentor Book of Short Plays* (Mentor)

- John Stephens, ed., *Ten Canadian Short Plays* (Dell).

See other suggestions in Chapter Eight.

b.   Analyze the dramatic elements that make the play successful. Keep your analysis in mind as you build your own drama in the remainder of this activity. *Note:* If you plan to co-write your play, read the interview with Jerome Lawrence and Robert E. Lee (page 308) before beginning.

2a.   Decide the dramatic elements—a conflict situation with potential for plenty of action, a main character (protagonist), and a foil (antagonist). Brainstorm many possibilities before deciding on a play suitable for your publication. Spontaneous role play may facilitate this process.

b.   Test your ideas from a practical performance perspective; for example, you'll want to limit the number of characters. Even though you're writing for publication, you may add a performance element. A one-act puppet play could be performed by dramatic arts students for a local kindergarten class.

3.   Get to know your characters inside out. Since conflict is drama's key force, focus on strong character contrasts. Compose a second point-form list or character sketch. *Tip:* Keep in mind George Bernard Shaw's comment: "My dialogue and characters are absolutely inextricable, each being the essence of the other."

4a.   Write your scenario—an outline with no dialogue describing action and visual impressions to carry the plot. Unfold the tale in the present tense with clear, concise phrasing. Begin at a high point of conflict; don't waste words on preliminaries. Complicate the conflict and resolve it.

b.   Check your plans: have you provided the who, what, when, where, why, and how in a logical cause-and-effect scenario? Read your scenario aloud or tell it, without looking at your draft. *Tip:* Share a secret with the audience—perhaps something one character knows but another doesn't. Coleridge commented that anticipation is more dramatically effective than surprise.)

5.   Draft the play, keeping these guidelines in mind:

· Show setting by building it into the dialogue.

· Show characterization through stage business as well as dialogue; build on action and reaction.

6.   If possible, arrange a play performance prior to publication. As actors rehearse, you may want to revise lines that read poorly. Remember, in drama seeing is believing. If performance is impossible, tape friends reading parts. Listening to the tape should help you "rehear" the play's possibilities.

Let's suppose you've been bitten by the stage-bug; you want to write for broadcast or screen. Where should you begin?

One way to build skills is to adapt a short story, narrative or dramatic poem, or a novel excerpt for broadcast or screen. For example, think about scripting strategies for the scene from Laurence's *The Stone Angel* in Chapter Four (page 164), or for the opening to Munro's "Thanks for the Ride."

The excerpt from Judith Guest's *Ordinary People* reprinted below and followed by the same scene from the screenplay by Alvin Sargent, may stimulate other ideas, too. After comparing these excerpts, which depict the same action in the novel and filmscript, move on to Activity Four. *Note:* The scene opens as Conrad and Karen meet for a coke. They haven't seen each other since they were patients in a mental hospital.

> Karen smiles at him. Deep dimples in her cheeks. He had forgotten that about her, had forgotten how she lowers her head when she is embarrassed or nervous. Nervous now as she sits down across from him in the narrow booth. It makes him feel protective. She doesn't have to be afraid of him.
> "Hi. How are you?"
> "Fine. And you?"
> He grins; shrugs his shoulders. "Not bad. Light, scattered paranoia increasing to moderate during the day." He means merely to jog her memory, but she frowns and looks away. He has offended her. "Hey, I'm only kidding. I'm fine. Really."
> She leans awkwardly to the side, shrugging out of her coat; folds it neatly beside her on the seat. She has gained weight since the hospital. It looks good on her. She used to wear her hair long and straight. She would tuck it

behind her ears while she talked. Now it is short, curling softly about her face. Dark feathers that brush against her cheeks.

"I like your hair that way."

"Thank you." She touches it. She touches and straightens her coat again. They look at each other. Slowly sinking in the awkwardness of the moment. He didn't want that to happen. They were good friends at the hospital. They still are. No reason to be uncomfortable, is there?

She asks, "When did you come home?"

"End of August." A place where they were both safe. They talked for hours on the stone bench outside the rec-room door. Sometimes Leo would come and sit with them, cracking jokes, finding out they were alive. Surely she must remember.

"It's great to see you," he says.

"Good to see you." Again she ducks her head. "I can't stay too long. I've got a meeting at school. Our drama club is doing *A Thousand Clowns*—the Neil Simon play—do you know it? We're going wild trying to get it together. I'm secretary this year, that's probably why we're so disorganized—

He says bluntly, "Well, don't let me hold you up, then."

Interior Soda Fountain—Conrad and Karen in a small booth. She is bright and warm. She smiles at him, but it is apparent she is nervous . . . awkward silence.

Karen: When did you come home?

Conrad: End of August. (*pause*) It's great to see you.

Karen: You too. (*looks at watch*) I'm sorry I can't stay long. I've got a meeting at school. Our drama club is doing *A Thousand Clowns*—do you know it? We're going wild trying to get it together. I'm secretary this year, that's probably why we're so disorganized . . .

Conrad: Don't let me hold you up, then.

Karen: No, it's okay. I really want to see you. Although I was sort of afraid. You seemed so down, over the phone.

Conrad: (*quickly*) Yeah, well, that was just a gray day. Actually, everything's going great. I'm back in school, and I'm swimming—

Karen: Oh, really? I'm glad.

Conrad: Well, we haven't had any meets yet. I could end up on the bench all year.

Karen: Oh, no, you'll do fine. I'm sure. And your folks'll be proud, too.

The counterman appears with their drinks. He puts the Cokes down, walks away. Conrad watches him, then leans toward Karen.

Conrad: (*re: counterman*) Definitely a low self-image day. (*Karen giggles. Conrad smiles at her. Then he drinks his drink. Studies her.*)

Conrad: You look beautiful.

Karen: You do, too.

Conrad: You miss it?

Karen: Miss what?

Conrad: The hospital?

Karen: No.
Conrad: Not even Mr. Minnow's goldfish trick?
Karen: (*laughs*) Oh . . .
Conrad: You were brilliant that day. You told everybody off. Even the judge.
Karen: I can't believe I ever did that.
Conrad: You did it, all right. I'll never forget it. And then we sneaked into the kitchen and talked all night, remember?
Karen: Yeah . . . Wow . . .
Conrad: Yeah . . .

Activity Four   Scripting for Radio, Television, and Film
Purpose

- to compare script and novel formats

- to compose "translation" guidelines

- to write a script for broadcast or screen

1a.   As a class, scrutinize the two treatments of the scene from *Ordinary People* above. List differences in the handling of material and account for each.
b.   If circumstances permit, view the film. How does this experience help you assess the scripting?
c.   Consider ways in which a radio script of this scene might differ from the film script. Account for differences.

2.   With a partner brainstorm guidelines for radio scripts, using your common sense, listening experience, advice from "The Sound of Muses" (Straczynski, page 317), and the following tips on scripting for television to assist you.

- Study the physical structure of a sample popular program. How many "acts" do you detect? Within each, how is the conflict begun, unfolded, and ended?

- Clarify in your mind the core idea of the story-line. Link dialogue tightly to this core.

- Clearly show the passage of time, the setting and unfolding of characters through action, reaction, and dialogue.

- Draw a plot graph (see Chapter Four) to represent the action.

- Make a chronological summary of the scenes within each act.

- Redraft until your script is highly polished.

3a.   Co-script a short opening scene for a teleplay or radio drama of Lessing's "Through the Tunnel" (page 96) or Callaghan's "All the Years of Her Life"

(page 299). Or work with a classic such as Austen's *Pride and Prejudice*. You may wish to read "Writing a Screenplay" (Cornish, page 303) before beginning.
b.   Compare work with others and assess your first draft against a class criteria checklist (page 392) before undertaking revisions.

4.   Draft a script for broadcast which is also suitable for your literary magazine. Invite dramatic arts students or classmates to read the parts; tape the reading. Work with a partner to assess the taped version and plan revisions.

OR

5a.   Review a favourite selection of New Journalism or a narrative poem such as Robert Frost's "Death of the Hired Man" or Earle Birney's "David." Consider whether either work would lend itself to scripting for radio or television.
b.   Prepare a short dramatization for radio, television, or stage. Scripting one of these ideas may appeal:

- An anecdote or brief episode from a popular history book by Pierre Berton or a biography by Peter C. Newman

- An interview with an author such as Aldous Huxley (page 367), Mordecai Richler (page 359), or Jean Little (page 361).

The Poetry Corner

As poetry editor of *WHAT IF?* Sasha was asked by the group for submission guidelines. The video tracked this discussion which unfolded into an informal poetry-reading session.

Sasha: I'm having trouble. There are so many types. And I feel uneasy evaluating poetry. It's so . . . personal.
Tarvo: Yeah, people feel very . . . attached to their creations. Just listen to this one by Joan Fern Shaw.

Delivery

I gave birth
to a healthy nine-pound
poem
this morning

I feel great
but need some rest
after ten hours
of labour

Before long
the little fellow
will be screaming
and shaking his fists
demanding
a bellyful of editing.

Craig: Well, I can relate to that feeling of ownership. But don't feel awed just because it's verse. As Louise Brogan says, poetry isn't born to you on "the wings of the dove." It requires hard work.

Tarvo: That's right, you know. And I've read some really good verse by students. Listen to "Beyond the Garden Gate" by Bridget Newson; it's in *Inkslinger*.

Beyond the Garden Gate

I walk into the garden
and to my surprise
am addressed by one of the Vegetables.
It has left the compost pile
to take its place among
the hybrids   Beefsteak
                Peaches and Cream
                Mountain of Snow
to take in carbon dioxide
    and give off oxygen
        and carry on a conversation
            with a wholesale charm
                of its own.

I was afraid before
of that far corner of the garden
but now I walk between the rows,
    enjoy the greenery,
and know
    it is not for me
        to thin them out.

Kirsten: Hey Tarvo, *I* found *Inkslinger*. Great title, huh? Read Zenovia Sadoway's "Blue Mountains" . . . the "folds of satin" lines are wonderful.

Blue Mountains

Even when I sit here
in the middle of the prairie,
    blue mountains
ripple across the horizon;

Folds of satin
stretched and pleated,
sprinkled with salt and cinnamon.
   To climb
the fine stone weave
   until I reach the point
where I can turn around . . .
and see the plains no more.

Tarvo: And the best are unintimidating. Here's an untitled one I like by
Anne Malcolm.

sometimes I wonder
if all those spiders I've squished
have ghosts

Sasha: This makes me feel a little better. . . . But I like narrative poetry
best. Is there one in *Inkslinger*, Tarvo?
Tarvo: This one by Melanie Misanchuk is dramatic:

Zucchinis at Harvest

It was the last day
of late night shopping
before Christmas.
Friday, 8:30 pm
It's cold and wet outside,
hot and stuffy in the zoo
they call a mall
where I'm shopping.
People hustle along,
frenetic last minute grabbing rules.
Searching for
"the perfect thing for him"
and
"Oh, gosh, she'll love this"
I myself am rushed
tired, and nowhere near done
the endless task of gift-buying
I am pushed from behind
Angrily, I turn around
and yell
"Why don't you watch
where you're going, lady?"
and am immediately silenced.
It is a Hutterite woman,
one from the colonies

outside of Saskatoon who come into
the city every so often.
She explains to me
in heavily accented English,
that she can't find her little boy.
I abandon my less important task
of gift finding
to help the mother search for her son.
He's six,
she says
and I pity the kid
lost in this bedlam.
We fight to get to a cashier
and she announces his name,
Peter.
The mother waits as I go off to find him
on my own.
He probably looks the same
as any other Hutterite boy,
black pants, dark checked shirt,
black coat and dark hat
But he'd stand out
among the city kids.
I come upon him,
cowering in a corner
his cowboy hat pulled far down
over his face,
and try to explain that I'll take him home.
He speaks no English,
so I pick him up and carry him,
crying,
to his mother.
She thanks me again and again,
with promises of meat pies
and zucchinis at harvest
and I resume my brutal quest
for the perfect gift.
They walk off, huddled together
and I wonder if they ever get lonely.

My foot is crushed by an anxious shopper,
my arm nudged.
They don't know what they're missing.

Craig: That rings so true and yet it could happen to anyone.

Kirsten: Yeah, but the poet's heightened the experience—really focused it—like this one, by Ali Norman:

Between You and Me

I'll tell you a secret:
Those girls
    over there
    are pointing this way
    'cause they like me!
and that group of boys
    playing tag
    knew better than to ask me to join.
    I'm too grown-up for tag.
The kids
    playing baseball
    can tell I don't feel like playing
    or I would have been picked first.
If you think these are tears
    in my eyes,
    you're mistaken.

Sasha: Everybody understands rejection. That's why the poem's so alive and unpretentious. That's why I like found poetry.
Kirsten: What's that?
Sasha: Verse that you . . . just find, maybe in a magazine article or words on a cereal box, a comic cover, or a historical document. You start with a great image or phrase and go from there.
Tarvo: Last year we used great ideas from Canadian poets—sound poetry and word association and haiku. I'm going to look for the book. That'll give us ideas to experiment with.

The book Tarvo is referring to—*When Is A Poem*, compiled and written by Florence McNeil for The League of Canadian Poets—helped these students focus their interests.

Begin by warming up to verse in Activity Five before exploring form in Activity Six.

Activity Five   Playing with Verse
Purpose

- to warm up for poetry writing

- to enjoy words—sounds, shapes, and textures

- to experiment with words in verse form

1.   Warm up to words. Take turns reading aloud humorous verse such as "Gus: The Theatre Cat" (page 68) and Dennis Lee's "Mister Hoobody" printed below. Enjoy the interplay of sounds and mental images. Since colour enhances creativity, you might view an art book or even colour charts or paint samples as you listen.

Mister Hoobody

There's a grubby sort of fairy
With the manners of a pig;
He isn't very little
And he isn't very big.
He lives inside our
Furnace, and he
Guzzles and he
Grunts.
His name is Mister Hoobody.
I've only seen him once.

He sneaks around and
Teaches children
What a fairy's for:
If you've eaten too much candy,
He always brings you more;
And when you're reading late, he tells you
"Why not read all night?"
And he keeps a pile of dimes
For kids that bite.

He's fat and fun and famous
And he doesn't wash his socks;
He wears a furry parka, just in
Case the furnace stops.
He drinks an awful lot, I guess to
Keep his stomach clean,
And when your parents come
He can't be seen.

Once I peeked inside the furnace, while he
Barbecued his toes:
The flames were red and crackly
Like his famous glowing nose;
He flickered through the shadows
Like a whizz-bang in a well,
Then he grinned a crooked grin
And made a smell.

A burp, a bounce, a guzzle
From his tiny whiskey keg,
Then the chubby little rubbydub
Spun quickly on one leg
Till, speeding up, he vanished
Like the vapour from a jet—
And as he went he thumped his chest:
"They haven't caught me yet!"

I hope that
Mister Hoobody will
Come back soon again.
Suppose I bounce a ball too high
And bend a window pane,
Or else my pen starts leaking
On the carpet
Like a sieve—
I hope that Mister Hoobody
Remembers where I live!

2a.   Explore poetry's non-verbal dimensions:

· What colour is each poem?

· What shape, texture, odour, and taste does each evoke?

· What dance, tune, or rhythm complements each?

· "Doodle-draw" the poem with a computer graphics program or just a pencil.

b.   In your Writer's Notebook, try to account for your associations.

3a.   Read aloud together bill bissett's poem, "i'll tell you a storee she sd" (page 70). With the book closed, freewrite in your Writer's Notebook about your *sense* of the poem.
b.   Repeat this choral reading at least three times, allowing the poem to flow into chant if you wish. Tape your reading. Replay it. How has your sense of the poem altered since you began?

4.   In *When Is a Poem*, Canadian poets suggest these warm-up word association exercises:

· Brainstorm many associations with a common word; then compose a poem about the "core word," using your associations.

· Create a class poem in a spontaneous poetry-writing session.

· One person suggests an idea; then everyone writes a line or two about the idea on separate pieces of paper which are collected and randomly arranged.

5.   Penn Kemp describes the process of writing a sound poem such as "Levity" as "tracking sound." The poem is "a play with language and an interest in language for its own sake just to see where it would go with tracking an inner associative process." Repeat the sequence of activities from question 3 using the first stanza from Kemp's "Levity."

> U
> U more
> humour or
> humour or less
> humour or lesson
> humour or less undo
> humour or less undo what
> humour or less undo what U
> humour or less undo what U D
> humour or less undo what U D sir
> humour or less undo what U D serve

6a.   Read aloud May Swenson's "Analysis of Baseball." Experiment with word positioning on the computer screen. Does this process alter meaning? Play with ideas for a concrete poem of your own.

Analysis of Baseball

> It's about
> the ball,
> the bat,
> and the mitt.
> Ball hits
> bat, or it
> hits mitt.
> Bat doesn't
> hit ball, bat
> meets it.
> Ball bounces
> off bat, flies
> air, or thuds
> ground (dud)
> or it
> fits mitt.
>
> Bat waits
> for ball
> to mate.
> Ball hates

to take bat's
bait. Ball
flirts, bat's
late, don't
keep the date.
Ball goes in
(thwack) to mitt,
and goes out
(thwack) back
to mitt.

Ball fits
mitt, but
not all
the time.
Sometimes
ball gets hit
(pow) when bat
meets it,
and sails
to a place
where mitt
has to quit
in disgrace.
That's about
the bases
loaded,
about 40,000
fans exploded.

It's about
the ball,
the bat,
the mitt,
the bases
and the fans.
It's done
on a diamond,
and for fun.
Its about
home, and it's
about run.

b.   Gary Geddes suggests imagining each word of a poem as a related part of a whole verbal "community"; how does each word bind the poetic structure? Does any word fail to "carry its load"? Justify.

7.   Write one or more humorous verses, perhaps using rhyme. Or experiment with acrostic form: "A composition, often in verse form, in which one or more sets of letters, as in the initial or final letters of the lines, taken in order, form a word or words." This may be a good group-writing exercise.

An acrostic may be read three ways; ancient Greeks called it "boustrophedon" ("as the ox turns in plowing"). This anonymous acrostic uses words instead of letters.

Your Face Your Tongue Your Wit

Your face	Your tongue	Your wit
so faire	so smooth	so sharp
first drew	then mov'd	then knit
Mine eye	Mine eare	My heart
thus drawn	thus mov'd	thus knit
affects	hangs on	yeelds to
Your face	Your tongue	your wit.

Activity Six   Exploring Verse Forms
Purpose

- to identify a variety of popular verse forms

- to note common elements of good poetry

- to identify resources and approaches for in-depth study

Note: Consider inviting a local poet to discuss writing verse before you begin this exercise. Or enlist the services of a parent or neighbour who experiments with verse.

1a.   Working with a partner, select a variety of poems you enjoy from several anthologies.
b.   Use prior knowledge, a dictionary, and this book to help you identify the form or type of poetry each represents.

2a.   Vivid imagery—diction that helps you *imagine*—is one sign of strong poetry. List additional qualities of good poetry; work with your samples and personal experience with verse.
b.   Do you agree with these criteria? A good poem is:

- fresh, concise, thoughtful

- illuminating, surprising

- unique and graceful.

Justify your response.

3a.   Regroup according to interests. For example, your grouping might look like this (you'll notice some overlapping).

Group One   HAIKU   Modern haiku derives from an ancient Japanese form, but observes looser rules. It is a vivid, imagistic verse about a particular experience, but with no narrative comment, and is usually related to a season. Generally its three lines have approximately five, seven, and five syllables. The following article will help you in the writing of this kind of verse.

17 Things Haiku Isn't

Lorraine Ellis Harr, consulting editor of *Dragonfly: A Quarterly of Haiku*, and founder of the Western World Haiku Society, offers this advice on how *not* to write haiku:

• Haiku isn't a prose sentence divided into three lines. It also isn't just any three- or four- or five-line poem.

• Haiku isn't padded with adjectives and modifiers to make the five-seven-five syllable count. Nor are *a* and *the* ignored; we use them in everyday speech.

• Haiku isn't always divided into five-seven-five syllable lines. Japanese *onji*, on which the haiku is based, are different from syllables. A short/long/short form is usually preferred, however.

• Haiku isn't a simile or metaphor. Simile and metaphor turn haiku into English language poetics.

• Haiku isn't a telegram. Haiku should flow from line to line. Read haiku aloud!

• Haiku isn't rhymed, unless the rhyme happens naturally.

• Haiku isn't a poem as much as it is a playful phrase. Use strong but simple words and images.

• Haiku isn't of human values, morals, judgments. But it can be of human *living*.

• Haiku isn't anthropomorphic. Don't humanize nature. No personification. Rather, naturalize man.

• Haiku isn't a generalization about something. Haiku is a specific thing/time/place/season/event.

• Haiku isn't a story. It is a sketch, an indication of deeper thoughts and emotions that are not stated.

• Haiku isn't vague. Be specific: Tree? What kind?

• Haiku isn't obscure. Give the reader clues. Include season words.

• Haiku isn't just anything that comes to mind. Haiku comes from direct experience.

• Haiku isn't a formula poem. Haiku is a way of life. *The poet lives the haiku.*

- Haiku isn't one-dimensional. It is an interplay between two or more objects.

- Haiku isn't easy to write. But when you get hooked you will be glad you tried it. The discipline and study will sharpen your perceptions and improve all other fields of writing. Haiku is what is.

Group Two   FREE VERSE   Modern lyric poetry with no end-of-line rhyme or metre is popular. Often imitative of speech rhythms, good free verse uses vivid images and sound patterns. In style, it resembles poetic prose, although it is written in lines and may be composed of one or more stanzas (e.g., students' poems on pages 275-279).

Group Three   NARRATIVE POETRY   It tells a story using exposition and often a combination of narration and dialogue. This ancient form includes full-length epics such as the *Iliad*, the *Odyssey*, and *Beowulf*. Modern examples include Frost's "Death of the Hired Man" and Birney's "David."

Group Four   BALLADS   A form of narrative poetry from an ancient oral tradition, ballads were the stories sung by travelling minstrels. Many were communal compositions. Ballads rely on strong action and usually have repetition through their refrains. An example is "The Rime of the Ancient Mariner" by Samuel Taylor Coleridge.

Group Five   DRAMATIC POETRY   This form recreates experience of a story through dialogue and action—the techniques of drama. Plays written in verse and dramatic monologues (poetry written in the speaker's diction) fall into this category. Examples are Shakespeare's plays and the following poem by Frank Davey:

She'd Say

'I'll never reach 40,' my mother would say,
'I have a short life-line,' she'd say,
holding out her palm solemnly
& pointing, 'I went to a fortune-teller
before the war,' she'd say, 'at the Exhibition,
& she took one look at my hand & she gasped
& said "Oh my dear, I'm so sorry,
you shouldn't have come in here," & I said
"What is it, can't you tell me?" & she said
"No, I can't bear to tell you.
oh you poor dear," she said.
& she threw her arms around me
& she hugged me just like that,' she'd say.
'& it was only later,' she'd say,
'that Genevieve told me about my life-line.'
'It was the same thing,' she'd say.

'with Dr. McCready, he'd be listening to my heart
& a sad look would come over his face,
& he'd put his arms around me & hold me tight
just for a minute, & afterward
he'd smile as if nothing had happened
& say I was okay, but I always knew
what he'd been thinking,' she'd say.
'I always knew,' she'd say.

'What will you do when I'm gone,' she'd say
when I brought a sock to be darned
or a book to be mended. Or to my dad
as she bustled around the kitchen.
'You're going to have to learn to cook
when I'm gone,' she'd say.
& when he growled 'Don't talk rubbish, honey,'
she'd say cheerily 'I know what you're thinking,
you're going to get yourself
a cute young floozie after I'm gone.'

'I nearly died when I had you,' she said.
'Dr. McCready didn't think I'd make it,' she said.
'He never said so but I could tell
by the way he looked at me,' she said.
'Look at my pot belly,' she said.
'That's what you did to me but it was worth it,'
she said. 'You were wanted,' she said.
'When I told Dr. McCready I was expecting
he put his arms around me & said
"Oh no, Jeannie, you're not."
& he looked sadly out the window & then said

"Well, we'll do the best we can,
but you're not to have another, you hear,
you be a good girl now, & don't have another." '
& my father would sit silently
when she talked like this,
but sometimes she'd keep going & ask
why he had not yet bought their burial plot.
'You can put me wherever you want,' she'd say.
'You'll have someone else to go in your double plot,'
she'd say. 'She won't want me,' she'd say.
'She'll sure make you toe the line,' she'd say.

& when they argued, or when she & I argued,
'You can count on one thing,' she'd say.
'You won't have me around much longer,' she'd say.
'You'll be able to have your own way soon,' she'd say.

She'd hold out her palm & say 'It's right here,
you can look at it,' she'd say. 'The fortune teller
was really upset,' she'd say.
'She took me in her arms & said "You poor thing,"
& sobbed on my shoulder,' 'I'll never make 50,'
she'd say.

Note: Lyric poetry appears in various forms, some of which are represented in the above list. They include haiku, free verse, hymns, sonnets, and songs. The speaker or narrator-voice narrates the verse, using musical language to express personal thoughts and feelings about a specific experience.

b.   In your groups, read aloud many sample poems, listening actively to language that appeals. A tape recorder facilitates this process. Experiment with the look of a variety of arrangements on the word processor screen. Note how form and meaning function in unison.

4.   Working from samples, deduce "rules" or guidelines for writing this type of poetry. Note, for example, the use of

- diction
- rhythm
- division of stanzas
- end or internal rhyme
- formation of lines
- figurative language

And, perhaps, look at narrative techniques (dialogue, characters) and rhyme scheme as well. Check your guidelines in a reliable source such as *New Horizons* (pages 259-261) or *Poems to Remember* (pages 553-556).

5.   In your Writer's Notebook,
a.   Brainstorm subjects or topics for poems appropriate to your publication(s).
b.   Freewrite in prose or free verse about several ideas.
c.   Play with words, composing word-association poems, found poems, rhyming couplets, or an abecedarian.

6.   Write verse for your publication. If the form lends itself to collaborative writing (e.g., the ballad, narrative poetry), join forces with a like-minded poet. Experiment with word order and placement of lines.

7.   In your Writer's Notebook, freewrite about your experience with writing poetry. If you wish, respond to one of these quotations:

John Keats   "... if poetry comes not naturally as the leaves to a tree, it had better not come at all."

Matthew Arnold   "Poetry is nothing less than the most perfect speech ... in which [one] comes nearest to being able to utter the truth."

Features

At their next meeting, Tarvo and his group are completing their plans for a department featuring humour and selections for children.

Craig: Profiles should be easier this time. If we use student writers, or neighbourhood artists or cartoonists, readers will love it. You know, Matthew Arnold's tribute to Shakespeare sort of inspired me. What if we write a modern one about a school personality? Listen to Arnold's first:

> Others abide our question. Thou art free.
> We ask and ask: Thou smilest and art still,
> Out-topping knowledge. For the loftiest hill
> That to the stars uncrowns his majesty,
> Planting his steadfast footsteps in the sea.
> Making the Heaven of Heavens his dwelling-place,
> Spares but the cloudy border of his base
> To the foil'd searching of mortality:
> And thou, who didst the stars and sunbeams know,
> Self-school'd, self-scann'd, self-honour'd, self-secure,
> Didst walk on earth unguess'd at. Better so!
> All pains the immortal spirit must endure,
> All weakness that impairs, all griefs that bow,
> Find their sole voice in that victorious brow.

Sasha: Great . . . but this time, let's not wait until the last minute to ask for interviews. That's why the profile story for the newspaper was late.
Tarvo: Okay, I get the message. So let's decide on the other material. . . . Dennis Lee's "Mister Hoobody" is the kind of verse kids love.
Kirsten: Why don't we do non-fiction for kids? Lots of ten-year-olds are interested in famous scientists and computers, and kids love animals.
Craig: Sure, but not too heavy. Let's try some witty sayings or short fillers . . . something clever . . .

Craig would probably find the following answers to the question, "How do I love thee?" by A. Ross Eckler just the thing:

- The cardiologist: with all my heart

- The contortionist: head over heels

- The psychoanalyst: unshrinkingly

- The dieter: through thick and thin

- The wheelwright: tirelessly

- The elephant trainer: roguishly

- The farmer: whole hog

- The couturier: in my fashion

If you're including writing for children and pre-teens, Activity Seven offers pointers.

Activity Seven   Writing for Children and Pre-Teens
Purpose

- to identify literature children enjoy

- to write for various age groups

- to share writing with a live audience

Note: Questions 2 through 7 may be completed with a partner.

1.   In your Writer's Notebook:

a.   Reflect on literature which appeals to children, beginning with personal favourites. Freewrite about stories and mental images. Why are these memories special?

b.   Reflect on the development of children's tastes and interests. At what age did you begin to read books of no interest to the opposite sex?

2a.   Vera and Bill Cleaver, co-writers of more than a dozen books for young readers, note the importance of conflict and quick pacing. Do the samples of children's literature in this book meet these criteria?

b.   Account for children's love of classics such as *The Tale of Peter Rabbit*, "Mister Hooboody," and "How the Camel Got His Hump." For what age group is each most appropriate? Justify.

3.   Account for the popularity of Judy Blume's books with girls aged eight through eleven. For clues, read the following excerpt* from *Tiger Eyes* aloud, listening carefully for how tone is created:

> It is the morning of the funeral and I am tearing my room apart, trying to find the right kind of shoes to wear. But all I come up with are my Adidas, which have holes in the toes, and a pair of flip-flops. I can't find my clogs anywhere. I think I packed them away with my winter clothes in a box in the attic. My mother is growing more impatient by the second and tells me to borrow a pair of her shoes. I look in her closet and choose a pair with three-inch heels and ankle straps.

4a.   After reading "Writing for the Beginning Reader" (page 307), brainstorm many ideas for stories of interest to young readers.

b.   Draft a story or poem for young readers, using personal experience and

---

* Reprinted with permission of Bradbury Press, an affiliate of Macmillan, Inc., from *Tiger Eyes* by Judy Blume. Copyright © 1981 by Judy Blume.

Krueger's advice to guide you. If possible, read it to your audience before completing a polished version for publication.

5a.   Draft a poem or non-fiction article for children of a different age group. In conference with others, assess its suitability for your target audience.
b.   In your Writer's Notebook, explain how you have adapted your work from questions 4b. and 5a. to your readers' age.

6.   Invite an elementary class to join you for several sessions of story-writing; kindergarten children enjoy telling a story to someone who will write it down. And they'll draw wonderful pictures for your publication.

Activity Eight   Humour and Miscellany
Purpose

· to identify and write suitable types of humour

· to search for and create appropriate visual humour

· to prepare miscellaneous material

1.   What forms of humour are appropriate for your literary magazine? Name humorists who appeal to the whole family: they may be cartoonists, entertainers who write their own material, or authors. Identify common elements in their humour.

2a.   Would satire, parody, wit, or irony be appropriate forms of humour for your publication? Justify.
b.   Estimate the likelihood that this cartoon would be popular with your readers.

© 1988 by Munro Ferguson, distributed by Universal Press Syndicate.

c.   Locate or create appropriate visual humour for your publication.

3a.   Warm up your "funny bone" by reading appealing selections. Which techniques of humour can you identify in your reading: surprise, repetition, familiarity, incongruity or the reversal of expectations, absurdity? Share samples with your group.

b.   Collect ideas for humorous situations from cartoon collections such as "Cathy" or "Garfield," or watch television cartoons such as the classic "Jeremy the Bear." Could one be adapted to your needs—perhaps a limerick or nonsense verse? Credit the source of your inspiration.

4.   Draft material in a form of your choice. Don't forget the possibility of anecdotes, puns, and witticisms. If you're writing for children, use rhyme and your sense of the delightful and the ridiculous.

5.   If you're inviting reader participation, consider including one of these forms:

- **Word Power**   A cross-word puzzle based on local events may entertain your readers.

- **For Our Culture Vultures**   A fill-in-the blank quiz challenges trivia buffs. For example, What poem ends with these lines . . . ? Name the cartoonist/screenwriter/artist who . . .

- **Witticisms**   *Books in Canada*'s "CanWit" provides an amusing illustration. Each month, readers are invited to submit witticisms on a specific theme. For example, "CanWit 126" requested definitions of Canadian place names. The winner, Marvin Goody, submitted *Guelph* (vb.): To nip into a parking space that someone else spotted first; and *Maniwaki* (n.): A strike by public transit employees.
      Lois Grant of Calgary won an honourable mention with *Moose Jaw* (n.): Swelling of the lower part of the face brought on by expelling excessive amounts of hot air during political campaigns; and *Nipigon* (n.): That sinking feeling when you accidentally lock your keys in the trunk of your car.

C. AFTER-WORDS

Responding to Reading

1.   Bring to class a book you enjoyed as a child or pre-teen. After reviewing storytelling techniques (Chapter Four), tell the story to a small group. Or explain why you continue to remember it fondly. If the book is popular with contemporary children, explain its enduring appeal.

2a.   Peruse a collection of your favourite short stories, poems, or other literary form.

b.   Share one selection with a partner or small group.

3.   After reading at least one additional short story by Doris Lessing, Morley Callaghan, and Carson McCullers:

a. Identify consistent qualities of style and thematic preoccupations.

b. Speculate about what each writer's prose fiction exemplifies for students of writing.

c. Decide whose work you most enjoy and share your appreciation with a partner.

4. With a partner, read aloud a one-act play of your choice. Then complete the following oral activities. Taping your interaction may be instructive.

a. In an informative style, deliver a plot summary (approximately 100 words) to two selected classmates. Ask them for a written assessment based on a criteria checklist (e.g., page 389).

b. In a rhetorical style, convince the same classmates of the play's merits or flaws. Limit yourselves to one and a half minutes each. Request a written evaluation based on pre-established criteria.

c. Identify the special challenges of writing a one-act play. Justify with references to two plays.

5. (Re)read at least four student poems from this book. Role play with a partner your responses to three of the poets' works. Ask your partner for feedback about the quality of your work as a peer reviewer.

The Writing Folder

1. Revise and polish drafts from activities in this chapter.

2a. Script *The Tale of Peter Rabbit* or another children's classic for television (a cartoon special) or a radio play. Or compose a sequel. *The T.V. Scriptwriter's Handbook* (Alfred Brenner, Writer's Digest Books, 1980) offers detailed instruction.

b. Compose a parody in verse for adults, working from a children's tale—perhaps a classic nursery rhyme or fairy tale. See, for example, Roald Dahl's *Revolting Rhymes*. The first three lines to his "Little Red Riding Hood and the Wolf" go like this:

> As soon as Wolf began to feel
> That he would like a decent meal,
> He went and knocked on Grandma's door.

3. After (re)reading Flannery O'Connor's "Writing Short Stories":

a. Argue or support one point in letter or standard essay format.

b. Review one or more short stories you've written, checking for how you created a strong sense of place. Consider revisions.

c. Read a story by Flannery O'Connor. In an interpretive essay, estimate the extent to which she takes her own advice.

4. Test a screenplay or a scene you've prepared against the advice from Straczynski or Cornish; consider revisions.

5.   Write a short story or a play for children. Your protagonist might be a toy or an animal. The first paragraph from Margery Williams's popular *The Velveteen Rabbit* may stimulate ideas:

> There was once a velveteen rabbit, and in the beginning he was really splendid. He was fat and bunchy, as a rabbit should be; his coat was spotted brown and white, he had real thread whiskers, and his ears were lined with pink sateen. On Christmas morning, when he sat wedged in the top of the Boy's stocking, with a sprig of holly between his paws, the effect was charming.

Independent Study

1.   Write a play for a specific audience or group of actors; keep in mind their strengths and the limitations of production facilities as you write. Direct and produce your play. Your actors may be students from a drama class or a local elementary school, or members of a community theatre group. Report on how production enhanced your understanding of writing drama and working with people. R. Hull's *How to Write a Play* (Writer's Digest Books, 1983) and J.M. Straczynski's *The Complete Book of Script Writing* (Writer's Digest, 1983) offer practical instruction.

2.   Study the fictional letter in short stories and/or novels. Write a short story composed exclusively of letters. You might begin your research with Henry James's "A Bundle of Letters," the opening of which appears below:

FROM MISS MIRANDA HOPE IN PARIS TO MRS ABRAHAM C. HOPE AT BANGOR MAINE   September 5, 1879.

My Dear Mother,
      I've kept you posted as far as Tuesday week last, and though my letter won't have reached you yet I'll begin another before my news accumulates too much. I'm glad you show my letters round in the family, for I like them all to know what I'm doing, and I can't write to every one, even if I do try to answer all reasonable expectations. There are a great many unreasonable ones, as I suppose you know—not yours, dear mother, for I am bound to say that you never required of me more than was natural. You see you're reaping your reward: I write to you before I write to anyone else.

These sources provide useful instruction: *Technique in Fiction* (Robie Macauley and George Lanning, revised edition, 1987, St. Martin's Press) and *How to Write Short Stories That Sell* (Louise Boggess, Writer's Digest, 1980).

3a.   Compare several textbook versions of an incident or event in history (e.g., building the CPR, the trial of Louis Riel, a significant conference or battle). Is each author's style forceful and lively? Reflect on specific changes that can be made to enhance the impact of each selection, e.g., active voice, shorter sentences and/or paragraphs, narrative techniques.

b.   Rewrite the historical event you've chosen in script form, or bring it to life in a dramatic non-fiction article or narrative poem. (*Tip:* You might examine techniques Pierre Berton uses to enrich Canadian history.)

4.   Write a dramatic non-fiction story or a collection of anecdotes about your community's history, using techniques of New Journalism. (For practical instruction, see *How to Write and Sell the 8 Easiest Article Types* by H. Schellenberg Barnhart, Writer's Digest Books, 1985.)

5.   Read many fables, taking note of the form; you might begin with Rudyard Kipling's *Just So* stories. Write several fables accompanied by poems as Kipling did. See, for example, "How the Camel Got His Hump" (page 306).

6.   Investigate the radio play; read and listen to many samples. Write a play and tape it with sound effects. "The Sound of Muses" excerpt (page 317) is a good place to begin "how-to" research.

7.   Read and view several plays. Review the performances, keeping in mind Lee and Lawrence's comments about their profession in "An Interview with Jerome Lawrence and Robert E. Lee" (page 308). Follow standards of reputable reviewing. The criteria checklist on page 391 may be of assistance.

8.   Investigate and write literature for children of a specific age. For example, a short story or book-length poem suitable for a pre-school child is an excellent project for a student with artistic ability. *The Children's Picture Book* by Ellen E.M. Roberts (Writer's Digest Books, 1981) provides "how-to" tips. Lee Wyndham's *Writing for Children and Teenagers* (Writer's Digest Books, revised by Arnold Madison, 1980) caters to older readers.

9.   Investigate a mode such as mystery writing, science fiction, or fantasy. Write a short story or play reflecting your learning. *Writing and Selling Science Fiction* by the Science Fiction Writers of America (Writer's Digest Books, 1976) and *Mystery Writer's Handbook* by the Mystery Writers of America (ed. Lawrence Treat; Writer's Digest Books, 1976) offer helpful instruction. Or adapt Gene Perrot's tips about effective speechwriting (*How to Hold Your Audience with Humour*, Writer's Digest Books, 1984) to writing humorous articles, stories, and plays written in verse.

10.   Compare the style and structure of lyrics in modern and traditional ballads. Accompany your essay with an original ballad which reflects your learning about the form. *The Craft of Lyric Writing* by Sheila Davis (Writer's Digest Books, 1985) may help.

The Writer's Notebook

1.   In your Writer's Notebook, freewrite in response to one of these statements by writers about their writing process:

Shirley Faessler   "I hate [writing]. I mistrust it. I'm scared of it, it frightens me. . . . [But] I love it. I can't keep away from it."

Maria Jacobs   "Why writing hurts . . . I don't know. Everything about it hurts: getting started, sticking to it, fine-tuning . . . even letting go is painful."

Kurt Vonnegut   "I used my daughter's crayons for each main character."

2.   If you were to submit a piece of your writing for publication, which would it be? Justify and suggest a suitable audience and publication.

3.   Do your writing processes differ with the genre in which you're composing? Do you feel that non-fiction, fiction, or poetry result from different mental processes?

4a.   Reflect on your growth as a peer editor and conference partner. What improvements in skills and attitudes have you noted?
b.   Revise your Writer's Portrait for the last time. Go back and reflect on growth since day one. Was there a turning point in your development? How well have you met personal goals established at the beginning of your course? What skills and attitudes have you acquired which may help you continue to grow as a writer in the post-secondary world?

READINGS 6

To Begin, To Begin

Clark Blaise

*"Endings are elusive, middles
are nowhere to be found, but
worst of all is to begin, to begin, to begin."*

—Donald Barthelme

The most interesting thing about a story is not its climax or dénouement—both dated terms—nor even its style and characterization. It is its beginning, its first paragraph, often its first sentence. More decisions are made on the basis of the first few sentences of a story than on any other part, and it would seem to me after having read thousands of stories, and beginning hundreds of my own (completing, I should add, only about fifty), that something more than luck accounts for the occasional success of the operation. What I propose is theoretical, yet rooted in the practice of writing and of reading-as-a-writer; good stories *can* start unpromisingly, and well-begun stories can obviously degenerate, but the observation generally holds: the story seeks its beginning, the story many times *is* its beginning, amplified.

The first sentence of a story is an act of faith—or astonishing bravado. A story screams for attention, as it must, for it breaks a silence. It removes the reader from the everyday (no such imperative attaches to the novel, for which the reader makes his own preparations). It is an act of perfect rhythmic balance, the single crisp gesture, the drop of the baton that gathers a hundred disparate forces into a single note. The first paragraph is a microcosm of the whole, but in a way that only the whole can reveal. If the story begins one sentence too soon, or a sentence too late, the balance is lost, the energy diffused.

It is in the first line that the story reveals its kinship to poetry. Not that the line is necessarily "beautiful," merely that it can exist utterly alone, and that its force draws a series of sentences behind it. The line doesn't have to "grab" or "hook" but it should be striking. Good examples I'll offer further on, but consider first some bad ones:

> Catelli plunged the dagger deeper in her breast, the dark blood oozed like cherry syrup. . . .
> The President's procession would pass under the window at 12:03, and Slattery would be ready. . . .

Such sentences can be wearying; they strike a note too heavily, too prematurely. They "start" where they should be ending. The advantages wrested will quickly dissipate. On the other hand, the "casual" opening can be just as damaging:

> When I saw Bob in the cafeteria he asked me to a party at his house that evening and since I wasn't doing much anyway I said sure, I wouldn't mind. Bob's kind of an ass, but his old man's loaded . . .

Or, *in medias res:* "Linda, toast is ready! Linda, are you awake?"

Now what's wrong with these sentences? The tone is right. The action is promising. They're real, they communicate. Yet no experienced reader would go past them. The last two start too early (what the critics might call an imitative fallacy), and the real story is still imprisoned somewhere in the body.

Lesson One: as in poetry, a good first sentence of prose implies its opposite. If I describe a sunny morning in May (the buds, the wet-winged flies, the warm sun and cool breeze), I am also implying the perishing quality of a morning in May, and a good sensuous description of May sets up the possibility of a May disaster. It is the singular quality of that experience that counts. May follows from the sludge of April and leads to the drone of summer, and in a careful story the action will be mindful of May; it must be. May is unstable, treacherous, beguiling, seductive, and whatever experience follows from a first sentence will be, in essence, a story about the May-ness of human affairs.

What is it, for example, in this sentence from Hugh Hood's story "Fallings from Us, Vanishings" that hints so strongly at disappointment:

> Brandishing a cornucopia of daffodils,
> flowers for Gloria, in his right hand,
> Arthur Merlin crossed the dusky
> oak-panelled foyer of his apartment
> building and came into the welcoming
> sunlit avenue.

The name Merlin? The flourish of the opening clause, associations of the name Gloria? Here is a lover doomed to loneliness, yet a lover who seeks it, despite appearances. Nowhere, however, is it stated. Yet no one, I trust, would miss it.

Such openings are everywhere, at least in authors I admire:

> The girl stood with her back to the bar, slightly in everyone's way. (*Frank Tuohy*)
> The thick ticking of the tin clock stopped. Mendel, dozing, awoke in fright. (*Bernard Malamud*)
> I owe the discovery of Uqbar to the conjunction of a mirror and an encyclopedia. (*Jorge Luis Borges*)
> For a little while when Walter Henderson was nine years old, he thought falling dead was the very zenith of romance, and so did a number of his friends. (*Richard Yates*)
> Our group is against the war. But the war goes on. (*Donald Barthelme*)
> The principal dish at dinner had been croquettes made of turnip greens. (*Thomas Mann*)
> The sky had been overcast since early morning; it was a still day, not hot, but tedious, as it usually is when the weather is gray and dull, when clouds have been hanging over the fields for a long time, and you wait for the rain that does not come. (*Anton Chekhov*)
> I wanted terribly to own a dovecot when I was a child. (*Isaac Babel*—and I didn't even know what a dovecot was when I started reading.)

At least two or three times a day a story strikes me in the same way and I read it through. By then I don't care if the climax and dénouement are elegantly turned—chances are they will be—I'm reading it because the first paragraph gave me confidence in the power and vision of the author.

Lesson Two: art wishes to begin, even more than end. Fashionable criticism—much of it very intelligent—has emphasized the so-called "apocalyptic impulse," the desire of fiction to bring the house down. I can understand the interest in endings—it's easier to explain why things end than how they began, for one thing. For another, the ending is a contrivance—artistic and believable, yet in many ways predictable; the beginning, however, is always a mystery. Criticism likes contrivances, and has little to say of mysteries. My own experience, as a writer and especially as a "working" reader is closer to genesis than apocalypse, and I cherish openings more than endings. My memory of any given story is likely to be its first few lines.

Lesson Three: art wishes to begin *again*. The impulse is not only to finish, it is to capture. In the stories I admire, there is a sense of a continuum disrupted, then re-established, and both the disruption and reordering are part of the *beginning* of a story. The first paragraph tells us, in effect, that "this is how things have always been," or at least, how they have been until the arrival of the story. It may summarize, as Faulkner does in "That Evening Sun":

> Monday is no different from any other weekday in Jefferson now. The streets are paved now, and the telephone and electric

companies are cutting down more and more of the shade trees. . . .

or it may envelop a life in a single sentence, as Bernard Malamud's often do:

> Manischevitz, a tailor, in his fifty-first year suffered many reverses and indignities.

Whereupon Malamud embellishes the history, a few sentences more of indignities, aches, curses, until the fateful word that occurs in almost all stories, the simple terrifying adverb: *Then*.

Then, which means to the reader: "I am ready." The moment of change is at hand, the story shifts gears and for the first time, *plot* intrudes on poetry. In Malamud's story, a Negro angel suddenly ("then") appears in the tailor's living room, reading a newspaper.

> Suddenly there appeared . . .
> Then one morning . . .
> Then one evening she wasn't home to greet him . . .

Or, in the chilling construction of Flannery O'Connor:

> . . . there appeared at her door three young men . . . they walked single file, the middle one bent to the side carrying a black pig-shaped valise . . .

A pig-shaped valise! This is the apocalypse, if the reader needs one; whatever the plot may reveal a few pages later is really redundant. The mysterious part of the story—that which *is* poetic yet sets it (why not?) above poetry—is over. The rest of the story will be an attempt to draw out the inferences of that earlier upheaval. What is often meant by "climax" in the conventional short story is merely the moment that the *character* realizes the true, the devastating, meaning of "then." He will try to ignore it, he will try to start again (in my story "Eyes" the character thinks he can escape the voyeurs—himself, essentially—by moving to a rougher part of town); he can't of course.

Young readers, especially young readers who want to write, should forget what they're taught of "themes" and all the rest. Stories aren't written that way. Stories are delicate interplays of action and description; "character" is that force which tries to maintain balance between the two. "Action" I equate with danger, fear, apocalypse, life itself; "description" with quiescence, peace, death itself. And the purest part of the story, I think, is from its beginning to its "then." "Then" is the moment of the slightest tremor, the moment when the author is satisfied that all the forces are deployed, the unruffled surface perfectly cast, and the insertion, gross or delicate, can now take place. It is the cracking of the perfect, smug egg of possibility.

All the Years of Her Life

Morley Callaghan

They were closing the drugstore, and Alfred Higgins, who had just taken off his white jacket, was putting on his coat and getting ready to go home. The little gray-haired man, Sam Carr, who owned the drugstore, was bending down behind the cash register, and when Alfred Higgins passed him, he looked up and said softly, "Just a moment, Alfred. One moment before you go."

The soft, confident, quiet way in which Sam Carr spoke made Alfred start to button his coat nervously. He felt sure his face was white. Sam Carr usually said, "Good night," brusquely, without looking up. In the six months he had been working in the drugstore Alfred had never heard his employer speak softly like that. His heart began to beat so loud it was hard for him to get his breath. "What is it, Mr. Carr?" he asked.

"Maybe you'd be good enough to take a few things out of your pocket and leave them here before you go," Sam Carr said.

"What things? What are you talking about?"

"You've got a compact and a lipstick and at least two tubes of toothpaste in your pockets, Alfred."

"What do you mean? Do you think I'm crazy?" Alfred blustered. His face got red and he knew he looked fierce with indignation. But Sam Carr, standing by the door with his blue eyes shining brightly behind his glasses and his lips moving underneath his gray moustache, only nodded his head a few times, and then Alfred grew very frightened and he didn't know what to say. Slowly he raised his hand and dipped into his pocket, and with his eyes never meeting Sam Carr's eyes, he took out a blue compact and two tubes of toothpaste and a lipstick, and he laid them one by one on the counter.

"Petty thieving, eh, Alfred?" Sam Carr said. "And maybe you'd be good enough to tell me how long this has been going on."

"This is the first time I ever took anything."

"So now you think you'll tell me a lie, eh? What kind of a sap do I look like, huh? I don't know what goes on in my own store, eh? I tell you you've been doing this pretty steady," Sam Carr said as he went over and stood behind the cash register.

Ever since Alfred had left school he had been getting into trouble wherever he worked. He lived at home with his mother and his father, who was a printer. His two older brothers were married and his sister had got married last year, and it would have been all right for his parents now if Alfred had only been able to keep a job.

While Sam Carr smiled and stroked the side of his face very delicately with the tips of his fingers, Alfred began to feel that familiar terror growing in him that had been in him every time he had got into such trouble.

"I liked you," Sam Carr was saying. "I liked you and would have trusted you, and now look what I got to do." While Alfred watched with his alert, frightened blue eyes, Sam Carr drummed with his fingers on the counter. "I don't like to call a cop in point-blank," he was saying as he looked very worried. "You're a fool, and maybe I should call your father and tell him you're a fool. Maybe I should let them know I'm going to have you locked up."

"My father's not at home. He's a printer. He works nights," Alfred said.

"Who's at home?"

"My mother, I guess."

"Then we'll see what she says." Sam Carr went to the phone and dialed the number. Alfred was not so much ashamed, but there was that deep fright growing in him, and he blurted out arrogantly, like a strong, full-grown man, "Just a minute. You don't need to draw anybody else in. You don't need to tell her." He wanted to sound like a swaggering, big guy who could look after himself, yet the old, childish hope was in him, the longing that someone at home would come and help him. "Yeah, that's right, he's in trouble." Mr. Carr was saying. "Yeah, your boy works for me. You'd better come down in a hurry." And when he was finished Mr. Carr went over to the door and looked out at the street and watched the people passing in the late summer night. "I'll keep my eye out for a cop," was all he said.

Alfred knew how his mother would come rushing in; she would rush in with her eyes blazing, or maybe she would be crying, and she would push him away when he tried to talk to her, and make him feel her dreadful contempt; yet he longed that she might come before Mr. Carr saw the cop on the beat passing the door.

While they waited—and it seemed a long time—they did not speak, and when at last they heard someone tapping on the closed door, Mr. Carr, turning the latch, said crisply, "Come in, Mrs. Higgins." He looked hard-faced and stern.

Mrs. Higgins must have been going to bed when he telephoned, for her hair was tucked in loosely under her hat, and her hand at her throat held her light coat tight across her chest so her dress would not show. She came in, large and plump, with a little smile on her friendly face. Most of the store lights had been turned out and at first she did not see Alfred, who was standing in the shadow at the end of the counter. Yet as soon as she saw him she did not look as Alfred thought she would look: she smiled, her blue eyes never wavered, and with a calmness and dignity that made them forget that her clothes seemed to have been thrown on her, she put out her hand to Mr. Carr and said politely, "I'm Mrs. Higgins. I'm Alfred's mother."

Mr. Carr was a bit embarrassed by her lack of terror and her simplicity, and he hardly knew what to say to her, so she asked, "Is Alfred in trouble?"

"He is. He's been taking things from the store. I caught him red-handed. Little things like compacts and toothpaste and lipsticks. Stuff he can sell easily," the proprietor said.

As she listened Mrs. Higgins looked at Alfred sometimes and nodded her head sadly, and when Sam Carr had finished she said gravely, "Is it so, Alfred?"

"Yes."

"Why have you been doing it?"

"I been spending money, I guess."

"On what?"

"Going around with the guys, I guess," Alfred said.

Mrs. Higgins put out her hand and touched Sam Carr's arm with an understanding gentleness, and speaking as though afraid of disturbing him, she said, "If you would only listen to me before doing anything." Her simple earnestness made her shy; her humility made her falter and look away, but in a moment she was smiling gravely again, and she said with a kind of patient dignity, "What did you intend to do, Mr. Carr?"

"I was going to get a cop. That's what I ought to do."

"Yes, I suppose so. It's not for me to say, because he's my son. Yet I sometimes think a little good advice is the best thing for a boy when he's at a certain period in his life," she said.

Alfred couldn't understand his mother's quiet composure, for if they had been at home and someone had suggested that he was going to be arrested, he knew she would be in a rage and would cry out against him. Yet now she was standing there with that gentle, pleading smile on her face, saying, "I wonder if you don't think it would be better just to let him come home with me. He looks a big fellow, doesn't he? It takes some of them a long time to get any sense," and they both stared at Alfred, who shifted away with a bit of light shining for a moment on his thin face and the tiny pimples over his cheekbone.

But even while he was turning away uneasily Alfred was realizing that Mr. Carr had become aware that his mother was really a fine woman; he knew that Sam Carr was puzzled by his mother, as if he had expected her to come in and plead with him tearfully, and instead he was being made to feel a bit ashamed by her vast tolerance. While there was only the sound of the mother's soft, assured voice in the store, Mr. Carr began to nod his head encouragingly at her. Without being alarmed, while being just large and still and simple and hopeful, she was becoming dominant there in the dimly lit store. "Of course, I don't want to be harsh," Mr. Carr was saying. "I'll tell you what I'll do. I'll just fire him and let it go at that. How's that?" and he got up and shook hands with Mrs. Higgins, bowing low to her in deep respect.

There was such warmth and gratitude in the way she said, "I'll never forget your kindness," that Mr. Carr began to feel warm and genial himself.

"Sorry we had to meet this way," he said.

"But I'm glad I got in touch with you. Just wanted to do the right thing, that's all," he said.

"It's better to meet like this than never, isn't it?" she said. Suddenly they clasped hands as if they liked each other, as if they had known each other a long time. "Good night, sir," she said.

"Good night, Mrs. Higgins. I'm truly sorry," he said.

The mother and son walked along the street together, and the mother was taking a long, firm stride as she looked ahead with her stern face full of worry. Alfred was afraid to speak to her, he was afraid of the silence that was between them, so he only looked ahead too, for the excitement and relief was still pretty strong in him; but in a little while, going along like that in silence made him terribly aware of the strength and the sternness in her; he began to wonder what she was thinking of as she stared ahead so grimly; she seemed to have forgotten that he walked beside her; so when they were passing under the Sixth Avenue elevated and the rumble of the train seemed to break the silence, he said in his old, bluster-way, "Thank God it turned out like that. I certainly won't get in a jam like that again."

"Be quiet. Don't speak to me. You've disgraced me again and again," she said bitterly.

"That's the last time. That's all I'm saying."

"Have the decency to be quiet," she snapped. They kept on their way, looking straight ahead.

When they were at home and his mother took off her coat, Alfred saw that she was really only half-dressed, and she made him feel afraid again when she said, without even looking at him, "You're a bad lot. God forgive you. It's one thing after another and always has been. Why do you stand there stupidly? Go to bed, why don't you?" When he was going, she said, "I'm going to make myself a cup of tea. Mind, now, not a word about

tonight to your father."

While Alfred was undressing in his bedroom, he heard his mother moving around the kitchen. She filled the kettle and put it on the stove. She moved a chair. And as he listened there was no shame in him, just wonder and a kind of admiration of her strength and repose. He could still see Sam Carr nodding his head encouragingly to her; he could hear her talking simply and earnestly, and as he sat on his bed he felt a pride in her strength. "She certainly was smooth," he thought. "Gee, I'd like to tell her she sounded swell."

And at last he got up and went along to the kitchen, and when he was at the door he saw his mother pouring herself a cup of tea. He watched and he didn't move. Her face, as she sat there, was a frightened, broken face utterly unlike the face of the woman who had been so assured a little while ago in the drugstore. When she reached out and lifted the kettle to pour hot water in her cup, her hand trembled and the water splashed on the stove. Leaning back in the chair, she sighed and lifted the cup to her lips, and her lips were groping loosely as if they would never reach the cup. She swallowed the hot tea eagerly, and then she straightened up in relief, though her hand holding the cup still trembled. She looked very old.

It seemed to Alfred that this was the way it had been every time he had been in trouble before, that this trembling had really been in her as she hurried out half-dressed to the drugstore. He understood why she had sat alone in the kitchen the night his young sister had kept repeating doggedly that she was getting married. Now he felt all that his mother had been thinking of as they walked along the street together a little while ago. He watched his mother, and he never spoke, but at that moment his youth seemed to be over; he knew all the years of her life by the way her hand trembled as she raised the cup to her lips. It seemed to him that this was the first time he had ever looked upon his mother.

Author's Commentary to "All the Years of Her Life"

Some of the stories were very easy to write, and some were hard, and I used to wonder why this was so. Years later I thought I had figured out why. When a story came easily for me it seemed to mean that I had suddenly found a structure, or an incident that drew out of me an emotion or a view of things that I had been nursing for a long time. Not that the incident or the person in the story I came upon made me think, "I've often brooded over this kind of a relationship." No. There would be no awareness at all of the long-nurtured emotion. That's why the form of the story would come easily. The story would come along, I would be sure I was exploring something that was new for me. . . .

A writer is very lucky when someone tells him a little story that is half complete. What has been given to him in this way seems to set his imagination off, and almost at once he finds himself completing the story in his mind. The story about the old priest was told to me as a kind of joke. I forget who told it to me. Whoever told it, as I recall, was amused that an old priest in his parish had managed to administer the last rites of the church to a sick young wife in spite of her husband's fierce resentment. About a week after hearing the story, I remember, I got to thinking about what might have gone on in the mind of the old priest after he left the couple. I seemed to know at once. This was the thing I must have been thinking of for a long time before I heard the first part of the story. I used to work on a little typewriter I could carry under my arm. I sat down at the kitchen table, wrote the story in about two and a half hours and knew it was right. I doubt that I ever changed a word.

The story "All the Years of Her Life" came out of a scene that had been very real to me. I saw a middle-aged woman who had just saved her son from some trouble with the law. Her simple effortless dignity, which was all she had to protect her son, had been overwhelm-ing. It had actually embarrassed the man who had proposed to prosecute her son. Of course the mother afterwards was really rattled. The son at first didn't understand her strange magic. His wonder was in his face. I knew about this story for a long time before I wrote it. Then one day I seemed to know what went on in the boy's heart as he watched his mother at home, having a cup of tea after the battle, and he tried to understand the years of her life—his own mother, his own life with her.

I started to write this story late one afternoon. I had finished it by dinner time. I knew that the whole success or failure of the story had to come in the last paragraph. So I kept the story around for about a week, repeating it aloud, and knew I didn't want to change any of it.

There was no plotting or planning of these stories. They had to come out like poems; there had to be a total poignant impact, and first, of course, this impact had to be in me.

Write a Screenplay

M.L. Cornish

Entire books have been written about how to write a screenplay, but I'm going to condense that information into one succinct article which can get you started on the right track.

Getting the right format is extremely important. You want your screenplay to be as professional-looking as possible. Producers read innumerable scripts in the course of a year and they're reluctant to waste time on something that looks amateurish. They're just too busy to be bothered. So an amateurish-looking script will mean one strike against you before anyone's even started to read it.

You can usually count on one page of a script having a one-minute running time. An hour-long program will run roughly 60 pages. A feature-length filmscript can range from 90 to 130 pages. A 30-minute situation comedy runs closer to 45 pages because comedy has to move at a faster pace. But make sure you don't hand somebody a script that falls somewhere in no-man's land, at 73 pages, for example, or 191. That tells the producers they're dealing with an amateur who doesn't even know what the proper length of a script should be.

Most beginning screenwriters worry about camera directions. Am I supposed to indicate a close-up or a zoom-in, they wonder. But you, as a screenwriter, don't have to worry about such things. Leave camera directions to the director.

Protect your script with a cover of light cardboard. Don't forget to include a title page with title of the script centred. In the bottom righthand corner put your name, address and telephone number. Never put a date on your script. Should it be rejected, you may want to send it to another producer. If the script bounces around for months (or, perish the thought, years) from one production office to another, you don't want a producer to think you've shown it to a thousand people already and nobody wanted it.

Don't staple together the pages of your script. Get a two- or three-hole punch and secure the pages with paper fasteners. That way, when the script is rewritten (as all scripts are rewritten!) pages can be added and dropped easily.

This, then, is your sample script, the one you're going to offer to producers. A sample script is imperative because, although you may say you can write a script, unless you have a finished product that proves it, you'll have a hard time finding anyone who will listen to you.

Your sample script can't be just as good as anything being shown on TV or in the theatres. It has to be better. Producers judge the unknown much more severely. After all, why should they risk a bundle of money on an unproven newcomer when a seasoned pro is ready and waiting to provide material?

Now to the actual writing. Obviously you're going to start with a premise. It should be something that interests you, but keep in mind that if you want your script to be produced it has to be producible. That means when you write your screenplay you should keep in mind the shooting budget. The less expensive the production, the better. Therefore avoid science fiction with expensive special effects or period pieces with elaborate sets and costumes. Think, too, about whether any special effects you're demanding are possible. Remember, somebody somewhere has to execute what you've written.

Once you've settled on your premise, you have to concentrate on two things—structure and character.

As far as structure goes, you simply have to determine what is at the core of your story and never lose sight of that. Have everything relate to it. Events must spin off that core centrifugally.

The beginning of your script is very important. After all, if you bore a producer to death in the first dozen pages, chances are he won't finish reading, even if it turns into true art by page 30. There's no formula for writing a grabby beginning. When I write, I simply think of what it would take to grab me so strongly that I wouldn't stop reading the script or turn to another channel if I were watching the story on TV.

Endings are every bit as important as beginnings. It's what the viewer has been anticipating, so if you build up to an ending that lets people down, they'll walk away disappointed and won't recommend your movie. The best ending is one that resolves the problems you've raised and fulfils the audience's expectations.

Now let's concentrate on the issue of subtext. Stories can work on more than one level. That which isn't stated in words but which is underlying and implied, is subtext.

For instance, I'm a big fan of the NBC series, "Remington Steele." In the first season, Remington and Laura were thrown together while working in a detective agency.

Each was attracted to the other but didn't want to let on. You can't have your characters say, "I'm attracted to you, but I don't want to let on that I am." But at the same time you want each of them to be aware of it and, more important, you want the audience to be aware of it.

So, at one point, while they're working on a kidnapping case, Remington says to Laura, "You're worried." She asks, "How can you tell?" He says, "You get this little crinkle on your nose when you're worried." She replies, "Really? You get a little crease across your forehead when you're worried." Then he makes a crack about them sounding like some British law firm—Crinkles and Crease—and they carry on with the case.

But the viewers are aware that they're not really discussing each other's habits or personal quirks. They're indicating an interest in each other, so much so that they watch each other closely and pick up on little things that most people wouldn't even notice. That is subtext. Film is a visual medium. Therefore you have to show, not tell, your story. That's what subtext is all about—showing something by actions or expressions or implications rather than having your characters spell everything out for the audience.

The second element, of course, is characters. I can't stress their importance enough. The main character has to be sympathetic. We have to be able to relate to him. Even if your main character is an anti-hero—for example, a person on the wrong side of the law or whatever—he still has to be sympathetic. Even if he's unlikable, he still has to have the respect of the audience. The audience has to care about the lead character in a movie.

Then there's the element of conflict. Whether it's within one character, or between characters, or between a character and nature, or all three—conflict is indispensable. Your main character has to have what some writers refer to as climax potential. Ask yourself this question: Is my character's conflict great enough to lead to an exciting, dramatic resolution? If the answer is no, then you'd better rethink your script.

When you introduce your characters, give a brief description of their personalities. However, don't give physical descriptions of your characters unless it's crucial to the story. You should allow the director to cast the parts without being confined by your descriptions.

While you can describe your characters in the script to a producer, you can't tell your audience about them in the same fashion. You have to show the audience what kind of a person your protagonist is through clothing, hobbies, speech patterns, attitudes, reactions, and even by the goals he or she sets.

Oh yes, your main character must have goals. Characters must all be motivated by something and their goals must be understandable or people will lose interest in them because they're unbelievable. And when characters are reaching for these goals, they must grow. Nothing is worse than a static character who goes nowhere and consequently prevents the movie from going anywhere.

Finally, we come to dialogue. Dialogue must be realistic, but not real. Let's face it, everyday conversation is full of "um's" and "er's," "you know's," and all kinds of banalities. To have to listen to real conversations in a movie would be deadly. So make your film characters' speech just a little more eloquent than most; but at the same time, make it believable, as natural as possible, and breathable.

So there it is—a quick lesson in writing a screenplay. Each of the elements I have discussed warrants an article devoted to itself. But if you're serious about writing a screenplay, what I've given you will provide the foundation upon which to build.

How the Camel Got His Hump

Rudyard Kipling

In the beginning of years, when the world was so new-and-all, and the Animals were just beginning to work for Man, there was a Camel, and he lived in the middle of a Howling Desert because he did not want to work; and besides, he was a Howler himself. So he ate sticks and thorns and tamarisks and milkweed and prickles, most 'scruciating idle; and when anybody spoke to him he said 'Humph!' Just 'Humph!' and no more.

Presently the Horse came to him on Monday morning, with a saddle on his back and a bit in his mouth, and said, 'Camel, O Camel, come out and trot like the rest of us.'

'Humph!' said the Camel; and the Horse went away and told the Man.

Presently the Dog came to him, with a stick in his mouth, and said, 'Camel, O Camel, come and fetch and carry like the rest of us.'

'Humph!' said the Camel; and the Dog went away and told the Man.

Presently the Ox came to him, with the yoke on his neck, and said, 'Camel, O Camel, come and plough like the rest of us.'

'Humph!' said the Camel; and the Ox went away and told the Man.

At the end of the day the Man called the Horse and the Dog and the Ox together, and said, 'Three, O Three, I'm very sorry for you (with the world so new-and-all); but that Humphthing in the Desert can't work, or he would have been here by now, so I am going to leave him alone, and you must work double-time to make up for it.'

That made the Three very angry (with the world so new-and-all), and they held a palaver, and an *indaba*, and a *punchayet*, and a pow-wow on the edge of the Desert; and the Camel came chewing milkweed *most* 'scruciating idle, and laughed at them. Then he said 'Humph!' and went away again.

Presently there came along the Djinn in charge of All Deserts, rolling in a cloud of dust (Djinns always travel that way because it is Magic), and he stopped to palaver and pow-wow with the Three.

'Djinn of All Deserts,' said the Horse, is it right for any one to be idle, with the world so new-and-all?'

'Certainly not,' said the Djinn.

'Well,' said the Horse, 'there's a thing in the middle of your Howling Desert (and he's a Howler himself) with a long neck and long legs, and he hasn't done a stroke of work since Monday morning. He won't trot.'

'Whew!' said the Djinn, whistling, 'that's my Camel, for all the gold in Arabia! What does he say about it?'

'He says "Humph!" ' said the Dog; 'and he won't fetch and carry.'

'Does he say anything else?'

'Only "Humph!"; and he won't plough,' said the Ox.

'Very good,' said the Djinn. 'I'll humph him if you will kindly wait a minute.'

The Djinn rolled himself up in his dust-cloak, and took a bearing across the desert, and found the Camel most 'scruciatingly idle, looking at his own reflection in a pool of water.

'My long and bubbling friend,' said the Djinn, 'what's this I hear of your doing no work, with the world so new-and-all?'

'Humph!' said the Camel.

The Djinn sat down, with his chin in his hand, and began to think a Great Magic, while the Camel looked at his own reflection in the pool of water.

'You've given the Three extra work ever since Monday morning, all on account of your 'scruciating idleness,' said the Djinn; and he went on thinking Magics, with his chin in his hand.

'Humph!' said the Camel.

'I shouldn't say that again if I were you,' said the Djinn; 'you might say it once too often. Bubbles, I want you to work.'

And the Camel said 'Humph!' again; but no sooner had he said it than he saw his back, that he was so proud of, puffing up and puffing up into a great big lolloping humph.

'Do you see that?' said the Djinn. 'That's your very own humph that you've brought upon your very own self by not working. To-day is Thursday, and you've done no work since Monday, when the work began. Now you are going to work.'

'How can I,' said the Camel, 'with this humph on my back?'

'That's made a-purpose,' said the Djinn, 'all because you missed those three days. You will be able to work now for three days without eating, because you can live on your humph; and don't you ever say I never did anything for you. Come out of the Desert and go to the Three, and behave. Humph yourself!'

And the Camel humphed himself, humph and all, and went away to join the Three. And from that day to this the Camel always wears a humph (we call it 'hump' now, not to hurt his feelings); but he has never yet caught up with the three days that he missed at the beginning of the world, and he has never yet learned how to behave.

The Camel's hump is an ugly lump
  Which well you may see at the Zoo;
But uglier yet is the hump we get
  From having too little to do.

Kiddies and grown-ups too-oo-oo,
If we haven't enough to do-oo-oo,
  We get the hump—
  Cameelious hump—
The hump that is black and blue!

We climb out of bed with a frouzly head
  And a snarly-yarly voice.
We shiver and scowl and we grunt and we growl
  At our bath and our boots and our toys;

And there ought to be a corner for me
(And I know there is one for you)
  When we get the hump—
  Cameelious hump—
The hump that is black and blue!

The cure for this ill is not to sit still,
  Or frowst with a book by the fire;
But to take a large hoe and a shovel also,
  And dig till you gently perspire;

And then you will find that the sun and the wind,
And the Djinn of the Garden too,
  Have lifted the hump—
  The horrible hump—
The hump that is black and blue!

I get it as well as you-oo-oo—
If I haven't enough to do-oo-oo !
  We all get hump—
  Cameelious hump—
Kiddies and grown-ups too !

Writing for the Beginning Reader

Susan L. Krueger

Times have changed since Dick, Jane and Sally delighted beginning readers, but the need for delightful material suitable for children just learning to read never changes. My first sales were two easy-reader stories, and I continue to score regularly in this market. You can, too, once you learn the requirements of writing for children who are eager to "read it by myself."

Easy-reader stories, used by such children's magazines as *Highlights for Children* and *Humpty Dumpty's Magazine*, are short: 200–600 words or so. To write them:

1. Use recurring elements in your story. Material becomes easy to read when the reader can predict what's ahead. When a phrase or refrain is repeated several times, the child soon skims over those words with the exhilaration we all feel when a demanding task becomes less so. My story "Where Can We Find a Button?" repeated the title phrase four times in its 200 words. Other simple phrases such as "the needle and the thread" and "I will sew it on" were repeated, as well. Because the child soon predicts the pattern of the story with its reassuringly repetitious sentences, the occasionally difficult word can be puzzled out without undue frustration.

2. Stick to what the readers know. You probably don't remember your first efforts to decipher those squiggly marks on the pages of a book. But you may remember the skinned knees and elbows you got from your early bicycle-riding efforts. Staying somewhat upright was enough of a challenge without the added hazards of rough terrain, heavy traffic, or the snapping jaws of the neighbor's dog. So it is with beginning readers. As they hack their way through a jungle of squiggles, additional obstacles are the last thing they need or want. Unfamiliar, complex or bizarre subject matter only makes the jungle seem impenetrable. Therefore, stick to subject matter the child is familiar with. Some of my own choices of subject matter have been: getting ready for bed, picking vegetables from a garden, getting a birthday puppy.

3. Put away your thesaurus. Use simple but natural language. Write your stories using the same words you hear (or imagine) young children using themselves. A visit to the easy-reader section in the library will give you some examples. Here are some sentences from stories I have sold: "In the first nest was one brown egg." "It's no fun to be a little boy." "Betsy walked up and down in the garden."

A simple story can be made even easier to read by using rebuses. A rebus is a story in which a picture of a cat will be inserted in place of the word *cat*. My "I Want to Be Something Fun" featured rebuses to replace the words *boy, fish, snake,* and *bird*. To make a rebus story marketable, merely include a variety of "picture" words in the text. You don't have to draw the pictures yourself or

even decide which words should be replaced with pictures. Do suggest to the editor the possibility of turning your story into a rebus.

4. Remember that the pictures that will accompany your story *can* do some of the talking. There is no room in a 200-word easy-reader story for description, no matter how well written. Rely on the illustrations that will be used with your story to depict the setting and your characters' physical attributes and facial expressions. Begin with action and use every one of those 200 words to carry your story forward. (Unless you're a professional artist, however, leave the illustration decisions to the editor. Those darling sketches by your Aunt Millie will not increase your chances of selling your story, and may actually hurt them.)

5. Write a real story. A predictable pattern of short sentences using simple words and a familiar content do not necessarily form a story. Even action will not save a tale that gasps and dies at the final word without a satisfying conclusion. Children revel in the surprise ending, the problem solved, the mystery explained or the joke shared. Arouse their curiosity with the first word and satisfy it with the last.

In other words, write a story worth reading.

An Interview with Jerome Lawrence and Robert E. Lee

Writer's Digest: Kurt Vonnegut once said he believes he's successful because he hasn't "mastered" writing yet, that he always approaches it as a beginner. It sounds like that's what you're saying.

Lawrence: Every play that Bob and I start to write together—or separately, which we do sometimes—we feel is really our first play and that we're starting from the beginning.

One reason that approach is good for all writers is that the so-called experienced writers don't take chances. They keep harking back to their wounds. And they say, "I did that, it was a flop, it didn't work." And that limits you. . . .

WD: You once said, Jerry, that a certain play wasn't "serious enough to be a comedy." How does humor enter into your own works?

Lawrence: We always say that all our serious plays are funny and all our funny plays are serious. It's more important that a comedy have something really basic to say because then you can take off and be funny about it. There are, alas, so many young playwrights who take themselves so seriously that they are afraid of humor. Wit might trivialize their profound work.

The best playwrights—Tennessee Williams, for instance—will puncture the most serious moment with an outrageous laugh. The audience delights in it. They need the relief. They need laughter—or what Norman Cousins calls "inner jogging"—for the joy of life. The more an audience laughs, the more it feels. Shakespeare knew this—there's comedy in his most serious plays. . . .

WD: How do you work together? What's a day with Lawrence and Lee like?

Lawrence: It depends on what we're working on. We try to work six days a week and, if we're lucky, get five pages down every day. When we're actively working on a play, we usually are face to face. Sometimes, when there's heavy traffic, we're on an open phone line. We dialogue together and we talk out plots and characters together. We try to be face to face as often as possible.

Lee: On prose, books, short stories, articles, we write individually. And sometimes, when we have to write a piece we both sign, one of us drafts it and the other one punches it up.

If one of us says no to an idea or some dialogue or whatever, he has the obligation to come up with something better. We work "positively."

Lee: A play has got to have more than a spine. It's got to have a motor.

Lawrence: Every *scene* has to have a motor in it. That's the best test. If a scene has drive, it goes somewhere.

WD: Both a spine and a motor?

Lee: It's a mixed metaphor—excuse us. A motor with a spine, or a spine with a motor is bad imagery.

WD: Is the spine "theme"?

Lee: The word *theme* is not a helpful word for a practical writer. Let the critics or the audience talk about the theme. You write the play because you are possessed. You're possessed by an idea, by a passion. You see, theme has a surgical feel to it.

Lawrence: *Theme* sounds like *thesis*—it's an academic word. Your play has got to have some solid structure, some *spine*. You couldn't walk around very well if you didn't have a spine. A play's a human being.

Lee: When Bob said each scene has a motor, it means you don't start and finish each scene in the same place. It has to have some thrust, some drive. It has to go someplace. It can't stand still. Stasis is dullness in the theatre.

Now we go beyond that to a spine, which means every scene in a play, and every play itself, must stand up. I think *spine* is a very good word.

Lee: *Spine* and *theme* are fancy Christmas-ball words. There's got to be that purring, driving brrrrrrrrrrrrrr.

Lawrence: The breath of life. . . .

When a student or someone asks me, "What should I write about?", I ask, "What turns your stomach? What gives you chills? What makes your hair stand on end? What makes you angry? What makes you cry? What makes you laugh?" Analyze that, and that's something to write about.

Lee: But if one word, one phrase is false, the whole bridge collapses. The entire illusion fails. Every character must be stringently consistent. Characters have got to be real right down to the grit under their fingernails. . . .

Lawrence: Keep writing, write every day, keep at it, keep going, keep doing some new works, new plays of size and meaning.

Lee: With motors.

Lawrence: Motors in every scene.

WD: What about subplots?

Lee: Don't think about plots. There is *no* such thing as a plot. There is only what interesting people do.

Lawrence: People are interested in people. The human animal.

Lee: You don't have to think in terms of a plot. Think of what do these people do. Then all of a sudden they will weave their own plot.

WD: I see formulas where you set up a couple of groups and they sort of interweave.

Lee: Strike the word *formula.* Never use the word *formula.* There is no "tao," no pattern, no modus from a "master."

Beginning Short Stories and Novels

Margaret Laurence

Short stories and novels seem to begin in very different ways in my mind. With a novel, the main characters come first; they grow slowly in the imagination until I feel I know them well; what happens to them arises out of what they *are.* Most short stories I've written seem to be triggered off by some event, either in my own life or something I've observed or read about. The characters in a short story seem just as real to me as the characters in a novel, but I have not seen them, in my mind, in as many situations—they are visualized more in relation to one main situation. Perhaps this points up some of the differences between a novel and a short story. One form is not better than the other. They simply do not serve the same function. I see a novel as a fictional form containing many themes, and when I am writing a novel, I feel rather like a juggle: trying to keep a dozen plates spinning up

there in the air. In my stories, on the other hand, there tends to be one central theme, although of course it may have ramifications. As with a novel, one hopes to set up echoes in the reader's mind, which will lead them beyond anything on the printed page.

Why does a writer put some things in novel form and others in short story form? Every writer might give a different answer to this question, and my answer probably sounds vague, but the closest I can come to an explanation is that some situations and characters are naturally meant for a novel, and others for a short story, depending upon the variety of themes and the emphasis one wants to give these. Actually, I don't decide by doing a long analysis or even by flipping a coin. It is a decision which seems to be taken partly at a subconscious level, perhaps for reasons related to what I've said about stories and novels. . . .

A Tree. A Rock. A Cloud.

Carson McCullers

It was raining that morning, and still very dark. When the boy reached the streetcar café he had almost finished his route and he went in for a cup of coffee. The place was an all-night café owned by a bitter and stingy man called Leo. After the raw, empty street the café seemed friendly and bright: along the counter there were a couple of soldiers, three spinners from the cotton mill, and in a corner a man who sat hunched over with his nose and half his face down in a beer mug. The boy wore a helmet such as aviators wear. When he went into the café he unbuckled the chin strap and raised the right flap up over his pink little ear; often as he drank his coffee someone would speak to him in a friendly way. But this morning Leo did not look into his face and none of the men were talking. He paid and was leaving the café when a voice called out to him:

'Son! Hey Son!'

He turned back and the man in the corner was crooking his finger and nodding to him. He had brought his face out of the beer mug and he seemed suddenly very happy. The man was long and pale, with a big nose and faded orange hair.

'Hey Son!'

The boy went toward him. He was an undersized boy of about twelve, with one shoulder drawn higher than the other because of the weight of the paper sack. His face was shallow, freckled, and his eyes were round child eyes.

'Yeah Mister?'

The man laid one hand on the paper boy's shoulders, then grasped the boy's chin and turned his face slowly from one side to the other. The boy shrank back uneasily.

'Say! What's the big idea?'

The boy's voice was shrill; inside the café it was suddenly very quiet.

The man said slowly: 'I love you.'

All along the counter the men laughed. The boy, who had scowled and sidled away, did not know what to do. He looked over the counter at Leo, and Leo watched him with a weary, brittle jeer. The boy tried to laugh also. But the man was serious and sad.

'I did not mean to tease you, Son,' he said. 'Sit down and have a beer with me. There is something I have to explain.'

Cautiously, out of the corner of his eye, the paper boy questioned the men along the counter to see what he should do. But they had gone back to their beer or their breakfast and did not notice him. Leo put a cup of coffee on the counter and a little jug of cream.

'He is a minor,' Leo said.

The paper boy slid himself up onto the stool. His ear beneath the upturned flap of the helmet was very small and red. The man was nodding at him soberly. 'It is important,' he said. Then he reached in his hip pocket and brought out something which he held up in the palm of his hand for the boy to see.

'Look very carefully,' he said.

The boy stared, but there was nothing to look at very carefully. The man held in his big, grimy palm a photograph. It was the face of a woman, but blurred, so that only the hat and the dress she was wearing stood out clearly.

'See?' the man asked.

The boy nodded and the man placed another picture in his palm. The woman was standing on a beach in a bathing suit. The suit made her stomach very big, and that was the main thing you noticed.

'Got a good look?' He leaned over closer and finally asked: 'You ever seen her before?'

The boy sat motionless, staring slantwise at the man. 'Not so I know of.'

'Very well.' The man blew on the photographs and put them back into his pocket. 'That was my wife.'

'Dead?' the boy asked.

Slowly the man shook his head. He pursed his lips as though about to whistle and answered in a long-drawn way: 'Nuuu' he said. 'I will explain.'

The beer on the counter before the man was in a large brown mug. He did not pick it up to drink. Instead he bent down and, putting his face over the rim, he rested there for a moment. Then with both hands he tilted the mug and sipped.

'Some night you'll go to sleep with your nose in a mug and drown,' said Leo. 'Prominent transient drowns in beer. That would be a cute death.'

The paper boy tried to signal to Leo. While the man was not looking he screwed up his face and worked his mouth to question soundlessly: 'Drunk?' But Leo only raised his eyebrows and turned away to put some pink strips of bacon on the grill. The man pushed the mug away from him, straightened himself, and folded his loose crooked hands on the counter. His face was sad as he looked at the paper boy. He did not blink, but from time to time the lids closed down with delicate gravity over his pale green eyes. It was nearing dawn and the boy shifted the weight of the paper sack.

'I am talking about love,' the man said. 'With me it is a science.'

The boy half slid down from the stool. But the man raised his forefinger, and there was something about him that held the boy and would not let him go away.

'Twelve years ago I married the woman in the photograph. She was my wife for one year, nine months, three days, and two nights. I loved her. Yes. . . ' He tightened his blurred, rambling voice and said again: 'I loved her. I thought also that she loved me. I was a railroad engineer. She had all home comforts and luxuries. It never crept into my brain that she was not satisfied. But do you know what happened?'

'Mgneeow!' said Leo.

The man did not take his eyes from the boy's face. 'She left me. I came in one night and the house was empty and she was gone. She left me.'

'With a fellow?' the boy asked.

Gently the man placed his palm down on the counter. 'Why naturally, Son. A woman does not run off like that alone.'

The café was quiet, the soft rain black and endless in the street outside. Leo pressed down the frying bacon with the prongs of his long fork. 'So you have been chasing the floozie for eleven years. You frazzled old rascal!'

For the first time the man glanced at Leo. 'Please don't be vulgar. Besides, I was not speaking to you.' He turned back to the boy and said in a trusting and secretive undertone: 'Let's not pay any attention to him. O.K.?'

The paper boy nodded doubtfully.

'It was like this,' the man continued. 'I am a person who feels many things. All my life one thing after another has impressed me. Moonlight. The leg of a pretty girl. One thing after another. But the point is that when I had enjoyed anything there was a peculiar sensation as though it was laying around loose in

me. Nothing seemed to finish itself up or fit in with the other things. Women? I had my portion of them. The same. Afterwards laying around loose in me. I was a man who had never loved.'

Very slowly he closed his eyelids, and the gesture was like a curtain drawn at the end of a scene in a play. When he spoke again his voice was excited and the words came fast—the lobes of his large, loose ears seemed to tremble.

'Then I met this woman. I was fifty-one and she always said she was thirty. I met her at a filling station and we were married within three days. And do you know what it was like? I just can't tell you. All I had ever felt was gathered together around this woman. Nothing lay loose in me any more but was finished up by her.'

The man stopped suddenly and stroked his long nose. His voice sank down to a steady and reproachful undertone: 'I'm not explaining this right. What happened was this. There were these beautiful feelings and loose little pleasures inside me. And this woman was something like an assembly line for my soul. I run these little pieces of myself through her and I come out complete. Now do you follow me?'

'What was her name?' the boy asked.

'Oh,' he said, 'I called her Dodo. But that is immaterial.'

'Did you try to make her come back?'

The man did not seem to hear. 'Under the circumstances you can imagine how I felt when she left me.'

Leo took the bacon from the grill and folded two strips of it between a bun. He had a gray face, with slitted eyes, and a pinched nose saddled by faint blue shadows. One of the mill workers signaled for more coffee and Leo poured it. He did not give refills on coffee free. The spinner ate breakfast there every morning, but the better Leo knew his customers the stingier he treated them. He nibbled his own bun as though he grudged it to himself.

'And you never got hold of her again?'

The boy did not know what to think of the man, and his child's face was uncertain with mingled curiosity and doubt. He was new on the paper route; it was still strange to him to be out in the town in the black, queer early morning.

'Yes,' the man said. 'I took a number of steps to get her back. I went around trying to locate her. I went to Tulsa where she had folks. And to Mobile. I went to every town she had ever mentioned to me, and I hunted down every man she had formerly been connected with. Tulsa, Atlanta, Chicago, Cheehaw, Memphis . . . For the better part of two years I chased around the country trying to lay hold of her.'

'But the pair of them had vanished from the face of the earth!' said Leo.

'Don't listen to him,' the man said confidentially. 'And also just forget those two years. They are not important. What matters is that around the third year a curious thing begun to happen to me.'

'What?' the boy asked.

The man leaned down and tilted his mug to take a sip of beer. But as he hovered over the mug his nostrils fluttered slightly; he sniffed the staleness of the beer and did not drink. 'Love is a curious thing to begin with. At first I thought only of getting her back. It was a kind of mania. But then as time went on I tried to remember her. But do you know what happened?'

'No,' said the boy.

'When I laid myself down on a bed and tried to think about her my mind became a blank. I couldn't see her. I would take out her pictures and look. No good. Nothing doing. A blank. Can you imagine it?'

'Say Mac!' Leo called down the counter. 'Can you imagine this bozo's mind a blank!'

Slowly, as though fanning away flies, the man waved his hand. His green eyes were concentrated and fixed on the shallow little face of the paper boy.

'But a sudden piece of glass on a sidewalk. Or a nickel tune in a music box. A shadow on a wall at night. And I would remember. It might happen in a street and I would cry or bang my head against a lamppost. You follow me?'

'A piece of glass . . . ' the boy said.

'Anything. I would walk around and I had no power of how and when to remember her. You think you can put up a kind of shield. But remembering don't come to a man face forward—it corners around sideways. I was at the mercy of everything I saw and heard. Suddenly instead of me combing the countryside to find her she begun to chase me around in my very soul. *She* chasing *me*, mind you ! And in my soul.'

The boy asked finally: 'What part of the country were you in then?'

'Ooh,' the man groaned. 'I was a sick mortal. It was like smallpox. I confess, Son, that I boozed. I fornicated. I committed any sin that suddenly appealed to me. I am loath to confess it but I will do so. When I recall that period it is all curdled in my mind, it was so terrible.'

The man leaned his head down and tapped his forehead on the counter. For a few seconds he stayed bowed over in this position, the back of his stringy neck covered with orange furze, his hands with their long warped fingers held palm to palm in an attitude of prayer. Then the man straightened himself; he was smiling and suddenly his face was bright and tremulous and old.

'It was in the fifth year that it happened,' he said. 'And with it I started my science.'

Leo's mouth jerked with a pale, quick grin. 'Well none of we boys are getting any younger,' he said. Then with sudden anger he balled up a dishcloth he was holding and threw it down hard on the floor. 'You draggle-tailed old Romeo !'

'What happened?' the boy asked.

The old man's voice was high and clear: 'Peace,' he answered.

'Huh?'

'It is hard to explain scientifically, Son,' he said. I guess the logical explanation is that she and I had fleed around from each other for so long that finally we just got tangled up together and lay down and quit. Peace. A queer and beautiful blankness. It was spring in Portland and the rain came every afternoon. All evening I just stayed there on my bed in the dark. And that is how the science come to me.'

The windows in the streetcar were pale blue with light. The two soldiers paid for their beers and opened the door—one of the soldiers combed his hair and wiped off his muddy puttees before they went outside. The three mill workers bent silently over their breakfasts. Leo's clock was ticking on the wall.

'It is this. And listen carefully. I meditated on love and reasoned it out. I reasoned it out. I realized what is wrong with us. Men fall in love for the first time. And what do they fall in love with?'

The boy's soft mouth was partly open and he did not answer.

'A woman,' the old man said. 'Without science, with nothing to go by, they undertake the most dangerous and sacred experience in God's earth. They fall in love with a woman. Is that correct, Son?'

'Yeah,' the boy said faintly.

'They start at the wrong end of love. They begin at the climax. Can you wonder it is so miserable? Do you know how men should love?'

The old man reached over and grasped the boy by the collar of his leather jacket. He gave him a gentle little shake and his green eyes gazed down unblinking and grave.

'Son, do you know how love should be begun?'

The boy sat small and listening and still. Slowly he shook his head. The old man leaned closer and whispered:

'A tree. A rock. A cloud.'

It was still raining outside in the street: a mild, gray, endless rain. The mill whistle blew for the six o'clock shift and the three spinners paid and went away. There was no one in the café but Leo, the old man, and the little paper boy.

'The weather was like this in Portland,' he said. 'At the time my science was begun. I meditated and I started very cautious. I would pick up something from the street and take it home with me. I bought a goldfish and I concentrated on the goldfish and I loved it. I graduated from one thing to another. Day by day I was getting this technique. On the road from Portland to San Diego———'

'Aw shut up!' screamed Leo suddenly. 'Shut up! Shut up!'

The old man still held the collar of the boy's jacket; he was trembling and his face was earnest and bright and wild. 'For six years now I have gone around by myself and built up my science. And now I am a master. Son. I can love anything. No longer do I have to think about it even. I see a street full of people and a beautiful light comes in me. I watch a bird in the sky. Or I meet a traveler on the road. Everything, Son. And anybody. All stranger and all loved! Do you realize what a science like mine can mean?'

The boy held himself stiffly, his hands curled tight around the counter edge. Finally he asked: 'Did you ever really find that lady?'

'What? What say, Son?'

'I mean,' the boy asked timidly, 'have you fallen in love with a woman again?'

The old man loosened his grasp on the boy's collar. He turned away and for the first time his green eyes had a vague and scattered look. He lifted the mug from the counter, drank down the yellow beer. His head was shaking slowly from side to side. Then finally he answered: 'No, Son. You see that is the last step in my science. I go cautious. And I am not quite ready yet.'

'Well!' said Leo. 'Well well well!'

The old man stood in the open doorway. 'Remember,' he said. Framed there in the gray damp light of the early morning he looked shrunken and seedy and frail. But his smile was bright. 'Remember I love you,' he said with a last nod. And the door closed quietly behind him.

The boy did not speak for a long time. He pulled down the bangs on his forehead and slid his grimy little forefinger around the rim of his empty cup. Then without looking at Leo he finally asked:

'Was he drunk?'

'No,' said Leo shortly.

The boy raised his clear voice higher. 'Then was he a dope fiend?'

'No.'

The boy looked up at Leo, and his flat little face was desperate, his voice urgent and shrill. 'Was he crazy? Do you think he was a lunatic?' The paper boy's voice dropped suddenly with doubt. 'Leo? Or not?'

But Leo would not answer him. Leo had run a night café for fourteen years, and he held himself to be a critic of craziness. There were the town characters and also the transients who roamed in from the night. He knew the manias of all of them. But he did not want to satisfy the questions of the waiting child. He tightened his pale face and was silent.

So the boy pulled down the right flap of his helmet and as he turned to leave he made the only comment that seemed safe to him, the only remark that could not be laughed down and despised:

'He sure has done a lot of travelling.'

Writing Short Stories

Flannery O'Connor

. . . A story is a complete dramatic action—and in good stories, the characters are shown through the action and the action is controlled through the characters, and the result of this is meaning that derives from the whole presented experience. I myself prefer to say that a story is a dramatic event that involves a person because he is a person, and a particular person—that is, because he shares in the general human condition and in some specific human situation. A story always involves, in a dramatic way, the mystery of personality. I lent some stories to a country lady who lives down the road from me, and when she returned them, she said, "Well, them stories just gone and shown you how some folks *would* do," and I thought to myself that that was right: when you write stories, you have to be content to start exactly there—showing how some specific folks *will* do, *will* do in spite of everything.

Now this is a very humble level to have to begin on, and most people who think they want to write stories are not willing to start there. They want to write about problems, not people; or about abstract issues, not concrete situations. They have an idea, or a feeling, or an overflowing ego, or they want to Be A Writer, or they want to give their wisdom to the world in a simple-enough way for the world to be able to absorb it. In any case, they don't have a story and they wouldn't be willing to write it if they did; and in the absence of a story, they set out to find a theory or a formula or a technique.

Now none of this is to say that when you write a story, you are supposed to forget or give up any moral position that you hold. Your beliefs will be the light by which you see, but they will not be what you see and they will not be a substitute for seeing. For the writer of fiction, everything has its testing point in the eye, and the eye is an organ that eventually involves the whole personality, and as much of the world as can be got into it. It involves judgment. Judgment is something that begins in the act of vision, and when it does not, or when it becomes separated from vision, then a confusion exists in the mind which transfers itself to the story.

Fiction operates through the senses, and I think one reason that people find it so difficult to write stories is that they forget how much time and patience is required to convince through the senses. No reader who doesn't actually experience, who isn't made to feel, the story is going to believe anything the fiction writer merely tells him. The first and most obvious characteristic of fiction is that it deals with reality through what can be seen, heard, smelt, tasted, and touched.

Now this is something that can't be learned only in the head; it has to be learned in the habits. It has to become a way that you habitually look at things. The fiction writer has to realize that he can't create compassion with compassion, or emotion with emotion, or thought with thought. He has to provide all these things with a body; he has to create a world with weight and extension.

I have found that the stories of beginning writers usually bristle with emotion, but *whose* emotion is often very hard to determine. Dialogue frequently proceeds without the assistance of any characters that you can actually see, and uncontained thought leaks out of every corner of the story. The reason is usually that the student is wholly interested in his thoughts and his emotions and not in his dramatic action, and that he is too lazy or highfalutin to descend to the concrete where fiction operates. He thinks that judgment exists in one place and sense-impression in another. But for the fiction writer, judgment begins in the details he sees and how he sees them. . . .

Meaning is what keeps the short story from being short. I prefer to talk about the meaning in a story rather than the theme of a story. People talk about the theme of a story as if the theme were like the string that a sack of chicken feed is tied with. They think that if you can pick out the theme, the way you pick the right thread in the chicken-feed sack, you can rip the story open and feed the chickens. But this is not the way meaning works in fiction.

When you can state the theme of a story, when you can separate it from the story itself, then you can be sure the story is not a very good one. The meaning of a story has to be embodied in it, has to be made concrete in it. A story is a way to say something that can't be said any other way, and it takes every word in the story to say what the meaning is. You tell a story because a statement would be inadequate. When anybody asks what a story is about, the only proper thing is to tell him to read the story. The meaning of fiction is not abstract meaning but experienced meaning, and the purpose of making statements about the meaning of a story is only to help you experience that meaning more fully.

Fiction is an art that calls for the strictest attention to the real—whether the writer is writing a naturalistic story or a fantasy. I mean that we always begin with what is or with what has an eminent possibility of truth about it. Even when one writes a fantasy, reality is the proper basis of it. A thing is fantastic because it is so real, so real that it is fantastic. Graham Greene has said that he can't write, "I stood over a bottomless pit," because that couldn't be true, or "Running down the stairs I jumped into a taxi," because that couldn't be true either. But Elizabeth Bowen can write about one of her characters that "she snatched at her hair as if she heard something in it," because that is eminently possible.

I would even go so far as to say that the person writing a fantasy has to be even more strictly attentive to the concrete detail than someone writing in a naturalistic vein—because the greater the story's strain on the credulity, the more convincing the properties in it have to be.

There are two qualities that make fiction. One is the sense of mystery and the other is the sense of manners. You get the manners from the texture of existence that surrounds you. . . .

An idiom characterizes a society, and when you ignore the idiom, you are very likely ignoring the whole social fabric that could make a meaningful character. You can't cut characters off from their society and say much about them as individuals. You can't say anything meaningful about the mystery of a personality unless you put that personality in a believable and significant social context. And the best way to do this is through the character's own language. . . .

The Sound of Muses

J. Michael Straczynski

Where Am I?

Of first concern to the radiodrama writer should be establishing a sense of place. To do this, you must develop an instinct for ambient sound. Unless your character is trapped in a hermetically sealed, soundproof room, there should be some telltale noises that will aid the listener in putting together a mental image of where the story is taking place. Is someone in the next room typing, or playing with toys, or watching television? If we're outside, can we hear the wind in the trees, a stream running nearby, construction work in progress?

Just about every scene should have at least one indication of ambient sound, particularly at the start of the scene—not only to give the listener an image of the surrounding scenery, but also to set the mood, and convey plot information.

Another function of sound is to give the listener a sense of specific location *within* a particular place.

Where Am I Going?

Sound effects—even the absence of sound —can be used to imply more extensive movement, including a transition from one location to another. A listener should be moved smoothly along the storyline, with a minimum of bumps, sidetrips, and other distractions. The task, then, is to make the transitions understandable without being obvious, to continue to set the scene, and to perpetuate the story's mood.

There are any number of ways to effect a transition, depending on how elaborate you want to get. The simplest is to do nothing at all . . . but of course to do nothing at all *just so*. Let's say we've got a plane to catch, and the next thing we hear will be a plane engine fading down under the dialogue. You can do the same with cars, trains—even drag in the old ticking clock gag.

But sound effects were never intended to substitute for dialogue. One effect after another, without commentary, can confuse the listener. So, as has been done throughout, your characters should indicate where they are and what they're doing, as long as you aren't painfully obvious in red-flagging the listener.

Once you become comfortable with using sound as a dramatic device—as much a part of the story as the dialogue and the characters—you can branch out, experiment.

The musical transition is, of course, the old stand-by in case nothing else works. A whole range of specific sound effects are available if you can tie them into the action.

The Pen of My Aunt

Josephine Tey

SCENE: A French country house during the Occupation by German forces in World War II. The lady of the house is seated in her drawing room.

Simone: (*approaching*) Madame! Oh, madame! Madame, have you—
Madame: Simone.
Simone: Madame, have you seen what—
Madame: Simone!
Simone: But madame—
Madame: Simone, this may be an age of barbarism, but I will have none of it inside the walls of this house.
Simone: But madame, there is a—there is a—
Madame: (*silencing her*) Simone. France may be an occupied country, a ruined nation, and a

conquered race, but we will keep, if you please, the usages of civilization.

Simone: Yes, madame.

Madame: One thing we still possess, thank God; and that is good manners. The enemy never had it; and it is not something they can take from us.

Simone: No, madame.

Madame: Go out of the room again. Open the door—

Simone: Oh, *madame!* I wanted to tell you—

Madame: —Open the door, shut it behind you—quietly—take two paces into the room, and say what you came to say. (*Simone goes hastily out, shutting the door. She reappears, shuts the door behind her, takes two paces into the room, and waits.*) Yes, Simone!

Simone: I expect it is too late now; they will be here.

Madame: Who will?

Simone: The soldiers who were coming up the avenue.

Madame: After the last few months I should not have thought that soldiers coming up the avenue was a remarkable fact. It is no doubt a party with a billeting order.

Simone: (*crossing to the window*) No madame, it is two soldiers in one of their little cars, with a civilian between them.

Madame: Which civilian?

Simone: A stranger, madame.

Madame: A stranger? Are the soldiers from the Combatant branch?

Simone: No, they are those beasts of Administration. Look, they have stopped. They are getting out.

Madame: (*at the window*) Yes, it is a stranger. Do you know him, Simone?

Simone: I have never set eyes on him before, madame.

Madame: You would know if he belonged to the district?

Simone: Oh, madame, I know every man between here and St. Estèphe.

Madame: (*dryly*) No doubt.

Simone: Oh, merciful God, they are coming up the steps.

Madame: My good Simone, that is what the steps were put there for.

Simone: But they will ring the bell and I shall have to—

Madame: And you will answer it and behave as if you had been trained by a butler and ten upper servants instead of being the charcoal-burner's daughter from over at Les Chênes. (*This is said encouragingly, not in unkindness.*) You will be very calm and correct.

Simone: Calm! Madame! With my inside turning over and over like a wheel at a fair!

Madame: A good servant does not have an inside, merely an exterior. (*comforting*) Be assured, my child. You have your place here; that is more than those creatures on our doorstep have. Let that hearten you—

Simone: Madame! They are not going to ring. They are coming straight in.

Madame: (*bitterly*) Yes. They have forgotten long ago what bells are for.

(*Door opens.*)

Stranger: (*in a bright, confident, casual tone*) Ah, there you are, my dear aunt. I am so glad. Come in, my friend, come in. My dear aunt, this gentleman wants you to identify me.

Madame: Identify you?

Corporal: We found this man wandering in the woods—

Stranger: The corporal found it inexplicable that anyone should wander in a wood.

Corporal: And he had no papers on him—

Stranger: And I rightly pointed out that if I carry all the papers one is supposed to these days, I am no good to God or man. If I put them in a hip pocket, I can't bend forward; if I put them in a front pocket, I can't bend at all.

Corporal: He said that he was your nephew, madame, but that did not seem to us very likely, so we brought him here. (*There is the slightest pause; just one moment of silence.*)

Madame: But of course this is my nephew.

Corporal: He is?

Madame: Certainly.

Corporal: He lives here?

Madame: (*assenting*) My nephew lives here.

Corporal: So! (*recovering*) My apologies, madame. But you will admit that appearances were against the young gentleman.

Madame: Alas, Corporal, my nephew belongs to a generation who delight in flouting appearances. It is what they call "expressing their personality," I understand.

Corporal: (*with contempt*) No doubt, madame.

Madame: Convention is anathema to them, and there is no sin like conformity. Even a collar is an offence against their liberty, and a discipline not to be borne by free necks.

Corporal: Ah, yes, madame. A little more discipline among your nephew's generation, and we might not be occupying your country today.

Stranger: You think it was that collar of yours that conquered my country? You flatter yourself, Corporal. The only result of wearing a collar like that is varicose veins in the head.

Madame: (*repressive*) Please! My dear boy. Let us not descend to personalities.

Stranger: The matter is not personal, my good aunt, but scientific. Wearing a collar like that retards the flow of fresh blood to the head, with the most disastrous consequences to the gray matter of the brain. The hypothetical gray matter. In fact, I have a theory—

Corporal: Monsieur, your theories do not interest me.

Stranger: No? You do not find speculation interesting?

Corporal: In this world one judges by results.

Stranger: (*after a slight pause of reflection*) I see. The collared conqueror sits in the high places, while the collarless conquered lies about in the woods. And who comes best out of that, would you say? Tell me, Corporal, as man to man, do you never have a mad, secret desire to lie unbuttoned in a wood?

Corporal: I have only one desire, monsieur, and that is to see your papers.

Stranger: (*taken off guard and filling in time*) My papers?

Madame: But is that necessary, Corporal? I have already told you that—

Corporal: I know that madame is a very good collaborator and in good standing—

Madame: In that case—

Corporal: But when we begin an affair we like to finish it. I have asked to see monsieur's papers, and the matter will not be finished until I have seen them.

Madame: You acknowledge that I am in "good standing," Corporal?

Corporal: So I have heard, madame.

Madame: Then I must consider it a discourtesy on your part to demand my nephew's credentials.

Corporal: It is no reflection on madame. It is a matter of routine, nothing more.

Stranger: (*murmuring*) The great god Routine.

Madame: To ask for his papers was routine; to insist on their production is discourtesy. I shall say so to your Commanding Officer.

Corporal: Very good, madame. In the meantime, I shall inspect your nephew's papers.

Madame: And what if I—

Stranger: (*quietly*) You may as well give it up, my dear. You could as easily turn a steamroller. They have only one idea at a time. If the Corporal's heart is set on seeing my papers, he shall see them. (*moving towards the door*) I left them in the pocket of my coat.

Simone: (*unexpectedly from the background*) Not in your *linen* coat?

Stranger: (*pausing*) Yes. Why?

Simone: (*with apparently growing anxiety*) Your *cream* linen coat? The one you were wearing yesterday?

Stranger: Certainly.

Simone: Merciful Heaven! I sent it to the laundry!

Stranger: To the laundry!

Simone: Yes, monsieur; this morning; in the basket.

Stranger: (*in incredulous anger*) You sent my coat, *with my papers in the pocket*, to the laundry!

Simone: (*defensive and combatant*) I didn't know monsieur's papers were in the pocket.

Stranger: You didn't know! You didn't know that a packet of documents weighing half a ton were in the pocket. An identity card, a *laisser passer*, a food card, a drink card, an army discharge, a permission to wear civilian clothes, a permission to go farther than ten miles to the east, a permission to go more than ten miles to the west, a permission to—

Simone: (*breaking in with spirit*) How was I to know the coat was heavy! I picked it up with the rest of the bundle that was lying on the floor.

Stranger: (*snapping her head off*) My coat was on the back of the chair.

Simone: It was on the floor.

Stranger: On the back of the chair!

Simone: It was on the floor with your dirty shirt and your pajamas, and a towel and what not. I put my arms round the whole thing and then—woof! into the basket with them.

Stranger: I tell you that coat was on the back of the chair. It was quite clean and was not going to the laundry for two weeks yet—if then. I hung it there myself, and—

Madame: My dear boy, what does it matter? The damage is done now. In any case, they will find the papers when they unpack the basket, and return them tomorrow.

Stranger: If someone doesn't steal them. There are a lot of people who would like to lay hold of a complete set of papers, believe me.

Madame: (*reassuring*) Oh, no. Old Fleureau is the soul of honesty. You have no need to worry about them. They will be back first thing tomorrow, you shall see; and then we shall have much pleasure in sending them to the Administration Office for the Corporal's inspection. Unless, of course, the Corporal insists on your personal appearance at the office.

Corporal: (*cold and indignant*) I have seen monsieur. All that I want now is to see his papers.

Stranger: You shall see them, Corporal, you shall see them. The whole half-ton of them.

You may inspect them at your leisure. Provided, that is, that they come back from the laundry to which this idiot has consigned them.

Madame: (*again reassuring*) They will come back, never fear. And you must not blame Simone. She is a good child, and does her best.

Simone: (*with an air of belated virtue*) I am not one to pry into pockets.

Madame: Simone, show the Corporal out, if you please.

Simone: (*natural feeling overcoming her for a moment*) He knows the way out. (*recovering*) Yes, madame.

Madame: And Corporal, try to take your duties a little less literally in future. My countrymen appreciate the spirit rather than the letter.

Corporal: I have my instructions, madame, and I obey them. Good day, madame. Monsieur.

(*He goes, followed by Simone—the door closes. There is a moment of silence.*)

Stranger: For a good collaborator, that was a remarkably quick adoption.

Madame: Sit down, young man. I will give you something to drink. I expect your knees are none too well.

Stranger: My knees, madame, are pure gelatine. As for my stomach, it seems to have disappeared.

Madame: (*offering him the drink she has poured out*) This will recall it, I hope.

Stranger: You are not drinking, madame.

Madame: Thank you, no.

Stranger: Not with strangers. It is certainly no time to drink with strangers. Nevertheless, I drink the health of a collaborator. (*He drinks.*) Tell me, madame, what will happen tomorrow when they find that you have no nephew!

Madame: (*surprised*) But of course I have a nephew. I tell lies, my friend; but not *silly* lies. My charming nephew has gone to Bonneval for the day. He finds country life dull.

Stranger: Dull? This—this heaven?

Madame: (*dryly*) He likes to talk and here there is no audience. At Headquarters in Bonneval he finds the audience sympathetic.

Stranger: (*understanding the implication*) Ah.

Madame: He believes in the Brotherhood of Man—if you can credit it.

Stranger: After the last six months?

Madame: His mother was American, so he has half the Balkans in his blood. To say nothing of Italy, Russia and the Levant.

Stranger: (*half amused*) I see.

Madame: A silly and worthless creature, but useful.

Stranger: Useful?

Madame: I—borrow his cloak.

Stranger: I see.

Madame: Tonight I shall borrow his identity papers, and tomorrow they will go to the office in St. Estèphe.

Stranger: But—he will have to know.

Madame: (*placidly*) Oh, yes, he will know, of course.

Stranger: And how will you persuade such an enthusiastic collaborator to deceive his friends?

Madame: Oh, that is easy. He is my heir.

Stranger: (*amused*) Ah.

Madame: He is, also, by the mercy of God, not too unlike you, so that his photograph will not startle the Corporal too much tomorrow. Now tell me what you are doing in my wood.

Stranger: Resting my feet—I am practically walking on my bones. And waiting for tonight.

Madame: Where are you making for? (*as he does not answer immediately*) The coast? (*He nods*) That is four days away—five if your feet are bad.

Stranger: I know it.

Madame: Have you friends on the way?

Stranger: I have friends at the coast, who will get me a boat. But no one between here and the sea.

Madame: (*rising*) I must consult my list of addresses. (*pausing*) What was your service?

Stranger: Army.

Madame: Which regiment?

Stranger: The 79th.

Madame: (*after the faintest pause*) And your Colonel's name?

Stranger: Delavault was killed in the first week, and Martin took over.

Madame: (*going to her desk*) A "good collaborator" cannot be too careful. Now I can consult my notebook. A charming colour, is it not? A lovely shade of red.

Stranger: Yes—but what has a red quill pen to do with your notebook?—Ah, you write with it of course—stupid of me.

Madame: Certainly I write with it—but it is also my notebook—look—I only need a hairpin—and then—so—out of my quill pen comes my notebook—a tiny piece of paper—but enough for a list of names.

Stranger: You mean that you keep that list on your desk? (*He sounds disapproving.*)

Madame: Where did you expect me to keep it, young man? In my corset? Did you ever try to get something out of your corset in a hurry? What would you advise as the ideal quality in a hiding place for a list of names?

Stranger: That the thing should be difficult to find, of course.

Madame: Not at all. That it should be easily destroyed in an emergency. It is too big for me to swallow—I suspect they do that only in books—and we have no fires to consume it, so I had to think of some other way. I did try to memorize the list, but what I could not be sure of remembering were those that—that had to be scored off. It would be fatal to send someone to an address that—that was no longer available. So I had to keep a written record.

Stranger: And if you neither eat it nor burn it when the moment comes, how do you get rid of it?

Madame: I could, of course, put a match to it, but scraps of freshly burned paper on a desk take a great deal of explaining. If I ceased to be looked on with approval my usefulness would end. It is important therefore that there should be no sign of anxiety on my part; no burned paper, no excuses to leave the room, no nods and becks and winks. I just sit here at my desk and go on with my letters. I tilt my nice big inkwell sideways for a moment and dip the pen into the deep ink at the side. The ink flows into the hollow of the quill, and all is blotted out. (*consulting the list*) Let me see. It would be good if you could rest your feet for a day or so.

Stranger: (*ruefully*) It would.

Madame: There is a farm just beyond the Marnay crossroads on the way to St. Estèphe — (*She pauses to consider.*)

Stranger: St. Estèphe is the home of the singleminded Corporal. I don't want to run into him again.

Madame: No, that might be awkward; but that farm of the Cherfils would be ideal. A good hiding-place, and food to spare, and fine people—

Stranger: If your nephew is so friendly with the invader, how is it that the Corporal doesn't know him by sight?

Madame: (*absently*) The unit at St. Estèphe is a noncommissioned one.

Stranger: Does the Brotherhood of Man exclude sergeants, then?

Madame: Oh, definitely. Brotherhood does not really begin under field rank, I understand.

Stranger: But the Corporal may still meet your nephew somewhere.

Madame: That is a risk one must take. It is not a very grave one. They change the personnel every few weeks, to prevent them becoming too acclimatized. And even if he met my nephew, he is unlikely to ask for the papers of so obviously well-to-do a citizen. If you could bear to go *back* a little—

Stranger: Not a step! It would be like—like denying God. I have got so far, against all the odds, and I am not going a yard back. Not even to rest my feet!

Madame: I understand; but it is a pity. It is a

long way to the Cherfils farm—two miles east of the Marnay crossroads it is, on a little hill.

Stranger: I'll get there; don't worry. If not tonight then tomorrow night. I am used to sleeping in the open by now.

Madame: I wish we could have you here, but it is too dangerous. We are liable to be billeted on at any moment, without notice. However, we can give you a good meal, and a bath. We have no coal, so it will be one of those flat-tin-saucer baths. And if you want to be very kind to Simone you might have it somewhere in the kitchen regions and so save her carrying water upstairs.

Stranger: But of course.

Madame: Before the war I had a staff of twelve. Now I have Simone. I dust and Simone sweeps and between us we keep the dirt at bay. She has no manners but a great heart, the child.

Stranger: The heart of a lion.

Madame: Before I put this back you might memorize these: Forty Avenue Foch, in Crest, the back entrance.

Stranger: Forty Avenue Foch, the back entrance.

Madame: You may find it difficult to get into Crest, by the way. It is a closed area. The pot boy at the Red Lion in Mans.

Stranger: The pot boy.

Madame: Denis the blacksmith at Laloupe. And the next night should take you to the sea and your friends. Are they safely in your mind?

Stranger: Forty Avenue Foch in Crest; the pot boy at the Red Lion in Mans; and Denis the blacksmith at Laloupe. And to be careful getting into Crest.

Madame: Good. Then I can close my notebook—or roll it up, I should say—then—it fits neatly, does it not? Now let us see about some food for you. Perhaps I could find you other clothes. Are these all you—

(*The* Corporal's *voice is heard mingled in fury with the still more furious tones of* Simone. *She is yelling:*

*"Nothing of the sort, I tell you, nothing of the sort!"
but no words are clearly distinguishable in the angry
row. The door is flung open, and the* Corporal
bursts in dragging a struggling Simone *by the
arm.)*

Simone: (*screaming with rage and terror*) Let me
go, you foul fiend, you murdering foreigner,
let me go. (*She tries to kick him.*)

Corporal: (*at the same time*) Stop struggling,
you lying deceitful little bit of no-good.

Madame: Will someone explain this extra-
ordinary—

Corporal: This creature—

Madame: Take your hand from my servant's
arm, Corporal. She is not going to run
away.

Corporal: (*reacting to the voice of authority and
automatically complying*) Your precious servant
was overheard telling the gardener that she
had never set eyes on this man.

Simone: I did not! Why should I say anything
like that?

Corporal: With my own ears I heard her, my
own two ears. Will you kindly explain that to
me if you can.

Madame: You speak our language very well,
Corporal, but perhaps you are not so quick to
understand.

Corporal: I understand perfectly.

Madame: What Simone was saying to the
gardener, was no doubt what she was
announcing to all and sundry at the pitch of
her voice this morning.

Corporal: (*unbelieving*) And what was that?

Madame: That she *wished* she had never set
eyes on my nephew.

Corporal: And why should she say that?

Madame: My nephew, Corporal, has many
charms, but tidiness is not one of them. As you
may have deduced from the episode of the
coat. He is apt to leave his room—

Simone: (*on her cue, in a burst of scornful rage*)
Cigarette ends, pajamas, towels, bedclothes,
books, papers—all over the floor like a *flood.*
Every morning I tidy up, and in two hours it is
as if a bomb had burst in the room.

Stranger: (*testily*) I told you already that I was
sor—

Simone: (*interrupting*) As if I had nothing else
to do in this enormous house but wait on
you.

Stranger: Haven't I said that I—

Simone: And when I have climbed all the way
up from the kitchen with your shaving water,
you let it get cold; but will you shave in cold?
Oh, no ! I have to bring up another—

Stranger: I didn't ask you to climb the stairs,
did I?

Simone: And do I get a word of thanks for
bringing it? Do I indeed? You say: "*Must
you bring in that hideous jug; it offends my
eyes.*"

Stranger: So it does offend my eyes!

Madame: Enough, enough! We had enough of
that this morning. You see, Corporal?

Corporal: I could have sworn—

Madame: A natural mistake, perhaps. But I
think you might have used a little more
common sense in the matter. (*coldly*) And a
great deal more dignity. I don't like having my
servants manhandled.

Corporal: She refused to come.

Simone: Accusing me of things I never
said!

Madame: However, now that you are here
again you can make yourself useful. My
nephew wants to go into Crest the day after
tomorrow, and that requires a special pass.
Perhaps you would make one out for him.

Corporal: But I—

Madame: You have a little book of permits in
your pocket, haven't you?

Corporal: Yes, I—

Madame: Very well. Better make it valid for
two days. He is always changing his mind.

Corporal: But it is not for me to grant a
pass.

Madame: You sign them, don't you?

Corporal: Yes, but only when someone tells
me to.

Madame: Very well, if it will help you, I tell
you to.

Corporal: I mean, permission must be granted before a pass is issued.

Madame: And have you any doubt that a permission will be granted to my nephew?

Corporal: No, of course not, madame.

Madame: Then don't be absurd, Corporal. To be absurd twice in five minutes is too often. You may use my desk—and my own special pen. Isn't it a beautiful quill, Corporal?

Corporal: Thank you, madame, no. We Germans have come a long way from the geese.

Madame: Yes?

Corporal: I prefer my fountain pen. It is a more efficient implement. (*He writes.*) "For the 15th and the 16th. Holder of identity card number"—What is the number of your identity, monsieur?

Stranger: I have not the faintest idea.

Corporal: You do not know?

Stranger: No. The only numbers I take an interest in are lottery numbers.

Simone: I know the number of monsieur's card.

Madame: (*afraid that she is going to invent one*) I don't think that likely, Simone.

Simone: (*aware of what is in her mistress's mind, and reassuring her*) But I really *do* know, madame. It is the year I was born, with two "ones" after it. Many a time I have seen it on the outside of the card.

Corporal: It is good that someone knows.

Simone: It is—192411.

Corporal: 192411. (*He fills in the dates.*)

Madame: (*as he nears the end*) Are you going back to St. Estèphe now, Corporal?

Corporal: Yes, madame.

Madame: Then perhaps you will give my nephew a lift as far as the Marnay crossroads.

Corporal: It is not permitted to take civilians as passengers.

Stranger: But you took me here as a passenger.

Corporal: That was different.

Madame: You mean that when you thought he was a miscreant you took him in your car, but now that you know he is my nephew you refuse?

Corporal: When I brought him here it was on service business.

Madame: (*gently reasonable*) Corporal, I think you owe me something for your general lack of tact this afternoon. Would it be too much to ask you to consider my nephew a miscreant for the next hour while you drive him as far as the Marnay crossroads?

Corporal: But—

Madame: Take him to the crossroads with you and I shall agree to forget your—your lack of efficiency. I am sure you are actually a very efficient person, and likely to be a sergeant any day now. We won't let a blunder or two stand in your way.

Corporal: If I am caught giving a lift to a civilian, I shall never be a sergeant.

Madame: (*still gentle*) If I report on your conduct this afternoon, tomorrow you will be a private.

Corporal: (*after a long pause*) Is monsieur ready to come now?

Stranger: Quite ready.

Corporal: You will need a coat.

Madame: Simone, get monsieur's coat from the cupboard in the hall. And when you have seen him off, come back here.

Simone: Yes, madame.

(*Exit Simone*)

Corporal: Madame.

Madame: Good day to you, Corporal.

(*Exit Corporal*)

Stranger: Your talent for blackmail is remarkable.

Madame: The place has a yellow barn. You had better wait somewhere till evening, when the dogs are chained up.

Stranger: I wish I had an aunt of your calibre. All mine are authorities on crochet.

Madame: I could wish you were my nephew. Good luck, and be careful. Perhaps one day, you will come back, and dine with me, and tell me the rest of the tale.

(*The sound of a running engine comes from outside.*)

Stranger: Two years today, perhaps?

Madame: One year today.

Stranger: (*softly*) Who knows? (*He lifts her hand to his lips.*) Thank you and *au revoir*. (*turning at the door*) Being sped on my way by the enemy is a happiness I had not anticipated. I shall never be able to repay you for that. (*He goes out.*) (*off stage*) Ah, my coat—thank you, Simone.

(*Sound of car driving off.* Madame *pours out two glasses. As she finishes, Simone comes in, shutting the door correctly behind her and taking two paces into the room.*)

Simone: You wanted me, Madame?

Madame: You will drink a glass of wine with me, Simone.

Simone: With you, madame?

Madame: You are a good daughter of France and a good servant to me. We shall drink a toast together.

Simone: Yes, madame.

Madame: (*quietly*) To Freedom.

Simone: (*repeating*) To Freedom. May I add a bit of my own, madame?

Madame: Certainly.

Simone: (*with immense satisfaction*) And a very bad end to that Corporal!

Curtain

PART
C

Writers' Resources

C H A P T E R
Seven

Writers Writing

AFTER-WORDS ONLY

The questions and exercises in this chapter invite you to think about the role of writing and writers in society and to plan for your future. Instruction is divided into two sections:

- **I   Writers on Writing** is a collection of readings in which practising writers discuss their craft.

- **II   Working with Words** focuses on post-secondary experiences—education and career opportunities for people with strong verbal skills and interests.

To begin, read aloud the following poem by Richard Wilbur, and then read bill bissett's "poetree is for communikaysyun."

The Writer

In her room at the prow of the house
Where light breaks, and the windows are tossed with linden,
My daughter is writing a story.

I pause in the stairwell, hearing
From her shut door a commotion of typewriter-keys
Like a chain hauled over a gunwale.

Young as she is, the stuff
Of her life is a great cargo, and some of it heavy:
I wish her a lucky passage.

But now it is she who pauses,
As if to reject my thought and its easy figure.
A stillness greatens, in which

The whole house seems to be thinking,
And then she is at it again with a bunched clamor
Of strokes, and again is silent.

I remember the dazed starling
Which was trapped in that very room, two years ago;
How we stole in, lifted a sash

And retreated, not to affright it;
And how for a helpless hour, through the crack of the door,
We watched the sleek, wild, dark

And iridescent creature
Batter against the brilliance, drop like a glove
To the hard floor, or the desk-top,

And wait then, humped and bloody,
For the wits to try it again; and how our spirits
Rose when, suddenly sure,

It lifted off from a chair-back,
Beating a smooth course for the right window
And clearing the sill of the world.

It is always a matter, my darling,
Of life or death, as I had forgotten. I wish
What I wished you before, but harder.

poetree is for communikaysyun   why i write like ths

i spell phonetikalee bcoz i want th pome to look on th
page as close as possibul to th way it sounds in that
pome   correct spelling has almost no relaysyunship to
th sound uv th words we say   for me correct spelling
ignores n can almost eliminate sound wch is major element
in poetree

i want th pomes sumtimes to have shapes that ar not square
or rectangula   as life has infinit shapes so can all th
pomes   poetree can b instrumental in freeing us from central
control   not a meens uv furthr regimenting us to nothing
in big mac attack ium writing sumthing that reelee happend
so th process was is to go thru th drafts versyuns
until its as close to what happend   th dialog   sens uv
urgensee   as much as possibul   paring out th xtraneous   or
redundant   or awkward words   phrases   getting to th life
uv it   no mattr how manee versyuns that may take to it

with each pome thats th aim for me to get to th life uv
it let it shine thru how th line moovs wide less wide
spaces for breth paus emphasis can work bettr than commas
we seldom say th *e* in *the* we dont oftn say we ar going
to *the* store mor frequentlee we say we ar going to *th*
store we can drop th *e* if we want its interesting time
seeing wher all th places ar that english spelling can b
mor mor phonetik if we want closr to th sound itself

same spelling was gradualee considerd mor praktikul for
setting th lettr presses operaysyun previous to that era
peopul wud spell th same words diffrentlee evn in th same
correspondens chek th lettrs btween qween elizabeth first
n sir waltr raleigh diffrent spellings diffrent tones

diffrent emphasis sound all part uv th changing meenings
n ar diffrent informaysyuns poetree can b a form uv music
as well th changing n phonetik spellings help writing bcum
th operating tones uv scale notes phrasing rhythm

sins poetree dusint have to b specifikalee instruksyunal
on how to operate a compewtr cross a street tho it may
offr insites in thees n othr areas it can b freed to b
mor whatevr we want it to b poetree is a sours uv play
n reverens n informaysyun n speeking with wun anothr n
each sylabul a molecule like each stroke in painting
sum vocabularee responding to th invisibul eyes wher th
always living eyez reside poetree is meening color image
sound pictur rhythm partikular vois descripsyuns events
in th langwage n in our lives th length uv th line th width
changing with th stress n outreech uv each part uv th pome
th mytholojee uv th margin its an invensyun can help also
othr shapes can happn with th writing infinit shapes happn
a pome like big mac attack is fun to write cuz it happend
n its got a cawsyunaree note abt diet also yu can feel th
prson in th pome in ths case me walking thru th pome get
that cleen narrativ line in ther to dew that

i write 7 kinds uv poetree narrativ like th big mac attack
spiritual vizual sound politikul natur romantik all
thees approaches can have a lot in common n ar not so eezilee
split from each othr i think writing in as manee ways as
possibul helps make us strongr n mor flexibul in what we can
dew say

i think poetree helps us speek with each othr caringlee n sz
a lot uv important things that othrwize wud go unrecordid
unnotisd is an area wher we can comment direktlee if we want
on th mistakes uv our leedrs or theyr wisdoms our own lives
whos els ar they

correct grammar in poetree is not necessaree it is an opsyun
th tradishyunal grammar uv th predicate or subject acting on
th object thru th verb predicate is also onlee wun kind uv
presentaysyun it is mor imperialistik mor ego drivn n desire
for controlling we ar veree small creeturs n onlee within
natur we dont live in a vacuum if we destroy natur we kill
ourselvs poetree dusint live in a vacuum eith n can comment
on all thees th skies no limit

grammar constructs can change espeshulee for chants repeeting
say th ancient lord laydee uv th univers asks us to b ovr n
ovr agen othr sounds start to emerg n we can b singing it
n resonanses occur that help with th lungs bodilee being

th owl uv minerva flies by at midnite owls can turn theyr
hed rite around spinning mite miss th end uv th line totalee
like thees blocks uv words reeding them like watching tennis
ther ar othr shapes latelee teems uv snowee owls have showd
up at tennis games have bcum its biggest fans

I. Writers on Writing

Reading

The questions for discussion, writing, and research in this section are based on
the readings on pages 345 to 369.

1. Use your own knowledge as well as information from the readings to
   formulate generalizations about:
a. the role of the writer in society
b. challenges and rewards of the writing life
c. personal qualities which contribute to or detract from a writer's
   success.

2. Dramatize an anecdote or situation from one reading. For example, mime
   or role play:
a. a writer, whose novel is being made into a movie, visits the film shooting
   location
b. a young fan meets a favourite author at a book-signing event
c. a younger brother or sister composes a writing assignment; you
   empathize.

3. Imagine yourself as:
- a reporter interviewing an author

- a writer—with impaired vision

- a research assistant for a writer preparing an authorized biography of a living person.

a. Visualize how you would cope with the experience. If you wish, exchange responses with a partner.

b. What have you learned through your workshop experiences that might help you in the situation?

c. What additional measures could you take now to prepare for the experience?

Writing

1. Develop a piece of writing from your answer to either question 2 or 3 above.

2. Research and write a column for a national newspaper or magazine, the text for a dial-a-lecture, or a debate about an issue raised in one of the readings. These suggestions may help you begin:

- Canadians' reading habits (or perhaps develop a sample by surveying students at your school)

- Canadian readers' attitudes to their literary heritage

- the Canadian writer's lot today compared to the early 1950s

- "fair play" guidelines for writers profiling celebrities from sports, entertainment, or another field of interest

- Canada's financial support of a specific group such as writers, athletes, or special-interest groups.

3. Compose a parody or satire using an idea from question 2.

4. Build a piece of writing around one or more ideas from the following comments by and about writers. Consider using one of these formats:

a. a script in which two of the writers appear as characters

b. a letter, editorial, journal entry, or satirical poem

c. an anecdote about one or more writers

d. a passage of interior monologue or stream of consciousness writing, reflecting a writer's unspoken convictions.

- **Books in Canada** (May 1987) reported that, in a "studiously unscientific survey," readers' three favourite Canadian writers were Alice Munro, Margaret Atwood, and Timothy Findley.

- **Chekhov** urged young writers to toss out beginnings and endings of their work since the part that rings true usually lies in the middle.

- **Joan Didion** in "Why I Write" sees writing as an "act of saying I, of imposing myself upon other people, of saying listen to me. . . ."

- **William Faulkner** suggested that a creative person's worst fear is the sight of an empty page.

- **F. Scott Fitzgerald** urged his daughter, Scottie, to omit "dry stuff" from her journal. "Don't try to be witty . . . unless it's natural—just true and real."

- **Goethe** is reported to have said ". . . if any man wishes to write a clear style let him first be clear in his thoughts."

- **Graham Greene** notes in *Ways of Escape* that he learned to trust his mind's "divagations." He feels that the writer needs to let the shape of a piece "grow inside" itself.

- **Stephen King** told *Maclean's* magazine that his quintessential "middle American mind" accounts for his success. "I always write for an audience of one, myself."

- **Katherine Anne Porter** reportedly wrote her last paragraph first; then she aimed the rest of the story toward that paragraph.

- **Leo Tolstoy** alleged he could only write when he was in love: "now I am old I can't fall in love anymore, and that's why I've stopped writing."

- **Eudora Welty** in her autobiography *One Writer's Beginnings* explained the importance of the writer's "ear" for stories. Listening for the "unspoken as well as the spoken" truth as opposed to falsehood is part of a writer's training.

Independent Learning

1.   Research the techniques and strategies professional collaborators use for screenwriting, translating novels to the screen, and writing drama or feature stories. Your written work could be an analysis or a fictional portrayal of your learning.

2.   Read a writer's autobiography or collected letters. Construct a project around a focus of personal interest. You might consider:

- A.O. Bell and A. McNellie, eds., *The Diary of Virginia Woolf* (Penguin, 1984)

- Isak Dinesen, *Out of Africa* (Penguin, 1984)

- Robert Graves, *Goodbye to All That* (Penguin, 1985)

- Isaac Bashevis Singer, *Love and Exile: An Autobiographical Trilogy.*

3.   Read a biography about a writer or literary couple. Construct a project around a focus of personal interest. You might consider:

- Peter Ackroyd, *T.S. Eliot* (Abacus, 1986)
- Daniel Karlin, *The Courtship of Robert Browning and Elizabeth Barrett* (Oxford University Press, 1986)
- Judith Thurman, *Isak Dinesen: The Life of a Storyteller* (St. Martin's Press, 1982)

4.   Research differences in people's composing processes. You might interview other students. Or focus on the published accounts by professional writers. Develop a specific focus for your study. Or arrange a Co-operative Education project which includes working with a group of elementary school students or an educational researcher.

5.   Investigate the work of one or more of the writers cited on pages 334 and 335. Develop a specific focus for an analytical and/or creative project with the teacher.

6.   Make your own collection of "Jottings on Writers" for a specific audience and purpose; you could focus your work on Canadian writers or a specific aspect of the process of writing. For instance, your research may form the basis of lesson plans for writing students or a Canadian Literature class. If possible, include a database in the project.

Reflecting

1.   Speculate on which author you would interview, given the opportunity. Explore your reasoning.

2.   Free-associate, beginning with any comments that appeal to you from those on pages 334 and 335.

3.   Ruminate on an idea of interest from one of the readings. Respond to the idea in writing.

4.   Explore in writing one or more of these ideas:
a.   your learning from the shared experience of one or more writers
b.   an intriguing discussion or argument with a classmate about an idea from the readings
c.   what you learned about someone else through discussion.

5.   Compose several questions for one or more of the readings' authors. Assume the author's role and write monologue answers. Step out of role and give a rationale for each answer.

6.   Speedwrite about your writing process. One of these statements may help you begin:

- Robert Graves wrote a book entitled *The Reader over My Shoulder*. This title makes me think of/feel . . .

- Experimenting with possibilities is important in my composing process.
- I find out what I think by . . .
- Sometimes I need a couple of drafts before my meaning makes itself clear to me.
- If I feel anxious that I have nothing to say about a topic or assignment, I . . .
- Sometimes *things*—a book, a file of notes, a photograph, a quotation, a line from a song—help me to . . .
- If I think of the process of writing as a series of layers, I imagine . . .
- Reading seeds my composing process.
- When we co-write/collaborate, I often find myself . . .

II.   Working with Words

Reading

The questions below are based on the following:

- Career Search: Explore Your Options (page 339)
- "A Post-Secondary Preview" (page 354)
- "Investigative Reporting" (page 365).

1a.   What personal and professional qualities are the hallmark of a good book editor and/or reporter? Which of these qualities do you possess?
b.   How might the skills and attitudes outlined by McDayter and Hunter help you "break into print" or become an investigative reporter?

2.   Collect information for a dial-a-lecture about an interesting career. If facilities are available, store data on disc for possible use in a written piece.

3.   Complete the exercises following your reading of "Career Search: Explore Your Options."

4.   Examine several readings in this chapter for:
a.   effective statement of thesis
b.   clear transitions (if appropriate to format)
c.   use of "showing" techniques
d.   appropriate style and level of language for apparent audience and purpose.

Writing

1.   Persuade someone that you possess the personal and professional qualities to succeed at a specific career. Possible format includes: an anecdotal résumé and covering letter for an employer, a letter to a good friend, written text for an oral presentation, or a profile.

2.   Research the educational requirements for a career of interest. Report on your findings using a format and style similar to the entry for "Journalistic Reporters" on page 342.

3a.   In an informative style, write a dial-a-lecture about careers for a specific student audience.
b.   Use the same data to write a speech in an interpretive or rhetorical style.
c.   Append an analysis of how you've tailored language to purpose.

4.   Assume the role of a first-year university student. Depict one key aspect of your experience through a satirical skit or essay, a cartoon strip, a Letter to the Editor or to a trusted friend, or a short story.

5.   Write an employment advice column for your school newspaper; include both readers' queries and your replies.

6.   Write the narration for a videotape your student council is preparing for your school's Career Day.

Independent Learning

1.   Develop a topic from your own interests, perhaps an area uncovered as you worked through this chapter.

2.   Adapt a suggestion from questions 1 through 6 above.

3.   Research and arrange a co-operative education or work study placement under the guidance of your teacher and the Student Services Department.

4.   Working with a student services teacher, create a database to help students identify their career interests. Field test it under the supervision of your teacher and/or student services counsellor. Write a report, short story, or essay which reflects your learning.

Reflecting

1.   Speculate on an idea of interest from a reading or class discussion.

2.   Reflect on the role of language in your future. If your goals are in need of rethinking, plan to do so.

3.   Speedwrite in response to a personal concern about your future. You might begin with a statement such as:

"I want to know . . ."

"I'm concerned about . . ."

"How will I find out . . .".

Career Search: Explore Your Options

Ever since the elementary grades, you've heard this refrain: "English is important. Everybody needs to build language proficiency."

And in a vague sense, you know it's true. Words are a fundamental aspect of communication. As social beings, we use and abuse them daily. You can't imagine a future without language: so many pleasures are rooted in words—favourite lyrics, joking with friends, or winning an argument with parents. But when you get right down to it, how will working with words come in to your future? You're an aspiring graphic artist, film editor, or scientific researcher, not Farley Mowat, after all. Or perhaps you have strong verbal skills and are looking for practical suggestions to exploit your talents.

Regardless of your circumstances, you're invited to participate in actively thinking about your future—and the ways in which working with words may be part of it. You'll need the equipment and/or facilities outlined below:

- a high-school resource centre and/or public library

- a word processor and/or index cards

- a telephone and/or mail service

- a cassette tape recorder and blank cassettes

- a student services/guidance office in a high school, community college, or university

- a video camera and film (optional)

- standard writing supplies.

Warm-up

Note: This activity may be done with or without a word processor.

1a.   Speculate on your plans for next year or upon leaving your current educational institution. What do you see yourself doing? What can you hear yourself saying? Where do you hope to be? Freewrite for about ten minutes, recording your observations.

b.   Repeat the same process, but this time focus on one career option.

c.   Share your musings with a partner or in a small group.

2.   Read "A Post-Secondary Preview" by McDayter and Hunter (page 354). Of what value is the advice they offer in light of your plans?

3a.   Compose a master list of "Careers We're Considering" for the class. If you're working on disc, you may wish to begin a database.
b.   Subdivide the list into three sections, according to the *relative* importance of: working with *people*, working with *information/ideas*, working with *things*, as suggested in manuals such as *What Colour Is Your Parachute?* by Richard Bolles (Ten Speed Press, 1988).

4.   Form home groups of three. Beside each career, rank the importance of language usage from 1 (of little importance) through 10 (of extreme importance). Assign a different category to each home group member.

5.   Reformulate into specialist or expert groups, according to the category with which you're working.
a.   For each career, brainstorm for two minutes to get a general picture of its when, what, why, where, and how.
b.   Then list several specific occasions that language will be important for career success.
c.   Draw generalizations about this category of careers.

6.   In your home groups, share your work from question 4.

7.   Reflect on this activity.
a.   Do you find yourself drawn to one category of work more than another? Explain. Do your preferences bear any relationship to learning style?
b.   What have you learned about yourself, another member of your class, and/or the world of work that may prove useful in the present or future?

8.   Check your perceptions about the role of language in careers explored (question 3) with information from a local government employment centre or library. And/or invite your student services or guidance counsellor in to talk with your class.

You may wish to continue exploring career paths by completing the "Broadening Horizons" set of exercises below.

Broadening Horizons

1.   Investigate one or more careers or fields listed below. You might begin by checking with your student services counsellor about software that explores the field. Or consult a service such as SGIS (Student Guidance Information Service) for a computer print-out providing occupational descriptions and training information programs.

- campaign writer
- computer programmer
- diplomat
- police officer
- public relations officer
- salesperson
- sports writer

- communications officer
- desk-top publisher
- executive
- printer
- radio announcer
- speech pathologist

2a.   Rank the careers listed above in order of the importance of language in each. Justify each ranking with a twenty-five word annotation.
b.   Compare answers with other students.

3.   The career descriptions below are a sample of over seventy-five listed in two Career Selector manuals from the Government of Ontario Women's Bureau. The two manuals used are "Communication and Creative Arts" and "Community Service and Education." Peruse the material before attempting the questions which follow it.

- **Advertising Copywriters** write the words of advertisements promoting products or services so that the audience will notice and respond favourably.

   [They] work closely with other advertising personnel and, in some cases, with the client, to produce the most effective advertisement. [They] write the specifications, either to directions from the client or following the marketing plan the agency has prepared for the client. The theme, style and length of copy is determined by the advertiser's needs, budget and media limitations.

- **Announcers** introduce various types of programs, interview guests, read news bulletins and make other announcements for radio and television broadcasting. Work includes . . . reading prepared news bulletins, special announcements and advertisements, and conducting interviews . . . broadcasting weather, traffic conditions and general information.

- **Print Editors** The mass media have so many types of editors that it is difficult to find a definition typical of them all. Daily newspapers have editors for individual departments as well as for the newspaper; departmental editors are assisted by copy editors, photo editors, rewrite editors and layout editors. Radio stations have broadcast editors who write for the news departments; wire services have a variety of editors who sort through a great deal of information and select the news they think will be of interest to their clients. There are also book editors who work for publishing houses and publications editors who work for magazines that are directed at a particular audience such as a profession or an industry.

Newspaper editors direct the collecting, selecting and editing of local news for the newspaper. [They] assign reporting and photographic staff to cover various news events and receive and rewrite, or assign for rewriting, newscopy. Work includes editing the copy for conformity to accepted rules of style and syntax, and shortening or lengthening items to fit the allocated space on newspaper pages. [They] relay the copy to the composing room, and write or direct the writing of headlines.

Book editors evaluate manuscripts to determine their suitability for publication and supervise the preparation of the manuscript for publication. . . . [They] suggest changes in the manuscript and negotiate with the author regarding the details of publication, such as royalties, publication date, and number of copies to be printed.

Publications editors select, write and review material for the publication, plan layout, and supervise the editorial staff. . . . [They] write editorials and special articles . . . and [perhaps] news releases and brochures.

Copy editors edit and correct printed proof copy; [they] read the copy to detect errors in spelling, construction, punctuation and content; verify facts, dates and statistics.

- **Film Editors** view, analyse, and evaluate prints of film, and select scenes in terms of story continuity and dramatic and entertainment value. . . . [They are] responsible for arranging film segments in the sequence that presents the story with maximum effect.

- **Interior Designers and Decorators** plan and design aesthetic interiors for homes, industrial, commercial and institutional establishments and other structures. [They] analyse the functional requirements, the desired mood and the purpose of the interior, based on a client's needs and preferences.

- **Interpreters** repeat orally in one language what has been stated in another. . . . [They] use their knowledge and training in professional, technical and cultural terminology, combined with a thorough familiarity with the specific languages involved . . .

- **Journalist Reporters** research and prepare information for the print media, such as newspapers or magazines, or for radio or television broadcasts. [They] go to the scene of newsworthy events, gather the facts by interview, investigation or observation and write articles conforming to prescribed editorial techniques and format. . . . [They] may be technical writers who prepare manuals, bulletins and other literature for government information services, public relations firms and advertisers.

- **Broadcast Journalists** have responsibilities similar to those of the print journalist, but they make use of different equipment in order to disseminate the news they gather.

- **Public Relations People** plan, organize and carry out a program of information designed to influence the public favourably towards an employer's organization, product or services. Specific tasks may include attending social functions and competitions, dealing with the media and conducting opinion polls.

- **Career Counsellors** assist individuals and groups in decisions regarding educational and vocational planning and occupational selection, and teach job search techniques. . . .

- **Child Care Workers** work with emotionally disturbed children and adolescents.

- **Law Clerks** examine legal data for the preparation of briefs or arguments on statutory law or decisions. [They] search for and study legal records and documents to find the relevant information. [They] prepare rough drafts of briefs or arguments.

- **Lawyers** prepare and plead cases in court, draw up legal documents, and advise clients.

- **Psychologists** study human behaviour and mental processes and investigate and recommend treatment of psychological problems.

- **Psychometrists** administer and score intelligence, aptitude, achievement and other psychological tests. . . . With experience, [they] may undertake such functions as report writing, counselling and/or behaviour modification.

- **Social Workers** diagnose and treat problems that affect individuals, groups and communities.

- **Statisticians** plan, survey, collect, organize, interpret, summarize and analyse numerical data. . . . [Their] work may include developing questionnaires . . .

1.   According to the publication from which these job descriptions are taken, good communication skills are important for each of them.

- Which entries surprise you?

- Identify a situation in which strong communication skills would be important in any field you query. Consult a person working in the field or your student services teacher.

2.   Speculate as to the reasons people in these fields need good communication skills:

- package designer
- make-up artist
- medical illustrator
- pharmacist
- surgeon

3.   Identify fields in which oral skills are more important than writing abilities.

4.   Prepare a database for people interested in language-related careers.

5.   What are some of the ways the foregoing career descriptions could be useful to a student in grade nine?

6.   Speculate on one or more ways this career information could be useful in writing essays, short stories, plays, anecdotes, or résumés.

7.   Role play an interview for a position in which strong verbal skills are a prerequisite.

OR

Write a shooting script for a videotape of the job interview. Make the video for your student services department.

8.   Assume the role of someone working in one of the careers described above. Write a series of journal entries reflecting the first six months of employment in a career in which strong verbal skills are important.

READINGS 7

An Interview with William Faulkner

The interviewer has just asked William Faulkner if he thinks there is a formula for being a good writer.

Faulkner: Ninety-nine per cent talent . . . 99 per cent discipline . . . 99 per cent work. He must never be satisfied with what he does. It never is as good as it can be done. Always dream and shoot higher than you know you can do. Don't bother just to be better than your contemporaries or predecessors. Try to be better than yourself. An artist is a creature driven by demons. He don't know why they choose him and he's usually too busy to wonder why. He is completely amoral in that he will rob, borrow, beg, or steal from anybody and everybody to get the work done.

Interviewer: Do you mean the writer should be completely ruthless?

Faulkner: The writer's only responsibility is to his art. He will be completely ruthless if he is a good one. He has a dream. It anguishes him so much he must get rid of it. He has no peace until then. Everything goes by the board: honor, pride, decency, security, happiness, all, to get the book written. If a writer has to rob his mother, he will not hesitate; the "Ode on a Grecian Urn" is worth any number of old ladies.

Interviewer: Then could the *lack* of security, happiness, honor, be an important factor in the artist's creativity?

Faulkner: No. They are important only to his peace and contentment, and art has no concern with peace and contentment.

Interviewer: Then what would be the best environment for a writer?

Faulkner: Art is not concerned with environment either; it doesn't care where it is. . . . So the only environment the artist needs is whatever peace, whatever solitude, and whatever pleasure he can get at not too high a cost. All the wrong environment will do is run his blood pressure up; he will spend more time being frustrated or outraged. . . .

Interviewer: You mentioned economic freedom. Does the writer need it?

Faulkner: No. The writer doesn't need economic freedom. All he needs is a pencil and some paper. I've never known anything good in writing to come from having accepted any free gift of money. The good writer never applies to a foundation. He's too busy writing something. If he isn't first rate he fools himself by saying he hasn't got time or economic freedom. Good art can come out of thieves, bootleggers, or horse swipes. People really are afraid to find out just how much hardship and poverty they can stand. They are afraid to find out how tough they are. Nothing can destroy the good writer. The only thing that can alter the good writer is death. Good ones don't have time to bother with success or getting rich.

Interviewer: Can working for the movies hurt your own writing?

Faulkner: Nothing can injure a man's writing if he's a first-rate writer. If a man is not a first-rate writer, there's not anything can help it much. The problem does not apply if he is not first rate, because he has already sold his soul for a swimming pool.

Interviewer: Does a writer compromise in writing for the movies?

Faulkner: Always, because a moving picture is by its nature a collaboration, and any collaboration is compromise because that is what the word means—to give and to take. . . .

Interviewer: How do you get the best results in working for the movies?

Faulkner: The moving-picture work of my own which seemed best to me was done by the actors and the writer throwing the script away and inventing the scene in actual rehearsal just before the camera turned. If I didn't take, or feel I was capable of taking, motion-picture work seriously, out of simple honesty to motion pictures and myself too, I would not have tried. But I know now that I will never be a good motion-picture writer; so that work will never have the urgency for me which my own medium has.

Interviewer: You say that the writer must compromise in working for the motion pictures. How about his writing? Is he under any obligation to his reader?

Faulkner: His obligation is to get the work done the best he can do it; whatever obligation he has left over after that he can spend any way he likes. I myself am too busy to care about the public. I have no time to wonder who is reading me. I don't care about John Doe's opinion on my or anyone else's work. Mine is the standard which has to be met, which is when the work makes me feel the way I do when I read *La Tentation de Saint Antoine*, or the Old Testament.

Interviewer: So you never feel the need to discuss your work with anyone?

Faulkner: No, I am too busy writing it. It has got to please me and if it does I don't need to talk about it. If it doesn't please me, talking about it won't improve it, since the only thing to improve it is to work on it some more. I am not a literary man but only a writer. I don't get any pleasure from talking shop.

Interviewer: Could you explain more what you mean by motion in relation to the artist?

Faulkner: The aim of every artist is to arrest motion, which is life, by artificial means and hold it fixed so that a hundred years later, when a stranger looks at it, it moves again since it is life. Since man is mortal, the only immortality possible for him is to leave something behind him that is immortal since it will always move. This is the artist's way of scribbling "Kilroy was here" on the wall of the final and irrevocable oblivion through which he must someday pass.

An Interview with Robert Frost

*A regional poet who has achieved international stature, Robert Frost was born in San Francisco on March 26, 1874. He attended Dartmouth but could not abide the academic routine. At twenty-two he entered Harvard, specializing in Latin and Greek during his two years there. He then went to live on a farm in Derry, New Hampshire, teaching, doing occasional work for a local newspaper, and continuing to write his poems. It was a trip to England, however, in 1912, which gave his literary career its decisive push forward. There his first two books were published—*A Boy's Will *and *North of Boston. *When he returned to America in 1915, he was already well known, and his future as a poet and teacher was secure.*

*Mr. Frost received the Pulitzer Prize for poetry four times—in 1924, for *New Hampshire; *in 1931, for *Collected Poems; *in 1937, for *A Further Range; *and in 1943, for *A Witness Tree. *His latest collection, *In the Clearing, *was published in 1962.*

More than any other quality in Frost, his individualism stood out. He spurned what he called "the necessary group." As in other areas of life, he believed "there are too many gangs, cliques, or coteries in poetry. Maybe that's one of the ways they have to manage it. But I'm a lone wolf."

Robert Frost died on January 29, 1963.

Frost: I never write except with a writing board. I've never had a table in my life. And I use all sorts of things. Write on the sole of my shoe.

Interviewer: Why have you never liked a desk? Is it because you've moved around so much and lived in so many places?

Frost: Even when I was younger I never had a desk. I've never had a writing room.

Interviewer: The difficulty of your poetry is perhaps in your emphasis on variety in tones of voice. You once said that consciously or unconsciously it was tones of voice that you counted on to double the meaning of every one of your statements.

Frost: Yes, you could do that. Could unsay everything I said, nearly. Talking contraries —it's in one of the poems. Talk by contraries with people you're very close to. They know what you're talking about. This whole thing of suggestiveness and *double entendre* and hinting—comes down to the word "hinting." With people you can trust you can talk in hints and suggestiveness. Families break up when people take hints you don't intend and miss hints you do intend. You can watch that going on, as a psychologist. I don't know. No, don't . . . no don't you . . . don't think of me. . . . See, I haven't led a literary life. These fellows, they *really* work away with their prose trying to describe themselves and understand themselves, and so on. I don't do that. I don't want to know too much about myself. . . . I don't have hours; I don't work at it, you know. I'm not a farmer, that's no pose of mine. But I have farmed some, and I putter around. And I walk and I live with other people. Like to talk a lot. But I haven't had a very literary life, and I'm never very much with the gang. I'm vice-president, no, I'm Honorary President of the Poetry Society of America. Once in a great while I go. And I wish them well. I wish the foundations would take them all, take care of them all.

I look at a poem as a performance. I look on the poet as a man of prowess, just like an athlete. He's a performer. And the things you can do in a poem are very various. You speak of figures, tones of voice varying all the time. I'm always interested, you know, when I have three or four stanzas, in the way I *lay* the sentences in them. I'd hate to have the sentences all lie the same in the stanzas. Every poem is like that: some sort of achievement in performance. Somebody has said that poetry among other things is the marrow of wit. That's probably way back somewhere— marrow of wit. There's got to be wit. And

that's very, very much left out of a lot of this labored stuff. It doesn't sparkle at all. Another thing to say is that every thought, poetical or otherwise, every thought is a feat of association. They tell of old Gibbon—as he was dying he was the same Gibbon at his historical parallels. All thought is a feat of association: having what's in front of you bring up something in your mind that you almost didn't know you knew. Putting this and that together. That click.

Interviewer: Can you give an example of how this feat of association—as you call it—works?

Frost: Well, one of my masques turns on one association like that. God says, "I was just showing off to the Devil, Job." Job looks puzzled about it, distressed a little. God says, "Do you mind?" And, "No, no," he says, "No," in that tone you know, "No," and so on. That tone is everything, the way you say that "no." I noticed that—that's what made me write that. Just that one thing made that. . . .

Interviewer: Making couplets "offhand" is something like writing on schedule, isn't it? I know a young poet who claims he can write every morning from six to nine, presumably before class.

Frost: Well, there's more than one way to skin a cat. I don't know what that would be like, myself. When I get going on something, I don't want to just—you know . . . Very first one I wrote I was walking home from school and I began to make it—a March day—and I was making it all afternoon and making it so I was late at my grandmother's for dinner. I finished it, but it burned right up, just burned right up, you know. And what started that? What burned it? So many talk, I wonder how falsely, about what it costs them, what agony it is to write. I've often been quoted: "No tears in the writer, no tears in the reader. No surprise for the writer, no surprise for the reader." But another distinction I made is: however sad, no grievance, grief without grievance. How could I, how could anyone have a good time with what cost me too much agony, how could they? What do I want to communicate but what a *hell* of a good time I had writing it? The whole thing is performance and prowess and feats of association. Why don't critics talk about those things—what a feat it was to turn that that way, and what a feat it was to remember that, to be reminded of that by this? Why don't they talk about that? Scoring. You've got to *score*. They say not, but you've got to score, in all the realms—theology, politics, astronomy, history, and the country life around you.

Other People's Lives

John Goddard

"With a little slimming down and a snappy soft cover, it might rise to the best-seller list in the paperback trade," wrote Montreal poet Louis Dudek of Elspeth Cameron's biography on Hugh MacLennan in 1981. "But now we have it as a university press book, with three strikes against it as far as wide readership is concerned—fairly high price, modest edition, scholarly format. I hope it does find its readers anyhow."

It did. *Hugh MacLennan: A Writer's Life*, published by University of Toronto Press, was soon on the *Maclean's* best-seller list, remaining there for three months. Last April it went into paperback—all 421 pages. Praise from the critics was nearly unanimous. "Well-researched and beautifully written," said Dudek in his review for *Canadian Forum*. "A major work," said William French in the *Globe and Mail*. "A model for literary biographers," said Ken Adachi in the *Toronto Star*. The book was a finalist in 1981 for the Governor General's Award for non-fiction, won in the end by George Calef's *Caribou and the Barren-Lands*. Cameron won the University of British Columbia's medal for Canadian biography.

The editors at *Saturday Night* took notice, inviting Cameron to write book reviews, then major personality profiles, beginning with Peter C. Newman. The Newman profile won her the 1982 Fiona Mee Award for literary journalism. Articles on Jack McClelland and Timothy Findley followed as Cameron carved out a niche for herself as a chronicler of Canadian literary lives. Now she is nearly through writing a biography of Irving Layton, scheduled to be released this fall by General Publishing and almost guaranteed to attract a mass audience.

"I was astounded that [the MacLennan book] was in any way popular," Cameron says. "I was only aiming to be accurate in a scholarly sense."

At age 42, Elspeth Cameron has a firm, perfunctory handshake, a charming manner and stunning good looks, a mature version of what one high-school contemporary remembers as "smouldering, unusual beauty, like a heroine out of Hardy." On a bright, wintry day, she is in her office at New College, University of Toronto, where she teaches Canadian cultural history and is coordinator of a Canadian literature and language program. She has three writing projects on the go: a book review for *Saturday Night*; a profile for *Chatelaine* of Laura Legge, the first woman treasurer of the Law Society of Upper Canada; and the Layton biography, which is moving along at more than 2,000 words a day, three days a week. She also has three children, ages 14, 12 and 6—two by her second husband and one by her third, Paul Lovejoy, chairman of the history department at York University and a professor of African economic history. "And we have no housekeeper," Cameron says, laughing, as if wondering herself how she manages to keep up.

She does it, she says, by being a good administrator. "It may not look it" (there are boxes of file folders on the floor, on a chair, and on a desk) "but I could put my hand on anything in this room." Both her parents were administrators. Her father, now retired, was general administrator of the Royal Victoria Hospital in Barrie, Ont., where Cameron grew up, the eldest of three girls. Her mother took a job, when the youngest was 16, as secretary at the Simcoe County Museum and quickly rose to become its director.

"My parents were the kind of people who, when I asked about things, always told me the answers," Cameron recalls, sitting at her writing desk next to book shelves lined with Irving Layton books and supporting prints of Hugh MacLennan. "My curiosity was never stifled. They encouraged me to read about almost anything."

She was a top student, chosen in grade six to write her first book review (for a local radio station), and described by her former high-school English teacher as "unrelenting in pursuit of her goals." She was also a star athlete.

"I know it sounds odd," she says, "but writing to me feels like competitive swimming or playing basketball. I was very involved in sports. I was in ballet for 15 years, I was in skating, I have all the swimming stuff—you know, the bronze, silver, instructors', all that, both Royal Lifesaving and Red Cross. I set records in high jump and various track-and-field events in high school. And when I'm writing I feel the same kind of exhilaration, the feeling of moving forward, the sort of momentum that I used to feel when I was in sports. It's like, you know, three more laps to go."

In 1974, Cameron attended the Canadian literature sessions of the annual Learned Societies meetings in Toronto and heard poet Frank Davey speak passionately about the deplorable way in which bibliography and biography were being ignored in the study of Canadian writing. The speech struck a chord with her. By this time, she had acquired an honours B.A. in English at the University of British Columbia, an M.A. in Canadian literature at the University of New Brunswick,

and a Ph.D. in Victorian literature at McGill (on advice, which she continues to resent, that she would never get a teaching job with a Ph.D. in CanLit). She agreed with Davey that the so-called New Criticism, with its concentration on the study of themes and images, had to be balanced with work of factual substance, with information about the author.

Davey's talk inspired her to attempt what turned out to be the first major biography of a Canadian writer. She first thought to write about Robertson Davies. Her M.A. thesis was on Davies and she had written a short book about him, now out of print and lost, she says, among the plethora of short biographical books that hit the market around 1970 when CanLit courses became the rage. But by now she was living in Montreal, teaching Canadian literature at Loyola College, and as a single parent with two small children she thought she had better write about a Montrealer. "Hugh MacLennan was the obvious choice."

"A lot of people make the assumption that I must be a fan of MacLennan's or I must be a groupie of Layton's, but that's not so. I've never chosen any subject either from admiring them excessively or disliking them excessively, only from the fact that they're important figures and we need to know more about them.

"I basically set out to accumulate information about MacLennan that was otherwise going to be lost. And I know that's true, because a number of people I interviewed for MacLennan and now for Layton have since died. I wanted to know: How did he get where he is? Where did he come from? What are the facts? People make rash statements about famous people, and they in a sense fall for the public image without knowing what really happened."

MacLennan consented immediately to cooperate—to give interviews and turn over his papers and letters. "Frankly, I doubted if she would ever get through it," he said recently. "A lot of people had come to me before with the same idea, and nothing would ever come of it. But Elspeth is tremendously industrious, very intelligent. She went everywhere—to England, Germany. She met a whole lot of people I hadn't seen for years. She knew more about me than I could remember. And that book is longer than anything I've ever written."

The research, crammed in with her other duties, took six years, twice the time she had anticipated, although she banged out the manuscript in five months. In the process, she found MacLennan was an excellent essayist, and as a by-product of the biography she compiled a collection from 400 he had written, published as *The Other Side of Hugh MacLennan.*

The biography mainly deals with the events of his life, the excruciating sadness of his first wife's death, the books that influenced him, the people he knew and corresponded with, and the difficulties of trying to write for a living in the days when Canadian literature had no public following. The book includes an extensive analysis of MacLennan's writing, and occasionally delves into his eccentricities and curious obsessions.

"He literally moved out of his home at the age of twelve and slept in a tent in the back yard, summer and winter, until he graduated from university...," Cameron writes. "His Spartan father approved of the whole idea, thinking it would toughen him up...." She tells how MacLennan continued to write to his father after his father died, a series of six letters that speak of the great force that Dr. Sam MacLennan had exerted on his son for so long.

She also describes MacLennan's zeal for tennis. He rarely lost, but when he did, "his reactions could be spectacular: throwing his racket away, he would fall down on the grass and tear it up with his bare hands, or pitch himself in fury onto the wire fence that surrounded the court, such was his frustration at losing."

MacLennan was pleased with the book. "It astounded me," he wrote to Cameron after receiving the first copy. "It's meticulously accurate.... I'm lost in admiration." But he didn't remember his performances over losing at tennis and he remains strangely obsessive about the tennis passage. "That never happened," he insists. "I never tore the grass with my hands. I was probably lying on the grass because I was tired."

Cameron is not defensive about his objections and prefers not to argue the point. But when pressed she gives a philosophical explanation that says something of the hazards a biographer faces when writing about a living subject.

"I think it's sort of a symbolic thing. Nobody really wants to think that his life has been contained in 400 pages and I don't see how you can avoid a negative response on some level. The same if someone does a portrait of you, you feel, 'Well, I look better than that,' or 'It's not the way I see myself.' And I think that detail for him has become the outlet for the negative response. I did double-check it afterwards. There was more than one eyewitness. But if the tennis hadn't been mentioned, I think he'd have fixed on something else."

Writing about a living subject can be a "very tricky situation," says Clara Thomas, co-author of *William Arthur Deacon: A Canadian Literary Life.* "You have to get the person's trust, and that requires a special kind of temperament and patience, all kinds of charm and personal integrity. Elspeth has all that."

She needed all that to deal with the mercurial Irving Layton. Layton read the MacLennan biography, and in the fall of 1981, when he was writer-in-residence at the University of Toronto, he invited Cameron to write a biography about himself. Cameron had been toying with the idea of writing a mystery novel about a biographer who discovers her subject has committed a crime. But publishers were calling with offers for another biography, and Layton's invitation was too good to refuse.

At least, that's how Cameron remembers the events. Layton tells the story to his own advantage. "One day when I was writer-in-residence at U of T," he says, "she came over to me when I was having lunch and asked if she could write a biography about me. It took me by surprise, and I think my face registered surprise, but then it must have registered agreement. I had an idea she was letting herself in for a great deal of work, but I said, 'yes,' not something sensible like, 'Let me think it over for 24 hours.'"

Now Layton has reservations about the project. "I've read most of the profiles she's done, and I thought they were very well done. And the MacLennan book I thought was very good. But I've read a lot of biography, and hers is not so much a biography as a story. To me, she is telling about the external events of his life. Hugh's life was quiet, sedentary, untumultuous, compared to my cross-starred life. I thought, how was she going to be able to handle the compulsions, the obsessions, the dark spots, and the lighter spots too, to make it clear what it is that drives a person? Any biography should do something like that—how a writer's work comes out of the swamp, the matrix of his life, the sewer-laden stream, and gets transfigured into poetry."

One critic had had reservations similar to Layton's about the MacLennan biography. "[Cameron's] discreet accuracy is bought at a price: vitality," wrote Mark Abley in *Maclean's*. "The accumulation of orderly facts and the scarcity of disorderly anecdotes gives this biography a strangely abstract, bloodless quality. . . . Hugh MacLennan's inner life remains a closed book."

As if anticipating a shortfall in Cameron's work, Layton, while continuing to cooperate with her, has also begun writing his memoirs. *Waiting for the Messiah*, it is to be called, chronicling his youth to 1943. He says it will be in the book stores about the same time as Cameron's book.

Cameron is aware of the challenge of trying to capture Layton, and as she discusses this in the late afternoon at her office she illuminates the more creative, subjective side of her own personality, and something of the struggle a biographer goes through.

"I think that in MacLennan I was able to have the book reflect the person," she says, resting her chin on one hand. "The images in the chapter titles, for instance—The Voyage Out, Charting a Course, Storm at Sea—those are MacLennan's images, they reflect MacLennan. Writing a biography isn't just a question of chronicling facts, it's a question of representing the facts in such a way that they somehow express the personality. It's a question of getting the facts straight first and then somehow finding the form, style, pace, narrative, all the things you would associate with creative writing. I would not want to be creative to the point of skewing the facts, but I want to make it entertaining to read, like a novel, and to make the form and style expressive of the subject.

"Now, Layton is a completely different kind of person from MacLennan. Layton is a Rumanian Jew. MacLennan is a Nova Scotia Scot. Layton came from a very poor family. MacLennan came from a wealthy family. They're miles apart in terms of upbringing, the kinds of ideas that are going to be floating around, the kind of life options that are going to be presented, and so on. Even the pace Layton lived at is completely different from MacLennan. Therefore it seems to me the book on Layton has to be different in pace if the feeling of Layton is going to come through."

Faced with trying to convey the personality of the subject and the atmosphere of his times implicitly in the prose style, she says, a biographer virtually has to become the other person. "I try to be transparent, to drop away my own experiences and prejudices, and in a sense live the other person's life.

"It becomes a kind of obsession. You get to the point where you know in advance what that person would think on some subject, even when you don't know what the person actually said about it. If you asked me what would MacLennan think about something, or what would Layton think, I would probably be pretty accurate."

For Better or Worse: Ontario Cartoonist Wins Top Award

Lynn Johnston's directions were clear and it appeared that it would be just a short, uneventful jaunt from the North Bay airport to her home in the little town of Corbeil. But neither of us had counted on a cab driver with no memory or sense of direction. In a ride punctuated by jerky stops, impromptu U-turns and a growing feeling of hopelessness, the driver fixed me with a look in the rear-view mirror. "I worked in the printing business all my life. The dye went to my head. Killed my memory. Go 50 feet and forget where I'm going. You could tell me something," he said, appealing to my dwindling sympathies, "and five minutes later, it's gone. Now, where'd you say you were going?" I felt as if I'd unwittingly stumbled into one of Lynn Johnston's *For Better Or For Worse* comic strips.

Finally, I spotted the landmark blue mailbox. "There," I ordered, breathlessly. The cab screeched to a stop and rumbled down the gravel driveway leading to a beautiful log house. I bolted from the cab, but not before the cabbie had thrust his card into my hand with the words, "Call me. At least, now I know where to come to get you." A line from one of Johnston's strips sprang to mind, ". . . when elephants fly."

For better or for worse, I had arrived. And who better to understand the last frenetic 40 minutes than Lynn Johnston—the award-winning creator of the comic strip that brings a daily dose of humor and meaning to life's familiar trials, joys and frustrations? I reached out to shake the friendly hand extended in greeting. "Hi, I'm Rod, Lynn's husband," the tall, slender man said with a warm smile. The "Better" had begun.

This past April, Lynn Johnston was presented with the National Cartoonists Society's Reuben Award at an annual awards dinner in Washington, D.C. She is the first woman to receive the coveted award, named in honor of the late, great Reuben (Rube) Goldberg, a well-known cartoonist for the Hearst newspapers. Though Johnston's popular strip has been running for seven years in newspapers around the world and has generated books and television specials since, the award took her completely by surprise. "I was shocked," she says. "I still think of myself as a rookie—with the likes of Mort Walker (creator of *Hi & Lois* and *Beetle Bailey*) and Charles Schultz (*Peanuts*), who are veterans of the art. It felt great to have been nominated, but I thought Jim (Unger, creator of *Herman*), who had been nominated five times, would win. I was all set to congratulate him." It seems that the award took some members of the awards committee by surprise, too. Lynn's husband picked up a gold bracelet—gifts are traditionally given to spouses, usually female. "It fits me perfectly," Rod says.

Johnston's comic strip, *For Better Or For Worse*, stars John and Elly Patterson and their children, Michael and Lizzie, and their adorable sheepdog, Farley. It runs six days a week in the *Toronto Star*, as well as in more than 700 newspapers around the world. The characters do resemble her family—Rod at 37 is better looking than his comic strip character, John; Aaron, at 13, and Katie, at 8, are three years older than Michael and Lizzie, their respective strip characters. . . .

If panic was her first reaction to the responsibility of producing, it has been replaced by a sense of calm and trust that the work will eventually get done. "I still get my days of anguish. I walk around like a zombie, as if I've got the flu, because I can't think of anything. But I find if I'm in a familiar place, in familiar surroundings, and allow myself to sleep if that's what my body is telling me to do, then an idea will come. As long as I pit myself against the problem every day, then all of a sudden, whether it's two in the morning or the afternoon, it will come to me. There are times when it arrives on my plate like a gift from God and I say, Well, thanks, whoever wrote that last two weeks, thanks for the help!"

But she admits, with a sheepish grin, that she's easily distracted. "If my mother-in-law (who lives nearby) phones and screeches Garage Sale! I'm gone." Her output amounts to at least six comic strips, or a week's work, per day. "In the past, I've done three to four weeks in a day. I told that to Cathy Guisewite (creator of the popular comic strip, *Cathy*) and she almost cried with envy."

For Johnston, the writing is the first step in the process and the hardest. The pictures come later. "But I find that writing a strip in a series helps. It gives me time to develop a story. The series I'm working on right now involves John and Phil on a canoe trip that ends in a near-disaster. What I do is write several pieces of dialogue and then I say to myself, The guys are lost and Elly and Georgia are in a motel room. They can't sleep, they're upset. What are they saying to each other? The dialogue has to be real and meaningful but still positive and upbeat. My readers don't want me to dwell on the pain too long. So I imagine dialogue. I'm not Elly; I'm not in the bed looking out of her eyes. I'm like a fly on the wall, observing. But I have to write dialogue that is believable for those characters. It's sort of like writing a little screenplay because I do see the camera angles and feel the emotions and see the scene played out." Though Johnston is very protective of her family and does not base her strips on true family events, the series devoted to the canoe trip is based on a real occurrence. Her husband and three friends were in an aircraft accident and were missing for three days and nights in the wilderness of the Northwest Territories. They were eventually picked up by a search and rescue team. A great deal of the emotion found its way into the strip. "In one scene I've written, the two men are huddled around a campfire trying to keep warm at night. They're cold and uncomfortable and lonely and one of them says, Isn't it amazing how our entire focus is this little campfire and how all we want is to be fed and to be comfortable and warm . . . and last week, I wanted a Mercedes."

It is these poignant little truths laced with funny and tender irony that have won Johnston a loyal following. Though her intention is never to teach, only to share what she feels, her message continues to touch a worldwide audience. Her audience is made up of single and married people, with and without children. She is surprised at how seriously some people take her strip. Some write to catch her on spelling errors, others to berate her for suggesting that a character got a job without a degree. Most write to tell her how much they enjoy the strip. "Where do you live?" the letters ask. "Beneath my fridge? Behind my couch? How do you know what goes on in my house?" Letters come from men and women, ministers and priests. Some of her more illustrious fans—and friends— include Cathy Guisewite and Charles Schultz.

Her favorite letter is from the woman who wrote, "I am standing here in a bodycast making dinner for my family. Everyone's going to sit down but me. I haven't been able to sit down for weeks and I'm so miserable I'm eating canned pears out of a can. I'm feeling so sorry for myself. But I opened the newspaper and read your comic strip, and you made me laugh." Johnston was so touched by her letter that she looked up the day the woman wrote and sent her the original strip. . . .

As a child, Johnston wanted many things

for herself. She dreamed of being in the theatre, of being a comic, of travelling. Most of all, she wanted to have fun and laugh a lot. "I was the kind of kid who could never take things seriously and always got into trouble." She also wanted to be an artist. "My parents would say, Lynn, artists live in garrets, eat beans out of cans and starve. But I always knew I could make a living."

Life is sweet for the Johnston family. Their home sits on more than 100 acres of lush, green property and Rod has the airplane he's always wanted. As we drive down the gravel road—this time with Lynn at the wheel—she points out the gentle oasis of color: a field dotted with lavender, pink and purple lupins that she hopes to transplant into her own garden. For Lynn Johnston, success has never meant celebrity and fortune. In fact, Lynn and Rod opted for living in a remote area because it affords them the luxury of retreat from the celebrity whirl. "I never wanted that influence in my life," she says. "I wanted a loving family and I wanted to do what I love and love what I do. That's what I've done. I don't think I'll ever get tired of it."

Her many readers also hope she never tires of it.

A Post-Secondary Preview

Ghislaine McDayter
John Hunter

The authors attended high school in Scarborough, Ontario, and are recent graduates of the University of Toronto.

If you're preparing for post-secondary education but can't think of what you should be asking to get ready, don't worry. You're not alone. For many, the prospect of higher education is a bit intimidating. But after an initial settling-in period, most students adapt quite comfortably. We hope our experience and suggestions from post-secondary instruc-

tors will stimulate your own questions to help you plan for and cope with your future.

To focus our thinking, we interviewed instructors at Humber College of Applied Arts and Technology and University of Toronto about three broad areas of concern: communication and thinking skills, recommended preparation for senior secondary students, and attitudes to foster post-secondary success. We offer ten guidelines for your consideration.*

1. Think about your personal goals. What are your goals for post-secondary education? Know your personal expectations and work toward them. Adrian Adamson stressed this element; you'll get more out of your schooling if you pursue your own objectives, rather than settling for the institution's. Don't be upset if your goals alter drastically during your studies. Many students graduate from a program other than the one in which they began. Perhaps you're unsure of what you want. Gary Noseworthy, Adamson's colleague, suggests you postpone studies for a year or two. The experience will build confidence, enthusiasm and direction.

2. Open up your mind. This point can't be overstressed. If you don't do so already, start to read extensively and familiarize yourself with such media as film, music and the plastic arts. Each respondent stressed that students must extend their learning beyond course material. "Extra-curricular" learning builds a foundation for institutional learning. It also enhances cultural literacy, sharpens vocabulary and, most importantly, fosters a healthy critical attitude toward ideas.

. . . .

* The authors thank the following instructors who agreed to be interviewed for this article: Eleanor Cook and Julian Patrick, Department of English, University of Toronto; Adrian Adamson and Gary Noseworthy, Department of Human Studies, Humber College; Bonnie Kettel and Robert Deshman, Department of Anthropology, University of Toronto.

3. Deal with information actively. Question everything! The ability to *think independently* is the single most important piece of advice offered by our respondents. Learn to scrutinize and manipulate information—to analyze, synthesize, compare, contrast and evaluate. Robert Deshman concurs with Bonnie Kettel about the necessity to consider an argument's implications before committing yourself to it. *Creative thinking*—making ideas your own rather than regurgitating others' views—is vital to the process of learning.

Above all, *learn to take risks, innovate and speculate.* As Eleanor Cook emphasizes, education is "essentially an *active* occupation." To benefit, you must participate.

4. Learn to be an active listener and skilled note-taker. Learning to listen and extract main ideas and supporting evidence is essential; the lecture is the most common teaching style in post-secondary schooling. According to Cook, good note-taking is "the art of extracting the essence of a lecture"; this art requires an active response of the creative intelligence, not a passive recording of facts.

5. Learn to express yourself in writing. You knew it was coming and here it is: grammar, vocabulary and spelling. Apart from its intrinsic value, proficiency in the craft of writing is vital in post-secondary education for two reasons. First, you'll never be able to go beyond conventional modes of writing until you've mastered them. And second, you'll be evaluated frequently on your writing skills. In fact, written work—essays, reports, summaries, reviews, responses and exams—is the primary means of assessment in the early years when classes are large.

6. Express your enthusiasm in a piece of writing. Aside from knowing the mechanics of expression, you'll need to convey an enthusiasm for your subject in written work. As Adamson and Cook point out, lack of interest in an essay comes through to the audience. A mechanically correct but lifeless piece of writing is boring—for *you* and your reader. To get the most out of your education, you need to care about learning for its own sake. If you view these years exclusively as preparation for the job market, you're doing yourself a great injustice.

7. Be flexible. Your instructors come in all shapes, sizes and shades of opinion. This variety is good; it reflects many different ways of approaching the same subject. And teaching and communication styles differ markedly. Since you'll never be taught in quite the same way twice, you need to adapt your learning style to the instructor.

8. Ask for help before it's too late. Much is made of the "coldness" of post-secondary institutions; their size makes some of this inevitable. If you're unsure about something, ask questions of your instructor until it is resolved. Whatever their classroom manner may be, most are only too happy to help in one-to-one conversations. More than likely they've encountered your problem before and know how best to guide you.

9. Learn how to deal with stage fright. At some point, you're going to give an oral presentation. Julian Patrick observes that students' oral skills are better than they've been in many years. But keep these things in mind. Don't prepare your presentation as if you're writing an essay: you're going to talk to an audience and the experience of listening is very different from reading. Avoid simply reading or reciting a prepared text. Unless you're a very talented reader, you'll start to sound monotonous. Noseworthy emphasizes coherence and relevance as the two most important aspects of an effective presentation. Kettel notes that the best way to ensure these qualities is meticulous research and reading. If you suffer from plain old-fashioned terror, practice is the only solution.

10. DON'T BE AFRAID. You'll note we've emphasized creative and critical thinking and active participation. This focus extends beyond academic course material.

Patrick, Adamson and Kettel reiterated that students should never be reluctant to question their social and intellectual environment. *Innovation* and *creativity* are not born from passive acceptance of existing institutions and modes of thought.

This glimpse into the future may have answered some of your concerns. If it's provoked more questions, that's okay, too. Contact the institutions you're considering and start *asking*.

An Interview with Ernest Hemingway

George Plimpton

The walls are lined with white-painted bookcases from which books overflow to the floor, and are piled on top among old newspapers, bullfight journals, and stacks of letters bound together by rubber bands.

It is on the top of one of these cluttered bookcases —the one against the wall by the east window and three feet or so from his bed—that Hemingway has his "work desk"—a square foot of cramped area hemmed in by books on one side and on the other by a newspaper-covered heap of papers, manuscripts, and pamphlets. There is just enough space left on top of the bookcase for a typewriter, surmounted by a wooden reading board, five or six pencils, and a chunk of copper ore to weight down papers when the wind blows in from the east window.

A working habit he has had from the beginning, Hemingway stands when he writes. He stands in a pair of his oversized loafers on the worn skin of a Lesser Kudu—the typewriter and the reading board chest-high opposite him.

When Hemingway starts on a project he always begins with a pencil, using the reading board to write on onionskin typewriter paper. He keeps a sheaf of the blank paper on a clipboard to the left of the typewriter, extracting the paper a sheet at a time from under a metal clip which reads "These Must Be Paid." He places the paper slantwise on the reading

board, leans against the board with his left arm, steadying the paper with his hand, and fills the paper with handwriting which through the years has become larger, more boyish, with a paucity of punctuation, very few capitals, and often the period marked with an x. The page completed, he clips it face-down on another clipboard which he places off to the right of the typewriter.

Hemingway shifts to the typewriter, lifting off the reading board, only when the writing is going fast and well, or when the writing is, for him at least, simple: dialogue, for instance. . . .

Interviewer: Are these hours during the actual process of writing pleasurable?

Hemingway: Very.

Interviewer: Could you say something of this process? When do you work? Do you keep to a strict schedule?

Hemingway: When I am working on a book or a story I write every morning as soon after first light as possible. There is no one to disturb you and it is cool or cold and you come to your work and warm as you write. You read what you have written and, as you always stop when you know what is going to happen next, you go on from there. You write until you come to a place where you still have your juice and know what will happen next and you stop and try to live through until the next day when you hit it again. You have started at six in the morning, say, and may go on until noon or be through before that. When you stop you are as empty, and at the same time never empty but filling, as when you have made love to someone you love. Nothing can hurt you, nothing can happen, nothing means anything until the next day when you do it again. It is the wait until the next day that is hard to get through.

Interviewer: Can you dismiss from your mind whatever project you're on when you're away from the typewriter?

Hemingway: Of course. But it takes discipline to do it and this discipline is acquired. It has to be.

Interviewer: Do you do any rewriting as you read up to the place you left off the day before? Or does that come later, when the whole is finished?

Hemingway: I always rewrite each day up to the point where I stopped. When it is all finished, naturally you go over it. You get another chance to correct and rewrite when someone else types it, and you see it clean in type. The last chance is in the proofs. You're grateful for these different chances.

Interviewer: How much rewriting do you do?

Hemingway: It depends. I rewrote the ending to *Farewell to Arms*, the last page of it, thirty-nine times before I was satisfied.

Interviewer: Was there some technical problem there? What was it that had stumped you?

Hemingway: Getting the words right.

Interviewer: Is it the rereading that gets the "juice" up?

Hemingway: Rereading places you at the point where it *has* to go on, knowing it is as good as you can get it up to there. There is always juice somewhere.

Interviewer: But are there times when the inspiration isn't there at all?

Hemingway: Naturally. But if you stopped when you knew what would happen next, you can go on. As long as you can start, you are all right. The juice will come.

Interviewer: Thornton Wilder speaks of mnemonic devices that get the writer going on his day's work. He says you once told him you sharpened twenty pencils.

Hemingway: I don't think I ever owned twenty pencils at one time. Wearing down seven number two pencils is a good day's work.

Interviewer: Where are some of the places you have found most advantageous to work? The Ambos Mundos hotel must have been one, judging from the number of books you did there. Or do surroundings have little effect on the work?

Hemingway: The Ambos Mundos in Havana was a very good place to work in. This Finca is a splendid place, or was. But I have worked well everywhere. I mean I have been able to work as well as I can under varied circumstances. The telephone and visitors are the work destroyers. . . .

Interviewer: Would you suggest newspaper work for the young writer? How helpful was the training you had with the *Kansas City Star*?

Hemingway: On the *Star* you were forced to learn to write a simple declarative sentence. This is useful to anyone. Newspaper work will not harm a young writer and could help him if he gets out of it in time. This is one of the dustiest clichés there is and I apologize for it. But when you ask someone old tired questions you are apt to receive old tired answers.

Interviewer: You once wrote in the *Transatlantic Review* that the only reason for writing journalism was to be well paid. You said: "And when you destroy the valuable things you have by writing about them, you want to get big money for it." Do you think of writing as a type of self-destruction?

Hemingway: I do not remember ever writing that. But it sounds silly and violent enough for me to have said it to avoid having to bite on the nail and make a sensible statement. I certainly do not think of writing as a type of self-destruction, though journalism, after a point has been reached, can be a daily self-destruction for a serious creative writer.

Interviewer: Would you admit to there being symbolism in your novels?

Hemingway: I suppose there are symbols since critics keep finding them. If you do not mind I dislike talking about them and being questioned about them. It is hard enough to write books and stories without being asked to explain them as well. Also it deprives the explainers of work. If five or six more good explainers can keep going why should I interfere with them? Read anything I write for the pleasure of reading it. Whatever else you find will be the measure of what you brought to the reading. . . .

Interviewer: Could you say how much thought-out effort went into the evolvement of your distinctive style?

Hemingway: That is a long-term tiring question and if you spent a couple of days answering it you would be so self-conscious that you could not write. I might say that what amateurs call a style is usually only the unavoidable awkwardnesses in first trying to make something that has not heretofore been made. Almost no new classics resemble other previous classics. At first people can see only the awkwardness. Then they are not so perceptible. When they show so very awkwardly people think these awkwardnesses are the style and many copy them. This is regrettable.

Interviewer: How complete in your own mind is the conception of a short story? Does the theme, or the plot, or a character change as you go along?

Hemingway: Sometimes you know the story. Sometimes you make it up as you go along and have no idea how it will come out. Everything changes as it moves. That is what makes the movement which makes the story. Sometimes the movement is so slow it does not seem to be moving. But there is always change and always movement.

Interviewer: Is it the same with the novel, or do you work out the whole plan before you start and adhere to it rigorously?

Hemingway: *For Whom the Bell Tolls* was a problem which I carried on each day. I knew what was going to happen in principle. But I invented what happened each day I wrote.

Interviewer: We've not discussed character. Are the characters of your work taken without exception from real life?

Hemingway: Of course they are not. *Some* come from real life. Mostly you invent people from a knowledge and understanding and experience of people.

Interviewer: Could you say something about the process of turning a real-life character into a fictional one?

Hemingway: If I explained how that is sometimes done, it would be a handbook for libel lawyers.

Interviewer: Do you make a distinction—as E.M. Forster does—between "flat" and "round" characters?

Hemingway: If you describe someone, it is flat, as a photograph is, and from my standpoint a failure. If you make him up from what you know, there should be all the dimensions.

Interviewer: How do you name your characters?

Hemingway: The best I can.

Interviewer: So when you're not writing, you remain constantly the observer, looking for something which can be of use.

Hemingway: Surely. If a writer stops observing he is finished. But he does not have to observe consciously nor think how it will be useful. Perhaps that would be true at the beginning. But later everything he sees goes into the great reserve of things he knows or has seen. If it is any use to know it, I always try to write on the principle of the iceberg. There is seven-eighths of it underwater for every part that shows. Anything you know you can eliminate and it only strengthens your iceberg. It is the part that doesn't show. If a writer omits something because he does not know it then there is a hole in the story.

Interviewer: Archibald MacLeish has spoken of a method of conveying experience to a reader which he said you developed while covering baseball games back in those *Kansas City Star* days. It was simply that experience is communicated by small details, intimately preserved, which have the effect of indicating the whole by making the reader conscious of what he had been aware of only subconsciously. . . .

Hemingway: The anecdote is apocryphal. I never wrote baseball for the *Star*. What Archie was trying to remember was how I was trying to learn in Chicago in around 1920 and was searching for the unnoticed things that made emotions, such as the way an outfielder tossed his glove without looking back to where it fell, the squeak of resin on canvas under a fighter's flat-soled gym shoes, the gray color of Jack Blackburn's skin when he had just come out of stir, and other things I noted as a painter sketches. You saw Blackburn's strange color and the old razor cuts and the way he spun a man before you knew his history. These were the things which moved you before you knew the story.

Interviewer: Have you ever described any type of situation of which you had no personal knowledge?

Hemingway: A writer, if he is any good, does not describe. He invents or *makes* out of knowledge personal and impersonal and sometimes he seems to have unexplained knowledge which could come from forgotten racial or family experience. Who teaches the homing pigeon to fly as he does; where does a fighting bull get his bravery, or a hunting dog his nose? This is an elaboration or a condensation on that stuff we were talking about in Madrid that time when my head was not to be trusted.

Interviewer: How detached must you be from an experience before you can write about it in fictional terms? The African air crashes you were involved in, for instance?

Hemingway: It depends on the experience. One part of you sees it with complete detachment from the start. Another part is very involved. I think there is no rule about how soon one should write about it. It would depend on how well adjusted the individual was and on his or her recuperative powers. Certainly it is valuable to a trained writer to crash in an aircraft which burns. He learns several important things very quickly. Whether they will be of use to him is conditioned by survival. Survival, with honor, that outmoded and all-important word, is as

difficult as ever and as all important to a writer. . . .

An Interview with Mordecai Richler

Book Talk: It was good to see Jacob Two-Two again in *Jacob Two-Two and the Dinosaur*. How did you decide to use a dinosaur as a sidekick for Jacob?

MR: Well, I didn't really decide anything, it just occurred to me the way the other story occurred to me. I just took off from there. And I think all kids like dinosaurs.

BT: There was a generous sprinkling of political and social satire in the book. Do you think that kids appreciate satire or was it put in there for their parents?

MR: Well, I think kids enjoy that kind of thing. There was a certain amount of satire in the first Jacob Two-Two book. I think kids are much brighter than many people give them credit for.

BT: Is there is a message for kids in the book?

MR: No! It's just fun.

BT: How is writing a children's book different than writing an adult book?

MR: It really isn't any different. It's writing and it's just as difficult. It goes through as many drafts.

BT: How many drafts do you usually go through?

MR: Oh, this book's been easier than most; I guess about four drafts.

BT: I remember reading an interview with Philip Roth once and he said that he spends all morning putting in a comma, and all afternoon taking it out again. Do you go through that kind of agony when you write?

MR: Well, I know what he means. It's difficult sometimes, you know. I tend to write a great deal. Sometimes I go through ten, twelve drafts and then throw a good part of it out. I keep trimming it. I am never quite sure which way the plot's going until it's finished.

BT: Your writing style is very direct and yet the characters and plots are so complex. Is this interplay between style and substance deliberate?

MR: It's just the way I write. There is a great danger in examining these things too closely. Take the machine apart and you're not going to put it together again.

BT: In some of your books, you write about some pretty crude characters. Do you want to shock or shake up your readers?

MR: No. Those are the voices I hear. I don't do anything deliberately one way or another for the readers. You write to please yourself and hope as many people as possible will enjoy it. But you don't change your work by trying to ingratiate yourself with anybody.

BT: In *St. Urbain's Horseman*, the main character of Jake Hirsch is pushy, defensive, insecure. He often seems to go far beyond readers' sympathy. Is that character anything like you?

MR: There's no way of answering this to anybody's satisfaction because there are aspects of these characters that are part of me, but they are certainly not me. But certainly when I'm writing, I identify with them, and there are certain aspects of every character that approximate mine and there are other things that have nothing to do with me whatsoever. It's a bit of an amalgam.

BT: To push this point a little more, in *St. Urbain's Horseman*, you write that Jake is consumed with ambition and filled with self-hatred and doubts. He felt that he was an imposter and his work was a con. Do you ever have these feelings about being a writer?

MR: Well, it depends on what hour of the night. No novel is ever what you intended it to be, so in a sense they're all failures. There are times when you don't want to go back and re-read any of it. And there are other ones that make you feel good. To be honest with you, I'm somewhat pleased with them.

BT: Some authors say that when they're writing they get completely involved in their characters, that the characters seem to take on a life of their own. Does that happen when you're writing?

MR: Well, if it doesn't, you're in trouble. I mean, if it starts to chug along in a very predictable fashion, you're not getting anywhere. If it doesn't change while you're working on it, then there's no hope. A novel has to take on a life of its own.

BT: Is there one novel that in your mind stands out as your best one?

MR: I guess either *St. Urbain's Horseman* or *Cocksure*.

BT: In a very moving essay in *Home Sweet Home*, you wrote that your father was a lifelong failure. Did his failure have anything to do with your drive for success?

MR: Oh, of course. In some ways it makes life much easier when you can't do as badly as that. But I had a great affection for him and I'm sorry he died as early as he did.

BT: Let's talk about some of the movies that have been made from your books. *The Apprenticeship of Duddy Kravitz* and *Joshua, Then and Now* were both made into films. In an article you wrote some years ago, you said that you didn't like the movie-making process. Has there been any change in your attitude now that more of your books have been made into movies?

MR: No. It certainly can be profitable, but it's a group activity. Most writers enjoy writing novels more than anything else because they're in total control. Movie-making is subject to a lot of accidents, some of them very beneficial, but others amazingly harmful. There are so many people involved. Writers tend to work best alone. I was very pleased with the way the Duddy Kravitz movie came out. Still I'm a very private person and I prefer sitting up here and working on a novel.

BT: In the "Duddy" and "Joshua" movies, were there any surprises in the way the actors interpreted your lines?

MR: Well, I was very lucky in both cases

with Richard Dreyfuss and Jimmy Woods. I was pleased with what both of them did. "Duddy Kravitz" was a more successful film. It was a lot easier in that it didn't deal with an inner life. It was an episodic novel, whereas "Joshua" was such a complex novel, going to and fro in time. The failures in that film were largely my own; I tried to squeeze too much into it.

BT: Were you affected by the bad reviews for the movie "Joshua"?

MR: Well you know, it was an awful lot of work, it was a much more difficult script than "Duddy Kravitz." Sure, it was somewhat disappointing. But you give it your best shot and you get on with something else. You can't brood over these things anyway.

BT: Any special memories from making "Joshua"?

MR: No. I don't hang around once the film is being made. A writer is really redundant once they start shooting, and there's nothing quite as boring as a film shoot. It takes half the day to shoot someone getting out of a car.

BT: Do you think a writer has any responsibility to his readers?

MR: Well, I think he has a responsibility to be as honest and as good as he can be, but that's about all you can do. And you work with the talent that's available to you. None of us are geniuses. You try and do it as honestly as you can and as well as you can. And when you're very tired, you send it to the publisher.

BT: Is your readers' approval important to you, or do you mainly write for yourself?

MR: Well, it's a bit complicated—you write for yourself and for your friends, but you hope to have as many readers as possible but always on your own terms.

BT: What about critics?

MR: Some critics are important to me and others aren't. I certainly read the reviews. I think the critic's relationship is with the reader and not with the writer. By the time those reviews come out, the novel has been finished for about a year. There are certain critics who I have respect for, and others who are insulting whether they like the book or not. So there's no hard rule for critics.

BT: Do you think Canadians support their own culture enough?

MR: I think they give it tremendous support. Novelists, such as Margaret Atwood, and Robertson Davies, and Alice Munro, and myself, sell far more in proportion to population here than we would if we were in the United States. I think there is too much crying and self-pity. I think that there is enormous support for Canadian writing. There is a lot of government support too. There is very little to complain about.

BT: If an aspiring writer asked you for advice, what kind of advice would you give them?

MR: Work hard. Writing is hard work and you've got to be prepared to work—not just write when you feel like it. And learn to write in your own way so that your voice cannot be mistaken for anybody else's.

Play It Again, SAM: A Profile of Jean Little

Barbara Wade Rose

A chilly autumn wind blows open the last pink roses of the year in the sunny garden behind the small black-and-white cottage on a street in downtown Guelph. Inside, children's novelist Jean Little stirs the lemon meringue filling that cooks on the stove for a pie she and her mother will share with a guest for lunch. "I'm sure it was two cups of liquid," she says, taking the box of mix into an adjoining room. A magnificent golden Labrador named Zephyr picks himself up from the kitchen floor and follows her. Jean Little places the box under a device similar to the microfiche readers found in public libraries. When she switches on the light, the print on the box is suddenly magnified many times over. "There, two cups—that's right," she says, satisfied. Zephyr thumps his tail in appreciation.

It has been a good year for Little, 53. Her new novel for eight- to 12-year-olds, *Lost and Found* (Penguin), has just been published. *Mama's Going to Buy You a Mockingbird* (Penguin), last year's spare, moving novel about a boy's learning to cope with the death of his father, won Little the Canadian Library Association Children's Book of the Year Award and the Canadian Booksellers' Association Ruth Schwartz Award. During almost 25 years of writing for children, Little's realistic books have been translated into nine foreign languages. In particular, writes Meguido Zola in the periodical *Language Arts*, Little was "in the vanguard" of writing about handicapped children. "That is the real thrust of Jean Little's novels, recognizing and mastering the enemy within, rather than tilting at the one without." But perhaps her foremost accomplishment since she won the Canada Council Children's Literature Award in 1977 has not yet appeared in print. Little has been mastering a formidable enemy within herself.

A well-planted and sunny-natured woman, she was born in Taiwan in 1932 to J.L. and F.G. Little, who were medical missionaries. When they discovered in Jean's infancy that she had about 10 per cent of normal sight, it was some improvement on the diagnosis of absolute blindness at birth, and the family rejoiced. It would be one of the things that made Jean special. One of the first words she learned, after "mommy" and "daddy," was "book." When the family settled in Guelph when Jean was seven, the girl with the thick glasses who loved to read was transferred from a school for the visually handicapped to a regular children's class.

"It was awful," Little recalls. She is sitting on an overstuffed chair in the front room of the cottage, a room filled with extra chairs for visitors. Paintings reminiscent of the landscape around her Muskoka cottage dot the walls. "They called me names, they chased me home from school. . . ." Her voice trails off.

The child retreated even further into the world of books, holding them a scant three inches from her nose in order to read the print.

Jean also began to write stories herself. Her first "book" was written in an orange scribbler when she was in grade five, an adventure tale about a boy and his dog Lad who live on the top of a mountain and, after a series of adventures, save the boy's mother when she has an accident. Her father purchased a special large-print typewriter for Jean as soon as he learned of her talent. Something of a writer himself—Little remembers he religiously kept a diary and insisted she date her poetry—he arranged to have a book of her poems published privately when she turned 15.

"Every writer should have a father like that," says Little now (he died when she was 21). She can recall him sending two of her poems to *Saturday Night* magazine two years later and the subsequent thrill of seeing them in print. The cheque for $30 bought her a few yards of green velvet for a party dress. When a letter to the editor appeared in the next issue inquiring politely about the interesting poet named Jean Little and asking for further details about her, Little's mother took one look at her husband and coolly said. "You didn't!" "He did," says Little, hooting with laughter—he had even gone to Oakville to mail the letter under an assumed name.

After graduating with honours in English from the University of Toronto, Little met her first published author at a seminar in Utah, where she was attending a special course on teaching handicapped children. Virginia Sorensen was principally known as a children's writer, so that's what Little decided to be—never believing it would become something she could afford to do full-time. She returned to Guelph and began to teach a class of children with cerebral palsy, writing as a hobby.

"I discovered there were no books with real

children with cerebral palsy as characters," she says. "The children who had any kind of handicap were either miraculously cured at the end or they died." It was 1961 when she wrote *Mine for Keeps*, about a young girl named Sally Copeland and the crutches that transport her to school, the little dog Susie who teaches her responsibility, and the secret place beside the fence that makes her feel special. Little showed it to a local librarian who suggested submitting the manuscript for the $1,000 Little, Brown Canadian Children's Book Award. Little won, and her first book was in stores and libraries the following year. "That's embarrassing," she now recalls with a smile. "When I'm travelling and people ask me whether I had any trouble getting my first book published, I almost hate to answer—they get so mad!"

Another eight books followed as Little's two brothers and a sister married and began raising 11 nieces and nephews for her to observe and enjoy. She has mixed feelings about never having raised any children of her own, but concedes that being an aunt has had its benefits. "I think I enjoy it better because you can always give them back. You enjoy it, but you can always sit and say to yourself, 'My, that child is turning out to be a selfish one,' and you don't feel responsible." The children in her own books have always reflected Little's keen observations. Margaret Laurence, writing in *Canadian Children's Literature* in 1976, said: "One can always be certain with Jean Little's characters, of true feelings and characteristics. There are no good guys and bad guys; all are ambiguous mixtures."

Jean Little laughs sometimes at the way in which those characters develop. "When I wrote *One to Grow On* [Little, Brown, 1969], there was a character in it that I did not like at all—she was a very nasty child. I finally sent her to Europe with her parents to get rid of her. I was sitting typing the finish of the book—my heroine was up in Muskoka and her godmother and her best friend were

coming as a surprise. So I typed 'Tilly got out of the car' and 'Pam got out of the car'—and then my hands typed 'and Lisa got out of the car.' I just sat there staring and said right out loud, 'She can't! She's in Europe with her parents!'"

Along the way to critical acclaim Little's left eye began giving her trouble: it was diagnosed as glaucoma and corneal edema "and it blistered and became so painful that I had to have it out." It was replaced by a glass eye, with Little cheerfully removes for curious audiences of schoolchildren, "although the teachers," she adds, "tend to sort of faint away in the aisles." Her 10 per cent vision was reduced by half. Editing and retyping manuscripts became an increasingly tedious process; Little would hold a page to her nose to read it, and then try to find what point she was at on her typewriter. Still, during the 1970s she published four more books, won the Vicky Metcalf Award in 1974 for her achievements to date, went on a whim with a friend to Japan to study Japanese for two years, and spent her spare time leading children's groups such as Explorers and Canadian Girls in Training.

Then, in 1977, professional success met head-on with her personal handicap. *For Anna* (Fitzhenry & Whiteside, 1972), about a German immigrant girl coping with anti-German sentiment after the Second World War, had been so successful that Little wrote a sequel. Hailed by the *New York Times Book Review* as "first-rate," *Listen for the Singing* (Clarke Irwin) garnered her highest honour yet: the Canada Council's annual award for best children's author. Shortly afterwards, bad news struck. "Within three days [of winning the award], I found I had glaucoma in my remaining eye and thought I would be blind within a year and a half—because that's what happened with the first eye.

"That was a very bad time," she now says quietly of the eight years it took to finish another book. "I did pretty well stop writing for a while—I just didn't know how to do it. I would come out of the depression for a while and try to write, doing absolutely ridiculous things. I taped a bell to the space bar on my typewriter and used a tape recorder so that when I stopped to think, I counted the number of keys I had hit between the bell ringings to try to figure out what the last word I'd typed was. It was absolutely insane."

Little eventually turned to dictating her work on a tape recorder, adding punctuation so that a typist could record her intentions faithfully. (Even now, she says, she silently punctuates story-telling on the radio or on her favourite "reading," the Canadian National Institute for the Blind's series of tape-recorded books.)

Mama's Going to Buy You a Mockingbird took 97 cassette tapes and the tenacity of Little's editor, Shelley Tanaka of Penguin Books, to bring the story of Jeremy Talbot to life. "She was fantastic," Little says of Tanaka. In order to edit the book, Tanaka would read the manuscript to Little, and both would suggest revisions. On the dedication page Little credits Tanaka's "patience, incisive skill and mounting excitement" for the book's success, and adds, "Jeremy and I would never have made it without her."

During this time another helpful colleague came along in the form of Zephyr, a thoroughly trained, friendly guide dog who snores in church and follows Little wherever she goes. ("It can be a bit embarrassing in public washrooms," Little admits, "when people come along and see Zephyr's tail thumping away under one of the cubicles.") She was afraid she would not qualify for a guide dog, not being totally blind—"one of the few times in my life," she says wryly, "that I thought I might have too much sight."

The latest addition to the cottage she shares with her 82-year-old mother and bedridden aunt—and the saving grace to Little's writing—arrived in June. SAM, a colloquial name for the Synthetic Audio Microcomputer on which Little now writes her books, sits in a quiet corner of her office with a printer donated by the local Lion's Club. Developed by David Kostyshyn, an enterprising blind businessman in Hamilton, Ont., SAM can tell Little what letters, words, or even phonetics she is typing, and repeats, in a gravelly, electronically accented voice, any command she gives it. "It's made me more independent than I ever was—even when I could see much better," Little says with delight. "I'm just like any writer. Now I can insert and delete without thinking I'm going to have to redo the entire page." SAM's only drawback is a visitor who pays more attention to the computer than to her.

Little's vision has held at around five per cent with the aid of a special contact lens that prevents blisters from forming on her right eye. Her imaginative vision is ever-expanding. "I love fantasy myself," she says over salad and lasagna prepared by her active mother. She declines to write fantasy, however, because "there are lots of children's books that I love to read that are outside my scope as a writer. I've read a lot of writers who say that because *they* write a certain type of children's book that's the type of book kids should read. I think children need all kinds of books."

Although her kind of books are about real children whose parents die or who find pets they have to give up, Little dislikes writing novels solely to depict a human dilemma. "When I came along there were lots of things you didn't mention, like death and divorce. That certainly has changed—there's nothing you can't write about for children if you do it well. But when somebody says, 'I think we should write a book for children about divorce' or 'we ought to write a book about prejudice against Jews,' it comes out that way, like a sermon. There's a lot of young adult fiction that is like that. It's so problem-oriented that the story didn't get to the writer first, the propaganda did."

Her face lights up when she recalls the books she loved as a child—Frances Hodgson

Burnett's *The Secret Garden* and *The Little Princess.* "I asked my mother when I was about 11 to tell me the name of a perfect book and she told me *The Little Princess.* After that I had great respect for my mother's opinion." Many of the children in Little's books, handicapped or otherwise (and there are plenty of both), share a love of the "secret place" where "no adult comes. That's very, very magical."

She feels a commitment to the world of children's books because "you go so intently into them" as a child. "You're not thinking you should really be doing something else. You may be hoping that no one will catch you and *make* you do something else, but otherwise, as far as you're concerned, you're living right in that book.

"So many people grow up and stop reading children's books, then complain and complain because they read Margaret Atwood and it may not be what they want to read just then. They don't want to look at that world, they want to look at a different world, and they won't find it in adult fiction."

That different world remains with Little as an adult. Her childhood memories are among her strongest, partly because she was handicapped and partly because of her writer's perspective on life. "I have one particular memory of being eight and starting regular school," she says. "The strain of it was so great I was going temporarily *bald,* of all things. One morning my mother said, 'The house is cold, stay in bed for a while longer and I'll bring you an orange.' I was sitting looking at these pretty orange boats reflected in the window and I was suddenly conscious that memory fades. So I said to myself, 'I am going to remember this moment, always.' That memory is very strong."

As Little comes outside the house to say goodbye, she points with pride to the brilliant orange sunflowers, bursting with black seeds, at the bottom of the garden. They stand six feet high next to the green wooden shed where Little once kept her own "secret place," a

room furnished with bed, wood-burning stove, and a table for writing when the pressures of the outside world became too intense. The room is quiet and empty. Next spring, when it is warm enough to work there, her family plans to hook up an electrical system so she may take SAM out from the main house and resume her writing in a place where no other adults come. We peer in at the door of the shed. It has been bereft of Jean Little's imagination for too many years.

Investigative Reporting

Ted Thurston

Grass roots journalism is facing a crisis in Canada, and the challenge to preserve a distinguished tradition rests with the working newsmen, not their managements.

Journalism graduates of college and university courses often come to their first job asking what is required of them to become investigative reporters.

Too many young reporters have a misguided impression of what constitutes an investigative reporter. Many visualize a special breed of newsman, working in a specialized field, as the only one worthy of carrying this title.

Of course every newsman should be an investigative reporter. To think otherwise is to accept mediocrity.

Aspiring reporters must learn not to accept anything at face value. They must be prepared to build their stories on details beyond those facts determined and dictated by some public servant. To serve only as a mouthpiece is to deprive readers of pertinent information.

Consider the hypothetical situation of a fatal train-car crash.

The reporter visits the police station to obtain details. The police report will give the basic facts: when, where, who, and how. The question "why?" is never answered. It is for the reporter to determine why. This is the basic ingredient of investigative journalism.

Not satisfied with basic facts, a good reporter attempts to develop the story—so on goes the investigative-reporter hat. Unfortunately many young reporters may seek to round out their stories with only such details as the cause of death as ruled by the coroner, whether the victim was dead on arrival at the hospital, or whether the victim ever regained consciousness.

Such details are not proof of good investigative reporting. Rather, they merely attempt to satisfy some readers' appetites for gory detail, and are simply sensationalism.

An investigative reporter must uncover facts which serve the well-being and interests of the readers, not just their curiosity.

In the case of the fatal train-car crash, the public interest would be better served if the reporter were to consider the issue of safety at the crossing. A little work would uncover any history of similar crashes. A further call would ascertain whether police were trying to determine exactly how fast the train was travelling at the time of the accident.

Raising the question of safety at the crossing, or neglect in enforcing speed limits, could result in improved controls and enforcement, thereby benefiting the public.

Historically, a newspaper's main responsibility is to inform and serve. Most newspapers were founded for exactly that purpose.

Because political revolution played a greater role in the histories of the US and Great Britain than it did in Canada, the peoples of those nations maintain a greater tradition as newspaper readers than do Canadians.

In a Canadian city with a population of fifty thousand, it has long been impossible for more than one daily paper to exist. Prior to the economic turmoil of the last decade, however, a US city of the same size often supported two and even three dailies because American readers demanded more than one source of local news.

Canada's best newsmen and major newspapers are a good as the best of any nation, but at the grass roots of journalism a crisis of responsibility to the reader looms.

Canadian readers can depend on newspapers of the *Toronto Star*'s stature, but can they depend on their local paper when investigative reporting is becoming an art form reserved for national newspapers?

Investigative reporting should be the substance of all the many small-city daily and weekly newspapers read by millions of Canadians. But it is not. The problem lies not only in the failure of the Canadian economy to support competing newspapers in a market, but in the failure of the average Canadian reader to act as the watchdog of his or her local media.

Competition demands investigative reporting for success, but monopolies settle for mediocrity as more profitable.

As more community newspapers in today's economy find themselves in a monopoly situation, or controlled by profit-oriented company monopolies, readers all too frequently are deprived of hard-nosed reporting of local news.

When a choice exists, managements often sacrifice costly and time-consuming investigative reporting for easily obtained, telephone-pickup, fluff pieces.

Those spaces around the advertisements can be filled by fewer staff if the number of stories is increased by reducing the time spent investigating each of them.

Too many community newspapers are moulding young editorial staffs to believe that their journalistic duty is to get as many stories as possible, as quickly as possible, while depending solely upon the telephone to complete their investigations.

At least one chain has elevated the image of investigative reporting to such a high and specialized level in the minds of its reporters that many believe such work is the domain of Toronto newspapers only.

As community newspapers have elevated the ideal of investigative reporting to supposedly unattainable heights, its actual use has been demoted to a costly and expendable luxury.

Journalism instructors in Canadian colleges and universities must make their students aware of the crisis. The instructors have a greater responsibility than just preparing their students for jobs, they must also instill a sense of dedication to the profession itself.

We are all investigative reporters, and if we aren't we should be.

It would be too arrogant, and probably inaccurate, to profess that the public demands this of us, but certainly the public does, and should expect it of us.

An Interview with Aldous Huxley

George Wickes
Ray Frazer

Interviewers: Would you tell us something first about the way you work?

Huxley: I work regularly. I always work in the mornings, and then again a little bit before dinner. I'm not one of those who work at night. I prefer to read at night. I usually work four or five hours a day. I keep at it as long as I can, until I feel myself going stale. Sometimes, when I bog down, I start reading—fiction or psychology or history, it doesn't much matter what—not to borrow ideas or materials, but simply to get started again. Almost anything will do the trick.

Interviewers: Do you do much rewriting?

Huxley: Generally, I write everything many times over. All my thoughts are second thoughts. And I correct each page a great deal, or rewrite it several times as I go along.

Interviewers: Do you keep a notebook, like certain characters in your novels?

Huxley: No, I don't keep notebooks. I have occasionally kept diaries for short periods, but I'm very lazy, I mostly don't. One should keep notebooks, I think, but I haven't.

Interviewers: Do you block out chapters or plan the over-all structure when you start out on a novel?

Huxley: No, I work away a chapter at a time, finding my way as I go. I know very dimly when I start what's going to happen. I just have a very general idea, and then the thing develops as I write. Sometimes—it's happened to me more than once—I will write a great deal, then find it just doesn't work, and have to throw the whole thing away. I like to have a chapter finished before I begin on the next one. But I'm never entirely certain what's going to happen in the next chapter until I've worked it out. Things come to me in driblets, and when the driblets come I have to work hard to make them into something coherent.

Interviewers: Is the process pleasant or painful?

Huxley: Oh, it's not painful, though it is hard work. Writing is a very absorbing occupation and sometimes exhausting. But I've always considered myself very lucky to be able to make a living at something I enjoy doing. So few people can. . . .

Interviewers: When you start out on a novel, what sort of a general idea do you have? How did you begin *Brave New World*, for example?

Huxley: Well, that started out as a parody of H.G. Wells' *Men Like Gods*, but gradually it got out of hand and turned into something quite different from what I'd originally intended. As I became more and more interested in the subject, I wandered farther and farther from my original purpose. . . .

Interviewers: Some writers hesitate to talk about their work in progress for fear they'll talk it away. You aren't afraid of that?

Huxley: No, I don't mind talking about my writing at all. In fact, it might be a good practice; it might give me a clearer notion of what I was trying to do. I've never discussed my writing with others much, but I don't believe it can do any harm. I don't think that there's any risk that ideas or materials will evaporate.

Interviewers: Do you think that certain occupations are more conducive to creative writing than others? In other words, does the work you do or the company you keep affect your writing?

Huxley: I don't believe there is an ideal occupation for the writer. He could write under almost any circumstance, even in complete isolation. Why, look at Balzac, locked up in a secret room in Paris, hiding from his creditors, and producing the *Comédie Humaine*. Or think of Proust in his cork-lined room (although of course he had plenty of visitors). I suppose the best occupation is just meeting a great many different kinds of people and seeing what interests them. That's one of the disadvantages of getting older; you're inclined to make intimate contacts with fewer people.

Interviewers: What would you say makes the writer different from other people?

Huxley: Well, one has the urge, first of all, to order the facts one observes and to give meaning to life; and along with that goes the love of words for their own sake and a desire to manipulate them. It's not a matter of intelligence; some very intelligent and original people don't have the love of words or the knack to use them effectively. On the verbal level they express themselves very badly.

Interviewers: What about creativeness in general?

Huxley: Yes, what about it? Why is it that in most children education seems to destroy the creative urge? Why do so many boys and girls leave school with blunted perceptions and a closed mind? A majority of young people seem to develop mental arteriosclerosis forty years before they get the physical kind. Another question: why do some people remain open and elastic into extreme old age,

whereas others become rigid and unproductive before they're fifty? It's a problem in biochemistry and adult education.

Interviewers: Some psychologists have claimed that the creative urge is a kind of neurosis. Would you agree?

Huxley: Most emphatically not. I don't believe for a moment that creativity is a neurotic symptom. On the contrary, the neurotic who succeeds as an artist has had to overcome a tremendous handicap. He creates in spite of his neurosis, not because of it.

Interviewers: You've never had much use for Freud, have you?

Huxley: The trouble with Freudian psychology is that it is based exclusively on a study of the sick. Freud never met a healthy human being—only patients and other psychoanalysts. Then too, Freudian psychology is only concerned with the past. Other systems of psychology, that concern themselves with the present state of the subject or his future potentialities, seem to me to be more realistic. . . .

Interviewers: To return to writing, in *Point Counter Point* you have Philip Quarles say, "I am not a congenital novelist." Would you say the same of yourself?

Huxley: I don't think of myself as a congenital novelist—no. For example, I have great difficulty in inventing plots. Some people are born with an amazing gift for storytelling; it's a gift which I've never had at all. One reads, for example, Stevenson's accounts of how all the plots for his stories were provided in dreams by his subconscious mind (what he calls the "Brownies" working for him), and that all he had to do was to work up the material they had provided. I've never had any Brownies. The great difficulty for me has always been creating situations.

Interviewers: Developing character has been easier for you than creating plots?

Huxley: Yes, but even then I'm not very good at creating people; I don't have a very wide repertory of characters. These are difficult things for me. I suppose it's largely a question of temperament. I don't happen to have the right kind of temperament.

Interviewers: By the phrase "congenital novelist" we thought you meant one who is only interested in writing novels.

Huxley: I suppose this is another way of saying the same thing. The congenital novelist doesn't have other interests. Fiction for him is an absorbing thing which fills up his mind and takes all his time and energy, whereas someone else with a different kind of mind has these other, extracurricular activities going on. . . .

Interviewers: Then in some of those early novels you also make use of musical effects, much as Gide does.

Huxley: The marvelous thing about music is that it does so easily and rapidly what can be done only very laboriously in words, or really can't be done at all. It's futile to even attempt to write musically. But I've tried in some of my essays—in *Themes and Variations*, for instance. Then I've used the equivalent of musical variations in some of my stories, where I take certain traits of character and treat them seriously in one personage and comically, in a sort of parody, in another. . . .

Interviewers: How do you convert a real person into a fictional character?

Huxley: I try to imagine how certain people I know would behave in certain circumstances. Of course I base my characters partly on the people I know—one can't escape it—but fictional characters are oversimplified; they're much less complex than the people one knows.

Interviewers: Even though you have been writing fewer novels in recent years, you don't think less highly of the art of fiction than you used to?

Huxley: Oh, no, no, no. I think fiction, and biography and history, are *the* forms. I think one can say much more about general abstract ideas in terms of concrete characters and situations, whether fictional or real, than one can in abstract terms. . . .

CHAPTER
Eight

Workshop Supplement

This chapter gathers supplementary material in a half-dozen Writers' Resources for use with Chapters One through Seven. Contents include sample forms, organizers, and checklists. *Students are encouraged to devise their own forms, organizers, and checklists.* The samples are intended to be sources of ideas, not models. If word processing facilities are available, consider building a database of forms which may be adapted to accommodate your development.

Writers' Resource One   Building Your Workshop

"Writing is one art form that can be practised almost anywhere at any time," Theodore M. Bernstein sagely informs his readers in *The Careful Writer* (p. vii). You need only a piece of paper and a writing implement. Indeed, children know that a twig and a patch of sand or a wall and a fat red crayon serve the purpose nicely. However, a carefully organized curriculum and well-stocked studio smooth the process of thinking through writing.

Underlying Goals

First, effective organization and design require a sense of the educational philosophy or broad goals underlying your curriculum. The workshop program goes beyond building "the good writer." Activities foster your

- self-motivation
- communication and thinking skills
- creative problem-solving abilities
- collaborative skills
- overall personal growth.

As you work through your program, keep these goals in mind.

A Supportive Atmosphere

Second, you'll want to build a positive atmosphere which invites collaboration. To facilitate group interaction, keep in mind five strategies advocated by successful leaders.

- Set realistic group and individual goals; then chip away at them bit by bit.
- Recognize that growth is a slow process requiring patience and mutual support; the pace and manner of change differs among individuals.

- Build team commitment; a feeling of shared ownership ensures everyone has a stake in success.

- People function best when their needs for recognition, autonomy, control, emotional support, praise, challenge, and variety are met.

- Believe that collaboratively designed creative solutions can move virtually any rock.

Physical Set-up and Resources

Third, if you meet in a standard classroom or a computer lab used by other classes, you'll need to work closely with your teacher to create a comfortable atmosphere. You may wish to keep in mind the following suggestions.

- **Quiet work area**—a section of the room where students can work individually; carrels are ideal.

- **Central community area**—an arrangement of desks or chairs and tables which can be moved to aid face-to-face discussion; long cafeteria-style tables may work well too.

- **Supply station**—a stock of coloured pens and pencils, lined and plain paper, and implements for self-publishing such as cardboard and twine or dental floss.

- **Audio-visual centre**—a supply of standard equipment supplemented with cassette and record players, and music to write by.

- **Word processing station(s)**—one word processor per student is ideal; even one computer and a printer is useful for demonstrations.

- **Reference station**—a collection of single-copy resources such as those listed below is a valuable classroom resource.

Miscellaneous

- **Dictionaries**: *Funk and Wagnalls Standard College Dictionary* (Canadian Edition) and *The Concise Oxford Dictionary of Current English*

- **Thesaurus**

- Bartlett's *Familiar Quotations* (Toronto: Little, Brown and Co., 1980)

- Paul McLaughlin, *Asking Questions* (Toronto: Self-Counsel Press, 1986)

- Kirk Polking, ed., *Writer's Encyclopedia* (Cincinnati: Writer's Digest Books, 1986)

- **Periodicals/magazines/subscriptions**: *Books in Canada*, the *Globe and*

Mail, Canadian Author and Bookman, Maclean's, Canadian Forum, Quill &
Quire, Content, Saturday Night, Cross Canada Writers' Quarterly, and
Writer's Digest.

A Variety of Activities

Finally, this list suggests a variety of learning experiences to brighten class
interaction. If you're planning a seminar or presentation, use it to devise a
well-rounded experience.

appreciating	polishing
assessing	proof-reading
brainstorming	reading aloud
choral reading	reflecting
collaborating	researching
conferencing	revising
creating	role playing
debating	sharing
decision-making	simulating
discussing	speaking
editing	(story) telling
experimenting	teaching
imaging	valuing
listening	viewing
planning	visualizing
playing with language	writing

Writers' Resource Two   Tips for Successful Conferences

Meeting Individual Needs

Effective conferences don't just happen; they grow from a foundation of
learning about human interaction, honed through guided experimentation.
Important skills and attitudes include:

- a sincere desire to assist a partner's writing growth

- an awareness of a partner's learning preferences

- an ability to communicate your interest and knowledge

- an ability to motivate and reinforce growth.

This Writers' Resource guides your interaction. You may also benefit from
(re)reading the Forsythe-Hollyer interview about teamwork (page 72) and

from practising communication techniques suggested by your instructor or manuals such as:

- Robert and Isabel Hawley, *Developing Human Potential: A Handbook of Activities for Personal and Social Growth* (Amherst, Mass: ERA Press, 1975)

- Jack Canfield and Harold Wells, *100 Ways to Enhance Self-Concept in the Classroom* (Englewood, NJ: Prentice-Hall, 1976)

- Geraldine Ball, *Innerchange: A Journey into Self-learning Through Group Interaction* (San Diego, Calif: Human Development Training Institute Inc.)

The first principle in organizing a successful peer conference is balancing candour with tact. Anticipating your partner's sensitivities and avoiding hostile responses are vital to this process.

HERMAN®

"A lot of men would
love to be 7 feet tall."

"Herman" © 1989 Universal Press Syndicate. Reprinted with permission. All rights reserved.

An awareness of preferred communication styles may enhance the sensitivity with which you and your writing partner(s) interact. The four styles outlined below apply the work of Jean M. Kummerow, Ph.D. (Center for Applications of Psychological Type) and Bernice McCarthy, Ph.D. (Excel Corporation). If one approach flounders, experiment with another or combine elements until the mix is right for you and your partner.

*For partners like **Tarvo:*** *respect the high value they place on people and feelings.*

- show you care about individuals; for example, devote a few minutes to casual conversation before getting down to business
- determine their preferences for the conference
- begin with discussion; follow up with comments on forms such as the Peer Conference Dialogue Organizers
- emphasize strengths before outlining general suggestions—avoid nit-picking
- honour their writing's emotional integrity
- indicate your availability for informal follow-up
- over a period of time, encourage objective self-evaluation

*For partners like **Kirsten:*** *respect their high regard for logic, facts, and expert opinion.*

- offer written comments before a sit-down conference
- get down to business
- present reasoned comments succinctly and objectively
- honour their writing's logical integrity and organization
- deal calmly with emotional issues
- validate suggestions with "expert" opinion
- encourage imaginative experimentation in writing

*For partners like **Sasha:*** *respect their practicality and concern for real-life issues.*

- get down to business
- present concise, step-by-step suggestions
- offer new writing strategies within a familiar context
- make suggestions concrete (give examples)
- emphasize the practical value of suggestions
- honour their writing's factual integrity
- encourage imaginative risk-taking in writing

*For partners like **Craig:*** *respect their individuality and creative experimentation.*

- determine their perception of writing needs
- offer main suggestions first—avoid an abundance of detail
- downplay routine approaches to the assignment

- invite them to articulate ambiguous passages
- honour the intuitive integrity and vision of their writing
- encourage them to test the feasibility of ideas

If you're wondering how these ideas translate into practice, eavesdrop on two conferences in progress. You'll likely acquire tips about how to proceed.

Setting

- After several months of classwork, students are increasingly self-confident about peer conferences. They've worked with different conference partners, but rely most frequently on the pairing described below.

- They're discussing revisions for Tarvo's and Kirsten's formal essays. Kirsten has already completed a self-conference, using an organizer similar to the one on page 379. Tarvo prefers to leave the self-conference strategy until after his discussion with Sasha.

- The following snippets reflect what you'd see and hear if you observed them in action.

What They Sound Like

Sasha *says things to* **Tarvo** *like . . .*

- So how's your job in the daycare going?
- Do you like this draft better than the last one?
- Where do you want to begin?
- I'm impressed with how you keep personal feelings out of this; I know that's hard for you.
- Even though you don't use "I" a lot, it's great—it really sounds like you.
- You've shown fantastic insight about the characters, especially when you say . . .

Tarvo's *responses include comments like . . .*

- I'm glad you noticed my writing's more objective.
- You're good at picking up details that slip my mind. What have you noticed so far?
- Okay, I'll think about which idea I want to emphasize.

Craig *says things to* **Kirsten** *like . . .*

- I think the analysis of characters' relationships is fine.

- Your first two reasons are the strongest because . . .
- I wonder if the main idea is a bit bogged down with detail.
- What would you think of ending this with a . . . ?
- This book gives a good example of . . .

Kirsten's responses include comments like . . .

- You've made a good point about facts—the main idea got lost.
- Maybe the quotations are slowing down this section . . .
- Your essays are so lively. What do you think I could do about mine?

What They Look Like

Sasha *and* Tarvo

- They sit facing each other.
- Tarvo reads his work aloud to Sasha.
- They sometimes hold their conference at a word processor where Sasha teaches Tarvo how to enter revisions.

Craig *and* Kirsten

- They sit side by side in the quiet of the library if possible.
- Kirsten takes notes—sometimes on the word processor—as Craig reiterates his written comments.

Forms, Organizers, and Checklists

Use organizers and checklists such as those below to guide your conference preparation and subsequent interaction.

Writers' Planner

Purpose   To set goals and experiment with writing folder work.

- *Area of interest*: "I am interested in experimenting with . . ."
- *Background reading*: Samples of work by professionals, advice from practising professionals, or samples of work by peers.
- *Media and other (re)sources*: Programs and community contacts.
- *Other pre-writing preparation*: Journal writing, follow-up from previous writing, investigation of audience, language remediation, or vocabulary building.

- *"Newness" for me*: Form, genre, style, audience, tone, and purpose.

Self-Conference Organizer

Purpose   To prepare for peer conferences by reflecting on work to date.

- How do I *feel* about this draft?
- Am I interested in my work?
- In what ways is the work different from what I envisaged? Am I generally pleased with its evolution?
- When I read my writing aloud, what sounds and images stick in my mind?
- What about the piece strikes me as especially lively or vivid, "off," unexpected, apt, new for me, or in need of attention?
- What do I want my partner(s) to focus on in conference?
- What points do I anticipate my partner(s) will make?

Conference Summary Organizer

Purpose   To encourage accurate recordkeeping.

Conference record for   (title/topic of work)

_____   _____

1. Summary of suggestions for REVISING   Date _____

_____

_____

Conference partner(s) _____

2. Summary of suggestions for EDITING   Date _____

_____

_____

Conference partner(s) _____

3. Summary of suggestions for POLISHING   Date _____

_____

_____

Conference partner(s) _____

Peer-Conference Response Organizers

Purpose   To guide conference dialogue about works-in-progress prior to completing written checklists.

Note: The number of conferences and questions dealt with in each should be adapted to meet your developmental needs.

Dialogue Organizer One–Revision

Purpose   To explore a preliminary (rough) draft.

Warm up by stressing the positive.

1.   "I particularly like. . . ." Focus on an idea, phrase, or interpretation.

2.   "I am interested in. . . ." Note a concept or writing strategy you'd like to know more about.

3.   "This writing made me think about/feel. . . ." Share your associations—a thought or feeling it initiated.

Move on to mutual concerns.

4.   "Where would you like to begin?" Determine the writer's major concerns.

5.   "In terms of your purpose, I think you've. . . ." Indicate whether the purpose is clearly communicated.

6.   "In terms of your audience. . . ." Share your reactions about the work's suitability for the audience.

7.   "Your main point is. . . ." Paraphrase your perception of the theme, thesis, or unifying vision.

8.   "I am confused by. . . ." Point out ambiguities. Help determine causes and possible remedies.

9.   "Another point you could consider is. . . ." Suggest information or another way of looking at the topic.

10.   "The assignment stipulates. . . ." If you are working with an assigned topic, establish that the draft meets the instructor's criteria.

Sum up on a strong note.

11.   "You might strengthen this draft by. . . ." Summarize your ideas about diction, structure and organization, style and voice, and content/ideas.

Note: Complete written comments on a form such as the Revision Checklist (page 382).

Dialogue Organizer Two–Editing

Purpose   To provide feedback about the growth of writing.

Warm up by stressing progress.

12.   "How do you like this draft now that you've. . .?" Explore the writer's sense of the revised piece.

13.   "You've done a great job reorganizing. . . ."

Look closely at key issues.

14.   "The language in this draft seems more suitable because. . . ." Establish examples of apt language level and indicate diction which still needs work.

15.   "This new phrasing clarifies your purpose. . . ." Is the wording consistently appropriate for the purpose?

16.   "Your tone is stronger here. . . ." Check for consistent tone.

17.   "The mental pictures are stronger now because. . . ." Find examples of vivid, fresh wording. Note problems—clichés, verbal vagueness, and other improprieties.

18.   "The style in this part really sounds like you. . . ." Share your perceptions of the writer's voice—characteristic phrases and rhythms. Note phrasing that may not "ring true."

19.   "The answer to this grammatical problem is in. . . ." Suggest a text or computer software for a chronic grammar fault.

20.   "Perhaps this figure of speech would work better if. . . ." Are figures of speech/rhetorical techniques appropriately employed?

21.   "These sentences are much clearer now because you've. . . ." Note improvements in general sentence structure.

22.   "I like the sentence variety you've created in this draft. . . ." Mention strengths and concerns too.

Review structure and organization.

23.   "By altering your emphasis/point of view, you've more clearly. . . ." If the revised work has benefited from restructuring, indicate why. Suggest further paragraph reorganization or sequencing if necessary.

24. "The transitions in this draft are stronger because...." Communicate about the overall flow of the piece.

25. "The beginning and ending...." Identify strengths and concerns.

Note: Complete written comments on a form such as the Editing Checklist.

Dialogue Organizer Three—Polishing

Purpose   To fine-tune style until the writing sparkles like a newly polished gem.

Has my partner ...

- selected the most vivid and precise diction
- eliminated (ineffective) repetition
- avoided mixed metaphors, stale similes, and the like
- appealed to the senses (if appropriate for audience and purpose)
- attended to details of punctuation and spelling
- employed a consistently apt level of language (for example, contractions, slang, colloquial language, and short forms of words should not appear in formal essays)
- used suitable techniques of showing/evidence
- eliminated inconsistencies in verb tenses, voice, and subject-verb agreement
- built in smooth transitions?

Note: Complete a written form such as Checklist for Polishing.

Dialogue Organizer Four—Proof-Reading

Purpose   To run a final check for careless errors and omissions.

Has my partner ...

- attended to the details of polishing
- stated the title, audience, and purpose on the final draft
- appended required forms (e.g., checklists, self-assessments)?

Revision Checklist

Purpose   To provide a written summary of dialogue about broad issues and preliminary impressions.

Focus on Writing Variables

- Is the **purpose** clearly stated at the top of the draft?
- Does the draft communicate its purpose as you read it?
- When you finish reading the draft, are you left with the feeling that the writer had the stated purpose in mind throughout?
- Is the **audience** clearly stated at the top of the draft?
- Is the audience selected appropriate for the writer's purpose?
- Is the **language**—level of formality, figures of speech—appropriate for the stated purpose and audience?
- Does the language convey a clear and consistent tone?
- Is the **style** appropriate for audience and purpose?
- Does the style meet the terms of the assignment?
- Is the **tone** clear and appropriate for the purpose and audience?
- Is the writer's **voice** apparent?

Focus on Content

- Is there a clear **organizing idea**—a thesis or central theme?
- Does the organizing idea sustain itself throughout the draft?
- Is the organizing idea significant (worth exploring) and imaginative?
- Is the **elaboration** of the organizing idea relevant, clear, thoughtful, well developed, and valid?

Focus on Form

- Is the overall **structure** logical, clear, and appropriate? Does it enhance or obscure the thought of the draft?
- Is each **paragraph** appropriately structured with a topic sentence, development, and a closing sentence?
- Does each paragraph clearly relate to the organizing idea of the draft?
- Are the paragraphs sequenced in the most effective order for meaning and significance to emerge?
- Are the **sentences** *generally* clear, without major flaws, and of appropriate length and level for audience and purpose?
- Is the **word choice** *generally* appropriate to the work's purpose, audience, and desired tone?

Leave all fine points for the editing stage.

Editing Checklist

Focus on Form

- Is the **diction** at the appropriate level for audience and purpose(s), consistent in tone, idiomatic, and clear and concise?

- Is the diction also fresh and lively (vivid verbs and precise nouns); does it reflect the writer's voice?

- Is it non-inclusive and correctly spelled?

- Are the **sentences** varied in structure and clear and concise?

- Are they expressed without inconsistent verb tenses, disagreement of subject and verb, and faulty structures such as dangling participles, fragments, and comma splices?

- Are the **paragraphs** clearly linked through transitions, logically sequenced, and appropriately developed for the form, audience, and purpose?

Focus on Content

Review the questions asked in the revision phase; this time, explore each in more depth.

A Summative Peer-Assessment Organizer

Purpose   To record an overview of polished work.

Assessment for (name of writer): _____

Peer assessor: _____

Assignment title/topic: _____

1. I have helped this writer with _____ drafts of this work. The improvements are summarized below.

2. I have proof-read the final draft. My evaluation according to the criteria developed in our workshop is given below. (Rank each item from 1–7, assigning 7 to the strongest feature. Then add a comment.)

- Overall suitability for intended audience

- Imaginative handling of topic

- Appropriate structure and organization

- Clear and concise throughout

- Pleasing unity, emphasis, and coherence

- High quality of thought/analysis

Summative Assessment Organizer

Purpose   To assess peer contributions; to develop summative self-analysis and provide the instructor with an overview of progress.

Name: _____

Assignment title/topic: _____

Intended audience: _____

Purpose(s): _____

My partner(s) and the assistance provided (circle appropriate response):

- **Revision**

  Excellent   Good   Satisfactory   Unhelpful

- **Editing and/or polishing**

  Excellent   Good   Satisfactory   Unhelpful

- **Proof-reading**

  Excellent   Good   Satisfactory   Unhelpful

1.   Comment on the growth of your work.

2.   Assess the final draft's strengths and weakness.

3.   What have you discovered from writing this work which may help you with future assignments?

4.   What steps have you taken to resolve persistent problems?

5.   Outline help you would like to receive from the instructor.

Writers' Resource Three   Challenging Your Writing Potential

To challenge your writing potential, you'll want to engage in a variety of stimulating activities. This resource outlines strategies to integrate the growth of your imaginative and critical capacities; use them to explore and expand options, try new approaches, and see new patterns and possibilities. *Tip:* Consider beginning a database for your class, or share ideas with other classes in the network.

Reading Prompts: Anecdotes, Quotations, and Cartoons

Collect anecdotes, quotations, and cartoons for your classroom. Post samples on the bulletin board. They offer excellent starting-points for discussion and writing.

For example, read the anecdotes about Pratt (printed below) and Leacock (page 161). Then brainstorm or speedwrite about ideas they stimulate. Or consult *The Little, Brown Book of Anecdotes* or *The Broadview Book of Canadian Anecdotes*, from which these tales are reprinted.

This anecdote about E.J. Pratt (1882-1964) may inspire ideas for a satirical skit about differences in Canadian English.

The Newfoundland poet, author of *The Titantic, Brébeuf and His Brethren,* and other long narrative poems had a cottage near Bobcaygeon, Ontario, to which he would retreat each summer after classes ended at University of Toronto where he taught. Before closing up the place one season and returning to the city, he contracted with a local builder to make a private "dock" on the property. He had used the term as it was used in Newfoundland, to mean a small enclosed dock, suitable for a child to swim in. When he returned the next summer, however, he found a "dock" in the mainland Canadian sense: a pier or wharf "big enough to moor a Kawartha lakes steamer—and with a price to match." Thus was it brought home once again that Newfoundland and Canada are separated by a common language, that English Canada plus French Canada plus Newfoundland equal two and one-half solitudes.

Cartoons and famous quotations may help you begin speedwriting on days when your store of ideas seems empty. Peruse cartoons in this book or quotations from sources such as *Bartlett's Familiar Quotations, Peter's Quotations: Ideas for Our Time,* and *Colombo's Canadian Quotations.*

Viewing Prompts: Audio-Visual Resources

Collect these audio-visual resources for your classroom, or order them for special use.

- Store postcards and photographs in shoeboxes for easy reference, or post them on a bulletin board.

- Display attractive posters and large photographs.

- Order films and videotapes through your instructor.

Whether you're beginning an essay, revising a poem, or searching for a new challenge, viewing a film or clips stimulates thinking. Watching a film with the sound track turned off is an effective strategy to unleash creativity. Fairy tales and other children's stories, particularly animated versions, are especially useful.

Additional Exercises to Heighten Awareness

You may also wish to experiment with the techniques proposed by Linda Verlee Williams in *Teaching for the Two-Sided Mind* (Prentice-Hall, 1982) outlined below.

- Explicate through metaphor—perhaps a concept or experience to a partner or small group.

- Draw and/or colour or sculpt your impressions of a word, poem, emotion, person, or event.

- Identify key words which communicate a work's essence; build a found poem, map, or cluster with them (see below).

- Summarize information in a chart, or plan a short story with a plot diagram or time line.

- Express ideas in a mind map. Using the technique of *clustering*, write the main idea in the centre of a page and circle it; then scatter secondary ideas around the central concept, circling each and representing connections and relationships with arrows.

  With *mapping* or *branching*, the central idea is placed in a box centred on the page; lines ("branches") show supporting information.

  For another mind-mapping technique, called a *mandala*, create a graphic symbol which expresses something important about the meaning of a piece of your writing. The mandala takes the form of one or more images enclosed in a circle which may or may not be subdivided into sections.

- Plan writing through idea sketches or stick-figure cartoons.

- Explore a concept, character, or writing style through fantasy; for example, you may feel more at ease with a history assignment about the hero in American society of the 1920s if you imagine yourself in the role.

- Plan collaborative writing by dramatizing the central mood, theme, or thesis in a tableau (a "freeze-frame" of an action).

Planning for Critical and Creative Thinking

The trigger verbs listed below may stimulate ideas for writing topics, research projects, and class/group discussion. For example, design questions about readings in this book with them.

The six categories into which these verbs are divided reflect increasingly complex thinking functions, according to the work of researchers Bloom and Guilford. You'll benefit most from exercises concentrating on the highest levels of thinking—analysis, synthesis, and evaluation.

Knowledge   *Emphasis on (factual) recall.*

define	label	quote	record
distinguish	list	read	state
draw	outline	recite	trace

Comprehension   *Emphasis on grasp of meaning.*

differentiate	extend	infer	predict
draw	extrapolate	interpolate	rewrite
estimate	generalize	paraphrase	summarize

Application   *Emphasis on use of learning in new situations by application of principles.*

apply	demonstrate	illustrate	practise
choose	discover	modify	predict
classify	examine	organize	restructure

Analysis   *Emphasis on breakdown of knowledge into parts, determining relationships and structural components.*

analyze	group	recognize	subdivide
categorize	illustrate	relate	transform
compare/contrast	order	select	
detect	point out	separate	

Synthesis   *Emphasis on combining parts (ideas, principles) into a new whole.*

combine	deduce	generate	relate
compile	design	integrate	revise
compose	develop	plan	synthesize
create	document	propose	tell

Evaluation   *Emphasis on forming a judgement based on stated criteria.*

appraise	decide	justify	standardize
argue	discriminate	interpret	support
assess	evaluate	measure	test
conclude	grade	rank	validate
critique	judge	recommend	verify

Criteria Checklists for Self- and Peer-Assessment

These criteria checklists invite you to practise the highest level of thinking—evaluation. They highlight what to look for in specific styles and forms of writing. For self- and peer-assessment, use them *in conjunction with* generic forms, organizers, and checklists.

Notes:

- Criteria may overlap and not be valued equally in the final assessment.

- Justify your ranking for each criteria with a brief comment.

Style Clusters—Major Criteria

Rank each item within a cluster from 1 (low)—10 (high). (See also Chapter Three, especially the style summary on page 117.)

Informative Style

- informs/records/explains

- avoids opinions, interpretations, and bias

- neutral denotative language

Interpretive Style

- persuades/interprets/argues

- language appeals to reason

- argument conforms to rules of logic

Rhetorical Style

- effective use of rhetorical devices

- emotive language of eloquence

Poetic Style

- effective expressive/figurative language

- sensual language with illumination

Stream of Consciousness

- sensual, emotive language

- imitates patterns of uncensored thought

- impressionistic, episodic

- audience not acknowledged

Interior Monologue

- similar to stream of consciousness, but acknowledges external audience

The Précis/Summary

- summary of the work's essence
- meaning clear without reading the original
- absence of interpretation and opinion
- original emphasis respected
- unity and coherence
- informative style (unless otherwise instructed)
- formal standard English (unless otherwise instructed)
- length one-third of original (approximate)

The (Generic) Essay

- clear, significant thesis
- logical structure
- introduction, body, and conclusion
- pleasing unity, coherence, and emphasis
- apt style for purpose and audience
- fresh, lively diction
- appropriate rhetorical techniques
- suitable "show, don't tell" techniques
- high-quality proof or illustration
- intellectual curiosity/imagination
- writer's voice

The Profile/Biographical Sketch

- vivid impression of subject
- appealing attributes/qualities portrayed
- identification or empathy invited

- accurate information
- vivid techniques of showing (e.g., anecdotes, dialogue)

The Report

- informative or interpretive style
- terse, clear language
- language appropriate for specialized audience
- absence of "buzz words" and unnecessary jargon
- summary of information/research findings
- sources noted (citations, references)
- diagrams, charts, tables (optional)
- apt level of idiomatic English (usually formal)
- headings and sub-headings (optional)

The Review

- clear sense of work without reading/viewing original
- supporting evidence for interpretation and assessment
- work treated within context/framework
- author's intentions respected
- flavour and texture of work communicated (e.g., direct quotations)

The Seminar/Presentation

- on topic
- (cooperative) planning
- (collaborative) research
- imaginative handling of assignment
- audience participation invited
- intellectual stimulation/enjoyment ("whole-brain" thinking)
- audio-visual aids
- clear articulation and standard English; appropriate body language and imaginative non-verbal touches

- depth of handling/level of thought
- key content/concepts and skills communicated
- instructions followed (e.g., timing, sign-out of equipment)

The Debate

- (collaborative) planning
- (collaborative) research
- conventions of form respected, such as opening statement, order of speakers
- clarity of resolution
- on topic
- quality of evidence and rhetoric in the argument
- delivery—clarity of speech; minimal reference to notes; appropriate language and gestures; appealing tone, pitch, and pace of voice; poise
- rebuttal and/or summation

The One-Act Play

Adapt for skits and other dramatic forms.

- effective stage business
- senses and intellect engaged
- setting built through direct and indirect techniques, such as dialogue, props, stage business
- characterization through dialogue, action, reaction
- unity of central vision or theme
- dialogue—ensure that: it is composed of clear, vivid, concise speech; supports the uniqueness of each character; and imitates natural pauses
- plot and conflict—moves smartly through a beginning, middle, and end

The Short Story

- writer's voice
- style appropriate for audience and purpose
- unifying vision or theme(s)
- dialogue (see play)

- setting built through indirect (e.g., dialogue) and direct (description) techniques
- intellectually and emotionally satisfying plot
- episodic conflict builds to climax and resolution
- characterization through action, reaction, and dialogue

Active Reading

Another practical and pleasurable stimulus for high-level thinking is active reading; you learn strategies to interact with the printed text. Practising these skills can enhance your writing performance and help you get the most out of your reading.

First, assess your present reading behaviour by ranking each statement on the following scale:

1 = does not describe me at all   5 = describes me very well

Then make a conscious effort to practise selected strategies.

Active Reading Checklist

Before reading I . . .

- predict content of a work by its title
- reflect on how this work may enhance my prior knowledge

While reading I . . .

- pause after an introductory section to mentally note the main idea and first impressions, reflect on surprises, and note fulfilled expectations
- repeat several times the steps outlined in question 3
- think of: additional examples and illustrations, alternative phrasing, contradictions, inconsistencies, ambiguities, and biases
- analyze how ideas and concepts interrelate and the validity and/or artistic integrity of the work
- visualize the content
- imagine the sounds of words and listen for pace, rhythm, tone, author's voice, and so on.

After reading I . . .

- imagine other approaches to writing the work (e.g., style, organization, the ending).

- mentally summarize earlier reflections and note intriguing issues.

- share my responses, or reflect privately in my Writer's Notebook.

Writers' Resource Four   Independent Study

What Is It?

The role of independent study in your program varies according to curriculum requirements and local circumstances. Your instructor and/or teacher librarian can help you adapt suggestions.

Independent study describes a process of learning which invites you to develop personal potential through:

a.   *individual inquiry*   and   b.   *interaction with others*

This process functions optimally when viewed as an opportunity for growth within a framework of "structured flexibility." That is, the *balance* between teacher-direction and individual choice is tailored according to readiness for independent work.

How Is It Assessed?

You and your instructor are likely to observe progress in specific areas, such as your ability to:

- initiate and execute an appropriate inquiry question (project)

- assume responsibility for your progress

- make learning personally meaningful

- use a variety of human and material resources

- think critically and creatively

- solve problems and make decisions with increasing independence.

Preparing Yourself

Early in your course, you may wish to take this self-assessment quiz. It highlights factors which promote successful independent learning. After responding in your Writer's Notebook, speculate on the significance of several factors and think of possible personal implications. For self-assessment purposes, assign yourself a number rating:

1 = does not describe me at all   5 = describes me very well

Note that items may overlap.

1.   I enjoy learning through new experiences—experimentation and risk-taking which does not endanger my safety or that of others.

2.   I am self-motivated.

3.   I enjoy meeting challenges.

4.   I have strong problem-solving skills.

5.   I can define goals appropriate to my skills and circumstances.

6.   I nearly always finish what I begin.

7.   I have strong organizational skills, including time management.

8.   I possess sound work habits.

9.   I am a curious person with a variety of interests.

10.   I possess realistic self-assessment skills.

11.   I am aware of my preferred learning style and its implications.

12.   I have developed the ability to learn in a variety of ways.

13.   I know how to use many resources to complete research, including:
a.   prior knowledge, skills, and interests
b.   expertise and contacts of family and friends
c.   library facilities (local and inter-library loans).

14.   I know when to:
a.   ask for help
b.   bail out and try something new.

15.   I learn from my mistakes.

An Overview of Independent Learning

Whether your plans for the future include post-secondary education and/or work experience, independent learning builds relevant skills and attitudes. The collaborative approach outlined below enhances your potential as a self-directed member of society who functions well alone or on a team.

Consult with your instructor to determine:

· content and form (including purpose, audience, and style)

· how you will proceed (process)

· final form (product)

· when, where, and how to collaborate with others (classmates, contacts in the community or workplace)

· assessment.

Dividing the process of independent learning into four major phases may make your work more manageable. However, as you complete the task, you'll likely move back and forth among phases and steps. Don't be discouraged; the learning process resembles more of a zig-zag than a straight line. Remember to use your Writer's Notebook to reflect on your experience-in-progress.

Note: Complete each phase in collaboration with your instructor and partner or learning group.

Phase One   *Searching*

- Identify a suitable inquiry question/problem/topic by exploring many possibilities.

Phase Two   *Forming and Doing*

- When research and/or reading are complete, form an imaginative product.

Phase Three   *Sharing*

- "Show and tell" selectively in a creative format.

Phase Four   *Reflecting and Assessing*

- Reflect on peer responses and estimate your success.

Defining an appropriate task challenges your creative and critical thinking abilities. You are looking for a project which:

- is of personal interest
- challenges your growth
- is feasible
- meets course requirements.

The three-step process outlined below may help you begin the search.

- **Review** givens—course requirements, local constraints, time allocations, and so on.
- **Reflect** on your interests, strengths, and future plans. Do they suggest avenues for further investigation?
- **Ruminate** on many possibilities.

Ideas may come from many sources including Writer's Notebook entries, peers, your instructor, and suggestions for adaptation in Chapters One through Seven. The following authors have rated highly with students of literature, language, and the writing process. Your teacher-librarian may help you select appropriate titles.

Chinua Achebe	Thomas Hardy
Edward Albee	Anne Hébert
Isaac Asimov	Lillian Hellman
Jane Austen	Ernest Hemingway
Russell Baker	O. Henry
Ann Beattie	Jack Hodgins
Samuel Beckett	J. Turner Hospital
Saul Bellow	Aldous Huxley
Constance Beresford-Howe	Henrik Ibsen
Pierre Berton	John Irving
Earle Birney	Shirley Jackson
Karen Blixen	Franz Kafka
Irma Bombeck	Martin Luther King
Ray Bradbury	Rudyard Kipling
Charlotte Brontë	Joy Kogawa
Emily Brontë	Margaret Laurence
Anthony Burgess	D.H. Lawrence
Morley Callaghan	John Le Carré
Roch Carrier	Laurie Lee
Lewis Carroll	Doris Lessing
Truman Capote	C.S. Lewis
Emily Carr	Malcolm Lowry
Willa Cather	Hugh MacLennan
Anton Chekhov	Somerset Maugham
Kate Chopin	Arthur Miller
Agatha Christie	A.A. Milne
Joseph Conrad	Rohinton Mistry
Robertson Davies	W.O. Mitchell
Charles Dickens	Brian Moore
Joan Didion	Alberto Moravia
Gerald Durrell	Farley Mowat
Max Ferguson	Alice Munro
M.F.K. Fisher	Iris Murdoch
F. Scott Fitzgerald	V.S. Naipaul
Robert Frost	Joyce Carol Oates
Mavis Gallant	Edna O'Brien
John Galsworthy	Frank O'Connor
Gabriel Garcia Marquez	Eugene O'Neil
William Golding	George Orwell
Nadine Gordimer	John Osborne
Mary Gordon	Alan Paton
Katherine Govier	Harold Pinter
Graham Greene	Edgar Allan Poe

Al Purdy
Thomas Pynchon
Mary Renault
Mordecai Richler
Erika Ritter
Gabrielle Roy
J.D. Salinger
William Shakespeare
George Bernard Shaw
Isaac Bashevis Singer
Elizabeth Smart
Alexander Solzhenitsyn
Raymond Souster
Muriel Spark
John Steinbeck

Tom Stoppard
David Suzuki
James Thurber
J.R.R. Tolkien
Mark Twain
John Updike
Kurt Vonnegut, Jr.
H.G. Wells
Eudora Welty
Edith Wharton
E.B. White
Oscar Wilde
Tennessee Williams
P.G. Wodehouse
William Zinsser

The Research Process—Starting Points

Certain projects require in-depth research of primary and secondary sources and may include interviews. These general suggestions may facilitate your work. Consult your teacher-librarian for further guidance.

As senior students, you're likely familiar with the set-up and organization of card catalogues, vertical files, and computer facilities. However, a knowledge of popular indexes and reference books may save you valuable research time.

- An **index** is a reference book listing periodicals which contain articles. *The Reader's Guide to Periodical Literature* is an excellent starting place for locating concise information about your project.

- An **encyclopedia** is a reference book which summarizes general information. Although it may build basic knowledge, you'll need to focus on in-depth works—essays and full-length books.

- A **handbook** or **dictionary** of . . . offers similar information. Familiarize yourself with several of special use to students of language and literature.

Of particular use when preparing a biographical sketch or profile are the following:

- *Who's Who*

- *Who's Who in Canada*

- *Dictionary of American Biography*

- *Current Biography*

- *British Authors of the Nineteenth Century*
- *Something About the Author*
- *Contemporary Novelists*
- *Reader's Encyclopedia*
- *Oxford Companion to American Literature*
- *Oxford Companion to Canadian History and Literature*
- *Oxford Companion to Classical Literature*
- *Oxford Companion to English Literature*
- *Brewer's Dictionary of Phrase and Fable*
- *Handbook of Literature*
- *Great Books of the Western World*
- *Book Review Digest*
- *Writer's Encyclopedia*

If an interview is part of your research, these forms may help you get organized.

Interview Organizer

Preliminaries

- Discuss plans with the instructor.

- Research background information—subject, subject's area(s) of interest or work.

- Contact the subject, clearly explaining your affiliation, purpose and scope of the requested interview, and willingness to be flexible about timing.

- Follow up with a confirmation letter outlining specific arrangements—time, place, date, use of tape recorder—copied to the workshop instructor.

- Obtain written permission for the prospective meeting from your instructor and/or the administration.

Preparations

- Draft tentative questions. Effective questions are respectful of individual privacy and sensitivities, clearly and concisely worded, and on topic. In addition, they should be open ended (discourage yes-no answers) and reasonable, given the individual's expertise and time limitations.

- Revise questions after feedback from peers and the instructor.
- Practise with your writing group—brush up on active listening skills and rehearse the interview through role playing.
- Prepare equipment and appropriate attire for the occasion.

On Interview Day

- Double-check directions and allow plenty of transit time.
- Remember equipment (e.g., tape recorder, clip board).
- Introduce yourself and express appreciation for the interview.
- Ask questions in a clear, firm voice.
- Sum up and determine the individual's availability if follow-up clarification by telephone is needed.
- Reiterate thanks and leave at the preappointed time.

Follow-up

- Write a letter of thanks.
- Send the final version for the subject's approval.
- Reflect in your Writer's Notebook about your learning.
- Discuss the experience with your writing group/partner.

Forms and Organizers for Independent Study

Forms such as these may facilitate the design, execution, and assessment of your projects.

Independent Study Planner

A page such as this stored in the independent study section of your Writer's Notebook provides a handy overview of a long-term project.

A. Submission Dates

Preliminary Contract Due Date: _____

Firm Contract Due Date: _____

Written Project Due Date: _____

Oral Component Due Date: _____

Other Submissions: _____

B.   Dates, Times, and Locations of Meetings

Peer Support Meetings:_____

Interviews with Instructor: _____

Research Appointments and Interviews:_____

Preliminary Contract

Early in your course, you may be asked to submit a tentative contract which might look something like the following. Ask your instructor about the extent to which you are bound by this submission.

1.   *Area of Interest*: Outline the topic or subject.

2.   *Purpose*: State briefly your objectives.

3.   *Rationale*: Explain your interest in the topic, its significance, and how it meets course requirements.

4.   *Methodology*: Explain steps in the *process* of completing the project.

5.   *Final product(s)*: Describe the final product's form; include both oral and written components, if relevant.

6.   *(Re)sources Consulted*: List books and articles read and people consulted to date.

7.   *Problem-solving*: Outline problems you've encountered and explain how you've tackled them.

8.   *Peer Support Partner/Group*: Name the classmate(s) who have agreed to act as your support for peer conferences and problem solving. Justify your choice(s).

9.   *Queries*: List questions you'd like to discuss with the instructor prior to or at your first interview, and predict problems.

10.   *Other*: What else do you need to communicate?

Sign and **date** your submission as instructed.

Independent Study Contract (Final)

After you and your instructor have reviewed your preliminary contract, you'll likely be asked to present a revised submission by a specific date.

1.   Under the categories of the Preliminary Contract, *revise* your ideas keeping in mind:

- your interview with the instructor

- discussions with contacts and peers

- findings of subsequent investigation and reflection.

2. Project: Final wording of the project.

3. Meetings: Dates of meetings with peer partner/group and instructor. Outline work to be prepared for each.

4. **Sign** and **date** your contract.

Note: Submit two copies for approval. Be sure to attach the Preliminary Contract to your revised submission.

Writers' Resource Five   Writing Essays

Mastering the art and craft of essay writing is important for post-secondary experience. This resource draws together and supplements materials found throughout the book to focus your study.

The Range of Essays

You'll have noticed that contemporary essays come in a potpourri of shapes, sizes, and colours. Before examining distinctions, let's review commonalities. An essay is:

- a short work of non-fiction

- generally written in prose

- controlled or unified by a central idea or thesis

- developed through argumentation, narrative, or description—or a combination of them

- composed of an introduction, body, and conclusion.

There are many approaches to examining differences among essays, none of them entirely satisfactory, as distinctions tend to blur in practice. However, you may find it instructive to examine how essays differ in their: purpose(s); audience; position of thesis or organizing idea; types of development or evidence; tone; level of formality (language); and writer's style and voice.

As you examine components, you'll want to identify their interrelationships—that is, how audience and purpose determine appropriate style and types of evidence, and so on.

You'll notice interrelationships such as these:

- *Formal essays* tend to be serious treatments of significant subjects. Written in formal standard English (no contractions or colloquialisms), they argue a case (interpretive style) or explain a phenomenon (informative style) or inspire to action through eloquent language (rhetorical style). A logical and orderly presentation of evidence (facts, statistics, and quotations) is imparted with some measure of objectivity and detachment.

- *Informal essays* are more likely to be unabashedly familiar and subjective. Often humorous and light, they reflect the writer's values and personality—voice—more directly than their formal counterparts, and invite a wide range of writing styles. Although logical organization is a constant in essay composition, the writer is likely to explore the subject with anecdotes, patches of dialogue, and other narrative techniques often associated with fiction.

This list highlights selections which may be especially helpful to your study of essay writing. Keep in mind, however, that the formal-informal continuum is only one way of exploring the essay.

See also the following activities and other resources: "Matching Writing Variables," Chapter Two (Activities Three, Four, Five, Six, Eight), Chapter Three (Activities Two, Three, Four, Five).

Argumentative Essays

Argumentative prose is particularly important in post-secondary experience and beyond. The two samples which follow, "Technopeasant Blues" by student Joanna Norland and "Illiteracy" by John Aitken, highlight important distinctions between informal and formal interpretive writing.

Technopeasant Blues

My friend Greg received a watch for his birthday. At least, he calls it a watch. And indeed, when the LCD face isn't displaying his timetable, measuring the temperature, playing one of eight possible tunes or calculating complex differential equations, it does actually tell the time. So Greg assures me, anyway.

"Hey, Greg," I said, pointing to the weighty tome tucked under his arm, "Is that the new chem textbook?"

"No way," he replied. "This is the quick-and-easy instructional manual for my watch."

We teenagers have enthusiastically embraced the golden age of technology. Many of us can lay claim to a staggering heap of sophisticated gadgetry. Our state-of-the-art sound systems virtually transport us to front row centre. Our scientific calculators have replaced the fingers-and-toes method in math class. Even English homework has its technological component: We type it up on word processors. Well, at least some of us type it up on word processors. Not me. I could never get my word processor to process words, or, for that matter, anything. This is why I am now the proud and still optimistic owner of an electronic typewriter.

My electronic typewriter, I have found, brings new challenge and excitement to the most menial assignments. Consider, for example, the essay I had to type. Before typing out my two-page essay, I had to read through a two-hundred-page, full-colour manual. Be they in fuchsia, crimson, chartreuse or royal, instructions for centring lines, printing in bold, shifting to the French mode, setting alternate tabs, repeating phrases, indenting paragraphs and correcting words, are not for the faint-hearted technopeasant. By the time I'd reached the lemon-yellow section, I waved a white flag. Before my cerulean eyes, the multicoloured text blurred into an illegible grey cloud. . . . Suddenly I noticed a button on my electronic typewriter. It read "MANUAL." Press it and voila! This 21st century electronic miracle transforms itself into a ten-finger-powered brontosaurus. Joyfully, I began to type. Just then my parents called down that it was midnight "AND WOULD I STOP THAT BANGING." So I copied out my essay with a ball point pen. It took me fifteen minutes.

Typing my essay to completion, my scientific calculator extrapolates, would have taken me 3.14 times as long as did writing it by hand . . . or did I accidentally press the Pi button?

Illiteracy

Joseph Weizenbaum, Professor Emeritus of computing science at the Massachusetts Institute of Technology, writes in a recent issue of MIT's *Technology Review* that "American schools are now failing miserably at their primary responsibility—to give every student the ability to communicate clearly in written and spoken English." He, in turn, quotes the head of a large corporation who complains that "fully half the high school graduates who apply for work . . . cannot read well enough to follow written instructions."

Weizenbaum speaks scathingly of his own students, whose computer programs, he says, are just as undisciplined and sloppy as the essays they write.

Prime Minister Brian Mulroney announced in September [1988] a $110 million federal literacy program which some observers regarded as an indictment of Canadian schools. Those who are involved in battling to help people learn to read and write were gratified.

Current studies reveal that one in four Canadians is functionally illiterate, a term which indicates inability to read and write at basic levels of comprehension. Other surveys indicate that one in five Canadians is simply illiterate, denoting a terrifying inability to read and understand instructions on a medicine bottle, fill out an application form, figure out the change on a lunch bill, or read a birthday card much less an insurance policy.

There is little to be gained by indulging in editorial outrage; this is a national tragedy which we have somehow permitted to happen. Nor can we blame immigrants for these appalling statistics; they have come from surveys of Canadians who were born and went to school here.

There are people and organizations who have been working at the problem for years. In 1986, Canada's book and periodical industry, with the help of seed money from Coles the Book People, formed the Canadian Give the Gift of Literacy Foundation. With donations from members of the industry and individuals and the support of Coles and booksellers across the country, the foundation raises money for community literacy groups.

Just as Kenneth Hare, University Professor Emeritus of University of Toronto, observed in another context, the public often takes action before governments do and "sooner or later, the politicians will budge and budge rapidly," so Hilary Marshall, now retired from the University of Toronto Press and treasurer of the literacy foundation, makes some observations of more than passing interest.

The foundation collects coins in canisters placed on bookstore counters across Canada, and the take from these now averages about $1,000 a week. The point is that these are not members of an intellectual elite but average people who like to read.

At a Coles branch in a mall in Burlington, Ontario, members of the sales staff told Marshall that the most frequent contributors were young people,

not adults. This, perhaps, is the most compelling argument that politicians—
if they truly cannot comprehend the dangers posed by an illiterate
populace—might heed. Young people themselves are not only aware but
willing to put their Big Mac money into a canister in the hope that it will
help others to learn to read.

This would be an absurd situation if it were not so deadly serious.

Note: A useful comparison between this editorial from *University of Toronto
Magazine* and the *Globe and Mail* editorial on the same subject (page 244) can be
made. Worth analyzing are their differences in

- style
- purpose
- clarity and placement of thesis
- use of transitions
- validity of argument

- level of formality
- audience
- structure and organization
- type and quality of proof

Writers' Resource Six   Glossary

Note: A chapter number following a definition designates where a concept or
skill is dealt with in depth.

abecedarian   A poem in which the first word of each line contributes a letter
from the alphabet, arranged from A through Z.

abstract   A brief summary of a scholarly essay's argument, often printed at
the beginning of the work. (Chapter Three)

adaptation   A revised version of material altered for publication or broadcast
in another medium. Copyright laws must be adhered to when planning an
adaptation. (Chapter Six)

allegory   One form of extended metaphor in which abstract concepts are
dramatized as characters in a narrative.

anecdote   A brief narrative about a person, place, or thing. (Chapter Four)

annotated bibliography   A list of sources consulted by a writer in preparing a
work that includes a brief summary and/or evaluation of each source.

antagonist   The person or force in conflict with the protagonist.

argumentation   A form of prose which endeavours to persuade the reader
through logic and verifiable evidence. (Chapter Three)

arrangement   The ordering or structuring of information. Three common
arrangements in non-fiction prose are: *causal*, in which material is presented in
terms of cause and effect; *chronological*, wherein events or experiences are
sequenced in order of their occurrence; and *climactic*, in which details are
presented in spiralling order of their importance or impact.

article   A term loosely used to refer to many forms of short non-fiction (essay) writing. (Chapter Five)

atmosphere   The overall emotional effect of a piece of writing on the audience; it is created by the writer's choice of setting and tone and such elements as description and dialogue.

audience   Intended readers and/or viewers of a piece of writing for which work should be tailored. (Chapter Three)

autobiography   A non-fiction account—usually a full-length work—of a person's life written by that person. An autobiography may be prepared by a "ghost-writer"—a professional hired to complete a manuscript who does not receive author credit. (Chapter Four)

biography   A non-fiction account of a person's life written by someone else. A biography may be authorized or unauthorized—that is, completed with or without the co-operation of the subject or his or her estate. (Chapter Four)

brainstorm   To record ideas without attempting to censor them or assess their validity.

business writing   A general term referring to various communications in the workplace. For example, memos, reports, and summaries are generally written in an informative style and may reflect the jargon of the field. (Chapters Two, Three, and Five)

by-line   A reporter whose name appears on a piece of journalism is said to have a by-line.

character   The people (and animals) of literature.

clichéd language   Over-used diction which obscures personal style. (Chapter Two)

collaborative writing   A process (also called co-writing) in which two or more authors jointly write a piece of work. Approaches include simultaneous composition with, for example, two keyboards and two computer screens or an arrangement whereby one person types or writes as others contribute ideas and phrasing (the scribe may contribute too). Another method is one in which a group or partners brainstorm ideas collectively, and one person is delegated to complete the first draft which may then be revised by other group members. (Chapters One and Two)

colloquial language   Informal phrasing used in everyday parlance which is generally inappropriate in formal speech or writing. (Chapters Two and Three)

conflict   The feeling of tension arising from the interaction of opposing forces and/or people. Conflict propels narrative toward its resolution. (Chapter Four)

connotation   Emotional overtones or implications associated with a word or phrase. Connotation goes beyond the dictionary definition of a word, and is, in some measure, subjective. Not all words have connotative values. (Chapter Three)

copyright   The exclusive right to communicate—publish or reproduce in any form—information, art, or other work.

crisis   The action/event which causes the climax. (Chapter Four)

denotation   A word's literal or dictionary definition. (Chapter Three)

diction   Choice of words. (Chapters Two and Three)

essay   A short work of non-fiction generally written in prose which treats one main subject. In contemporary parlance, an essay may take a variety of forms, each of which conforms to its own special conventions. Popular formats include interviews, profiles, memoirs, biographical or autobiographical sketches, speeches, and reports. (Chapters Two, Three, and Eight)

euphemism   A roundabout or inoffensive way of saying something.

figurative language   Fanciful expression which communicates through non-literal diction. It encourages a fresh perspective and may deepen response by, for example, comparing objects, concepts, or experiences.

figures of speech   Rhetorical devices which enhance speech or writing by making what is said or written more forceful and vivid. Figures of speech include allegory, metaphor, paradox, personification, simile, symbol, and vivification. See separate entries. (Chapter Three)

flashback   A glimpse at events that took place prior to the central story-line. This narrative device may be used in both fiction and non-fiction works.

foreshadowing   Hints or clues about the outcome of a non-fiction or fiction narrative.

found poem   A fragment of speech or writing recorded or transcribed by a writer who perceives it as a "diamond-in-the-rough" or ready-made poem.

freewrite/speedwrite   A technique of brainstorming on paper in which the writer composes non-stop for a set period of time—usually five to fifteen minutes. Thoughts are recorded spontaneously without regard for style or form. When speed is the object of the exercise, this technique is called speedwriting.

hyperbole   Purposeful exaggeration to make a point.

imagery   The content of a piece of writing or artistic endeavour which is perceived through the five senses. For example, figures of speech may convey mental images and associations which help make abstractions concrete. Imagery includes devices such as personification, metaphor, simile, and so on.

imagist poetry   Poetry marked by concrete language and figures of speech, modern subject matter, freedom in the use of meter, and the avoidance of romantic or mystic themes.

intuition   A form of perception which exists outside the rules of logic or factual evidence.

jargon   Language particular to a profession or field. (Chapter Two)

logic   Methods and principles used in deductive and inductive reasoning. Of the two basic forms of logical reasoning, *inductive* reasoning is the process whereby a conclusion is inferred from a number of verifiable facts. It cannot be judged to be valid or invalid, merely assessed as strong if it is consistent with the facts as we know them. In *deductive* reasoning a conclusion is presented first, followed by a number of verifiable facts to support it. It is said to be a valid argument if the conclusion follows necessarily from the premises. (Chapter Three)

logical fallacies   Arguments that mislead through the illusion of correctness but which transgress the rules of logic. (Chapter Three)

metaphor   Two apparently dissimilar things are identified with one another. This identification is often denoted by the linking of the two components by some form of the verb "to be" ("is" or "are"). An example is "All the world's a stage."

myth   A narrative of unknown origin which purports to explain a natural phenomenon or fundamental belief. (Chapter Four)

outline   A linear plan which sketches the structure for writing. Some writers compose outlines only after writing a rough draft. In either case, outlines are usually revised several times as a work takes shape. An outline for a scholarly essay begins with an *introduction* which includes a preliminary thesis statement and sentence stating how the essay will proceed. Following the introduction is the *body* which comprises the proof of the thesis, with arguments and proof supportive of the thesis. Finally, the *conclusion* summarizes the significance of the thesis. (Chapter One)

paradox   An apparently contradictory or absurd statement.

parallel structure   Words, phrases, or clauses which are of equal value or function are stated in a similar order or form.

persona   The mask adopted by a writer to create a desired literary result, for example, a specific tone.

personification   An inanimate or abstract object is described as having human qualities, such as emotions.

planning   A linear outline, mapping, clustering, or branching are techniques of this stage of thinking. (Chapter One)

point of view/narrative viewpoint   The perspective from which a writer tells the story. (Chapters Four and Six)

précis   A condensation of a work, generally one-third the original length. Formal précis conforms to specific conventions. (Chapter One)

premise   A proposition which forms the assumption in an argument. An argument may have more than one premise. (Chapter Three)

protagonist   The main character of a work. Most often used in reference to prose fiction and drama, but may also be found in New Journalism and some poetry. (Chapters Four, Five, and Six)

pun   A play on words in which, for the sake of humour, two words which sound the same but have different meanings are used so as to suggest both meanings.

repetition   Emphasis on a key word or phrase through purposeful reiteration.

rhetorical language   Words and phrases, often figurative expressions, crafted to stimulate specific audience responses, including *hyperbole, parallel structure, repetition,* and *rhetorical question*. See separate entries. Rhetorical styles are particularly important for speech-makers. See also *figurative language* and *sound appeal*. (Chapter Three)

rhetorical question   A question which is really a statement; that is, no answer is anticipated.

satire   Humour which ridicules human vices and foibles with the intent of instructing or warning about consequences.

setting   The time and place in a piece of writing. (Chapters Four and Six)

sight appeal   Literary techniques employed to heighten the visual quality of a piece of writing. (See figurative language.)

simile   An explicit comparison of two things linked by words such as "like" or "as."

slang   Informal language, sometimes known as "street talk," which may add colour, texture, and realism to writing such as in direct speech. (Chapter Two)

sound appeal   Literary devices which heighten the auditory quality of writing. Especially important in speeches and poetry, they include *alliteration*, in which two or more words used in succession or near succession begin with the same sound; *assonance*, which is repetition of internal vowel sounds; *dissonance*, a discordant combination of sounds in language; *euphony*, a pleasing combination of sounds in language; *onomatopoeia*, a device in which a word or phrase's sound imitates its meaning; and *rhythm*, the "beat" or cadence of language or flow of sound. (Chapter Three)

style   An individual's characteristic manner of expression which reflects a unique writer's voice. It is conveyed through the individual's idiosyncratic diction, cadence, rhythm, and so on. (Chapters Two and Three)

symbol   A thing (living or inanimate) with stands for something beyond its literal meaning.

theme   The main idea or central vision of a poem, short story, novel, or play. Literary works usually express more than one theme.

thesis   The main argument (claim) in a non-fiction work expressed as a statement. A strong thesis expresses a significant assertion. (Chapters Three and Eight)

tone   A writer's attitude toward a piece of work and its audience. Tone ultimately influences audience interpretation of content, just as tone of voice affects the impact of speech. Tone is conveyed through diction and should be tailored to purpose. (Chapters Two and Three)

transitions   Connective words or phrases that facilitate the flow of ideas between sentences or paragraphs. Appropriate transitions depend on their function. For example, "in other words" could be employed to reinforce an idea, whereas "on the other hand" signals a contrast. (Chapter Two)

vivification   Figure of speech in which non-human life is attributed to an inanimate object.

EPILOGUE

The Discovery

do not imagine that the exploration
ends, that she has yielded all her mystery
or that the map you hold
cancels further discovery

I tell you her uncovering takes years,
takes centuries, and when you find her naked
look again,
admit there is something else you cannot name,
a veil, a coating just above the flesh
which you cannot remove by your mere wish

when you see the land naked, look again
(burn your maps, that is not what I mean),
I mean the moment when it seems most plain
is the moment when you must begin again

—Gwendolyn MacEwen

SOURCES AND CREDITS

Chapter One

Page 8   Emily Carr, *Hundreds and Thousands.*

Page 8   Joan Didion, "On Keeping a Notebook."

Page 8   Anne Frank, *Diary of a Young Girl.*

Page 8   Penn Kemp, From "An Interview with Penn Kemp."

Page 9   Anaïs Nin, *Diary of Anaïs Nin,* vol. 1.

Page 20   Michael Schumacher, "Joyce Carol Oates and the Hardest Part of the Writing Process." Reprinted from *Writer's Digest,* April 1986.

Page 28   June Callwood, journalist.

Page 29   Phyllis Gotlieb, novelist.

Page 30   Peter C. Newman, author and editor.

Page 31   Workshop developed and taught by Penn Kemp in her course, "Exploring the Brain's Creative Potential."

Page 34   Jerome Bruner, *On Knowing: Essays for the Left Hand.*

Page 34   Charlotte Brontë, "The Editor's Preface" to Emily Brontë's *Wuthering Heights.*

Page 34   Gerhard Gollwitzer, *The Joy of Drawing.*

Page 34   Morton Hunt, *The Universe Within.*

Page 34   Aldous Huxley, *The Doors of Perception.*

Page 34   George Kneller, *The Art of Creativity.*

Page 34   Arthur Koestler, *The Sleepwalkers.*

Page 34   Edward Lindaman, *Thinking in the Future Tense.*

Page 34   Abraham Maslow, *Motivation and Personality.*

Page 34   David Suzuki, *An Introduction to Zen Buddhism.*

Page 35   Beverly Daurio, "A Chorus of Many Voices," *Cross-Canada Writers' Quarterly,* Vol. 9, No. 1, 1987.

Page 35   Alison Griffiths is quoted from an article by H.J. Kirchhoff, "Thoughts on 'Creative Non-fiction' and a Writer's Balancing Act," which appeared in the *Globe and Mail,* December 22, 1988.

Page 40   Marshall Cook, "Training Your Muse: Seven Steps to Harnessing Your Creativity," *Writer's Digest,* March 1986. Reprinted material is a collection of excerpts and not the complete article; for a fuller treatment of this subject Mr. Cook recommends *Becoming a Writer* by Dorothea Brande.

Page 45   Robertson Davies, "We Must Sing with the Voices God Gave Us," *Toronto Star,* September 19, 1987. Robertson Davies is the author of over 30 books; many of his novels have been translated in 12 foreign languages.

Page 47   Nancy Hathaway, "15 Great Creative-Block Busters," *New Woman Magazine,* June, 1987. Nancy Berman Hathaway is the author of *The Unicorn* and the co-author of *Giving Sorrow Words: How to Cope with Grief and Get on with Your Life* (Warner Books, 1990).

Page 52   Judy Keeler, "Three Days of Novel Writing," the *Globe and Mail,* August 30, 1986. Judy Keeler is a Toronto writer.

Page 54   Penney Kome, "There's a First Time for Every Day," the *Globe and Mail,* July 16, 1988. © Penney Kome.

Page 55   Carol McLeod, "Create Eccentrically." This article, written by Carol McLeod, originally appeared in the Spring 1985 issue of *Canadian Author & Bookman.*

Page 56   Alan Pearson, "The Joy of *Writing*," *Canadian Author & Bookman*, Spring, 1986.
Page 57   Lori Thicke, "Creative Writing Co-op." Reprinted with the author's permission. "Creative Writing Co-op" first appeared in *Canadian Author & Bookman*, Fall, 1985.
Page 60   Paul Wilson, "In the Mode: Personal Computers and Creativity." Toronto writer and translator Paul Wilson wrote "In the Mode" with the technical assistance of a Grand & Toy Roundedge ballpoint, a Dominion Blueline A 565 notebook, a Sony TC-150 tape recorder, a Kaypro 4 microcomputer using PerfectWriter Version 1.2, and a Berol Verithin E 41 blue pencil. The article first appeared in *Books in Canada*, Vol. 13, #3, March 1986, pp. 7-12.

Chapter Two

Page 68   T.S. Eliot, "Gus: The Theatre Cat." Reprinted by permission of Faber and Faber Limited from *Old Possum's Book of Practical Cats* by T.S. Eliot.
Page 70   Kate Chopin, *The Awakening*.
Page 70   bill bissett, "iul tell yu a storee she sd." By permission of the author.
Page 72   Greg Hollyer and Heather Forsythe, "Communicating with Style in the Workplace." By permission of Heather Forsythe, BSCh(Eng.), MBA, and Gregory Hollyer, BSCh(Eng.).
Page 73   Bruno Bettelheim, *A Good Enough Parent: A Book on Child-Rearing*. Copyright 1987 Random House. Reprinted by permission of Alfred A. Knopf, Inc.
Page 74   Joseph Conrad, *Lord Jim*. By permission of the Doubleday Publishing Company.
Page 74   Charles Dickens, *A Tale of Two Cities*.
Page 74   Lynne Hancock, *An Ape Came Out of My Hatbox*. Used by permission of the Canadian Publishers, McClelland and Stewart, Toronto.
Page 74   Dylan Thomas, *Quite Early One Morning*. Copyright 1954 by New Directions Publishing Corporation.
Page 75   William Zinsser, "Write As Well As You Can," *On Writing Well*. Copyright © 1976, 1980, 1985 by William K. Zinsser. Reprinted by permission of the author.
Page 77   William Faulkner, "On Receiving the Nobel Prize." From *The Faulkner Reader* by William Faulkner, Random House, New York. (a)
Page 77   Neil Graham, letter to the editor, the *Toronto Star*, August 24, 1987. By permission of Neil Graham. (b)
Page 77   Ernest Hemingway, *A Farewell to Arms*. Reprinted with permission of Charles Scribners Sons, a imprint of Macmillan Publishing Company, from *A Farewell to Arms* by Ernest Hemingway. Copyright © 1929 Charles Scribners Sons; copyright renewed 1957 Ernest Hemingway. (c)
Page 77   Margaret Laurence, *The Stone Angel*. Used by permission of the Canadian Publishers, McClelland and Stewart, Toronto.
Page 77   Blair Martin, "A Sailor's Moon." By permission of the author, Blair Martin.
Page 77   John Updike, "Wife-Wooing," *Pigeon Feathers and Other Stories*, Random House, New York. (f)
Page 77   Oscar Wilde, *The Picture of Dorian Gray*. (g)
Page 78   Joyce Carol Oates, *Marya: A Life*. Copyright 1986, E.P. Dutton, Inc.
Page 79   William Zinsser, *On Writing Well*.
Page 88   Eugene Forsey, letter in the *Globe and Mail*, Toronto, April 21, 1987.
Page 92   From "Collaborwriting" by Hal Blythe and Charlie Sweet in *Writers on Writing*, Thomas Waldrop, ed., Random House, 1985.
Page 93   William French, "Yuppies, Baby-Boomers Find Their Way into New Roget's," the *Globe and Mail*, April 18, 1988. By permission of the *Globe and Mail*.

Page **94**   Sally Gibson, "You Will *Not* Become a Writer When You Grow Up." Article first appeared in *Canadian Author & Bookman*, Spring 1987. Dr. Sally Gibson is the author of *More Than an Island: A History of the Toronto Island*, published by Irwin in 1984, and a freelance writer whose articles have appeared in a wide variety of Canadian periodicals.

Page **96**   Doris Lessing, "Through the Tunnel," *The Habit of Loving*. Copyright 1954 Doris Lessing. Reprinted by permission of Jonathan Clowes Ltd., London, on behalf of the author.

Page **102**   Excerpt from *The Handbook of Non-Sexist Writing* by Casey Miller and Kate Swift. Copyright © 1980 by Casey Miller and Kate Swift. Reprinted by permission of Harper & Row, Publishers, Inc.

Page **106**   Kurt Vonnegut, Jr., "How to Write with Style." Reprinted by permission of International Paper.

Chapter Three

Page **111**   Christie Blatchford, "Running: A Personal History." Excerpted from *Spectator Sports* by Christie Blatchford. Copyright © 1986 by Key Porter Books Limited.

Page **112**   Stephen Leacock, "Humour As I See It." Excerpt of an essay from *Further Foolishness* by Stephen Leacock, 1916. Used by permission of the Canadian Publishers, McClelland and Stewart, Toronto.

Page **113**   Farley Mowat, from *Never Cry Wolf*.

Page **113**   From "Golden Girl" by Janette Turner Hospital, in *Dislocations*. Used by permission of the Canadian Publishers, McClelland and Stewart, Toronto.

Page **114**   William Faulkner, from his Nobel Prize acceptance speech.

Page **115**   Margaret Atwood, *Survival: A Thematic Guide to Canadian Literature* (Toronto: House of Anansi Press, 1972). Reprinted by permission.

Page **115**   From *The McGraw-Hill Author's Book*; copyright © 1984 by McGraw-Hill. Used with permission of McGraw-Hill Publishing Company, New York.

Page **115**   John Kenneth Galbraith, *Economics, Peace and Laughter*. Copyright © 1971 by John Kenneth Galbraith. Reprinted by permission of Houghton Mifflin Company.

Page **118**   Humphrey, et al., "Can Blind Children Use Sonar Sensory Aids?" *Canadian Journal of Psychology*, 1988, 42 (2), 94-119. Copyright (1988), Canadian Psychological Association. Reprinted with permission.

Page **123**   W.H. Auden, "Anger," *The Seven Deadly Sins*.

Page **123**   Francis Bacon, "Of Marriage and Single Life," *Essays or Counsels, Civil and Moral*.

Page **123**   Ethel Strainshamps, "Our Sexist Language," *Women in Sexist Society*.

Page **123**   From "Rainy River Sturgeon: An Ojibway Resource in the Fur Trade Economy" by Tim E. Holzkamm, Victor P. Lytwyn, and Leo G. Waisberg, *The Canadian Geographer*, 32, No. 3 (1988), 194-205. © 1988 Canadian Association of Geographers/L'Association canadienne des géographes.

Page **127**   Tennessee Williams, *One Arm and Other Stories*. Copyright 1948, 1954 by Tennessee Williams. Reprinted by permission of New Directions Publishing Corporation.

Page **128**   Mark Twain, "Parody on Shakespeare." Found in Pembroke Press's *Words That Taste Good*, (Bill Moore).

Page **129**   Reprinted with permission of Charles Scribners Sons, an imprint of Macmillan Publishing Company, from *The Great Gatsby* by F. Scott Fitzgerald. © 1925 Charles Scribners Sons; copyright renewed 1953 Frances Scott Fitzgerald Lanahan.

Page 129   Gwendolyn MacEwen, "Dark Pines Under Water." Permission granted by the Estate of Gwendolyn MacEwen.

Page 130   Dorothy Livesay, "The Difference." Copyright Dorothy Livesay. Originally published in *Signpost*, 1932 (Macmillan).

Page 131   Judith Guest, *Ordinary People*. Copyright © 1976 by Judith Guest. All rights reserved. Reprinted by permission of Viking Penguin Inc.

Page 131   Blair Martin, "Independence Day." By permission of Blair Martin.

Page 133   Amnesty International, Canadian Section (English speaking).

Page 134   Humphrey, et. al., "Can Blind Children Use Sonar Sensory Aids?" Copyright (1988). Canadian Psychological Association. Reprinted with permission.

Page 137   W.H. New and W.E. Messenger, *The Active Stylist*.

Page 138   "Canadian Spoken Here" by Walter S. Avis from *Looking at Language* by M.H. Scargill and P.G. Penner (eds.). Copyright © 1966 W.J. Gage Limited. Reprinted by permission of Gage Educational Publishing Company.

Page 144   From *The Sound and the Fury* by William Faulkner. Reprinted with permission of Random House, Inc.

Page 145   William French, "Mr. Shaw Was Not at Home," the *Globe and Mail*, March 18, 1988. By permission of the *Globe and Mail*, Toronto.

Page 150   From *A Portrait of the Artist as a Young Man* by James Joyce. Copyright 1916 by B.W. Huebsch. Copyright 1944 by Nora Joyce. Copyright © 1964 by the Estate of James Joyce. All rights reserved. Reprinted by permission of Viking Penguin Inc.

Page 151   Martin Luther King, Jr., "A Christmas Sermon on Peace." From *Trumpet of Conscience* by Martin Luther King, Jr. (Harper & Row, Publishers, Inc.). Copyright © 1967 by Martin Luther King, Jr. Used by permission of Joan Daves.

Page 152   Cameron Stewart, student engineer.

Chapter Four

Page 160   Rudy Wiebe, "Introduction," *The Storymakers*. Reprinted by permission of the author. © Jackpine House Ltd., 1970.

Page 160   "The Mosquito and the Thunder" is an oral tale told by Nkamtci'nEmux and published in *Tales Told in Canada* by Edith Fowke. Copyright 1986 by Edith Fowke. Reprinted by permission of Doubleday, a division of Bantam, Doubleday, Dell Publishing Group, Inc.

Page 160   Al Purdy, "On Milton Acorn," *In Memoriam*. Copyright Al Purdy.

Page 161   "For What It's Worth," *The Little, Brown Book of Anecdotes*.

Page 161   Leslie Javorski, "Salt Cod, Anyone?" published in *The New Morningside Papers* by Peter Gzowski, McClelland and Stewart, 1987.

Page 161   "A Matter of Dress," *The Broadview Book of Canadian Anecdotes*. © Broadview Press Ltd.; reprinted with permission.

Page 164   From *The Stone Angel* by Margaret Laurence. Used by permission of the Canadian Publishers, McClelland and Stewart, Toronto.

Page 167   Judith Guest, *Ordinary People*. Copyright © 1976 by Judith Guest. All rights reserved. Reprinted by permission of Viking Penguin Inc.

Page 167   John Updike, "Wife-Wooing," *Pigeon Feathers and Other Stories*, Random House, New York.

Page 167   Reprinted with permission of Charles Scribners Sons, an imprint of Macmillan Publishing Company, from *The Great Gatsby* by F. Scott Fitzgerald. © 1925

Charles Scribners Sons; copyright renewed 1953 Frances Scott Fitzgerald Lanahan.

Page **172**   Louisa May Alcott, *Little Women.*

Page **172**   From *The Other Woman* by Colette, translated by Margaret Crosland, published by Peter Owen, London.

Page **172**   From *Mama's Going to Buy You a Mockingbird* by Jean Little. Copyright © Jean Little, 1984. Reprinted by permission of Penguin Books Canada Limited.

Page **174**   Charlotte Brontë, *Jane Eyre.*

Page **175**   Kate Chopin, "The Story of an Hour."

Page **178**   Sandra Birdsell is a short story writer, novelist, and playwright. "Why Do I Live Where I Live?" was written for broadcast on "Morningside," CBC.

Page **183**   Courtney Walker, University of Western Ontario; former Writer's Craft student; Contact North, Hearst, Ontario.

Page **184**   Debra Woods is a student at the University of Western Ontario. She is a former student of Writer's Craft. Contact North, Hearst, Ontario.

Page **184**   Charlotte Brontë, "The Editor's Preface" to Emily Brontë's *Wuthering Heights.*

Page **185**   Morley Callaghan, "On the Role of the Story and the Storyteller," an excerpt from Morley Callaghan's speech of acceptance on receiving the Royal Bank Award, June 15, 1970. Copyright Morley Callaghan.

Page **186**   "Lessons From the Kitchen Table," by Deborah C. Hecht, *Writer's Digest,* February, 1988.

Page **188**   Damon Knight, "It All Begins With Characters," *Writer's Digest,* December, 1985.

Page **192**   "The Secrets of Writing Powerful Dialogue," © 1987, Gary Provost; reprinted by permission of the author.

Page **197**   Rita Schepok, "The Set Up."

Page **198**   Beth Singleton, "The Opera Experience."

Page **199**   David Suzuki, "A Grim Fairy Tale," *Metamorphosis.* Reprinted by permission of Stoddart Publishing.

Chapter Five

Page **205**   Albert Camus, from *Resistance, Rebellion, and Death.*

Page **206**   Allan J. Lerner, *My Fair Lady.*

Page **207**   Blair Martin, "Le Piste: An Essay on Writing." By permission of the author.

Page **208**   From an article by Catherine Bauer, entitled "The Essay Is Alive and Well," which first appeared in the Fall 1984 issue of *Canadian Author & Bookman.*

Page **210**   June Callwood, reprinted from the *Globe and Mail,* July 16, 1986.

Page **215**   "Le Monde," *Guardian Weekly,* Paris section, May 17, 1987.

Page **215**   "Saved by a Scalpel of Light" by Marilyn Dunlop, the *Toronto Star,* August 28, 1987.

Page **215**   "Input" by Paula Danziger, the *Guardian,* August 12, 1987.

Page **215**   "Study the Forest Not the Trees" by David Suzuki, the *Globe and Mail.*

Page **215**   "Music Censorship Battle Never Ends" by Howard Kaman, *Fresh Perspective,* October, 1987. Reprinted with permission from Youth Communication/Toronto, *Fresh Perspective.*

Page **216**   From *News in America* by Frank Luther Mott, Harvard University Press.

Page **217**   "Integrated Sports: A Question of Fair Play," *Chatelaine,* February, 1988. By permission of Maclean Hunter, 1988, and by courtesy of the Ontario Women's

Hockey Association, dedicated to the advancement of females in hockey.

Page **220**   John Leo, "Journalese for the Lay Reader," *Time*, March 18, 1985. Copyright 1985 Time Inc. Reprinted by permission.

Page **223**   Norman Sims, "Introduction," *The Literary Journalists*, edited by Norman Sims, Ballantine Books, New York.

Page **224**   Peter Newman, quoted in H.J. Kirchhoff's, "Thoughts on 'Creative Non-Fiction' and a Writer's Balancing Act," *Globe and Mail*, December 22, 1988.

Page **228**   Richard Hoggart, *Speaking to Each Other*, Oxford University Press. Copyright © 1970 Richard Hoggart and Chatto & Windus.

Page **228**   Excerpts from cover quotations of Michele Landsberg's *Women and Children First*. © 1982. Reprinted by permission of Macmillan of Canada, a Division of Canada Publishing Corporation.

Page **229**   "What Can I Do?" Department of National Defence; reproduced with permission of the Minister of Supply and Services Canada.

Page **233**   John Allemang, "Winning Writing Contest Changed Mistry's Life," *Globe and Mail*, February 11, 1988. Courtesy of the *Globe and Mail*, Toronto.

Page **234**   Kevin J. Anderson, from "How to Write and Sell Book Reviews." © 1984 by Kevin J. Anderson; originally appeared in *Canadian Author & Bookman*, Winter 1984.

Page **235**   Michael J. Bugeja, "Making Your Article Leads Sparkle." Copyright 1987 by Michael J. Bugeja, reprinted with permission of *Writer's Digest*.

Page **238**   "The Language of Finance," from "Money Matters" by David C. Burrows, *Toronto's Midtown Voice*, March, 1988.

Page **238**   From "The Authors Behind the Back-Cover Blurbs" (review of *So to Speak*) by Marc Côté, *Globe and Mail*, March 5, 1988.

Page **239**   Lorene Hanley Duquin, "Setting a Good Example." Copyright 1988 by *Writer's Digest*. Reprinted by permission.

Page **243**   "I'm Sorry, I Don't Speak the Language," from OP ED page, the *Globe and Mail*, April 2, 1988. By permission of the *Globe and Mail*, Toronto.

Page **244**   "Tackling Illiteracy," editorial, the *Globe and Mail*, October 13, 1987. By permission of the *Globe and Mail*, Toronto.

Page **247**   Karim H. Karim, "Covering Refugees with Figures of Speech," *Content*. January/February, 1988. Reprinted with permission of *Content*.

Page **248**   Tom W. Parkin, "An Outdoor Journal." Courtesy of Tom W. Parkin. Article first appeared in *Canadian Author & Bookman*, Winter 1988 issue.

Page **249**   *The Royal Bank Letter*, "The Creative Approach," 1988. Courtesy of the Royal Bank of Canada.

Page **250**   William Safire, "Bizbuzz," *New York Times*, September 19, 1982. Copyright © 1982, the New York Times Company.

Page **255**   Robina Salter, "Write Science Stories Simply." The work of novelist and science writer Robina Salter appears regularly in *The Medical Post*, the University of Toronto's alumni magazine, and in other journals. She also contributes to CJRT's news journal. Her first novel, *Hannah*, was published last year, and her second is underway. She also writes for children. Robina Salter lives in Toronto. The article reprinted here first appeared in *Canadian Author & Bookman*, Fall 1986.

Page **257**   Diana Stout, "Recapture Your Feelings." Courtesy of Diana Stout, a freelance writer based in Tallahassee, Florida, and a member of Romance Writers of America. This material originally appeared in *Canadian Author & Bookman*, Winter 1988.

Chapter Six

Page 265   Farley Mowat, "What Makes a Writer?" By permission of Farley Mowat.

Page 265   By permission of Tanya Kanigan, *Inkslinger: An Aden Bowman Creative Writing Anthology.*

Page 266   Shel Silverstein, "Arrows." From *A Light in the Attic* by Shel Silverstein. Copyright © 1981 by Evil Eye Music, Inc. Reprinted by permission of Harper & Row Publishers, Inc.

Page 267   From *Dancing Girls and Other Stories* by Margaret Atwood. Used by permission of the Canadian Publishers, McClelland and Stewart.

Page 267   Blair Martin, "Fields." By permission of Blair Martin.

Page 268   Mordecai Richler, "The Art of Kissing." From *The Street* by Mordecai Richler. Used by permission of the Canadian Publishers, McClelland and Stewart.

Page 268   Alice Munro, "Thanks for the Ride." Copyright Alice Munro, 1968. Reprinted by permission of McGraw-Hill Ryerson Ltd.

Page 270   Joanna M. Glass, "Artichoke." Copyright 1979 by Joanna M. Glass. © Copyright 1971 by Joanna M. Glass as an unpublished dramatic composition. © Copyright 1966 by Joanna M. Glass (under the title, "Over the Mountain").

Page 272   Judith Guest, from *Ordinary People*. Copyright © 1976 by Judith Guest. All rights reserved. Reprinted by permission of Viking Penguin Inc.

Page 275   Joan Fern Shaw's "Delivery" was first published in *Canadian Author & Bookman*, Vol. 62.

Page 276   Bridget Newson, "Beyond the Garden Gate," *Inkslinger: An Aden Bowman Creative Writing Anthology.*

Page 276   Zenovia Sadoway, "Blue Mountains," *Inkslinger: An Aden Bowman Creative Writing Anthology.*

Page 277   Anne Malcolm, untitled poem, *Inkslinger: An Aden Bowman Creative Writing Anthology.*

Page 277   Melanie Misanchuk, "Zucchinis at Harvest," *Inkslinger: An Aden Bowman Creative Writing Anthology.*

Page 279   Ali Norman, "Between You and Me," *Inkslinger: An Aden Bowman Creative Writing Anthology.*

Page 280   "Mister Hoobody" by Dennis Lee from *Nicholas Knock and Other People*, published by Macmillan of Canada, © 1974, Dennis Lee.

Page 282   Penn Kemp, "Levity." By permission of Penn(y) Kemp, from *Incremental*, Pandas Press, 525 Canterbury Road, London, Ontario N6G 2N5.

Page 282   "Analysis of Baseball" by May Swenson is reprinted by permission of the author; copyright © 1971 by May Swenson.

Page 285   Lorraine Ellis Harr is editor of *Dragonfly: A Quarterly of Haiku* (1972-84) and founder of Western World Haiku Society. She is the author of six books of haiku, one of senryu, two of haibun, and two of children's poetry. Currently, she is also a consulting editor of *Dragonfly: East/West Haiku Quarterly.*

Page 286   "She'd Say" by Frank Davey; reproduced by permission of Frank Davey.

Page 289   Reprinted from *Word Recreations* by A. Ross Eckler, Dover Publications, Inc. 1979.

Page 292   Reprinted with permission of Marvin Goody.

Page 294   *The Velveteen Rabbit* by Margery Williams, 1958, Doubleday, a division of Bantam, Doubleday, Dell Publishing Group, Inc.

Page 294   Henry James, "A Bundle of Letters." By permission of Alexander R. James, Literary Executor.

Page **296**   Shirley Faessler, from "The Poor Literatus."

Page **299**   Morley Callaghan, "All the Years of Her Life." Reprinted by permission of Don
Congdon Associates Inc. Copyright © 1935, renewed by Morley Callaghan.

Page **303**   Morley Callaghan, Author's Commentary to "All the Years of Her Life."
Copyright Morley Callaghan.

Page **303**   Mary Lou Cornish is the editor of a hospital newspaper in London, Ontario.
She freelances as a scriptwriter and also writes poetry and short stories. "Write
a Screenplay" originally appeared in *Canadian Author & Bookman*.

Page **308**   From an interview of Jerome Lawrence and Robert E. Lee by Christopher
Meeks, entitled "The Greatest Sport in the World," which appeared in *Writer's
Digest*, March, 1986.

Page **310**   From Margaret Laurence's "Author's Commentary," first published in *Sixteen by
Twelve* by John Metcalf.

Page **310**   Carson McCullers, "A Tree. A Rock. A Cloud." from *The Ballad of the Sad Café
and Collected Short Stories* by Carson McCullers. Copyright © 1936, 1941, 1942,
1950, 1955 by Carson McCullers. Copyright © renewed 1979 by Floria V. Lasky.
Reprinted by permission of Houghton Mifflin Company.

Page **315**   "Writing Short Stories" from *Mystery and Manners* by Flannery O'Connor.
Copyright © 1969 by the estate of Mary Flannery O'Connor. Reprinted by
permission of Farrar, Straus & Giroux, Inc.

Page **317**   J. Michael Straczynski, "The Sound of Muses." Copyright © 1988 by Synthetic
Worlds, Inc. Reprinted by permission.

Page **317**   Josephine Tey, *The Pen of My Aunt.* Reprinted with permission of the Estate of
Josephine Tey and Messrs. Peter Davies Ltd.

Chapter Seven

Page **330**   Richard Wilbur, "The Writer," from *The Mind-Reader*; copyright © 1971 by
Richard Wilbur, reprinted by permission of Harcourt Brace Jovanovich, Inc.

Page **331**   bill bissett, "poetree is for communikaysyun   why i write like this;" writtn
espeshulee for *Thinking Through Your Writing Process* & other relatid process mss.
Copyright bill bissett.

Page **341**   Excerpted, with permission, from the publication, "Career
Selector—Communication and Creative Arts," produced by the Ontario
Women's Directorate.

Page **345**   "An Interview with William Faulkner," from *Writers at Work: The Paris
Interviews*, First Series, edited by Malcolm Cowley. Copyright © 1957, 1958 by
The Paris Review, Inc. All rights reserved. Reprinted by permission of Viking
Penguin Inc.

Page **346**   "An Interview with Robert Frost," from *Writers at Work: The Paris Interviews*,
Second Series, edited by George Plimpton. Copyright © 1963 by The Paris
Review, Inc. All rights reserved. Reprinted by permission of Viking Penguin Inc.

Page **348**   John Goddard, "Other People's Lives." Copyright © 1985 John Goddard. First
published under the title, "Other People's Lives" in *Books in Canada*, March,
1985.

Page **353**   "For Better of Worse: Ontario Cartoonist Wins Top Award," *Leisure Ways*,
October, 1986.

Page **354**   Ghislaine McDayter and John Hunter, "A Post-Secondary Preview." Reprinted
with the permission of the authors.

Page **358**   George Plimpton, "An Interview with Ernest Hemingway." from *Writers at Work: The Paris Interviews*, Second Series, edited by George Plimpton. Copyright © 1963 by The Paris Review, Inc. All rights reserved. Reprinted by permission of Viking Penguin Inc.

Page **359**   "An Interview with Mordecai Richler," from *Booktalk*, a free customer magazine, published by Coles Bookstores Ltd., Summer 1987 Issue.

Page **361**   Barbara Wade Rose writes for various Canadian magazines and has a master's degree from the University of Toronto.

Page **365**   Ted Thurston, "Investigative Reporting," *Canadian Author & Bookman*, Spring 1984.

Page **367**   George Wickes and Ray Frazer, "An Interview with Aldous Huxley," from *Writers at Work: The Paris Interviews*, Second Series, edited by George Plimpton. Copyright 1963 by The Paris Review, Inc. All rights reserved. Reprinted by permission of Viking Penguin Inc.

Chapter Eight

Page **386**   E.J. Pratt anecdote is from *The Broadview Book of Canadian Anecdotes*, by Douglas Fetherling, Broadview Press, 1988.

Page **404**   Joanna Norland, "Technopeasant Blues." Joanna Norland is a grade 12 student and a columnist for the *Ottawa Citizen*.

Page **405**   John Aitken, "Illiteracy," *University of Toronto Magazine*, Winter 1988.

Epilogue

Page **413**   Gwendolyn MacEwen, "The Discovery," from the collection, *The Shadow-Maker* (Mosaic Press). Permission to reprint granted by the Estate of Gwendolyn MacEwen.

INDEX TO AUTHORS

---

* Page numbers in roman type refer to excerpts from writers' works. Those italicized indicate citations for quotations by or references to writers.

The author gratefully acknowledges her indebtedness to the scholarship of researchers into learning theory and the process of writing. The pedagogy of *Thinking Through Your Writing Process* is based primarily on the work of:

Isabel Briggs Myers
Lucy Calkins
Merron Chorny
John Dixon

Brian Johnston
Keith Leithwood
Bernice McCarthy
Donald Murray

Peter Elbow
Toby Fulwiler
Donald Graves
Susan Hackman

Ian Reid
Harold Rosen
Leslie Stratta